Journal of the Early Book Society

for the Study of Manuscripts and Printing History

Edited by Martha W. Driver
Volume 20, 2017

ISBN: 978-1-935625-21-6
ISSN: 1525-6790

Member

Council of Editors of Learned Journals

The *Journal of the Early Book Society* is published annually. *JEBS* invites longer articles on manuscripts and/or printed books produced between 1350 and 1550. Special consideration will be given to essays exploring the period of transition from manuscript to print. Authors are asked to follow *The Chicago Manual of Style.* A Works Cited list at the end of the text should include city, publisher, and date. Manuscripts are to be sent, in triplicate, along with an abstract of up to 150 words, to Martha Driver, Early Book Society, Department of English, Pace University, 41 Park Row, New York, New York 10038. Only materials accompanied by a self-addressed, stamped envelope (or international reply coupon) will be returned. Members of the Early Book Society who are recent authors may send review books for consideration to Susan Powell, Reviews Editor, 7 Woodbine Terrace, Headingley, Leeds LS6 4AF, England. Brief notes on recent discoveries, highlighting little-known or recently uncovered texts and/or images, may be sent to Alexandra Gillespie, Centre for Medieval Studies, 125 Queen's Park, 3rd Floor, Toronto, ON MSS 2C7, Canada. Subscription information may be obtained from Martha Driver or from Pace University Press.

Those interested in joining the Early Book Society or with editorial inquiries may contact Martha Driver by post or e-mail (MDriver@Pace.edu). Information may also be found at <www.nyu.edu/projects/EBS>. For ordering information, call Pace University Press at 212-346-1405 or visit http://www.pace.edu/press. Institutions and libraries may purchase copies directly from Ingram Library Services (1-800-937-5300).

The editor wishes to thank Gill Kent, Julia Dillon, the Pace University Press Graduate Assistant Elliane Mellet, and Manuela Soares, Associate Director, Pace University Press, for their help and advice on this issue.

Journal of the Early Book Society
For the Study of Manuscript and Printing History

Editor:
Martha W. Driver, Pace University

Associate Editors:
Susan Powell, *University of Salford*
Alexandra Gillespie, *University of Toronto*

Editorial Board

Matthew Balensuela, *DePauw University*
Julia Boffey, *Queen Mary, University of London*
Cynthia J. Brown, *University of California, Santa Barbara*
Richard F. M. Byrn, *University of Leeds*
James Carley, *York University*
Joyce Coleman, *University of Oklahoma*
Margaret Connolly, *University of St Andrews*
Susanna Fein, *Kent State University*
Alexandra Gillespie, *University of Toronto*
Vincent Gillespie, *Lady Margaret Hall, Oxford University*
Ann M. Hutchison, *Pontifical Institute of Mediaeval Studies and York University*
Michael Kuczynski, *Tulane University*
William Marx, *University of Wales, Lampeter*

Carol M. Meale, *Bristol University*
Daniel W. Mosser, *Virginia Polytechnic Institute and State University*
Ann Eljenholm Nichols, *Winona State University*
Judy Oliver, *Colgate University*
Michael Orr, *Lawrence University*
Steven Partridge, *University of British Columbia*
Derek Pearsall, *Harvard University*
Alison Smith, *Wagner College*
Toshiyuki Takamiya, *Keio University*
Andrew Taylor, *University of Ottawa*
John Thompson, *Queen's University, Belfast*
Ronald Waldron, *King's College, University of London*
Edward Wheatley, *Loyola University*
Mary Beth Winn, *SUNY Albany*

Contents

At Work in the Anchorhold and Beyond: A Codicological Study of London, British Library, Cotton MS Nero A.xiv

MEGAN J. HALL

The thirteenth-century English manuscript London, British Library, Cotton MS Nero A.xiv ("Nero") is one of four complete thirteenth-century manuscripts of the well-known early Middle English text *Ancrene Wisse*, a guidebook for anchoresses.[1] Following its composition, sometime after 1215, the *AW* grew exponentially in popularity and over the next three centuries was adapted for and read not just by the small original audience of anchoresses for whom it was written, but by all kinds of religious—canons, canonesses, monks, and nuns—as well as by lay men and women, both literate and illiterate; it was also translated into French and Latin.[2] In short, the *AW* was the runaway bestseller of vernacular devotional guides in the thirteenth through sixteenth centuries. It marks the start of a rich Middle English tradition of vernacular anchoritic literature that continued into the fourteenth and fifteenth centuries with such works as Richard Rolle's *The Form of Living*, Walter Hilton's *Scale of Perfection*, the vernacular redaction of Aelred of Rievaulx's *De institutione inclusarum*, and the anonymous *Myrour of Recluses*.[3] A great deal, perhaps the bulk, of *AW* scholarship is carried out by scholars of the late Middle Ages because of the integral role the *AW* plays in the study of vernacular devotion and literacy in England in the fourteenth and fifteenth centuries.[4] Too, because so many *AW* manuscripts survive—seventeen in total—scholars have naturally been drawn in large part to critical editions from which they can derive textual studies, rather than working with specific manuscripts. As a result, individual manuscripts are typically elided, despite the critical information they can provide about the reception of the *AW*, particularly in its early stages. Investigations into fading Latin literacy, an increasing demand for vernacular literature, the adaptation of the *AW* for late medieval readers, and changes in readership over the history of the *AW* carried out by scholars who focus on late medieval England readership, such as Bella Millett, Catherine Innes-Parker, Christina von Nolcken, and Nicholas Watson, can be deepened and fruitfully complicated by considering not just codicological questions, but by asking such questions of the earliest manuscripts in the tradition.[5] Such study tells us much about, for example, the early uses of the text and the increasing popularity of the *AW*, and frames the late medieval vernacular readership with a larger understanding of the progress from Latinate to vernacular readers. Though the particular manuscript I examine here, Nero, is a bit earlier than the usual scope of this journal, it plays a critical role in the development of the *AW* into the form studied by scholars of Middle English texts and merits consideration.

Nero is textually the earliest witness to the *AW*, preserving as it does the reference to the three sisters still presumed to be the original audience, and was initially the surviving manuscript favored by scholars.[6] With Tolkien's interest in the AB language in the early twentieth century, though, attention swiftly shifted to Corpus ("A" of the AB manuscripts), with its fine production quality and better text as the preferred base-text for critical editions.[7] Growing interest in Corpus also coincided with an increased interest in material and manuscript studies, and so Corpus has benefited from a relatively good deal of codicological analysis.[8] Nero, conversely, fell out of favor before codicological studies became popular and has never received a thorough treatment. Despite its significant place in the *AW* tradition as one of the earliest manuscripts, the timing of its scholarly popularity along with its simple aesthetics—it is a small, plain manuscript, effectively undecorated, with nothing particular to recommend it outside of that reference to its original audience and the Wooing Group material found in its last quire—it has been overlooked. Mabel Day, editor of the EETS edition of the Nero manuscript, is, as far as I am aware, the only scholar to provide an extended codicological consideration of Nero in her introduction.[9] Even so, it runs to only fifteen pages, four of which are given over to her efforts to trace the manuscript's early provenance, and it functions on the whole more as a catalogue of major features than as an in-depth analysis. Some of the codicological features she notes are the mixed quality of the parchment, the dual ruling scheme, and the irregular nature of most of the quires. Still, she offers little analysis of these features and in fact she does not address a few very important items.

A close codicological look at the manuscript reveals a bevy of new, heretofore unremarked-on evidence that changes how we must perceive the history and use of the text and the manuscript. The evidence speaks to Nero's role as what I call here a working book, used in at least one anchorhold in its early years.[10] Its small size, the varying quality and state of the parchment, its contents and collation, and varied ruling scheme all suggest a utility-grade manuscript intended for heavy use. In further testament to that, the manuscript's leaves record the responses of three and possibly several more anonymous medieval readers and one identifiable early modern reader, Richard James, who was librarian to Sir Robert Cotton. Erasures throughout the main text also indicate possible censure of a reader or perhaps recycling of the manuscript for a later audience. Most importantly among these readers is the unknown anchoress for whom, I argue here, Nero was commissioned.[11]

Nero is a small, quarto-sized manuscript that could be easily held in one hand while reading. The small size is no surprise, given its function and production context. Michael Clanchy notes in *From Memory to Written Record* that from the mid-thirteenth century on, books became increasingly smaller, to accommodate the needs of mendicant friars, who would teach, preach, and hear confession (and who therefore needed portable books), as well as to accommodate those of university students and private lay readers. Nero, given its contents, authorship, and intended usage, was an ideal text for production as one of these smaller, portable volumes, and indeed, it was produced just as the trend for smaller books really got underway. It is not a volume for display but one for on-the-ground use. The internal structure of Nero strongly suggests an anchoress commissioned the manuscript for her use in enclosure.[12] The manuscript contains the complete text of the earliest version of the *AW* and is only one of two manuscripts that preserves material from the Wooing Group, together with the Apostles' Creed and two later Latin pieces, a short poem on death and a brief prose piece on the Cross, the *Sermo de Cruce Domini*—all pieces, naturally, of practical value to an anchoritic reader. The *AW* spans the first twelve quires, and the end of the twelfth quire and all of the thirteenth contain the additional material.[13] As Table 1 shows, the scribe made some effort to divide the eight parts of the text into their own quires, though anywhere from a few lines to a whole folio at the beginning or end of a quire were used to end or begin the previous or following part; however, the length of parts and presumably the layout of the exemplar and the size of the hand meant that, for economy's sake, not every part could exist in its own quire. Quire 1, for example, contains all of the Preface and Part 1, though the last fourteen lines of Part 1 spill over into the second quire. Similarly, quires 2 and 3 contain nearly exclusively Part 2; the same is true for quires 4 through 9. Quires 10 and 11 are roughly evenly split between two parts: quire 10 contains the last half of Part 5 and the first half of Part 6, while quire 11 contains the last half of Part 6 and the first half of Part 7. Quire 12 is split among the last half of Part 7, all of Part 8, and about two-thirds of W1. All the rest of the smaller collected pieces are added in the final quire.

At the time of Nero's copying, around the end of the twelfth and the beginning of the thirteenth century, quire structure was moving toward standardization; in the thirteenth and fourteenth centuries sexternios, or quires of six bifolia, became a much more common arrangement.[14] It appears that the scribe by choice did not follow such conventions and has instead adjusted the size of the quires in some places in an effort to keep each part roughly within its own quire.[15] The quires that make up Nero are most commonly quinternions (that is, made up of five bifolia or ten leaves), though seven of the thirteen range in length of leaves (see Table 1). Strikingly, 7 and 8 are two of the largest quires in the manuscript, containing eleven and twelve leaves respectively. Only quire 12 is larger, with thirteen leaves.[16]

The first two quires at their regular length of ten leaves could accommodate the Parts discretely: the ten leaves in quire 1 were sufficient to contain the Preface completely and Part 1 nearly completely (with the exception of the last fourteen lines), and the ten leaves of quire 2 could be devoted completely to Part 2, except for the top half of the first leaf. The scribe adjusted the size of quire 3 so that he could accommodate all of Part 2 within that quire; he pasted folio 29 onto the last leaf of a gathering of four bifolia allowing for Part 2 to be completed rather than run into a third quire. As he could fill all of quire 4 with Part 3, he had no need to add or remove leaves and chose a regular quinternion. In quire 5, however, he had to remove two leaves in order to keep the quire mostly containing Part 3, which takes up six leaves. Part 4 takes up the last two leaves. Perhaps the scribe chose not to utilize a ternion to keep the gathering strictly in Part 3, because the quire arrangement would have fallen further out of balance (this quire is the shortest in Nero as it is). The scribe had no such difficulties with quires 6 through 8, as they are all devoted entirely to Part 4. Yet the scribe has structured these quires in an irregular way, and it seems as though some planning was involved to spread Part 4 across the quires as has been done: quire 6 is a quaternion plus a singleton, quire 7 is a quinternion plus a singleton, while quire 8 is a sexternion. The scribe could have chosen an arrangement of two quinternions and one sexternion, much more regular and with no gluing on of extra leaves. The rationale is unclear. Particularly mysterious is the scribe's malformation of quires 6 and 7: at some point, he sliced off the last leaf of quire 6 and glued it to the start of quire 7, leaving both quires with an odd number of leaves. There is no disruption to the text, suggesting that the move was planned, though the motivation is not obvious.

After this point, the scribe seems to have settled for splitting the quires roughly between parts, though quires 9 and 12 are less evenly balanced than quires 10, 11, and 13. Oddly, as with quires 6 and 7, the scribe tipped in a leaf to quire 12 to make an irregular quire of thirteen leaves, giving over more of the quire to "Ureisun of ure Lefdi" than was necessary, as it would have fit more naturally into quire 13 with the other collected short works.

The last quire, 13, is similarly irregular, its nine leaves containing all of the non-*AW* material. This quire is rather pieced together, made up of three conjugate leaves and three singletons, one of which is tipped in at the start of the quire and forms folio 123a; the arranger nested the other two to create an ad hoc bifolium. Clemens and Graham point out that the use of such single leaves signals attention to economy, using the pieces of the prepared skin that remained after full sheets were cut. For strength and longevity, the sheets would be sewn in somewhere between the outer and innermost leaves, where they were less likely to be loosened and lost: here, they fall as expected in second and seventh positions in the quire, not counting the tipping-in of the first leaf.[17] The parchment of this quire is of a rougher quality generally than that of the *AW* quires, and its leaves are darker on the whole than those of the previous quires, suggesting that the leaves for quire 13 were pulled from quite a different batch of parchment, and that the *AW* likely circulated without quire 13 for a time.[18]

The keeping of each part of *AW* roughly in its own quire, with the exception of the shorter sections, and the manipulating of quire size to accommodate this, suggests deliberate planning of the manuscript into thematic chunks. It is possible the scribe was copying via a sort of *pecia* system and was given his exemplars one part at a time but overran the planned space, though that is not at all certain.[19] Nero lacks, for example, any of the signs of copying via *pecia* system that Dobson points out in the Cleopatra manuscript, such as blank leaves or double hatch marks to signal the end of sections.[20]

The distribution of the text among the quires of Nero could also suggest a deliberate arrangement allowing for circulation of the text in quires among anchorholds before the quires were bound together, as is suggested by the references to textual circulation in Part 4. The author warns that "Þe ancre þe wearnde anoþer a cwaer to lane, f[e]or ha hefde heoneward hire bileaue ehe"[21] ("The anchoress who refused another a quire on loan would have the eye of her faith turned far from here"[22]), and further advises that

> 3ef þu hauest cnif oðer clăd, oðer mete oðer drunch,
> scrowe oðer cwaer, hali monne froure, oðer ei oþer
> þing þet ham walde freamien, vnnen þet tu hefdest
> wonte þe seolf þrof, wið þon þet heo hit hefden.[23]

(If you have a knife or a garment, or food or drink, parchment or quire, the comfort of holy people, or anything else that would be of comfort to them, be willing that you might have want of it yourself, so that they might have it.)

Such advice from the author suggests that the readers of the early text, including Nero, would have expected to receive and use reading materials in quires rather than as bound books; it may account for the rough division of the text into discrete quires. The anchoress, or a professional scribe, might have copied the portions of the text as they became available, so that she compiled a full and more permanent manuscript gradually, but used individual quires in the meantime.

Another key piece of information about the deliberate quire structure comes in the form of quire marks, which are unusual enough to merit some extended discussion. Table 2 shows the quire structure of Nero, which I have compiled by examining the manuscript at length. The current binding is very tight, but the center stitching remains visible in most quires (2, 3, 10, and 12 are the exceptions); the stitching was redone during nineteenth-century conservation and, notably, the old sewing stations were not reused.[24] In a few spots physical evidence apart from the sewing thread confirms quire structure, such as the wormhole mentioned above, which reveals that folio 29 was adhered as a singleton to the end of the third quire. Other useful evidence is in the form of quire marks, discussed below. The binding is sufficiently tight to obscure a full and accurate description of quire arrangement in some instances. Where I cannot make a determination of my own, I follow Day's proposed quire structure, which she developed in consultation with Neil Ker.

Perhaps unusually for an early manuscript, and not noted before about Nero in the scholarship, signatures also survive on all quires, denoting the start of a new quire as well as the first half of the leaves within those quires. In further evidence that the leaves were rearranged after the ruling and adding of quire signatures, the signature for quire 7 appears not on its first leaf but on its second, folio 58, for the first leaf of quire 7 was originally the last leaf of quire 6. The reason behind this shift is unknown, for both quires contain sections of Part 4, and shifting leaves meant disrupting two regular quinternions.

The manuscript's arranger used a system of Roman and Arabic numerals to note the quire arrangement on the leaves, marking both the start of the quires and the arrangement of leaves within them.[25] Some of these marks have not survived the binder's trimming. Unusually, the arranger seems to have incised rather than inked or impressed marks at the start of quires. The start of all quires but 9 (and possibly 1, where it is so faint as to be perhaps not there at all) has been marked with Roman numerals that appear to be cut into the parchment, presumably with a penknife or other thin, sharp blade, or possibly with a fine stylus, so that the numerals are actually sliced in the parchment.[26]

The quire marks support the move of the last folio of quire 6 to the start of quire 7: folio 57a, the first leaf of quire 7, lacks a quire mark; the mark appears instead on folio 58a, the second leaf in the quire. This supports Day and Ker's asserted quire structure, confirmed in my own examination of the manuscript, that folio 57 once existed as the last leaf of quire 6, conjugate with folio 48, but was moved at some point to the start of quire 7, gummed to folio 67. A move to accommodate a shift from one part to another does not explain the move, for quires 6 and 7 fall squarely within Part 4, which spans quires 5 through 9. It is possible that folio 57 was added to complete the quire length needed for copying in the *pecia* system (or to move a leaf unneeded in copying the material in quire 6).[27]

Further, while the arranger used incised capital Roman numerals to differentiate the start of quires, he used another system to mark the leaves in order within the quires, at the bottom of the leaves, alternating minuscule letters with Roman numerals. Roman numerals mark the first half of the leaves in quires 1, 3, 5, 7, 10, 12, and 13.[28] Sequential letters mark those in quires 2, 4, 6, 8, 9, and 11. Peculiarly, the Roman numerals are used for odd-numbered quires through quire 7, and letters for even-numbered quires through 8, but this system changes at quire 9. The consistent system suggests one person prepared the parchment in quires. The change in system suggests that either that preparer got his quires out of order, or that a different person carried out the scribal work, deciding to rearrange for reasons unknown. Quires 9 and 10, the points at which the system switches, contain the same number of folios. Quire 9 contains Part 5; the first half of quire 10 is used to complete Part 5 while the second half contains the start of Part 6.[29]

It is rather mysterious. The scribal hand is uniform, and the corrections carried out to the main text are also in the same hand, so the evidence does not suggest that multiple scribes carried out the work. Perhaps the manuscript was indeed copied by *pecia* system, with the scribe attempting to plan in advance how the parts of the *AW* might need to be laid out.[30] Notably, the marking system also appears, though much less visibly (as in the first quire), in the final quire, which contains the shorter collected works, in a second scribal hand.

A third set of marks exists in Nero as well, though some have been lost through trimming. It is unclear whether the arranger added these marks, or whether a later reader did so. At the tops of most of the leaves, usually in the center or slightly to the right or left, a series of Roman numerals appears, added to indicate which Part of the text the leaf contains—e.g., iiij to indicate Part 4. These marks appear to have been added in ink, now very faded, on the recto of a number of leaves, particularly those in Part 4, the longest Part of the text. It is possible that the scribe added these marks, though it is also possible that a reader did so, as other indexing marks appear in the manuscript.[31]

In addition to the deliberate distribution of text among the quires, the shifting of leaves to create quires of odd sizes, and the creation of a final quire from several odd leaves, the ruling pattern suggests rearrangement as well. It also provides further evidence that Nero was produced as a working book, with limited concern for polish and sophistication and preference instead for utility, underscored by the co-opting of the ruling grid for the addition of readers' marginalia. The differing ruling patterns also show that Nero was produced during a time of changing standards.

In quire 1, ruling was carried out in leadpoint or a very fine, dark gray-brown minium; after quire 1 the minium changes to a reddish brown, typical for the time period.[32] The ruling grids are variably visible throughout the manuscript. On some leaves the grid remains dark, whereas on other leaves the grid was very lightly ruled in the first place or has simply faded. Some of the leaves are so worn that the ruling grid is no longer visible. On the leaves where the ruling pattern is dark and clear, it is evident the ruling was done rapidly with little care for neatness. On folios 55b and 56a, for example, where the ruling is highly visible, the horizontal lines of the text block are ruled unevenly—many of the ends run over into the margins and gutters, some go only through the double column bordering the text block, and some do not even reach to the inner line of the double column. The ruling pattern in Nero follows generally two types, which I have called A and B (see Table 3). The two types are distinguished primarily by the number of vertical columns. Both are based on Derolez ruling type 36 but are slightly modified.[33] In Type A, the scribe ruled for two columns in each vertical margin (outside the writing area), while in Type B, the scribe ruled for one column on each side of the writing area. On some leaves the ruling grid is no longer visible or has been trimmed so that determining the type used on every leaf is impossible. However, it is possible to identify the grid on most of the leaves, and thus determine, interestingly, that the leaves used for the *AW* text are ruled exclusively in Type A, while the leaves used for the short collected texts at the end of Nero almost always follow Type B. It is possible that the leaves that appear to be Type B in the last quire were trimmed so that the outermost "extra" line was removed. Nonetheless, the apparent pattern is striking and suggests that the *AW* and the shorter texts were joined together in Nero after both were copied separately. The *AW* ends about halfway down folio 120b, after which the text of W1 is added and continued on the next leaf, 121a, on which the Type B pattern begins.[34] Folio 21 is also the last conjugate leaf of quire 12; folio 122 is a singleton, attached to folio 121. As I discuss above, it is unclear why the scribe or compiler chose to attach a single leaf to quire 12, giving it an odd number of leaves, rather than adding the leaf to quire 13, which also contains an odd number of leaves (nine). In any case, these differing ruling patterns argue for separate circulation of the *AW* text and the shorter collected texts before they were all bound together in Nero. Such conclusion is strengthened by the fact that one scribe wrote out the *AW* and a second scribe wrote out the collected texts. Also notably, and strengthening the argument that quires of the *AW* themselves may have circulated separately for a time, is the fading of the ruling grid nearly completely at the opening folios of quires 1, 2, and 4.

Richard Morris notes that the texts in Q13 are "excellent specimens of the Hail Maries, Psalms, and Orisons alluded to in" the *AW*.[35] Nero appears to represent a custom book for an anchoress who wanted these particular texts appended for her devotion, either before or after she had obtained a copy of the *AW* for use in her cell. Notably, only two of the early *AW* manuscripts contain WG texts; Nero contains the largest number, three, while Titus contains only one, though Titus also contains three Katherine Group texts. Neither Cleopatra, Corpus, nor Vitellius contain any other anchoritic, KG, or WG texts. Though Titus was adapted for use by a male community, the inclusion of texts for devout female readers suggest the manuscript was produced for women, and the same is true for Nero, which was not adapted for male use.[36]

In addition to the variations in ruling pattern relative to the margins, Nero also exhibits variations in ruling for text above- and below-top-line. Quires 1–4 and 7–8 are ruled in the old style, with the text written above the top ruled line, while quires 5, 6, and 9–13 are ruled in the new style, with the text written below the top ruled line.[37] This feature is very often used to distinguish early thirteenth-century manuscripts (roughly pre-1230) from later thirteenth-century manuscripts and beyond.[38] Why the scribe chose to change his writing pattern is unclear, but the shift underscores the move, discussed above and further proven by quire marks, of folio 57 from quire 6, written in the new style (below top line), to quire 7, written in the old style (above top line).[39] Further, either the scribe or another user of the manuscript went through Nero at some later time and added a line, often in drypoint rather than plummet, above the top line of text in quires 1–4 and 7–8 to give those quires the surface appearance of having been ruled in the new style. This means that a shift in ruling style took place about halfway through the quires used for Nero, so that while the first four quires are old-style and the last five quires are new-style, the four in the middle are switched

(5 and 6 are new while 7 and 8 are old). Again, though the quire-marking system is the same throughout, it too was switched partway through the manuscript, as discussed above.

The evidence of the arrangement, quire marks, and ruling together suggest significant clues about the production of Nero. If the text circulated separately in quires for a time, it might have been because it took some time to acquire enough parchment to complete the manuscript, though since Nero is a small book the number of skins needed might not have been prohibitive.[40] On top of that the scribe would have required quills and ink as well as exemplars. If it took a significant amount of time to procure and pay for such materials, the *AW* could have been copied over several years' time. Unlike Corpus and the late-fourteenth-century Vernon manuscript, which were carefully and deliberately compiled with an eye for aesthetics and with the use of fine materials, Nero was put together as funds allowed, with what was available.

Employment of text both above- and below-top-line could reflect production over a stretch of time during which standards were changing. As Ker has noted, in the thirteenth century scribal practice regarding placement of the first line of text on the page shifted: the earlier standard called for text to be written above the first ruled line, while the later standard called for text to be started below it.[41] Michelle Brown narrows the transitional period between 1220 and 1240, while Jane Roberts pinpoints *c.*1220 as the distinctive turning point.[42] Nero, written out between 1225 and 1250 (according to Ker) but perhaps more specifically the 1240s (according to Malcolm Parkes), with its scribe's ambivalence about page-ruling fashions, appears to reflect this change. The scribe may, further, have not been entirely sure what convention was called for or did not have someone directing him or her—related perhaps to the unnecessary use of quire signatures on the versos of leaves.[43] The addition of a line to transform old-style pages into new-style ones might be an addition by Nero's compiler to bring quires written earlier into alignment with prevailing convention.

Additional evidence in the form of the appearance and feel of the parchment suggests that certain quires were produced separately, over time. For example, many of the leaves in the eighth quire appear to be from the same skin and are extremely pliant and silk-like (particularly fols. 68 and 69), suggesting they were made from a batch of parchment prepared at the same time and by the same parchmenter, possibly from a run of skins. Similarly, folios 120a and 120b show a stark contrast: folio 120a is light colored while folio 120b is much darker and dirtier. Folios 121a to 124a and 131b are also darker and dirtier while the others in quire 13 are lighter. Even the lighter leaves of quire 13, though, are darker than the light-colored ones of *AW* (through quire 12). This suggests that quire 13 was pulled from a different batch of parchment, and that the *AW* was used without that quire for some time.

Also of note is that while folios 121 and 110 appear to be conjugate, they do not feel like the same piece of parchment. It is possible folio 121 was subject to enough exposure, handling, dirt, and so forth to account for this difference; it is also possible that one of the two was pasted in: the binding is very tight and it is difficult to tell. Folios 121 and 110 do not seem completely consistent as conjugate leaves. It is possible that folio 121 has received a great deal more wear than folio 110, and they are more similar closer to the spine; however, the outer half of folio 121 is gray, heavily worn, and sueded, and in fact feels thinner and floppier than folio 110. Folio 120b, by contrast, is lighter than folio 121a, and the text is crisper. Likewise, folio 100a (the opening of a quire) shows wear. It is a bit darker and grayer, and more rubbed, than the folios that precede it. Interestingly, folio 99b is not. It appears fairly bright and clean, though folio 99a looks a little more like folio 100a in condition.

Further evidence is visible that the first quire almost certainly circulated on its own for some time. The coloring of the parchment overall in quire 1 is darker than elsewhere in the manuscript. The first leaf (fol. 1a) shows the wear, dirt, and dinginess associated with a quire that went without a protective cover, and the last folio of the quire (fol. 10b), while not as darkened as the first, is still darker than the next folio, 11a, which begins quire 2. There is indeed color variation in the leaves throughout the manuscript, but this evidence, together with another small piece, a blot of ink, suggests strongly this quire circulated alone. On the upper outer edge of folios iv and 1 to 10, a dot of ink, about two centimeters across, has soaked through. The ink does not continue on folio 11a, the start of quire 2. This ink blot suggests that quire 1, as well as the fourth medieval flyleaf, existed together for a time, apart from the manuscript.[44] All this evidence together argues strongly for a book built over some small period of time, custom ordered for an anchoress and prepared with expectation of its use as a working book and perhaps as a future exemplar.

The quality of Nero's parchment also reflects this intended usage. It is, overall, not very high grade. While the parchment is well scraped, with few traces of hair follicles remaining, as is typical of English preparation, the leaves are not well-matched in quality. They vary in thickness, from very thin to rather thick. Some leaves are more sueded than others. The coloration of the parchment also varies from a clean, creamy color typical of the majority of the *AW* text folios to a muddied gray, typical of the outer leaves, as well as the leaves that make up the last quire. Some of this may be due to circulation of portions of the folios as unbound quires, possibly true of the first quire at least, which shows evidence of having spent time apart from the rest of the *AW* text.

Further, a number of repairs were carried out on Nero at several stages in its medieval life. While many pages are completely intact, with no repairs, there are a number of pages that required some touching-up before use as book leaves; there is also evidence of later repairs. Altogether, the manuscript has gone through at least three stages of repair. Some pages evince medieval (and/or early modern, possibly) repairs, either through sewing of small tears or holes or gluing on of custom-cut parchment strips to make square pages out of inadequately sized or cut bifolia. Some of these repairs were carried out prior to the text's being copied in, while some were carried out at a later date, as some of the patches cover small portions of text. Some tears were serviced twice, once before the text was written in, by sewing a hole closed, and later by patching over with a parchment strip a hole whose stitching had partially gone or was taken out.[45] Additional evidence that parchment of middling quality was acceptable to the manuscript's preparer and/or commissioner is found on folio 29a, where two small wormholes are present at the bottom, one interrupting the last line of text and one just below that place. These holes do not appear on the adjacent leaves, and the scribe accommodated the hole by writing around it. Incidentally, this wormhole further supports the piecemeal quiring of the manuscript, that folio 29 was adhered as a singleton to the end of the third quire.

Useful comparison (though brief for the sake of space) may be made with other manuscripts in the same textual tradition to emphasize Nero's distinctiveness as a working book and the important information it reveals about the growth in popularity of the *AW*. Cleopatra and Titus were created within roughly the same quarter-century as Nero, with Cleopatra likely having been copied using the *pecia* system, as Dobson has demonstrated. Titus, like Nero, is composed of a number of irregular quires (only six of out the twelve quires containing *AW* material are or were designed as regular sexternions); the quires of Cleopatra are in large part made up of quaternions (twenty out of twenty-six). It is possible all three were custom ordered for individual anchoresses, though the evidence for this seems the strongest in Nero. The Corpus and Vernon manuscripts stand in contrast: both are later (Corpus slightly, Vernon significantly) and much more lavish productions, and it seems likely that both were created for religious communities rather than for individuals.

Corpus, produced in Malcolm Parkes's estimation in the 1270s or '80s—and thus roughly fifty years after Nero, Titus, and Cleopatra—is made up of higher-grade materials than the earlier manuscripts, and its layout is extremely regular, made up exclusively of quinternions (though the second quire now lacks the central leaf of the gathering; its ruling is also entirely uniform throughout).[46] It seems clearly to have been prepared at one blow, and carefully planned. A notation at the foot of the first folio (recto) establishes that Shropshire layman John Purcel gave Corpus to a house of canons at Wigmore Abbey (Herefordshire) sometime in the late thirteenth century; it is not clear whether Corpus was created for the canons directly or given to them after use elsewhere.

Production of Vernon appears to have begun in the 1380s and was continued possibly into the early 1400s.[47] Vernon is a hefty compilation volume of religious and moral instruction; the *AW* is only one of 370 texts contained in it. Unlike Nero, Titus, Cleopatra, and Corpus, all generally of a size to accommodate private reading, Vernon was designed for display, being of large dimensions (544 x 393 mm, contrasted with Nero's 144 x 106 mm); the manuscript is also illuminated. In addition to the lavish decoration, the layout on the page is tightly controlled just as in Corpus, and the quire structure is highly regular—almost exclusively quaternions—both indications of the careful planning not as evident in the earlier manuscripts.[48] Though the intended recipients of the manuscript are not known for certain, it is generally thought, particularly given the dialect, great expense, and dimensions of the book, to have been created for a female religious house in the West Midlands, though it is possible that the manuscript was made for a lay audience or patron.[49] What I wish to point out here is that, along the trajectory of this textual tradition (considering those manuscripts that contain the text in full or nearly in full, particularly the text that was revised for increasingly larger groups of readers in the later Middle English period), one sees that the *AW* grew in status, embodied in the thirteenth and fourteenth centuries in the humble, working-class manuscripts of Nero, Titus, and Cleopatra, likely intended for individual readers; next in the highly polished Corpus manuscript; and then, by the turn of the fifteenth century, in the deluxe Vernon manuscript. Broadly viewed, as the text grew increasingly important, so too did its vehicles.

A final point about Nero: the wealth of annotations appearing throughout the manuscript, in the margins as well as interlineally, provides the last layer of evidence that the Nero manuscript was created as a working book and was utilized as such from its beginnings. Because we do not know its earliest provenance, and more importantly because evidence in the text and the manuscript points to use by anchoresses, we must consider that the many marginal annotations surviving from Nero's first century of use were made by women readers. As I discuss the marginalia in detail elsewhere, I provide an overview of the details here.[50]

A number of readers have used this manuscript between the thirteenth and twentieth centuries, though some of their additions have been partially trimmed by later binders such as that of Robert Cotton. One of the early modern commentators was Richard James, Cotton's librarian. Of all annotations his are the most prominent; he wrote both on the flyleaves and within and around the text of the manuscript, adding comments of summary and cross reference and underlining extensively. The other early modern additions appear at folios 47a/b and 49a/b, in two different hands. The thirteenth- or fourteenth-century additions, executed in now very faded ink or minium, and at times in drypoint, are written in a generally informal or untutored protogothic script. More formal protogothic letter forms do appear; one hand is noticeably more formal, though it is not quite written in a book hand. Day indexes the more evident markings but does not mention most of these early annotations. The number and variety of early annotations is striking, especially contrasted with what is found in the other early manuscripts. These earliest annotators utilized the unusual ruling pattern as a grid for recording marginalia in a systematic way. (Whether the scribe deliberately designed the ruling pattern for this is unclear.) On many pages the ruling grid allowed for a meaty blank column in the outer margins of the leaves, which annotators used quite frequently. On some leaves, depending on how much trimming was performed, two columns in fact survive, providing copious room for annotation.[51] Comments survive in both Latin and English. Overall, I have identified comments in three different hands, together with a number of marginalia unattributable to a particular hand, and none appearing scholarly. As Michael Clanchy has pointed out, "The gloss took definite shape in the twelfth century and grew out of the practice of lecturers and students making explanatory notes on spare space around the texts they studied."[52] None of the marks are made in this kind of academic way; apart from two particular examples, none of these appear in the places one would expect scholastic glosses. Nor indeed would we expect to find elaborately laid out glosses here because this is neither a Bible, an academic treatise, nor a law book. The informality and variety of the marks suggest that Nero may have been passed from one anchoress to another—perhaps after an anchoress's death or withdrawal from the anchorhold—before, like the other early manuscripts, joining the library of a religious community. The early annotations that appear fall into several major categories: devotional or meditative glosses, indexing aids, navigational aids, and spontaneous glosses.

An odd feature among these annotations is underlining that has been roughly erased or partially erased throughout the manuscript. Altogether I have counted 111 instances of this phenomenon. As with a number of these odd features, I am not entirely sure to what I should attribute these scraped-away underlinings, though I tend to think either it was a result of some kind of censorship or of recycling for use by another reader. Censorship or recycling is further supported by the presence of additional erasures in marginal areas. In some of these areas traces of ink remain, suggesting that comments as well as underlinings were redacted.

The last medieval commentators make an appearance, albeit briefly, on folios 47a through 49b. Two different hands have underlined phrases in these folios and added words in the margins in a fifteenth- or early sixteenth-century script. The underlinings appear to pick out phrases and words of interest to the annotators, while the words, accompanying some of the underlining, presumably update the spelling of an underlined word. For example, on folio 47a, lines 28 and 29, which contain the word "sicnesse" are underlined; in the margin "syknisse" has been written with a different spelling.[53]

Nero remained a working manuscript well beyond the medieval period, having entered Sir Robert Cotton's oft-consulted manuscript collection by 1625.[54] At this stage it received its last and perhaps most copious set of annotations, by Richard James, librarian for the collection from about 1625 until 1638. Along with quite a few flyleaf scribblings, including two lists of contents, James added seventy-seven marginal comments together with at least 280 underlinings of words and phrases apparently of interest to him. His comments, written in both Latin and English, and his underlinings reflect his interest in antiquarian items and evidence of past religious practices. He notes on folio 12b, for example, that "Adam and Eve were in the torments of hell more than 4000 years" and on folio 19b that "In the time of this booke no Heresie in Englond."[55] James also indexed portions of the text topically, adding an index list on the final flyleaf, two tables of contents in the opening flyleaves, and page references in a number of his marginal comments. To complete this system he paginated each leaf in the upper outer corner.

Following James's lavish attention, Nero saw little augmentation of its markings beyond British Museum stamps and library markings, but as a member of a national collection available for consultation, Nero continues to work, though without the same visible record of its modern readers. While it is a necessary sacrifice for preservation's sake, it's still a bit sad to think that our marks will not join the living history of Nero as did James's, or as did those of the many unknown readers who thoroughly worked over this wonderful little manuscript. Their reading marks, together with the evidence in the parchment, text, and quires, tell a story not of a luxury display book like Vernon, produced for a large audience, nor a fine manuscript like Corpus, prepared with care from a well-established text, but of a manuscript much referenced, much used, over its lifetime. Nero was meant to be read privately by readers familiar with Latin as well as English and other vernaculars, and was intended for close, personal study by women. Nero shows evidence of heavy use, likely in an anchorhold, from its beginnings and retains marks of use by intelligent, responsive readers, very likely women. Above all, the evidence suggests very strongly that Nero was itself commissioned by or for an anchoress. It is imperative that scholars begin to examine more deeply the individual manuscripts of the *AW* rather than rely primarily on critical editions to recover something of both the spiritual and textual experiences of the earliest readers, worked out on the page. Over the two-hundred-year history from Nero to Vernon, the representation of the *AW* texts within these manuscripts tells a very important story about the popularity of the text and the experience of its readership from its earliest audience of three sisters to its widely varied late medieval readers.

The University of Notre Dame

Table 1: Contents of Nero and Corresponding Folios and Quires

QUIRE	FOLIOS	NO. OF LEAVES	TEXT
1	1-10	10	**AW Preface** (1a-4a) **1** (4a-end)
2	11-20	10	**1** (11a) **2** (11a-end)
3	21-28 + 29	9	**2** (21a-29a) **3** (29a)
4	30-39	10	**3**
5	40-47	8	**3** (40a-45b) **4** (45b-end)
6	48-56 - 57	9	**4**
7	57 + 58-67	11	**4**
8	68-79	12	**4**

9	80-89	10	4 (80a-80b)
			5 (80b-end)
10	90-99	10	5 (90a-95a)
			6 (95a-end)
11	100-109	10	6 (100a-105b)
			7 (105b-end)
12	110-121 + 122	13	7 (110a-114a)
			8 (114a-120b)
			WG1 (120b-end)
13	123 + 124/131 + 125 + 126-129 + 130	9	WG1 (123a-b)
			WG2 (123b-126b)
			WG3 (126b-128a)
			WG4 (128a-131a)
			AC (131a-b)
			L1 (131b)
			L2 (131b)

NOTE:

WG1	Þe Wohunge of ure Lauerd
WG2	Ureisun of God Almihti
WG3	"Lofsong of ure Lefdi"
WG4	"Lofsong of ure Louerde"
AC	Apostles' Creed
L1	Latin verse meditation on death
L2	Sermo de Cruce Domini

Table 2: Quire Structure of Nero

Table 3: The Two Ruling Patterns in Nero

TYPE A	TYPE B

NOTE: Not to scale.

Acknowledgments

I wish to express sincere thanks to the Institute of Historical Research of the University of London, which awarded me the Mellon Junior Dissertation Research Fellowship that funded my archival research. I also gratefully acknowledge the scholars who helped shape my work, including Jane Roberts, Kathryn Kerby-Fulton, Elaine Treharne, Michael Clanchy, and P. R. Robinson.

NOTES

1. The other three *AW* manuscripts are Cleopatra (London, British Library, Cotton MS Cleopatra C.vi, *c.*1225 to 1230); Corpus (Cambridge, Parker Library, Corpus Christi College MS 402, *c.*1225 to 1240); and Titus (London, British Library, Cotton MS Titus D.xviii, *c.*1225 to1250.

2. For example, Cambridge, Gonville and Caius College, MS 234/120 (*c.* 1250 to 1300) is in part a series of extracts from the *AW*, while Titus was adapted for use by men. Altogether the text survives in seventeen manuscripts (nine in English, four in French, and four in Latin). On these manuscripts see the descriptions in Bella Millett, *Ancrene Wisse, the Katherine Group, and the Wooing Group,* Annotated Bibliographies of Old and Middle English Literature 2 (Cambridge: D. S. Brewer, 1996), 6–15, and Millett, ed., *Ancrene Wisse: A Corrected Edition of the Text in Cambridge, Corpus Christi College, MS 402, with Variants from Other Manuscripts, drawing on the uncompleted edition by E.J. Dobson; with a glossary and additional notes by Richard Dance,* EETS o.s. 325–326 (Oxford: Oxford University Press, 2005–2006), II.xi–xix.

3. The broader body of vernacular spiritual literature extends beyond this, of course, including on the early end the works of the Katherine and Wooing Groups and on the later works of English mysticism and affective piety such as Julian of Norwich's *Shewings,* Margery Kempe's *Book,* other treatises by Rolle and Hilton, Robert Mannyng's *Handlyng Synne, A Talking of the Love of God,* and *The Prick of Conscience,* to name a few of the major representatives.

4. For an overview of major trends in *AW* scholarship, see Millett, *Ancrene Wisse, the Katherine Group, and the Wooing Group,* and the Introductions to both volumes of Millett's *Ancrene Wisse: A Corrected Edition of the Text.*

5. See, for example, the points raised in Millett, "*Mouvance* and the Medieval Author"; Innes-Parker, "The Legacy of *Ancrene Wisse*"; von Nolcken, "The *Recluse* and its Readers"; and Watson, "*Ancrene Wisse,* Religious Reform and the Late Middle Ages."

6. James Morton chose Nero as the base text for his 1853 edition of the *AW, The Ancren Riwle; a Treatise on the Rules and Duties of Monastic Life.*

Edited and Translated from a Semi-Saxon MS. of the Thirteenth Century, Camden Society Publications 57 (London, 1853).

7. See particularly J. R. R. Tolkien, "Ancrene Wisse and Hali Meiðhad," *Essays and Studies by Members of the English Association* 14 (1929): 104–126, and ibid., ed. *The English Text of the Ancrene Riwle, Ancrene Wisse, Edited from MS. Corpus Christi College Cambridge 402,* introd. Neil R. Ker, EETS o.s. 249 (London: Oxford University Press, 1962 for 1960). The preference for Corpus continues today: Bella Millett uses it for her seminal two-volume EETS critical edition, relied on for studies of the *AW* whether in the high or later Middle Ages.

8. The same is true for Cleopatra, thanks to E. J. Dobson's impressive critical introduction in his *The English Text of the Ancrene Riwle, Edited from B.M. Cotton MS. Cleopatra C.vi.,* EETS o.s. 267 (London: Oxford University Press, 1972).

9. *The English Text of the Ancrene Riwle, Edited from Cotton MS. Nero A.XIV, on the basis of a transcript by J. A. Herbert,* EETS o.s.225 (London: Oxford University Press, 1952 for 1946). Caroline Cole uses codicology to argue for the unity of the manuscript in "The Integrity of Text and Context in the Prayers of British Library, Cotton MS Nero A.XIV," *Neuphilologische Mitteilungen* 104.1 (2003): 85–94. Her analysis is thoughtful and thorough but still fairly brief and is used in service to her textual argument rather than as a codicological survey.

10. By this term I want to suggest manuscripts of the type that are small, portable, utility-grade, and heavily used by readers (marked in, worn out, repaired), in contrast to display copies or deluxe editions.

11. Nothing is known of the origins of the earliest *AW* manuscripts and only limited information is available about the early provenances of Cleopatra, which was in the hands of canonesses by about 1284, and Corpus, given to a house of canons near the end of the thirteenth century by a lay owner (Millett, *Ancrene Wisse: A Corrected Edition,* I.xiv and xi). It is quite possible Nero followed a similar path; Day proposes that Winchcombe Abbey in Gloucester possessed Nero by the late Middle Ages (xv–xvi).

12. Similar evidence suggests, as I argue in my Ph.D. dissertation, *Learning and Literacy Outside the Convent: Early Middle English Women Readers and the Ancrene Wisse,* that the Titus manuscript was custom made as well.

13. These pieces and their arrangements are noted in Table 1. For a comparative table of Wooing Group and Katherine Group texts distributed among the *AW* manuscripts, see Millett, *Ancrene Wisse: A Corrected Edition,* II.lvii.

14. Albert Derolez, *The Paleography of Gothic Manuscript Books: From the Twelfth to the Early Sixteenth Century* (Cambridge: Cambridge University Press, 2003), 32–33.

15. This is one of the major pieces of evidence, in my estimation, that the scribe was using or intended to use something like the *pecia* system in copying Nero. The intratextual references to the circulation of quires among anchorholds suggest that anchoresses might have loaned out their texts, or parts of them, to others for copying. If this is true for Nero, it may be that the creation of a utility-grade manuscript would have served not just as a working book in an anchorhold, but also as an easily used future exemplar.

16. As with quire 7, quire 12 has one singleton affixed to the regular gathering. In 7 this is added at the beginning, while in 12 this is added at the end.

17. Raymond Clemens and Timothy Graham, *Introduction to Manuscript Studies* (Ithaca: Cornell University Press, 2007), 14.

18. Tipping-in is also used for textual correction; however, the last quire does not show evidence of such a need. Smaller corrections are indicated in the usual way, by intralinear addition or marginal annotation; on folio 123b, notably, a missed line was written at the top of the leaf and marked for insertion by a *signe-de-renvoi* between lines 3 and 4.

19. Cole argues for Nero's "textual integrity," proposing that the two scribes of the manuscript copied from an existing exemplar, an archetype no longer extant (87). She relies on evidence from the structure of the manuscript as well as its "semantic and thematic intertextuality" (90).

20. On the use of the *pecia* system in Cleopatra, see Dobson, *English Text of the Ancrene Riwle*, xxix–xxxvi. On the *pecia* system itself, see Clemens and Graham, 22–24; Susan Uselmann, "Women Reading and Reading Women: Early Scribal Notions of Literacy in the Ancrene Wisse," *Exemplaria: A Journal of Theory in Medieval and Renaissance Studies* 16.2 (2004): 369–404, at 395; and Andrew Taylor, "Authors, Scribes, Patrons, and Books," in *The Idea of the Vernacular: An Anthology of Middle English Literary Theory*, 1280–1520, ed. Jocelyn Wogan-Browne et al. (University Park, PA: Pennsylvania State University Press, 1999), 354–365. Malcolm Parkes discusses it as well in "Book Provision and Libraries at Oxford," in *Scribes, Scripts, and Readers: Studies in the Communication, Presentation, and Dissemination of Medieval Texts* (London: Hambledon Press, 1991), 299–310 at 304–308. While scholars such as Destrez and Pollard have associated the *pecia* system strictly with the University, particularly in Paris (304), Parkes points out that at least in Oxford, non-University members used the system as well, and not just stationers hired out exemplaria (306). Particularly useful for this study is his conclusion that the Dominican and Franciscan convents kept exemplaria available for copying out (307); perhaps this is how Nero was produced. Though the term *pecia* has a specific meaning for the University of Paris, it is used more loosely by other scholars to describe

a system of lending out exemplars for writing out additional copies of texts. Dobson uses it, for example, to describe the system under which Cleopatra was produced; this manuscript was certainly not a university text but was very likely produced by friars. My use of *"pecia* system" is in this spirit.

21. Millett, *Ancrene Wisse: A Corrected Edition*, I.94.
22. All translations are mine.
23. Millett, *Ancrene Wisse: A Corrected Edition*, I.107.
24. This is visible, for example, at the gutter between folios 5 and 6, 7 and 8, and 119 and 120.
25. This might be an additional indication of the use of a *pecia*-like system.
26. This is unusual. The markings are very thin and fine and appear to cut through the parchment, rather than "bruise" it, as hardpoint usually does. The quire marking has been done with pressure enough to leave impressions on some subsequent leaves (mirrored on the verso of such leaves). It seems as though the slicing technique was carried out with the leaves of each quire stacked in order, unfolded, so that the marks carried through the first half of the stack.
27. Nothing in the text indicates missing material or the movement of a leaf for insertion.
28. The leaf marks in quires 1 and 7 are no longer visible, though the quire marks at the start of the quires are.
29. There is a small inconsistency in the system, though, whose significance is not apparent. In all quires but a few, the numbering of the individual leaves begins with the second leaf, ostensibly because the quire mark on the first leaf ensures that the first leaf is put in its correct place. In quires 5, 10, and 13, the first leaf, while not marked as such, begins the sequence of either Roman numerals or letters. On the face this may suggest some rearrangement of the size of the quires after marking; perhaps the incised quire marks were added to the first leaves after the individual leaves were marked, though this would mean that quires whose leaves were numbered with Roman numerals or letters starting with the second leaf risked falling out of arrangement.
30. See the discussion in Cole.
31. I discuss these markings at length in "Women's Latinity in the Early English Anchorhold," forthcoming in *Women Leaders and Intellectuals of the Medieval World*, ed. Kathryn Kerby-Fulton and Katie Ann-Marie Bugyis (University of Notre Dame Press). This system of carefully indexing the quires and parts was carried further by a thirteenth- or fourteenth-century reader, who added finding and indexing aids to the margins in a hand of that date as well.
32. Clemens and Graham, *Introduction to Manuscript Studies*, 17.

33. Albert Derolez, *Codicologie des manuscrits en écriture humanistique sur parchemin, Bibliologia, Elementa ad Librorum Studia Pertinentia 5–6* (Turnhout: Brepols, 1984), I.67.
34. Day describes the contents of quire 13 at xxii–iv; Cole examines the quire's unity with the rest of the manuscript.
35. Richard Morris, ed. and trans., *Old English Homilies and Homiletic Treatises (Sawles Warde, and Þe Wohunge of Ure Lauerd: Ureisuns of Ure Louerd and of Ure Lefdi, &c) of the Twelfth and Thirteenth Centuries, edited from MSS. in the British Museum, Lambeth, and Bodleian Libraries,* EETS o.s. 29, 34 (London, 1868), vii.
36. Oxford, Bodleian Library, MS Bodley 34, another thirteenth-century manuscript, and an important witness of writing of this milieu for women, contains all of the KG texts. One wonders if that is the sort of manuscript that might have accompanied Nero into the anchorhold, nearly completing the collection of KG/WG texts for an anchoritic reader.
37. For a discussion of this feature, see Day, ix.
38. Neil Ker, "From 'above top line' to 'below top line': A Change in Scribal Practice," Celtica 5 (1960): 13–16.
39. Day noted the shift of folio 57 from quire 6 to quire 7 by examining the ruling pattern but did not observe that the quire marks also confirm this shift.
40. The *AW* required fifty-eight bifolia and three singletons, which might have represented a significant number of animals, depending on the means of the patron or intended user. The short collected texts required three bifolia and three singletons, a much less significant expenditure.
41. "From 'Above Top Line' to 'Below Top Line'." This time period coincides with the arrival of the friars into England and the suggested date of composition for the *AW*.
42. Brown, "Mise-en-Page," *Understanding Illuminated Manuscripts: A Guide to Technical Terms*, British Library, Catalogue of Illuminated Manuscripts: Glossaries (London: British Library), accessed 3 Aug 2014; Roberts, *Guide to Scripts Used in English Writing up to 1550* (London: British Library, 2005), 106.
43. My thanks to Elaine Treharne for suggesting the scribe might have lacked a supervisor.
44. I have no easy explanation for why the flyleaf, too, is blotted with ink. It was once a pastedown so perhaps it served in an original binding of this *AW* text, or at least the first quire. Day suggests that the first parchment flyleaf (fol. i), but not the fourth, may have "originally been connected with the *Ancrene Riwle*" (xii).
45. See, for example, folios 55, 74, 76, 77, 86 (a particularly damaged page,

containing four repairs, including addition of a large parchment patch along the edge of the leaf), 92, 94, 96, 103, 105, and 127.

46. Neil Ker dates Corpus to the same time period as Nero, Titus, and Cleopatra. On the dating of the manuscript, see Millett, *Ancrene Wisse: A Corrected Edition*, I.xi.

47. See A. I. Doyle, "Codicology, Palaeography, and Provenance," esp. "2.2 Date and Provenance," in Wendy Scase and Nick Kennedy, *A Facsimile Edition of the Vernon Manuscript Oxford, Bodleian Library, MS. Eng. Poet. A. 1* (Oxford: Bodleian Library, 2011); and Arne Zettersten and Bernhard Diensberg, *The English Text of the Ancrene Riwle: the 'Vernon' Text*, Early English Text Society 310 (Oxford: Oxford University Press, 2000), ix–xvii.

48. On the great expense and heft of Vernon, as well as its regular quire structure, see A. I. Doyle, "Codicology, Palaeography, and Provenance," in Wendy Scase and Nick Kennedy, *A Facsimile Edition of the Vernon Manuscript Oxford, Bodleian Library, MS. Eng. Poet. A. 1* (Oxford: Bodleian Library, 2011).

49. A. I. Doyle reviews the range of possible houses in *The Vernon Manuscript: A Facsimile of Bodleian Library, Oxford, MS Eng. Poet. a. 1* (Cambridge: Brewer, 1987), 14–15. See also the discussion in Zettersten and Diensberg, *The English Text of the Ancrene Riwle: the 'Vernon' Text*, xiv–xvii. For an analysis of potential lay patronage, see Wendy Scase, "The Patronage of the Vernon Manuscript" in *The Making of the Vernon Manuscript: The Production and Contexts of Oxford, Bodleian Library, MS Eng. poet. a. 1*, ed. Wendy Scase, Texts and Transitions 6 (Turnhout: Brepols, 2013), 269–293.

50. For that discussion, see Hall, "Women's Latinity in the Early English Anchorhold."

51. See, for instance, folios 61b/62a and 76b/77a.

52. Clanchy, *From Memory to Written Record: England 1066–1307*, 3rd edition (Oxford: Wiley-Blackwell, 2012), 135. For examples of (likely) friars' hands, in contrast with the primarily nonprofessional annotations in Nero, see Oxford, Bodleian Library, MS Digby 2 (late thirteenth century) and London, British Library, Harley MS 913 (early fourteenth century).

53. This particular form is not recorded in the examples given by the *Oxford English Dictionary*, however, and is difficult to pin to a particular time period.

54. Nero was included in the catalogue of that same year, and James also added a note dated April 30, 1625, on a flyleaf of Nero, suggesting that he got his hands on Nero very soon after taking up his post.

55. Oddly, though, he consistently writes his comments a page or two ahead of where they should fall to correspond with the text.

WORKS CITED

Brown, Michelle. "Mise-en-Page." *Understanding Illuminated Manuscripts: A Guide to Technical Terms*. British Library, Catalogue of Illuminated Manuscripts: Glossaries. London: British Library. Accessed 3 Aug. 2014.

Clanchy, Michael. *From Memory to Written Record: England 1066–1307*. 3rd edition. Oxford: Wiley-Blackwell, 2012.

Clemens, Raymond, and Timothy Graham. *Introduction to Manuscript Studies*. Ithaca, NY: Cornell University Press, 2007.

Cole, Caroline. "The Integrity of Text and Context in the Prayers of British Library, Cotton MS Nero A.XIV." *Neuphilologische Mitteilungen* 104.1 (2003): 85–94.

Day, Mabel. *The English Text of the Ancrene Riwle, Edited from Cotton MS. Nero A.XIV, on the basis of a transcript by J. A. Herbert*. EETS o.s. 225. London: Oxford University Press, 1952 for 1946.

Derolez, Albert. *Codicologie des manuscrits en écriture humanistique sur parchemin*. Bibliologia, Elementa ad Librorum Studia Pertinentia 5–6. Turnhout: Brepols, 1984.

———. *The Paleography of Gothic Manuscript Books: From the Twelfth to the Early Sixteenth Century*. Cambridge: Cambridge University Press, 2003.

Dobson, E. J. *The English Text of the Ancrene Riwle, Edited from B.M. Cotton MS. Cleopatra C.vi*. EETS o.s. 267. London: Oxford University Press, 1972.

Doyle, A. I. "Codicology, Palaeography, and Provenance. *A Facsimile Edition of the Vernon Manuscript Oxford, Bodleian Library, MS. Eng. Poet. A. 1*. Edited by Wendy Scase and Nick Kennedy. Oxford: Bodleian Library, 2011.

———. *The Vernon Manuscript: A Facsimile of Bodleian Library, Oxford, MS Eng. Poet. a. 1*. Cambridge: Brewer, 1987.

Hall, Megan J. "Women's Latinity in the Early English Anchorhold." *Women Leaders and Intellectuals of the Medieval World*. Edited by Kathryn Kerby-Fulton and Katie Ann-Marie Bugyis. Notre Dame, Ind.: University of Notre Dame Press (forthcoming).

Innes-Parker, Catherine. "*Ancrene Wisse* and Þe Wohunge of Ure Lauerd: The Thirteenth-Century Female Reader and the Lover-Knight." *Women, the Book and the Godly: Selected Proceedings of the St. Hilda's Conference, 1993* I. Edited by Leslie Smith and Jane H. Taylor. Cambridge, Eng.: Brewer, 1995. 137–147.

Ker, Neil. "From 'above top line' to 'below top line': A Change in Scribal Practice." *Celtica* 5 (1960): 13–16.

Millett, Bella, ed. *Ancrene Wisse: A Corrected Edition of the Text in Cambridge, Corpus Christi College, MS 402, with Variants from Other Manuscripts, drawing on the uncompleted edition by E.J. Dobson; with a glossary and additional notes by Richard Dance.* EETS o.s. 325–326. Oxford: Oxford University Press, 2005–2006.

———. *Ancrene Wisse, the Katherine Group, and the Wooing Group.* Annotated Bibliographies of Old and Middle English Literature 2. Cambridge: D. S. Brewer, 1996.

———. "*Mouvance* and the Medieval Author: Re-editing Ancrene Wisse." *Late-Medieval Religious Texts and their Transmission.* Edited by A. J. Minnis. Cambridge, Eng.: Cambridge University Press, 1994. 9–20.

Morris, Richard, ed. and trans. *Old English Homilies and Homiletic Treatises (Sawles Warde, and Þe Wohunge of Ure Lauerd: Ureisuns of Ure Louerd and of Ure Lefdi, &c) of the Twelfth and Thirteenth Centuries, edited from MSS. in the British Museum, Lambeth, and Bodleian Libraries.* EETS o.s. 29, 34. London, 1868.

Morton, James. *The Ancren Riwle; a Treatise on the Rules and Duties of Monastic Life. Edited and Translated from a Semi-Saxon MS. of the Thirteenth Century.* Camden Society Publications 57. London, 1853.

von Nolcken, Christina. "The *Recluse* and its Readers: Some Observations on a Lollard Interpolated Version of Ancrene Wisse." *A Companion to Ancrene Wisse.* Edited by Yoko Wada. Woodbridge, Eng.: Brewer, 2003. 175–196.

Parkes, Malcolm. "Book Provision and Libraries at Oxford." *Scribes, Scripts, and Readers: Studies in the Communication, Presentation, and Dissemination of Medieval Texts.* London: Hambledon Press, 1991. 299–310.

Roberts, Jane. Guide to Scripts Used in English Writing up to 1550. London: British Library, 2005.

Scase, Wendy. "The Patronage of the Vernon Manuscript." *The Making of the Vernon Manuscript: The Production and Contexts of Oxford, Bodleian Library, MS Eng. poet. a. 1.* Edited by Wendy Scase. Texts and Transitions 6. Turnhout: Brepols, 2013.

"Sickness, n." *OED Online.* December 2016. Oxford University Press. Accessed 22 Dec. 2016.

Taylor, Andrew. "Authors, Scribes, Patrons, and Books." *The Idea of the Vernacular: An Anthology of Middle English Literary Theory, 1280–1520.* Edited by Jocelyn Wogan-Browne et al. University Park, PA: Pennsylvania State University Press, 1999. 354–365.

Tolkien, J. R. R. "*Ancrene Wisse* and Hali Meiðhad," *Essays and Studies by Members of the English Association* 14 (1929): 104–126.

———, ed. *The English Text of the Ancrene Riwle, Ancrene Wisse, Edited from MS. Corpus Christi College Cambridge 402.* Introduced by Neil R. Ker. EETS o.s. 249. London: Oxford University Press, 1962 for 1960.

Uselmann, Susan. "Women Reading and Reading Women: Early Scribal Notions of Literacy in the *Ancrene Wisse*." *Exemplaria: A Journal of Theory in Medieval and Renaissance Studies* 16.2 (2004): 369–404.

Watson, Nicholas. "*Ancrene Wisse*, Religious Reform and the Late Middle Ages." *A Companion to Ancrene Wisse*. Edited by Yoko Wada. Woodbridge, Eng.: Brewer, 2003. 197–226.

Zettersten, Arne and Bernhard Diensberg. *The English Text of the Ancrene Riwle: the 'Vernon' Text*. EETS o.s. 310. Oxford: Oxford University Press, 2000.

'All the Strete My Voyce Shall Heare': Gender, Voice, and Desire in the Lyrics of Bodleian MS Ashmole 176

CARISSA M. HARRIS

On the recto and verso of folio 98 in MS Ashmole 176, one scribe has copied together four "songs of wantonness" about gendered embodiment, violence, and desire. The cluster begins and ends with two poems about impotence, one from a dejected man's perspective and the other from a frustrated woman's. This corporeal emphasis is made all the more striking by the scribe's choice to bookend the bawdy lyric cluster with conventional courtly complaints in which anguished men bewail "the paynes of love" and lament their powerlessness against women's "false love" and "unkyndnes."[1] This understudied four-lyric group copied onto a single folio is the focus of this essay, as I argue that MS Ashmole 176's "songs of wantonness" speak fruitfully to one another as well as the male-voiced complaints that surround them in the anthology, and they shed light on the effects of bodies and desires coming into conflict with one another.

MS Ashmole 176: Manuscript, texts, and contexts
MS Ashmole 176's four lyrics—*My ladye hath forsaken me*, a never-before-printed obscene erotic poem; a singlewoman's pregnancy lament entitled *Up I arose in verno tempore*; *I can be wanton and yf I wyll*, a rape narrative; and *Let be wanton your busynes*, a short, female-voiced erotic lyric or scribal tag—are part of a collection of seventeen Tudor court songs written in a single, practiced secretary hand.[2] According to William A. Ringler, Jr., most of the songs were composed in the 1520s, and they were copied

together between 1525 and 1550.[3] The anthology is a slim booklet of five paper sheets, which were originally bound together and circulated on their own.[4] The booklet was later sewn into a larger quarto-size volume together with several other booklets consisting of astrological material, Latin prose treatises on the planets and signs of the zodiac, planetary tables, and nativity charts with birthdates from 1551 to 1631.[5] The seventeen English lyrics, which include ten male-voiced love complaints interspersed with songs about lost virility, unwanted pregnancy, sexual assault, and Henry VIII dancing with his young daughter Princess Mary at court, have not captured much critical interest until now.[6] Their authorship is largely unknown, save for one song by Tudor court composer William Cornish (d. 1523) and another by Henry Howard, Earl of Surrey (1516–1547). The anthology shares affinities with other manuscript collections of Tudor court songs about decorous love, bawdy desire, and sexual violence, most notably the Ritson Manuscript (British Library MS Additional 5665, copied before 1511), a trilingual English, French, and Latin choir repertory of sacred and secular songs associated with Exeter Cathedral, and the Henry VIII Manuscript (British Library MS Additional 31922, copied 1510–1513), which contains songs attributed to the lusty young king.[7] MS Ashmole 176's macaronic pregnancy lament *Up I arose in verno tempore* and the popular devotional lyric *Come over the borne, bessye* also survive in the Ritson Manuscript, where they are copied in the same hand on adjacent folios, suggesting more of a relationship between the two anthologies than has been previously acknowledged.[8] *Alas to whom shuld I complayne* was copied in longer form in British Library MS Harley 2252 (1517–1538), a commonplace book of moral, political, and didactic pieces belonging to London mercer John Colyn, as a politically-tinged elegy for Edward Stafford, Duke of Buckingham (executed 1521), then shortened to four lines and repurposed as a lovelorn complaint in MS Ashmole 176.[9] Cornish's leave-taking lament *Adew adew my hartis lust* survives in both MS Ashmole 176 and the Henry VIII Manuscript, and the incipit only of *Ravyshed was I that well was me* is copied with one of the earliest surviving lute-song settings in British Library Cotton MS Titus D.XI, a mid-fifteenth-century manuscript of Latin prose epistles by Walter Hilton and Thomas Becket containing two folios of early sixteenth-century music.[10] Surrey's popular lute-song *If care may cause men crye why doe I not complayne* was printed in variant form by Richard Tottel in *Songes and Sonettes* (1557), the earliest printed anthology of English poetry, and survives in two early seventeenth-century printed songbooks and four sixteenth-century manuscripts.[11] The remaining eleven poems survive in unique copies in MS Ashmole 176. We know nothing of the manuscript's provenance or early history before the astrologer William Lilly gifted it to the antiquarian Elias Ashmole in 1637.[12]

It belonged to the Ashmolean Museum after Ashmole's death in 1692 until it was moved to the Bodleian Library's collections in 1860.

The anthology's courtly lyrics focus on men's "payne"—a word that is repeated a total of seventeen times in the ten love complaints—and women's power. Three disconsolate lovers utter the phrase "she hathe reclaymed me to her lure," using a hawking metaphor to express feminine domination over men, as "reclayme" means "to make tame" or "subject somebody to one's control."[13] The songs emphasize men's "weping eeis" and "paynfull sighes," and they imagine the audience for their laments of lost or unrequited love as comprised chiefly of their fellow men.[14] *In a garden underneth a tre* explicitly stages this vision of masculine affective community: as the *chanson d'aventure* narrator wanders through a garden, he encounters "a man in paynes prest" sprawled on the grass (3). The narrator "ask[s] hym" to share his feelings (8), and the man responds with a doleful complaint. These courtly lyrics stand in stark contrast to the poems on folio 98, which shift their focus from men's emotional pain to women's embodied experiences of pregnancy, rape, and thwarted arousal.

Joshua Eckhardt has examined how the compilers of early modern verse miscellanies frequently copied polite love lyrics and obscene erotic verses alongside one another. He argues that this practice became "enormously popular" in the early decades of the seventeenth century, "particularly among young men at the universities and Inns at Court."[15] In proposing a model of "contextual reading," a methodology that I also use in this essay, Eckhardt argues that "[a] poem's full significance ... may extend beyond its text to the affiliations and resonances that it develops among other texts and in its various contexts, no matter how local or even physical."[16] He claims that "[b]y routinely countering or complementing love poetry with erotic or obscene verse, manuscript verse collectors arguably formed an unrecognized poetic genre" that he christens "anti-courtly love poetry."[17] MS Ashmole 176's juxtaposition of courtliness and obscenity demonstrates that this scribal practice identified by Eckhardt has a longer and richer history than previously acknowledged.

Scholars have explored the relationship between gender and lyric voice in manuscripts such as the Maitland Quarto (Cambridge, Magdalene College, Pepys Library MS 1408, *c.* 1586), a verse anthology containing amatory verse from women's perspectives that was associated with Mary (d. 1596) and Helen Maitland, daughters of the Scottish courtier Sir Richard Maitland of Lethington.[18] Mary and Helen were certainly among the collection's readers and may have participated in its production as composers, scribes, or editors. One of the Maitland Quarto's lyrics celebrates erotic love and friendship between women, while others portray women as accomplished poets, idealized objects of desire, and "filthie, faithless dame[s]" who "chus[e]" their lovers "for lance and speir."[19] Another verse anthology with links between female lyric voices and female composers and compilers is the Devonshire Manuscript (British Library, MS Additional 17492), copied by a coterie of women close to Henry VIII and Anne Boleyn in the 1530s.[20] Christopher Shirley discusses how Lady Margaret Douglas (1515–1578), one of the manuscript's scribes, annotated a cluster of misogynous poems for repeated re-reading. He christens this response "[m]isogynistic femininity, a performance of identity signaling worldliness, wit, and sophistication," showing how some sixteenth-century female readers responded to misogyny in ways that modern audiences might not expect.[21] Elizabeth Heale argues that the Devonshire Manuscript illuminates the wide range of subject positions available to first-person female speakers in early Tudor courtly verse, as its lyrics depict a range of women—from the faithless to the steadfast, from the insatiate to the chaste.[22] While we do not know anything about the gendered context of MS Ashmole 176's origins and earliest circulation history, its purposeful clustering of songs in women's voices in the midst of one male-voiced virility lyric and numerous polite male-voiced love complaints shares affinities with other sixteenth-century verse miscellanies that stage contrasting perspectives on gender, desire, and embodiment.

MS Ashmole 176's lyrics demonstrate how competing versions of gendered pain, power, and agency, when presented alongside one another, can speak back to one another in productive and illuminating ways. The courtly lyrics and the male-voiced erotic song on folio 98r assert that women possess all the "pleasure" in heterosexual erotic relationships by cruelly holding men "in cure" [in their power], while the three female-voiced "songs of wantonness" on folio 98v complicate this notion by vividly depicting various factors that constrain women's erotic agency: the threat of unplanned pregnancy, lack of reproductive choice, and sexual violence.[23] Like the lyrics in the Maitland Quarto and the Devonshire Manuscript, the anthology's songs provide a nuanced example of how women's desires could be represented in premodern lyric. Their emphasis on the immediacy and range of these desires, made both stronger and more complex through the scribe's choice to copy them together, betrays a focus that is relentlessly corporeal, as they highlight speakers' experiences of impotence, sexual competition, abandonment, pregnancy, and rape.

MS Ashmole 176's four "songs of wantonness"—one voiced by a man, and three voiced by women—are copied together in a self-contained cluster on the recto and verso of the booklet's second folio (98). The recto and verso of the booklet's first folio (97), which introduces the anthology, are occupied by the collection's longest lyric, the lute-song and courtly complaint *If care may cause men crye whye doe I not complayne.*[24] This framing of the bawdy songs through a courtly lens has important implications for how we read folio 98's lyric cluster. The song was written by the poet-aristocrat Henry Howard, Earl of Surrey, who along with Sir Thomas Wyatt was among the first to write sonnets in England before being beheaded for treason by an aging and paranoid Henry VIII.[25] The compiler's choice to open the collection with a lengthy, self-indulgent complaint about aristocratic male suffering and service directs the codex's readers to think about complaint, gender, and pain according to conventional courtly paradigms of women's power and men's suffering, only to offer a different perspective on the very next folio.

Surrey's complaint establishes the anthology's focus on male audiences and readers, as the speaker addresses his song not to his beloved but to his fellow men. He claims the complaint is a genre where "eche man may bewayle his woe" (2), a discursive space where men can voice their intimate feelings to one another. In setting up the anthology as a space where men share narratives about desire and suffering with other men, the scribe establishes a model of same-sex affective identification between gendered lyric voice and audience. Surrey's speaker, unable to separate himself from the gendered collective, sees his desires in comparison to other men's, exacerbating his doleful state: "And when I see some have their most desired sight / Alas thynke I eche man hathe well save I most wofull wight" (19–20), he sighs.[26]

By copying folio 98's cluster of mainly female-voiced lyrics about sexuality and desire in a group and bracketing them with complaints about men's powerlessness, MS Ashmole 176's scribe provides the opportunity for audiences to consider the various physical, social, and legal factors that thwart desire and obstruct erotic agency. There are several ties other than proximity that link folio 98's "songs of wantonness" and render them a distinct subgroup within the collection. One is gender and voice, since three of the four lyrics are voiced wholly or partially by women, in contrast to the other thirteen lyrics in the anthology, which are all voiced by men. Another factor that links the four songs is visual similarity: unlike some of the collection's other lyrics, they are copied without errors, hesitation, or cross-outs, each piece written in long lines punctuated by medial commas and neatly concluded with a "finis" and one or two *virgulae suspensivae*.[27] With their shared focus on explicit sexuality and female subjectivity, they contrast sharply with the anthology's complaints, which are devoid of bawdy corporeal references and focus instead on men's experiences of lost or unrequited love. And finally, all four are addressed to male audiences. The first is voiced by a man offering erotic counsel to his male peers; the second portrays an eavesdropping male narrator listening to a maiden's complaint of unwanted pregnancy; in the third, a woman challenges a man as he assaults her; and the fourth is voiced by a woman to her lover. All four emphasize women's desire and explore its social costs and consequences. They purport to enlighten male audiences about gendered corporeality and desire, just as the anthology's courtly complainers appeal to their same-sex peers with tales of heartfelt woe.

"Undoubted she desyreth muche": *My ladye hath forsaken me*

Folio 98r is occupied entirely by *My ladye hath forsaken me*, a six-quatrain, male-voiced erotic poem that has never been printed until now.[28] Its speaker narrates how his mistress of "this vij yeares and some deale more" (5) abandoned him for a new lover after he became physically unable to meet her voracious sexual demands. He addresses his fellow men and shares his narrative in graphic detail, representing his experiences of sex, impotence, and rejection as possessing the potential to edify his peers. His song is filled with the conventional courtly rhetoric of men's service and unstinting devotion, placing it in conversation with the manuscript's other love complaints in order to offer a contrasting perspective on gender and power.[29] The speaker deploys courtly rhetoric throughout the song but invests it with explicitly sexual meaning, as he imagines devoted "service" to his lady as entailing regular, vigorous intercourse. He recalls, "Her Servant when I first began, as then she dyd report / For trewe Servyce I bare the name among the rowte and sort" (9–10).[30] But it is not honeyed flattery and promises of devotion that constitute "trewe Servyce" according to this man, but rather the ability to provide his beloved with corporeal satisfaction. He describes a reciprocal relationship where men make careful, attentive efforts for which women recompense them: "with her I dyd take payne ... and ... she therfore rewarded me agayne," he relates (5–6).[31] He underscores the mutuality in their sexual relationship with the adverb "agayne" [in return, in exchange], and he uses rhyme to link "agayne" and "take payne" [to make an effort] to emphasize the reciprocity of their coital efforts.[32]

The speaker addresses his relationship narrative as a lesson to his male peers. He illustrates his sexual instructions with didactic proverbs, and he presents his experiences as an exemplum about men's bodies and women's desires. He warns his fellow men that excessive intercourse, particularly with a partner as ardently desirous as his former lady, leads to a permanent "lack[... of] Strengthe" (24), echoing other obscene instructive poems voiced by regretful men who have permanently squandered their potency.[33] In sharing his account of erectile misfortune with an audience of his peers and offering words of warning and counsel, the speaker teaches them about sexuality by sharing intimate details from his own experience. He candidly discloses his impotence when he states, "but nowe she feeles I faynt" (11), characterizing his physical state with a verb denoting enfeeblement and exhaustion due to exertion.[34] He purports to educate men regarding women's desire in his song's alliterating refrain, where he asserts that his lady seeks a lover "Lustye and full of Strengthe in Labour good at Lengthe" (4, 8, 12, 20).[35] He emphasizes the vigor that he no longer possesses by repeating the descriptors "lustye" and "full of strengthe" as bodily prerequisites for his former lady's next partner, and he insists that she desires a lover who is able to persist in "Labour" "at Lengthe," or "to the full extent, without cur-tailment." He identifies with his audience, imagining them all as potential partners of his lady: "Her appetyte ys suche," he relates, "marke who so Lust to trye" (21). By demanding that his peers "marke" his instructions about his lady's "appetyte" before they "trye" her themselves, the speaker portrays his obscene admonition as explicitly pedagogical, as he chooses an imperative verb that occurs frequently in didactic literature.[36]

It is easy to read this song as a misogynist lesson regarding the bottom-less capacity of women's desire, as the speaker voices common anxieties about impotence, rejection, and competition with other men prominent in the antifeminist poetry that proliferated during the late fifteenth and early sixteenth centuries.[37] Heale argues that, in the context of the early Tudor court, this enormously popular discourse of misogyny allowed women to "embody, or act as scapegoats for, deep-seated masculine fears and resent-ments, displacing the competition for royal service into an often antago-nistic game-world of amorous service."[38] *My ladye hath forsaken me* pres-ents women as fickle and insatiate, requiring more sex than any single man can provide and discarding their lovers for new ones once their potency is sapped. This representation of women's voracity and faithlessness is part of a larger discourse that demonized women in poems like John Lydgate's *Prohemy of a Mariage* (c. 1440–1460), another man-to-man didactic piece that represents female desire as both unquenchable "appetyte" (91, 391) and corporeal "sikenesse" (125). Lydgate's speaker says of one lustful woman, "She was hungry and wold have had hir mele" (390). This characterization of women's erotic yearning as bottomless hunger also appears in *My ladye hath forsaken me*, whose speaker names his beloved as "she unsacyate" (20) and declares, "undoubted she desyrethe muche" (18).[39] Similarly, in William Dunbar's *Tretis of the Tua Mariit Wemen and the Wedo* (c. 1507), the Wedo teaches her friends how she assesses potential lovers based upon whether they appear to be "forgeit … maist forcely to furnyse a bancat / In Venus chalmer" [forged most strongly to furnish a banquet in Venus's chamber] and compares sexual activity to a "cury" [concoction, cooked dish], while in *The Freiris of Berwik* (c. 1461–1482), an amorous woman addresses "hir cunt" directly to say, "Thir mullis of youris ar callit to ane feist" [These lips of yours are invited to a feast].[40] These antifeminist poems portray men's fears that women will sap their potency before rejecting them for their more virile and vigorous peers, and they give voice to the speakers' anxieties about intra-masculine competition.

The speaker addresses his fellow men with familiarity and appeals to their shared body of gendered wisdom by using proverbs to illustrate his lesson:

> Ye knowe that newe brome Swepeth cleane, as
> many mens sainge ys,
> And hackneyes that be comon oftymes tyred ys
> And so shall he be that servethe my Ladye
> Although he nowe have strengthe, she wyll hym
> tyre at Lengthe (13–16)[41]

His reference to the collective authority of "many mens sainge" to bolster his claims invokes a same-sex oral community of advice and instruction regarding erotic matters. He uses two different proverbs as tools to illustrate his lesson. He imagines a common corpus of sexual knowledge: "Ye knowe," he states in his lesson about bodies, capacities, and desires. While the speaker traffics in common antifeminist stereotypes of women's insatiability, he presents his lady as justified in her decision to take up with a new lover, since he is no longer able to perform his carnal service. He closes his song with a warning to his peers: "Thus he who lacketh strengthe," he cautions in the final line, "she lettethe him slyp at lengthe" (24).

If read alone, this song would perhaps be simply another misogynous lyric about women's voraciousness, exemplified by the widespread popularity of poems like Lydgate's didactic pieces advising men against marriage. However, its material context here in MS Ashmole 176 opens up new interpretive possibilities. The song depicts a woman who has ardent physical desires and chooses her partners based on their capacity to fulfill those desires, challenging the anthology's courtly complaints' portrayal of women's choices as motivated by "disdayne" and "lacke [of] pytye."[42] Its depiction of women's longing as unquenchable physical "appetyte" is in turn challenged by the songs copied onto the subsequent verso (folio 98v), in which women's voices tell male audiences that they want much more than a man who is "Lustye and full of Strengthe in Labour good at Lengthe."

"*Alas, quid faciam?*": Choice and complaint in
Up I arose in verno tempore

The next three lyrics in the anthology, all voiced wholly or partially by women, are copied on folio 98v, and their depictions of desire offer a useful counterpoint to the portrayal of women's unmitigated ravenousness in *My ladye hath forsaken me* on the preceding recto. Their presence together here is particularly significant because all the other lyrics in the collection are voiced by men. *Up I arose in verno tempore*, a macaronic pregnancy lament, is the first of the three, setting the tone for the verso's focus on women's voices protesting sexual violence, lack of reproductive choice, and thwarted desire.[43] The scribe pays careful attention to punctuating folio 98v's three lyrics, ending each with two *virgulae suspensivae*, in contrast to the single *virgula* he typically writes at the end of the anthology's courtly songs; alternatively, these similarities could mean that he copied them from the same exemplar. Regardless of their origin, the double *virgulae* encourage readers to pause for an extra moment to digest the female-voiced songs on folio 98v.[44]

Up I arose in verno tempore, copied at the top of the verso, is a single woman's narrative about sex and abandonment that gives voice to her agonized deliberations about her unplanned pregnancy.[45] Like the maidens in other English pregnancy laments, she depicts herself as a victim of clerical predation: "with me hath layne, *quidam clericus* [a certain clerk]," she relates (3).[46] The lyric is macaronic, with the first and third quarters of each long line in English and the second and fourth quarter-lines in Latin, the half-lines separated by commas. Ad Putter notes how, in many Latin-English macaronic carols, the different languages perform different functions, as in a pair of bawdy macaronic carols from *c.* 1500; in these songs, the English lines narrate a sexual and pedagogical relationship between a friar and a nun, while the interspersed Latin lines ("*Inducas, inducas… in temptationibus*" [Lead us, lead us, into temptation]) are a perverse echo of the Lord's Prayer.[47] The song's linguistic hybridity is echoed in some pastourelles, with the cleric speaking in Latin and the peasant girl speaking in the vernacular in order to emphasize the social and educational disparities between the two speakers. In *Up I arose in verno tempore*, the maiden speaks in both languages, and she uses the Latin of the clerk who abandoned her to criticize his exploitative behavior and critique the lack of options available to women who become pregnant against their will.[48]

The *chanson d'aventure* opens with a (presumably) male first-person speaker enjoying an idyllic spring morning when he happens upon "a mayd, *sub quadam arbore*" [under a tree] (1) and listens to her song of abandonment.[49] The opening line is the only time the eavesdropper appears in the song, and his subsequent absence places the focus solely on the maid's complaint. The framing fiction of the *chanson d'aventure*, a popular lyric form in the later Middle Ages, reinforces the song's didactic potential. It renders the maiden's lament as offering the man edification or didactic instruction: as Judith Davidoff argues, the genre would have been typically understood as "a generalized *exemplum* whose *moralitas* would become clear in the poem's didactic core."[50] This lyric stages a young woman's voice teaching a male audience about the results of insufficient sexual knowledge and lack of reproductive options using personal narrative and affective language. By emphasizing her desperation—"What shal I say?" she wonders (3)— and highlighting the physical manifestation of her grief with the statement "*incipio flere*" [I begin to weep] (6), the woman encourages her audience to empathize with her plight and to recognize the social conditions that have led to it.

The narrator characterizes the young woman's lament as "a mayd['s] complayn[t]" (1), both aligning it and setting it in direct contrast with MS Ashmole 176's ten male-voiced complaints. The anthology is filled with complaining men: "Alas, to whom shuld I complayne?" wonders one.[51] Another sighs, "I may complayne as one in payne"; a third characterizes his song as "paynfull playnt"; and a fourth declares, "with double sorowes complayne me I must."[52] Those complaints bemoan love lost through parting, feminine falseness, or the woman's failure to reciprocate the speaker's affections, whereas this female-voiced complaint details the social and bodily consequences of the cleric's selfish desire and callous abandonment, forcing audiences to consider how the differences between men's and women's grievances are shaped by larger conditions of inequality. In addition to denoting a heartfelt expression of grief, as is suggested here through its pairing with the phrase "*in suo pectore*" [in her breast] (2), the verb "complayne" contains legal valences, meaning "to make a complaint, accusation, or appeal."[53] This introduces the maiden's narrative of abandonment, mistreatment, and lack of reproductive agency as a legal complaint, or the reporting of a crime committed against her, much as the speaker in the verso's next lyric frames her narrative of assault as an act of raising the hue and cry against her rapist. By characterizing the song as "complayn[t]," the song's framing speaker not only underscores lyric's affective capacity to encourage audiences to identify with the terror, panic, and sorrow resulting from the maiden's unplanned pregnancy, but he also highlights the lyric's ability to stage social protest, as the young woman can be read as delivering an official grievance regarding her experience. Her complaint issues a sharp challenge to the conditions that allow the unnamed "*clericus*" to escape unscathed while she prepares to suffer abuse and abandonment from her loved ones once her pregnancy is revealed.

In the poem's final two lines, the maiden considers how she will proceed with her pregnancy and weighs the options available to her: "with this said child alas, *quid faciam* [what shall I do], shall I yt kepe, *vel interficiam* [or shall I kill it], / yf I yt sley, *quo loco fugiam* [whither shall I flee], I shall lose god and *vitam eternam* [eternal life]" (7–8). She considers multiple courses of action rather than resigning herself to raising an unwanted child and accepting the accompanying social costs, which indicates that she is attempting to frame motherhood in terms of volition rather than biological imperative. She underscores the acute difficulty of her dilemma with the sorrowful interjection "alas," which recurs repeatedly in the collection's courtly complaints.[54] When the speaker considers abortion or infanticide, she renders that option in Latin ("*interficiam*") as well as in English ("sley"), while she imagines "kepe[ing]" the child in English alone, indicating that the former is the option to which she is giving greater weight.[55] By vividly detailing the consequences she will suffer for her pregnancy—beatings from parents, public shaming and disparagement, verbal abuse, loss of playmates—the maiden encourages her eavesdropping listener to have compassion for her potential choice to avoid those consequences regardless of the cost.

Wantonness and resistance: *I can be wanton and yf I wyll*

The second lyric copied onto folio 98v, *I can be wanton and yf I wyll*, is voiced by a woman proclaiming her right to "be wanton" and "be merye" before she is brutally assaulted.[56] She challenges her attacker and details her increasingly forceful attempts to fight his aggression. She promises to stop crying out and "lye styll" (2) in the final line after he has physically overpowered her, as she shifts her focus from preventing the assault to surviving it. While one could read this song as illustrating the rape myth that women's refusal can be overcome with persistence and brute force, I am more interested in reading it as illuminating the different forms of women's resistance—physical, verbal, and legal—to sexual violence during the period. The speaker repeatedly represents her song as an act of "cry[ing] howe" (1, 7, 12) or raising the hue and cry in response to rape, forcing readers to bear witness to her suffering and rendering them complicit in her legal outcry against her assailant.

This lyric makes bold claims about female desire, asserting a woman's right to be "wanton" and "merye" without being subjected to unwanted sexual attention (1–2) and establishing women as erotic subjects who are entitled to bodily integrity and freedom from harm. The song allows for a woman's desperate negotiations with her rapist—she threatens to raise the hue and cry, then "warant[s]" him to come near her as long as he remains unseen by others (4), before demanding that he "syt farre from [her]" because he seems dangerous (5) and refusing to kiss him—to be interpreted as "mixed messages" and used to discredit her claims of coercion, if one chooses to read the song in that way. Or it can be read, as I suggest here, as a literary version of a legal outcry, compelling audiences to serve as witnesses to the speaker's violation. Copied on folio 98v between *Up I arose in verno tempore*, a poem about a woman's yearning for tenable reproductive choices, and *Let be wanton your busynes*, a poem about a woman's frustrated lust, *I can be wanton and yf I wyll* voices a woman's desire to express wantonness and merriment without suffering the violence of unwanted "touche."

The poem opens with the speaker confidently articulating her right to engage in merriment without being perceived as sexually accessible, to express lighthearted enjoyment and flirtation without violation of her bodily autonomy. She declares in the first two lines, "I can be wanton and yf I wyll, but yf yowe touche me I wyll crye howe / I can be merye & thynke no evell, but yet beware one cometh I trowe" (1–2). She defends her prerogative to be "merye" and "wanton," and she insists that this does not mean that men can "touche" her as they please. She invokes the law on her side, threatening to raise the hue and cry if any man should misconstrue her playful "wantonness" as availability. Her repeated use of the verb "can," with its implications that she is right and justified in her assertions, grounds her claim.[57] The stanza's layout on the manuscript page further authorizes her pronouncement of erotic agency: "I can be" begins each of the poem's first two lines, the first-person I's oversized, with circular looped ascenders and long, trailing descenders.

At the same time that she declares her right to express wantonness and merriment, the speaker expresses a fear of violence as retribution for this expression. She anticipates the unwanted "touche" that she might suffer, twice using the conjunction "but" when she cautions, "*but* yf yowe touche me I wyll crye howe … *but* yet beware one cometh" (1–2; emphasis mine). She offers a stern warning to men who presume to touch her without permission by threatening to invoke the law's protection against rape. Her use of the verb "beware," indicating the presence of danger, to characterize the approach of a man who has chosen to misconstrue her merry manner as an amorous invitation indicates that she immediately—and correctly, as we soon see—perceives him as a potential threat.[58] She uses "beware" again five lines later when she declares, "me semeth youe should be wylde … I wilbe ware of suchelyke wylde men," depicting certain men's "wylde"-ness and refusal to govern their desires as a threat to her safety (5, 7). "Wylde," which contains valences of wickedness, lasciviousness, and lack of sexual governance, frequently occurs in alliterative pairings with "wanton," another adjective denoting lecherousness and lack of restraint that she applies pejoratively to her assailant (6).[59] This highlighting of a woman's fears of violence alongside her assertion of sexual agency underscores the physical risk that accompanies women's expressions of desire. It illuminates the inequalities that are elided in courtly discourse, directly contradicting the anthology's complainers' assertions that women are their "governour[s]," as one man tearfully puts it.[60] The woman acknowledges the fear she feels as a result of living under the threat of violence, and she chooses to assert her right to wantonness and merriment in spite of that fear. The subsequent five quatrains validate her concerns with chilling specificity, as she encounters a man who refuses to honor her desires.

I can be wanton and yf I wyll emphasizes the social and legal power of women's voices by focusing on the act of "cry[ing] howe," or raising the hue and cry, a response to rape in which the aggrieved party publicly declares that she has been criminally assaulted.[61] In "cry[ing] howe," women's voices acquire formal legal power. Caroline Dunn notes that "rape was one of the few crimes that women—even married women—could prosecute independently," and thus "cry[ing] howe" was a tool for demanding justice available to any woman with a voice.[62] This understanding of "crying howe" as resistance is reflected in a parliamentary record from 1423, which characterizes "hewe [and] cry" as "resistence making."[63] In the very first line, the speaker promises, "yf youe touche me I wyll crye howe" (1), then declares, "I wilbe ware of suchelyke wylde men for when they touche me I doo crye howe" (7). The song returns to the hue and cry in its final lines, as the woman concludes her outcry by telling her assailant after he has overpowered her, "I wilbe styll and crye howe no more" (12).

The speaker invokes the presence of laws that ostensibly protect women from the harm of nonconsensual touch, but she ultimately demonstrates the ineffectiveness of these laws by sharing a step-by-step narrative of her assault in spite of the fact that she is following legal procedures. In telling her story, the speaker issues a sharp critique of the law's capacity to protect women from violence despite its purported claims to do so. In addition to exposing the law's ineffectuality and shedding light on the stark gap between legal provision and lived experience, the woman's song rhetorically positions itself as a formal legal speech act of protest. Her threefold repetition of the formula "crye howe," and her use of it as a framing mechanism for her song, positions the song itself as an act of raising the hue and cry. It serves as a testimony to the crime committed against its speaker, encouraging audiences to empathize with her fear and anguish. The song insistently draws attention to the fact that she follows legal procedure and fights back with every strategy she can muster, and yet she is still assaulted.

The speaker opposes the man's aggression with words as well as fists, demonstrating how women were imagined to fight sexual violence during the period. As part of raising the hue and cry, women were expected to produce evidence of resistance to violence through blood, torn clothing, and other signs of physical struggle. The woman's deployment of multiple strategies—blunt refusal, negotiation, heartfelt pleading, and physical violence as self-defense—functions as the legal proof victims needed to support their act of "cry[ing] howe."[64] She declares her opposition to sexual contact with the man in no uncertain terms when she insists, "ye may me kyll as soone as kysse" (8), using alliteration to reinforce her equation between being killed and kissed by her assailant. She switches to polite pleading and negotiation by begging, "I pray youe awaie and let me be" (9), using the supplicatory verb "pray." She calls upon the power of public shaming by threatening to testify about her assault: "In faith all the world wyll speake of this," she promises

(10), then declares, "I crye, that all the strete my voyce shall heare" (13). She turns to physical aggression as her final tactic of resistance in the poem's last quatrain, where she exclaims, "By god I strike youe with my fyste" (11).

After punching her assailant, the woman chooses survival at all costs in the final line, portraying the choice to survive as its own resistance: "But for all that doe what youe lyst, / And I wilbe styll and crye howe no more," she tells her attacker (12). While one could read this as signifying the speaker's consent, if they choose to interpret her statement as articulating her acquiescence to sex, I am more interested in reading the degree to which she is still resisting here. She tells her assaulter to "doe what *youe* lyst" (emphasis mine), refusing to voice her complicity in what is about to happen. She recognizes that there are no other means of resistance available to her, as no witnesses have responded to her cries. Since she sees no other options, she makes the choice to survive the assault. In framing her song as an act of "crying howe," the speaker puts the onus on her audience to respond to her assault by bearing unflinching witness to her violation and laying bare the social attitudes that authorize it.

Thwarted desire: *Let be wanton your busynes*

Folio 98's fourth and final lyric, *Let be wanton your busynes,* takes the previous two songs' portrayal of women's victimization in an unexpected direction, as it stages a woman confidently issuing sexual instructions to her lover. In this single quatrain, which can be read either as a short lyric or as a scribal tag responding to what has just been copied, a woman voices her frustration at her lover's impotence: "Let be wanton your busynes for in good faith youe are to blame / To put me thus in this distris, Seing that your best lymme ys lame."[65] The scribe's placement of *Let be wanton your busynes,* a song voicing unabashed female desire, at the bottom of folio 98v directly after a song voiced by a rape survivor serves an important purpose here, as it reminds readers that women can articulate erotic volition even after assault. The term "wanton," which appeared so prominently in the previous song, here functions as a noun of direct address for the man who has aroused the speaker with his amorous "busynes" but is unable to consummate the encounter due to his penile "lame[ness]"; in this context, "wanton" means "a lustful or lecherous person," or "a flirt."[66] The woman chastises her lover for his failure to please her through penetration, much as the titular lady in *My ladye hath forsaken me* discards her partner for a new, more virile one. The woman emphasizes her displeasure with the man's impotence, using alliteration to underscore the link between the genital euphemism "lymme" and the descriptor "lame" [weak, ineffectual], and she expresses her irritation by naming his flaccid penis sarcastically as his "best lymme."

The speaker's imperative tone and frank voicing of arousal is particularly notable as it comes just after a woman's assertions of erotic subjectivity were punished with rape. She opens her song with a command—"Let be," she orders—and she issues instructions to her lover about how to please her. In voicing her frustration by characterizing her state of thwarted arousal as "this distris," she echoes the anthology's courtly complainers, who make utterances such as "thus mourne J may in paynes allway, both nyght and day in great distress."[67] Like the other desiring voices on folio 98, the speaker attaches corporeal significance to the discourse of courtly love that dominates the collection, rendering "distris" a state of physical rather than emotional suffering.

Songs of wantonness: Possibilities

I categorize all four of MS Ashmole 176, folio 98's lyrics as "songs of wantonness," because the term "wanton" is repeated multiple times on the folio and provides a useful governing principle for the songs' explorations of gender, voice, desire, and embodiment.[68] The term's ever-shifting valences across the four lyrics shed light on the pleasures and dangers attached to it, and all four songs focus on the contexts and consequences of sexual activity. In *I can be wanton and yf I wyll,* the speaker asserts her prerogative to "be wanton" (1), invoking the term's valences of playful, unrestrained merriment. She presents wantonness as lighthearted enjoyment and flirtation that is *not* necessarily sexual. Several lines later, she invokes the term's sexual meaning and applies it negatively to men in particular when she warns her attacker, "by suche wanton men as youe be yonge maydes are sometymes begyled" (6). Here she aligns men's wantonness with deceptiveness and overt harm. She echoes didactic warnings to young women against unscrupulous men, and she underscores the threat of men's ungoverned lasciviousness to maidens whose youth, power disadvantage, and lack of knowledge make them prime targets for exploitation and coercion.[69] She presents wantonness as pleasure and danger, as prerogative and threat. Finally, in *Let be wanton your busynes,* "wanton" names a lover who strives to please his mistress with erotic "busynes" but is unable do to so because of penile indisposition; here, the speaker uses "wanton" to signify the promise of carnal satisfaction without the capacity to deliver it. Together, the four songs emphasize the corporeal joys and risks of wantonness.

When folio 98's four lyrics are read in order, they exhibit a circular logic. We can imagine the frustrated speaker in the folio's last lyric as the amorous lady described in the folio's first poem, as the two pieces portray differing gendered perspectives on desire and impotence. *Let be wanton your busynes* can be read as a response to *My ladye hath forsaken me,* or it can be interpreted as offering an alternate perspective. Even if the lyrics were not necessarily read in order, the scribe's choice to copy the cluster together and embed it within a collection of polite courtly lyrics depicts bodies and desires coming into conflict with one another. In contrast to the courtly lyrics' emphasis on women's power and men's pain, these four songs focus on men's and women's experiences of embodied subjectivity. The female-voiced lyrics copied together on folio 98v all articulate women's desires—to have satisfying erotic "busynes," to have control over their reproductive bodies, to laugh and flirt and "be merye" without suffering violence—and shed light on the impediments to the realization of those desires. They challenge the portrayal of women's desire in the impotence lyric copied on the recto just before them, with its claims that women most want lovers "Lustye and full of Strengthe in Labour good at Lengthe." All four lyrics on the folio challenge the anthology's courtly complaints about women's absence or hardheartedness that bracket them in the manuscript by illuminating a far more corporeal, unequal, and potentially violent erotic universe.

Temple University

Acknowledgments

I am grateful to Claire Falck, Marissa Nicosia, and Thomas Ward for their helpful feedback on the very earliest draft of this piece. I also wish to thank the University of Virginia's Medieval Colloquium for their generous comments, questions, suggestions, and warm hospitality in October 2016. I am indebted to the Weston Library's staff, especially Colin Harris, for assistance in helping me search for information regarding MS Ashmole 176's provenance. The archival research for this essay was made possible by a College of Liberal Arts Research Award from Temple University.

This essay is dedicated to my lioness rampant, whose survival, resilience, and powerful testimony were at the forefront of my mind throughout the writing process.

NOTES

1. *Sans remedye endure must I*, line 8; *Thoughe ye my love were a ladye fayr*, line 5; *Ah my hart ah*, line 4.
2. For the most recent, albeit brief, appraisal of the manuscript, see William A. Ringler, Jr., *Bibliography and Index of English Verse in Manuscript 1501–1558* (London and New York: Mansell, 1992), 41. This booklet is Part III of the largely astrological collection of booklets that comprise MS Ashmole 176. Bernard Wagner provides transcriptions of eleven of

the lyrics in "New Songs of the Reign of Henry VIII," *Modern Language Notes* 50.7 (1935): 452–455. John Stevens includes a short entry on the manuscript and calls it "[t]he only known late source of the words of early Tudor court-songs," *Music and Poetry in the Early Tudor Court* (London: Methuen, 1961), 462.

3. Ringler, *Bibliography*, 41. William Cornish, the composer of *Adewe adewe my hartes lust*, died in 1523; *Come over the borne, bessy*, survives in manuscripts as early as the fifteenth century (Cambridge, Trinity College, MS O.2.53, fols. 55v–56r); and *Ravyshed was I that wel was me*, which features Catherine of Aragon lovingly watching Henry VIII dance with Princess Mary and closes with a prayer that God "send [Mary] shortlye a brother to be Englandes righte heire" (12), was composed between 1516 and 1527, according to Ringler.

4. The five-folio anthology (folios 97–101) appears to consist of two individually folded bifolia (the first sheet is folios 97–98 and the second is folios 99–100), with folio 101 as a single sheet that was sewn at the end of the booklet. A different but roughly contemporary hand has copied a nativity chart with a 1551 birthdate on the remaining space on folio 100r after *Ravyshed was I that well was me*, the collection's final song, and a third, slightly later hand, with ink matching the manuscript's subsequent contents, has written another nativity chart for 1551 on folio 100v, suggesting that the booklet was bound with the astrological material by the early seventeenth century.

5. For a listing of the whole volume's contents, see William Henry Black, *A Descriptive, Analytical, and Critical Catalogue of the Manuscripts Bequeathed unto the University of Oxford by Elias Ashmole* (Oxford: Oxford University Press, 1845), 120–122.

6. The anthology's seventeen songs, in order, listed by their *Digital Index of Middle English Verse* (*DIMEV*) and Ringler *Index of English Verse in Manuscript 1501–1558* (TM) numbers, are Surrey's *If care may cause men crye* (TM 712); *My ladye hath forsaken me* (*DIMEV* 3618.5; TM 1050); *Up I arose in verno tempore* (*DIMEV* 6118; TM 1785); *I can be wanton and yf I wyll* (*DIMEV* 2145; TM 635); *Let be wanton your busynes* (*DIMEV* 3053; TM 882); *Thoughe ye my love were a ladye fayr* (*DIMEV* 5895; TM 1714); *Alas myne eye whye doest thu bringe* (*DIMEV* 291; TM 102); *Adewe pleasure welcome mournyng* (TM 68); *Ah my hart ah this ys my songe* (*DIMEV* 128; TM 82); *Sans remedye endure must I* (*DIMEV* 4780; TM 1383); *Parting parting I may well synge* (*DIMEV* 126; TM 1309); *Alas to whom should I complayne* (*DIMEV* 300; TM 108); Cornish's *Adewe adewe my hartes lust* (*DIMEV* 221; TM 64); *O what a treasure ys love certayne* (*DIMEV* 4090; TM 1248); *Come over the borne bessye* (*DIMEV* 5227; TM 1505); *In a garden underneth a tre* (*DIMEV*

2447; TM 749); and *Ravyshed was I that well was me* (*DIMEV* 4440; TM 1349). Eleven of the lyrics are printed in Wagner, "New Songs of the Reign of Henry VIII." *Ravyshed was I that well was me* is printed in *Reliquiae Antiquae*, eds. Thomas Wright and James Orchard Halliwell, 2 vols. (London: William Pickering, 1841–1843), 1:258; variant versions of *Up I arose in verno tempore* and *Come over the borne bessye* from the Ritson Manuscript are printed in Stevens, *Music and Poetry in the Early Tudor Court*, 390 and 348; and Cornish's *Adew adewe my hartes lust* was printed most recently in *The Lyrics of the Henry VIII Manuscript*, ed. Raymond G. Siemens (Renaissance Text Society, 2013), 28. This particular version of Surrey's *If care doe cause men crye* has never been printed, nor has *My ladye hath forsaken me* or *Let be wanton your busynes*.

7.   Cornish's *Adewe adewe my hartes lust* is copied in MS Ashmole 176 as well as MS Additional 19122, folios 23v–24r. For an edition of the manuscript's lyrics, see *The Lyrics of the Henry VIII Manuscript*, ed. Raymond G. Siemens (Renaissance Text Society, 2013); for a facsimile, see David Fallows, *Facsimile of The Henry VIII Book* (Oxford: Oxford University Press for DIAMM, 2014). Nineteen of the English lyrics from the Ritson Manuscript are printed in Stevens, *Music and Poetry in the Early Tudor Court*, 338–350, and the Latin songs are printed with music in *The Ritson Manuscript: Liturgical Compositions, Votive Antiphons, and Te Deum*, ed. Nick Sandon (Moretonhampstead, U.K.: Antico Editions, 2001).

8.   *Up I arose in verno tempore and Come over the borne, bessye* are copied on folios 145v–146r and 143v–144r in MS Additional 5665.

9.   Carol Meale discusses how MS Ashmole 176's *Alas to whom shuld I complayne* is excerpted from a longer political poem linked to Edward Stafford, Duke of Buckingham, who was executed in 1521, underscoring MS Ashmole 176's connections to the world of the Tudor court and demonstrating how lyrics could circulate and be repurposed for different uses in that milieu. Carol Meale, "London, British Library, Harley MS 2252: John Colyn's 'Booke': Structure and Content," *English Manuscript Studies 1100–1700* 15 (2009): 65–122, at 92; also Julia Boffey, *Manuscripts of English Courtly Love Lyrics* (Cambridge: D. S. Brewer, 1985), 84–85.

10.   *Adew adew my hartis lust,* in MS Additional 31922, folio 23v–24r. *Ravyshed was I that wel was me,* in MS Cotton Titus D.XI, folio 56v, along with the fragmentary song *Coll standyth* (TM 318) and the Latin hymn *O lux beata trinitatis* (fols. 55v–56v).

11.   For the print and manuscript history of Surrey's poem see TM 712 and Ringler, *Bibliography and Index of English Verse Printed 1476–1558* (London and New York: Mansell, 1988), TP 825. For a discussion of the song's manuscript circulation in seventeenth-century Scotland, see

A. S. G. Edwards, "Manuscripts of the Verse of Henry Howard, Earl of Surrey," *Huntington Library Quarterly* 67.2 (2004): 283–293.

12. According to a note at the beginning of the manuscript, the codex was a gift from William Lilly to Elias Ashmole on 27 November 1637. For background on Lilly and Ashmole, close friends who shared an interest in astrology, see Patrick Curry, "Lilly, William (1602–1681)," *Oxford Dictionary of National Biography,* Oxford University Press, 2004, http://www.oxforddnb.com.libproxy.temple.edu/view/article/16661, and Michael Hunter, "Ashmole, Elias (1617–1692)," *Oxford Dictionary of National Biography,* Oxford University Press, 2004, http://www.oxforddnb.com.libproxy.temple.edu/view/article/764.

13. The phrase "she hath reclaymed me to her lure" occurs in *Ah my hart ah* (9) and *In a garden underneth a tree* (16), and the speaker in *Sans remedye endure must I* tells his beloved, "doutles ye may reclayme me" (10). *MED* s.v. "reclaimen" (v.), 1(b), 2(d) and "lure" (n.[1]), (b). For "payne(s)" see *If care do cause men crye* (2, 10, 51), *Alas myne eye why doest thou bringe* (2), *Adewe pleasure welcome mournyng* (1), *Ah my hart ah* (7, 9), *Sans remedye endure must I* (1, 3, 4, 8, 10, 11), *Parting parting I may well synge* (1, 3, 7), and *In a garden underneth a tree* (3). The speaker in *My ladye hath forsaken me* claims that he "did take payne" to ensure his lady's sexual satisfaction (5).

14. *Ah my hart ah,* lines 1–2. A few of the lyrics are addressed to the female object of desire, but most refer to "my lady," "my love," or "my sweting" in the third person, imagining an audience composed of the speaker's male peers.

15. Joshua Eckhardt, *Manuscript Verse Collectors and the Politics of Anti-Courtly Love Poetry* (Oxford: Oxford University Press, 2009), 4.

16. Eckhardt, *Manuscript Verse Collectors,* 14.

17. Eckhardt, *Manuscript Verse Collectors,* 5.

18. For a recent edition of the Maitland Quarto with a thorough introduction, see *The Maitland Quarto: A New Edition of Cambridge, Magdalene College, Pepys Library MS 1408,* ed. Joanna M. Martin (Edinburgh: Scottish Text Society, 2015), esp. 28–30. For more on the manuscript's gendered textual community, see Julia Boffey, "The Maitland Folio Manuscript as a Verse Anthology," in *William Dunbar the Nobill Poyet: Essays in Honour of Priscilla Bawcutt,* ed. Sally Mapstone (East Linton: Tuckwell, 2001), 40–50; Sarah Dunnigan, "Feminising the Early-Modern Erotic: Female Voiced Lyric and Mary Queen of Scots," in *Older Scots Literature,* ed. Sally Mapstone (Edinburgh: John Donald, 2005), 441–466; Evelyn S. Newlyn, "A Methodology for Reading Against the Culture: Anonymous Women Poets and the Maitland Quarto Manuscript (c. 1585)," in *Women and the Feminine in Medieval and Early*

Modern Scottish Writing, eds. Sarah M. Dunnigan, C. Marie Harker, and Evelyn S. Newlyn (New York: Palgrave Macmillan, 2004), 89–102.

19. See *As Phoebus in his spheiris hicht, If Sapho saige for saphic songe so sueit,* and *Ane new fairweill a strainge gudnicht,* in *The Maitland Quarto,* ed. Martin, 182–183, 262–263, and 258–260, line 19 and 45.

20. For an edition of the Devonshire Manuscript, see Lady Margaret Douglas and Others, *The Devonshire Manuscript: A Woman's Book of Courtly Poetry,* ed. Elizabeth Heale (Toronto: Centre for Renaissance and Reformation Studies, 2012).

21. Christopher Shirley, "The Devonshire Manuscript: Reading Gender in the Henrician Court," *English Literary Renaissance* 45.1 (2015): 32–59, at 44.

22. Heale, "'Desiring Women Writing': Female Voices and Courtly 'Balets' in some Early Tudor Manuscript Albums," in *Early Modern Women's Manuscript Writing: Selected Papers from the Trinity/Trent Colloquium,* eds. Victoria E. Burke and Jonathan Gibson (Aldershot: Ashgate, 2004), 9–31. See also Raymond Siemens and Johanne Paquette, "Drawing Networks in the Devonshire Manuscript (BL Add. MS. 17492): Toward Visualizing a Writing Community's Shared Apprenticeship, Social Valuation, and Self-Validation," in *New Ways of Looking at Old Texts, V: Papers of the Renaissance English Text Society, 2007–2010,* ed. Michael Denbo (Tempe, AZ: Arizona Center for Medieval and Renaissance Studies, 2014), 113–151.

23. The speaker in *Ah my hart ah* laments, "I have the payne & she the pleasure" (9). *MED* s.v. "cure" (n.[1]), 3(b): "*haven in cure,* to have (sth.) under one's control, have in one's power"; *In a garden underneth a tree,* line 14.

24. For more on Surrey's work and the literary contexts which produced it, see Heale, *Wyatt, Surrey, and Early Tudor Poetry* (London and New York: Longman, 1998), esp. 88; for more on the poem see William A. Sessions, *Henry Howard, Earl of Surrey* (Boston: G.K. Hall & Co, 1986), 91–92. The most commonly copied version of *If care do cause men cry* is printed in *Tottel's Miscellany,* edited by Amanda Holton and Tom MacFaul (New York: Penguin, 2011), 41–42.

25. For more on Surrey's life and work, see Jessie Child, *Henry VIII's Last Victim: The Life and Times of Henry Howard, Earl of Surrey* (London: Jonathan Cape, 2006) and Sessions, *Henry Howard, The Poet Earl of Surrey: A Life* (Oxford: Oxford University Press, 1999).

26. Elsewhere the speaker compares his pain to that of his fellow men and sighs, "amonge them all I dare well say ys none / So farre from joye so full of woe nor have more cause to mone" (3–4).

27. For more on the significance of *virgulae suspensivae* and commas, see M. B. Parkes, *Pause and Effect: An Introduction to the History of Punctuation in the West* (Berkeley: University of California Press, 1993), 303 and 307. The other lyrics in the collection are not as free of errors. "Were" is erroneously copied twice in the first line of *Though ye my love were a ladye fayr* on folio 99r, and "blynde" is written, then crossed out, in the first line of *Alas myne eye whye doest thou bringe*, also on folio 99r.

28. The first four lines are printed in Wagner, "New Songs," 452; otherwise, the lyric has remained unprinted.

29. The speaker in *If care do cause men crye* relates his beloved's "strangenes when I sued first her servant for to be" (32), and he resolves "to serve and suffer pacyently" at his song's close (46).

30. The aristocratic appellation "my Ladye" appears in lines 1 and 15, and also appears in *O what a treasure ys love certeyn* (2) and *Though ye my love were a ladye fayr* (1). *MED* s.v. "ladi" (n.), 8(a): "A lady to whom a knight pays his homage in chivalric love; —often in direct address."

31. *MED* s.v. "pein" (n), 7(d); *OED* s.v. "pain" (n.), 5(b).

32. *MED* "ayen" (adv), 7(a).

33. These laments for lost virility include *Ich have ydon al myn youth* (*DIMEV* 3685), in *Medieval English Lyrics and Carols*, ed. Duncan, 65; *Elde makith me geld* (*DIMEV* 1183), in *The Texts of BL MS Harley 913, 'The Kildare Manuscript,'* ed. Thorlac Turville-Petre (Oxford: Oxford University Press for the Early English Text Society, 2015), 74–76; and *Burgeys, thou haste so blowen atte the cole* (*DIMEV* 896), in Rossell Hope Robbins, "A Warning Against Lechery," *Philological Quarterly* 35 (1956): 90–95, at 93–95.

34. *MED* s.v. "feinten" (v.), 3(a).

35. *OED* s.v. "length" (n.), 14(a).

36. *MED* s.v. "marken" (v.[1]), 8(c): "to take note mentally; take note of (somebody or something), give heed to."

37. Francis Lee Utley, *The Crooked Rib: An Analytical Index to the Argument about Women to the Argument about Women in English and Scots Literature to the End of the Year 1568*, 2nd ed. (New York: Octagon Books, 1970), 64. Heale discusses the role of misogyny in courtly verse in *Wyatt, Surrey, and Early Tudor Poetry*, 46–49.

38. Heale, *Wyatt, Surrey, and Early Tudor Poetry*, 48.

39. John Lydgate, *Prohemy of a Mariage Betwixt an Olde Man and a Yonge Wife, and the Counsail* (*DIMEV* 139), in *The Trials and Joys of Marriage*, 103–129. See also Lydgate's *Payne and Sorowe of Evyll Maryage*, another misogynistic didactic poem addressed to "yonge men," on 211–218, and Edward Gosynhyll's *A dialogue bytwene the commune secretary and jalowsye, touchynge the unstablenesse of harlottes* (London: John Kynge, 1556).

40. *The Tretis of the Tua Mariit Wemen and the Wedo* (*DIMEV* 6134), in *The Poems of William Dunbar*, ed. Priscilla Bawcutt, 2 vols. (Glasgow: Association for Scottish Literary Studies), 1:41–55, lines 430–431 and 455. *The Freiris of Berwik* (*DIMEV* 726), in *Ten Bourdes*, ed. Melissa M. Furrow (Kalamazoo, MI: Medieval Institute Publications for TEAMS, 2013), 84–109, lines 139, 142.

41. For more on the popular proverb "a new broom sweeps clean," see Whiting, *Proverbs, Sentences, and Proverbial Phrases*, B563. For the phrase "to labor like a hackney," see H6.

42. *Ah my hart ah*, line 7.

43. The song's *chanson d'aventure* opening and ventriloquizing of an abandoned young woman's lament also occurs in the lyrics *Nou sprinkes the sprai* (*DIMEV* 614; *Medieval English Lyrics and Carols*, ed. Duncan, 70) and *In wyldernes* (*DIMEV* 2666; Stevens, *Music and Poetry in the Early Tudor Court*, 346–347).

44. The only exception to this is *Alas to whom should I complayne* on folio 100r, which is punctuated with two *virgulae*; otherwise, all the anthology's lyrics are punctuated with a single *virgula*. According to Parkes, a single *virgula suspensiva* was "used to mark the briefest pause or hesitation in a text," and "[t]he double form // was used as a direction for... a final pause" (*Pause and Effect*, 307).

45. The pregnancy lament, a popular lyric genre in fourteenth- and fifteenth- century England, is discussed in Neil Cartlidge, "'Alas, I go with chylde': Representations of Extra-Marital Pregnancy in the Middle English Lyric," *English Studies* 5 (1998): 395–414, and Bennett, "Ventriloquisms," 196–197. Other pregnancy laments include *This enther day I met a clerke* (*DIMEV* 5679; *The Early English Carols*, ed. Greene, 277), *The last tyme I the well woke* (*DIMEV* 5369; *Medieval English Lyrics and Carols*, ed. Duncan, 283–284), *Ladd y the daunce a myssomur day* (*DIMEV* 3544; *Medieval English Lyrics and Carols*, ed. Duncan, 281–283), *As I went on yol day* (*DIMEV* 635; *Medieval English Lyrics and Carols*, ed. Duncan, 182–183), and *Al this day ic han soght* (*DIMEV* 393; *Medieval English Lyrics and Carols*, ed. Duncan, 280–281).

46. This convention of cleric as seducer and abandoner appears most vividly in *As I went on Yol Day* and *This enther day I met a clerk*, but it is a generic feature of nearly all the surviving English pregnancy laments.

47. *Ther was a frier of ordur gray* (*DIMEV* 5593) and *The nunne walked on her prayer* (*DIMEV* 4526), both in P. J. Croft, "The 'Friar of Order Gray' and the Nun," *Review of English Studies* 32, no. 125 (1981): 1–16, at 15–16. Ad Putter discusses a pair of trilingual verse epistles from around 1400 that purport to be a lover's invitation and a lady's reply, in "The French of English Letters: Two Trilingual Verse Epistles in Context," in

Language and Culture in Medieval Britain: The French of England c. 1100–c. 1500, ed. Jocelyn Wogan-Browne with Carolyn Collette, Maryanne Kowaleski, Linne Mooney, Ad Putter, and David Trotter (York: York Medieval Press, 2009), 397–408, at 400. For an overview of the robust tradition of macaronic poetry in premodern England, see Elizabeth Archibald, "Tradition and Innovation in the Macaronic Poetry of Dunbar and Skelton," *Modern Language Quarterly* 53, no. 1 (1992): 126–149.

48. Macaronic pastourelles include the *Carmina Burana*'s Latin-German *Tempus adest floridum, surgunt namque flores*; the French-Latin *L'autrier matin el moys de may* and *En may, quant dait e foil e fruit*; and the Latin-German *Ich was ein chint so wolgetan*. *The Medieval Pastourelle*, ed. Paden, 1:148–151, 186–193 and 76–83; *Anthology of Ancient and Medieval Woman's Song*, ed. Anne L. Klinck (New York: Palgrave Macmillan, 2004), 95–96.

49. Judith M. Davidoff discusses the genre conventions of the *chanson d'aventure* in *Beginning Well: Framing Fictions in Late Middle English Poetry* (Rutherford: Farleigh Dickinson University Press, 1988), esp. 36–59. See also Helene Estabrook Sandison, *The 'Chanson d'Aventure' in Middle English* (Bryn Mawr, PA: Bryn Mawr College Press, 1913).

50. Davidoff, *Beginning Well*, 59.

51. *Alas to whom should I complayne*, line 1.

52. *Sauns remedye endure must I*, line 3; *If care may cause men crye*, line 12; *Adewe adewe my hartes lust*, line 2.

53. *MED* s.v. "compleinen" (v.), 1(a) and 4(a); *OED* s.v. "complain" (v.), 1(a): "To bewail, lament, deplore"; and 8(a): "To make a formal statement of a grievance *to* or *before* a competent authority; to lodge a complaint, bring a charge."

54. "Alas" recurs repeatedly in the male-voiced complaints, including *If care do cause men crye* (9, 37, 53), *Alas myne eye why doest thu bringe* (1), *Adewe pleasure welcome mournyng* (1), *Ah my hart ah* (twice in 7), *Sans remedye endure must I* (12), *Alas to whom should I complayne* (1), and *Adewe adewe my hartes lust* (twice in 2). Its use here, given the context, is striking, as it forces readers to consider the relationship between sexual difference and lament in the anthology.

55. Bennett and Amy M. Froide note that "the majority of women accused of infanticide [during the period] were single women" in "A Singular Past," in *Singlewomen in the European Past 1250–1800*, eds. Bennett and Froide (Philadelphia: University of Pennsylvania Press, 1999), 1–37, at 36 n. 77. Laura Gowing provides a good historical overview of the issue, albeit with cases from a slightly later period, in "Secret Births and Infanticide in Seventeenth-Century England," *Past and Present* 156 (1997): 87–115.

56. Wagner, "New Songs of the Reign of Henry VIII," 452–453.

57. *MED* s.v. "connen" (v.), 2: "To be in a position (to do or be something); be justified or right (in doing something); be possible or right under the circumstances."
58. *OED* s.v. "beware" (v.), 1: "to take care, take heed, in reference to a danger."
59. *MED* s.v. "wild" (adj.), 1(c); *OED* s.v. "wild" (adj.), 7(b): "Giving way to sexual passion; also, more widely, licentious, dissolute, loose."
60. *In a garden underneth a tre*, line 18.
61. *MED* s.v. "heue" (n.[2]), c: "*law.* A loud outcry of alarm raised at the occurrence of robbery, assault, etc." Caroline Dunn discusses the role of raising the hue and cry in rape cases in *Stolen Women in Medieval England: Rape, Abduction, and Adultery*, 1100–1500 (Cambridge: Cambridge University Press, 2013), 68. For more on the hue and cry, see John H. Baker, *An Introduction to English Legal History*, 4th ed. (Oxford: Oxford University Press, 2005), 503–504.
62. Dunn, *Stolen Women*, 53.
63. *Rotuli Parliamentorum, ut et petitiones, et placita in Parliamento*, ed. John Strachey, 6 vols. (London, 1767–77), 4.198b.
64. Dunn, *Stolen Women*, 56.
65. *DIMEV* 3053. This short poem has never been printed until now, and can be read in relation to a similar four-line female-voiced obscene erotic song of impotence and frustrated from the early thirteenth century, *Ate ston-castinge my lemman I ches* (*DIMEV* 728), in Theo Stemmler, "More English Texts from MS Cambridge University Library Ii.III.8," *Anglia* 93 (1975): 1–16, at 9.
66. *OED* s.v. "wanton" (adj. and n.), B. 2.
67. *Sans remedye endure must I*, line 4.
68. *OED* s.v. "wanton" (adj. and n.), 3: "Lustful; not chaste, sexually promiscuous. Of a person (esp. a woman)"; 4(a): "Of a person: playful; unrestrained in merriment, jovial; inclined to joking; carefree. Also of behavior." *MED* s.v. "wantoun" (adj.), (c): "Of a person: given to excessive pleasure-seeking, overexuberant, rowdy"; (d): "pertaining to sexual indulgence, lewd, lascivious; of a person: given to lechery, lustful; promiscuous, of easy virtue."
69. Bennett sees this line as "particularly s[eeking] the attention of single-women in the audience." "Ventriloquisms," 202.

WORKS CITED

Archibald, Elizabeth. "Tradition and Innovation in the Macaronic Poetry of Dunbar and Skelton." *Modern Language Quarterly* 53, no. 1 (1992): 126–149.

Baker, John H. *An Introduction to English Legal History*. 4th ed. Oxford: Oxford University Press, 2005.

Barratt, Alexandra, ed. *The Knowing of Woman's Kind in Childing*. Turnhout: Brepols, 2001.

Bennett, Judith M. "Ventriloquisms: When Maidens Speak in Middle English Songs, c. 1330–1500." In *Medieval Woman's Song: Cross-Cultural Approaches*. Edited by Judith M. Bennett and Ann Marie Rasmussen. Philadelphia: University of Pennsylvania Press, 2002. 187–204.

———— and Amy M. Froide. "A Singular Past." In *Singlewomen in the European Past 1250–1800*. Edited by Bennett and Froide. Philadelphia: University of Pennsylvania Press, 1999. 1–37.

Black, William Henry. *A Descriptive, Analytical, and Critical Catalogue of the Manuscripts Bequeathed unto the University of Oxford by Elias Ashmole*. Oxford: Oxford University Press, 1845.

Boffey, Julia. "The Maitland Folio Manuscript as a Verse Anthology." In *William Dunbar the Nobill Poyet: Essays in Honour of Priscilla Bawcutt*. Edited by Sally Mapstone. East Linton: Tuckwell, 2001. 40–50.

————. *Manuscripts of English Courtly Love Lyrics*. Cambridge: D. S. Brewer, 1985.

Cartlidge, Neil. "'Alas, I go with chylde': Representations of Extra-Marital Pregnancy in the Middle English Lyric," *English Studies* 5 (1998): 395–414.

Child, Jessie. *Henry VIII's Last Victim: The Life and Times of Henry Howard, Earl of Surrey*. London: Jonathan Cape, 2006.

Croft, P. J. "The 'Friar of Order Gray' and the Nun." *Review of English Studies* 32, no. 125 (1981): 1–16.

Curry, Patrick. "Lilly, William (1602–1681)." *Oxford Dictionary of National Biography*, Oxford University Press, 2004, http://www.oxforddnb.com.libproxy.temple.edu/view/article/16661.

Davidoff, Judith M. *Beginning Well: Framing Fictions in Late Middle English Poetry*. Rutherford: Fairleigh Dickinson University Press, 1988.

Digital Index of Middle English Verse. Edited by Linne R. Mooney, Daniel W. Mosser, and Elizabeth Solopova, with Deborah Thorpe and David Hill Radcliffe, www.dimev.net.

Douglas, Lady Margaret, and others. The Devonshire Manuscript: A Woman's Book of Courtly Poetry. Ed. Elizabeth Heale (Toronto: Centre for Renaissance and Reformation Studies, 2012).

Dunbar, William. *The Poems of William Dunbar*. Ed. Priscilla Bawcutt. 2 vols. Glasgow: Association for Scottish Literary Studies, 1998.

Duncan, Thomas, ed. *Medieval English Lyrics and Carols*. Cambridge: D. S. Brewer, 2013.

Dunn, Caroline. *Stolen Women in Medieval England: Rape, Abduction, and Adultery, 1100–1500*. Cambridge: Cambridge University Press, 2013.

Dunnigan, Sarah. "Feminising the Early-Modern Erotic: Female Voiced Lyric and Mary Queen of Scots." In *Older Scots Literature*. Edited by Sally Mapstone. Edinburgh: John Donald, 2005. 441–466.

Eckhardt, Joshua. *Manuscript Verse Collectors and the Politics of Anti-Courtly Love Poetry*. Oxford: Oxford University Press, 2009.

Edwards, A. S. G. "Manuscripts of the Verse of Henry Howard, Earl of Surrey." *Huntington Library Quarterly* 67.2 (2004): 283–293.

Erb, Peter C. "Vernacular Material for Preaching in MS Camb. Univ. Lib. Ii.III.8." *Mediaeval Studies* 33 (1971): 63–84.

Fallows, David, ed. *Facsimile of The Henry VIII Book*. Oxford: Oxford University Press for DIAMM, 2014.

Furrow, Melissa M., ed. *Ten Bourdes*. Kalamazoo, MI: Medieval Institute Publications, 2013.

Gosynhyll, Edward. *A dialogue bytwene the commune secretary and jalowsye, touchynge the unstablenesse of harlottes*. London: John Kynge, 1556.

Gowing, Laura. "Secret Births and Infanticide in Seventeenth-Century England." *Past and Present* 156 (1997): 87–115.

Greene, Richard Leighton, ed. *The Early English Carols*. 2nd ed. Oxford: Clarendon Press, 1977.

Halliwell, James Orchard, and Thomas Wright, eds. *Reliquiae Antiquae: Scraps from Ancient Manuscripts*. 2 vols. London: William Pickering, 1841–1843.

Heale, Elizabeth. "'Desiring Women Writing': Female Voices and Courtly 'Balets' in some Early Tudor Manuscript Albums." In *Early Modern Women's Manuscript Writing: Selected Papers from the Trinity/Trent Colloquium*. Edited by Victoria E. Burke and Jonathan Gibson. Aldershot: Ashgate, 2004. 9–31.

———. *Wyatt, Surrey, and Early Tudor Poetry*. London and New York: Longman, 1998.

Holton, Amanda, and Tim McFaul, eds. and intro. *Tottel's Miscellany: Songs and Sonnets of Henry Howard, Earl of Surrey, Sir Thomas Wyatt, and Others*. New York: Penguin, 2011.

Hunter, Michael. "Ashmole, Elias (1617–1692)." *Oxford Dictionary of National Biography*, Oxford University Press, 2004, http://www.oxforddnb.com.libproxy.temple.edu/view/article/764.

Klinck, Anne L., ed. *Anthology of Ancient and Medieval Woman's Song*. New York: Palgrave Macmillan, 2004.

Kurath, Hans, and Sherman M. Kuhn, eds. *Middle English Dictionary*. 13 vols. Ann Arbor: University of Michigan Press, 1952–2001, http://quod.lib.umich.edu/m/med/.

Martin, Joanna M., ed. *The Maitland Quarto: A New Edition of Cambridge, Magdalene College, Pepys Library MS 1408*. Edinburgh: Scottish Text Society, 2015.

Meale, Carol. "London, British Library, Harley MS 2252: John Colyn's 'Booke': Structure and Content." *English Manuscript Studies 1100–1700* 15 (2009): 65–122.

Newlyn, Evelyn S. "A Methodology for Reading Against the Culture: Anonymous Women Poets and the Maitland Quarto Manuscript (*c.* 1585)." In *Women and the Feminine in Medieval and Early Modern Scottish Writing*. Edited by Sarah M. Dunnigan, C. Marie Harker, and Evelyn S. Newlyn. New York: Palgrave Macmillan, 2004. 89–102.

Oxford English Dictionary Online. Oxford University Press, 2016, www.oed.com.

Paden, William, ed. and trans. *The Medieval Pastourelle*. 2 vols. New York: Garland, 1987.

Parkes, M. B. *Pause and Effect: An Introduction to the History of Punctuation in the West*. Berkeley: University of California Press, 1993.

Putter, Ad. "The French of English Letters: Two Trilingual Verse Epistles in Context." In *Language and Culture in Medieval Britain: The French of England c. 1100–c. 1500*. Edited by Jocelyn Wogan-Browne with Carolyn Collette, Maryanne Kowaleski, Linne Mooney, Ad Putter, and David Trotter. York: York Medieval Press, 2009. 397–408.

Ringler, Jr., William A. *Bibliography and Index of English Verse in Manuscript 1501–1558*. London and New York: Mansell, 1992.

———. *Bibliography and Index of English Verse Printed 1476–1558*. London and New York: Mansell, 1988.

Robbins, Rossell Hope. "A Warning against Lechery." *Philological Quarterly* 35 (1956): 90–95.

Salisbury, Eve, ed. *The Trials and Joys of Marriage*. Kalamazoo: Medieval Institute Publications for TEAMS, 2002.

Sandison, Helene Estabrook. *The 'Chanson D'Aventure' in Middle English*. Bryn Mawr, PA: Bryn Mawr College, 1913.

Sessions, W. A. *Henry Howard, The Poet Earl of Surrey: A Life*. Oxford: Oxford University Press, 1999.

———. *Henry Howard, Earl of Surrey*. Boston: G.K. Hall & Co, 1986.

Shirley, Christopher. "The Devonshire Manuscript: Reading Gender in the Henrician Court." *English Literary Renaissance* 45.1 (2015): 32–59.

Siemens, Raymond G., ed. *The Lyrics of the Henry VIII Manuscript*. Renaissance Text Society, 2013.

Siemens, Raymond, and Johanne Paquette, "Drawing Networks in the Devonshire Manuscript (BL Add. MS. 17492): Toward Visualizing a Writing Community's Shared Apprenticeship, Social Valuation, and

Self-Validation." In *New Ways of Looking at Old Texts, V: Papers of the Renaissance English Text Society*, 2007–2010. Edited by Michael Denbo. Tempe, AZ: Arizona Center for Medieval and Renaissance Studies, 2014. 113–151.

Stemmler, Theo. "More English Texts from MS. Cambridge University Library Ii.III.8." *Anglia* 93 (1975): 1–16.

Stevens, John. *Music and Poetry in the Early Tudor Court*. London: Methuen, 1961.

Strachey, John. *Rotuli Parliamentorum, ut et petitiones, et placita in Parliamento*. 6 vols. London, 1767–1777.

Turville-Petre, Thorlac, ed. *The Texts of BL MS Harley 913, 'The Kildare Manuscript.'* Oxford: Oxford University Press for the Early English Text Society, 2015.

Utley, Francis Lee. *The Crooked Rib: An Analytical Index to the Argument about Women to the Argument about Women in English and Scots Literature to the End of the Year 1568*. 2nd ed. New York: Octagon Books, 1970.

Wagner, Bernard M. "New Songs of the Reign of Henry VIII." *Modern Language Notes* 50.7 (1935): 452–455.

Whiting, Bartlett Jere, and Helen Prescott Whiting. *Proverbs, Sentences, and Proverbial Phrases from English Writings Mainly Before 1500*. Cambridge, MA: Belknap Press, 1968.

APPENDIX: LYRICS OF MS ASHMOLE 176, FOLIO 98r-v

folio 98r
My Ladye hathe forsaken me that longe hathe bene her man
Yet she her selfe retayned me and covenunte first beganne
But nowe I haue espyed some other she hathe tryed
Lustye and full of strength in Labor good at Lengthe

This vij yeares and some deale more wth her I dyd take payne
and cannot say but she therfore rewarded me agayne
but nowe I am forsaken another she hathe taken
Lustye & full of strengthe in Labour good at Lengthe

Her Servant when I first began, as then she dyd report
for trewe Servyce I bare the name amonge the rowte & sort
but nowe she feeles I faynt, wth some she dothe acquaynt
Lustye & full of strengthe in Labour good at Lengthe /

Ye knowe that newe brome Swepeth cleane, as many mens sainge ys,
and hackneyes that be comon oftymes tyred ys

and so shall he be that servethe my Ladye
although he nowe have strengthe, she wyll hym tyre at Lengthe

Vndoubted she desyrethe muche in labour to endure
she sparethe not for ache nor stytche, but allwaye she ys sure
thus she vnsacyate, hathe obteyned for a mate   Lustye &c

her appetyte ys suche, marke who so Lust to trye
a springing founteyne she wyll lurche & clearlye drawe hym drye
And as the springe dothe quayle, lykewyse her love shall fayle
thus he that Lackethe strengthe, she lettethe hym slyp at lengthe /

folio 98v
Vp J arose, in verno tempore, & found a mayd, sub quadam arbore,
that dyd complayne, in suo pectore, sainge J feele, puerum movere,

what shall J say, meis parentibus, þᵗ wᵗʰ me hath layne, quidam clericus,
they wyll me beate, virgis & fustibus, & me deprave, coram hominibus /

Adewe playfers, antiquo tempore, full ofte wᵗʰ youe, solebam ludere,
but for my mysse, mihi deridere, wᵗʰ right full cause, incipio flere,
wᵗʰ this said child alas, quid faciam, shall J yt kepe, vel interficiam,
yf J yt sley, quo loco fugiam, J shall lose god & vitam eternam // finis

J can be wanton & yf J wyll, but yf youe touche me J wyll crye howe
J can be merye & thinke no evell, but yet beware one cometh J trowe

Yf any come in faith I crye, þᵗ all the strete my voyce shall heare
take hede that no man doe youe espye, & J then warant youe come
verye nye

But yf youe come syt farre from me for me semeth youe should be wylde
and by suche wanton men as youe be yonge maydes are sometymes
begyled

J wilbe ware of suchelyke wylde men for when they touche me I doo
crye howe
kysse me ye should, I beshrewe me then by crist not for my mothers
blacke cowe

ye may me kyll as soone as kysse, J pray youe awaie & let me be
in faith all the world wyll speake of this, J say ye play þᵉ foole wᵗʰ me

By god J strike youe wth my fyste I shall make yo*ur* cap fall on the flower
But for all that doe what youe lyst, & I wilbe styll & crye howe no more
fynis / /

Let be wanton yo*ur* busynes for in good faith youe are to blame
 to put me thus in this distris seing þ^t yo*ur* best lym*m*e ys lame/
finis /

'Ce petit amas de rymes': Musicality in Jeanne de Marnef's Edition of Pernette du Guillet's Poetry

JESSIE LABADIE

In 1545, Lyonnais printer Jean de Tournes published seventy poems of a recently deceased young woman from Lyon, France, named Pernette du Guillet. Virtually all of the information that we have regarding Du Guillet's life and the publication of her poetry comes to us via the paratext of this first edition.[1] Du Guillet's works were re-edited and republished several times in the sixteenth century: Parisian printer Jeanne de Marnef published editions of the work in 1546 and 1547, and Tournes published an emended version of his first edition in 1552.[2] Five of Du Guillet's poems appear in sixteenth-century songbooks as well.[3] After 1552, no complete edition of Pernette du Guillet's *Rymes* appeared until the nineteenth century.[4]

The first two editions of Pernette du Guillet's verse were published by different editors and present the works in contrasting ways. Jean de Tournes's two editions of Pernette du Guillet's works are the versions scholars consider first, while Jeanne de Marnef's two editions are relegated to a secondary status. It is clear that Marnef was working from the Tournes edition as she included much of its paratext. This essay explores how Marnef shaped Du Guillet's work to her own vision of how the poetry should be read. Marnef made several changes to Du Guillet's work that change the way readers interact with it. Specifically, Marnef's editorial choices underline the importance of the musical nature of the text. While the Tournes edition has references to music, Marnef's insists on Du Guillet's poetry as lines to be set to music or sung, rather than ones to be read silently.

Twenty-first-century readers have the tendency to refer to Du Guillet's poetry as "lyric" and understand that term to be related to the subjectivity of the poet. The sixteenth-century meaning of "lyric," however, should not be forgotten when we read Du Guillet's verse. In a 2015 essay, Jean Vignes reminds us that when we say "lyric" without referring to music, we marginalize the original meaning:

> Mais le succès de cette acception dans la langue critique moderne ne conduit-il pas à minorer ce que ces poètes de la Renaissance doivent encore à la conception traditionnelle (c'est-à-dire musicale) de la lyrique, tournée vers la performance musicale, la seule acception du terme qui ait cours au XVIe siècle? A l'époque de Ronsard, un recueil de *vers lyriques* rassemble des pièces pour leur forme strophique destine au chant, avec accompagnement instrumental.[5]

This essay seeks to draw our attention back to the musical nature of Du Guillet's lyric poetry. While we often read poetry silently and solitarily today, sixteenth-century poets conceived of their poetry in musical terms.

Jeanne de Marnef took over the print shop of her husband, Denis Janot, upon his death in 1544 and printed at least seven works either on her own or with other printers. By 1548, she had married another printer, Estienne Groulleau, and she probably continued to work alongside her new husband.[6] Marnef published *Rithmes de gentile, et vertueuse dame D. Pernette du Guillet Lyonnoise Avecq' le Triumphe des Muses sur Amour: Et autres nouvelles composicions* (henceforth *Rithmes*) in Paris in 1546, only one year after Jean de Tournes's *Rymes de gentile, et vertueuse dame D. Pernette du Guillet Lyonnoise* (henceforth *Rymes*). Marnef followed this previous version closely, but she did not simply reproduce it. In addition to many paratextual changes, she appended ten anonymous poems with the collective title *Le Triumphe des Muses sur Amour: Et autres nouvelles composicions* (see Fig. 1) to Du Guillet's poetry.[7] These additions alter the way we interact with the book and encourage the reader to receive the work as a songbook.

Scholarship that focuses on Jeanne de Marnef's editions of Du Guillet's verse is scant. To date, only one scholar, Leah Chang, has published research that considers the full 1546 edition.[8] Two other scholars, Beatrice H. Beech and George T. Beech, have jointly published two articles concerning one of the ten poems appended to Du Guillet's work "Les obsèques d'amour."[9] All three of these critical works engage with gender studies: Chang reads Marnef's edition as a "gendered publication," while the Beeches were

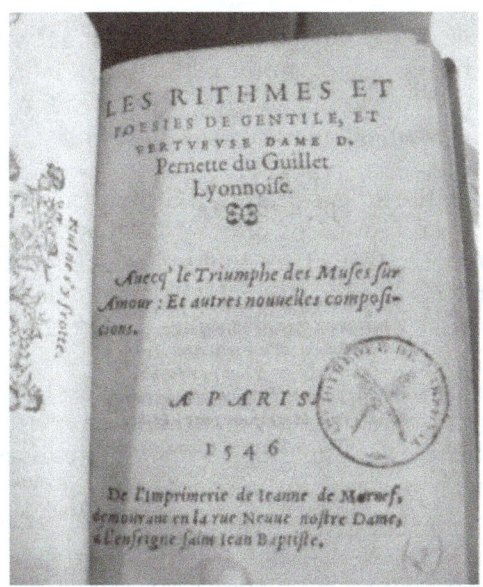

Figure 1. Title page, *Les Rithmes et poesies…*, ed. Jeanne de Marnef, 1546. Bibliothèque Nationale de France (Arsenal, cote 8-BL-8767).

interested in the relationship between the poem and the *affaire des Dames de Paris* that began in 1529 (Chang, 99; Beech and Beech, "Les obsèques," 243).[10] Both arguments are convincing, and these studies offer insight into certain aspects of the edition's genesis and production. No critical work on the *Rithmes*, however, has addressed the way in which Marnef's edition presents the musicality of Du Guillet's verse. I argue that, in addition to reading the Marnef edition as a "gendered publication," we can read it as a musical one. Paratextual elements including titles and page layout, as well as the inclusion of the ten additional poems, are signs that Marnef's edition harkened back to the first appearance of Du Guillet's poetry in songbooks in the early 1540s.[11]

Antoine du Moulin's prefatory letter, present in the Tournes and the Marnef editions, encourages this reading. In his letter addressed *Aux Dames Lyonnoises*, Du Moulin praises Du Guillet for her talent for and devotion to music:

> [V]eu le peu de temps, que les Cieulx l'ont laissée
> entre nous, il est quasi incroyable comme elle a
> peu avoir le loysir, je ne dy seulement de se rendre
> si parfaictement asseurée en tous instrumentz
> musiquaulx, soit au Luth, Espinette, et autres,

> lesquelz de soy requierent une bien longue vie à se
> y rendre parfaictz, comme elle estoit, et tellement,
> que la promptitude, qu'elle y avoit, donnoit cause
> d'esbahissement aux plus experimentez.[12]

Du Moulin takes the time to praise Du Guillet's musical expertise before going on to praise her knowledge of other languages, and then finally her writing. In this letter, Du Guillet is presented as a musician first and a writer second. Furthermore, the way in which Du Moulin describes Du Guillet's poetry could also point to a musically inclined work:

> [S]on affectionné mary a trouvé parmy ses brouillars
> en assés povre ordre, comme celle, qui n'estimoit
> sa facture estre encor digne de lumiere jusques à
> ce, que le temps la luy eust par frequent estude et
> estendue, et lymée. Et pource en la mesme sorte que
> luy, et moy avons trouvé Epygrammes, Chansons, et
> autres diverses matieres de divers lieux, et plusieurs
> papiers confusément extraictz, les vous avons icy,
> quasi comme pour copie, mis en evidence, tant pour
> satisfaire à ceulx, à qui privément en maintes bonnes
> compaignies elle les recitoit à propos, comme la plus
> part faictz à leur occasion, que aussi pour ne vouloir
> perdre soubz silence d'eternel oubly chose, qui vous
> peust non seulement recreer, mais faire honneur à
> vous, Dames Lyonnoises (111–112).[13]

When the 1545 editors found it, the work was in a disorganized, un-polished state. This could have signaled to Marnef that the work should be considered musically. Du Moulin refers to the work's fragmentary state in this passage as "brouillars en assés povre ordre" and "plusieurs papiers confu-sément extraictz" ["scattered papers" and "numerous pages pulled haphazardly together"]. Earlier in the letter, Du Moulin calls the work "ce petit amas de rymes" ["this little bundle of rhymes"]. This unorganized state would be typical of poetry written to be sung.[14] Indeed, we find evidence of oral per-formances in Du Moulin's prefatory letter about Du Guillet's previously un-published work. He states that he is printing the works in part due to requests he has received from Du Guillet's oral audiences—"pour satisfaire à ceulx, à qui privément en maintes bonnes compaignies elle les recitoit à propos" (Du Guillet, 111–112, "to satisfy those to whom she recited them whenever the occasion arose in many a private gathering of good company"). Du Guillet, like many other poets of her time, would have been performing her works and circulating them orally or in manuscript form for others to sing. I argue that Marnef noticed these references in the preface, as well as the makeup of the poetry and the prior publication of at least three of Du Guillet's poems in songbooks, and decided based on these characteristics that she would market her book by highlighting the musical qualities of the work.

Poets at this time often thought of their works as musical. This musicality is both figurative and literal in French Renaissance verse. Mentions of musical instruments and singing are not merely poetic devices; these references demonstrate strong links between poetic composition and music.[15] We continually see poets who link musical instruments with literary production. We find, for example, in the "Avertissement au Lecteur par l'imprimeur Ambroise de La Porte," which precedes the *Supplément musical* to Pierre de Ronsard's 1552 *Amours,* the following affirmation: "[Ronsard] a daigné prendre la peine de les mesurer sur la lyre" [Ronsard deigned to go to the trouble of measuring them on the lyre].[16] Here, music is part of the conception of poetry. Ronsard would have tried out his lines on a lute. In 1565, Ronsard writes in his *Abrégé de l'Art poétique*: "[L]a poésie sans les instrumens, ou sans la grace d'une seule ou plusieurs voix, n'est nullement aggreable, non plus que les instruments sans estre animez de la melodie d'une plaisante voix" ("Poetry without instruments, or without the charm of one or several voices, is not at all agreeable, no more than instruments that are not livened up by a pleasant voice," Ronsard, 9). Poetry needed music to be best experienced.

We find this connection between music and poetry in the works of many Renaissance poets, including Louise Labé and Pernette du Guillet. Many of Labé's sonnets and elegies, as well as the poems written in praise of her at the end of the *Œuvres*, refer to music and singing. Du Guillet also refers to her audible voice and to music-making in her poetry. For example, in the second poem in the collection, she says: "Je me trouvay de liesse si pleine / (Voyant desjà la clarté à la ronde) / Que commençay louer à voix haultaine / Celuy qui feit pour moy ce Jour au monde" (["Such joy full suddenly did me amaze / (Seeing how light already round me swirled), / That with exalted voice I began to praise / Him who formed me such a Morn in the World," Du Guillet, 118). In the penultimate line of this *dixain*, the poet praises her lover out loud ("à voix haultaine"). This praise would be the singing or the reciting of the poem at hand. In the second elegy, the poet casts herself as a Diana figure who will seduce her admirer with lute-playing: "Mais je vouldrois lors quant, et quant avoir / Mon petit Luth accordé au debvoir, / Duquel ayant cogneu, et pris le son, / J'entonnerois sur luy une chanson" ("Oh, yes, and I should like to have close by / My precious Lute, well tuned to gratify: / Familiar with its sounds, I would erelong / Begin to sing for him a tender song", Du Guillet, 153–154). The paratextual prose framing Du Guillet's poetry endeavors to convince readers of their strong connections to music and of the importance of music to their edification.

Musical education became more and more democratized across the sixteenth century and was an important part of young noblemen and noblewomen's formations.[17] In Baldassare Castiglione's *Il libro del cortegiano* (1528), a widely read book that was both descriptive and prescriptive of proper behavior for men and women, the Count remarks, "Gentlemen, I must tell you that I am not satisfied with our courtier unless he is also a musician and unless as well as understanding and being able to read music he can play several instruments."[18] The Count's perfect Lady would also have knowledge of music to a certain degree: "[T]he musical instruments that she plays ought to be appropriate …. Consider what an ungainly thing it would be to see a woman playing drums, fifes, trumpets, or other like instruments" (Castiglione, 210). Castiglione's perfect Lady played the lute or the clavichord, instruments that would be played to accompany lyric verse. These two instruments could often be found in sixteenth-century studies (Zecher, 3). Music was an acceptable pastime for sixteenth-century laywomen in France. Sixteenth-century readers may have been more receptive to a female musician than to a female author *tout court*.

With these societal pressures, it is not surprising that the Jeanne de Marnef edition of Du Guillet's poetry insists on the musicality of the work. Even the change in title compels the reader to consider the poems as songs. The title *Rithmes* recalls the Greek word ῥυθμός (rhythmos) while at the same time it distances Du Guillet's work from Petrarch's *Rime sparse,* to which the 1545 title pays homage. Marnef adds *"et poesies"* to *"Rithmes"* in the title. This addition leads the reader to think that some of the works would be "poesies" while others would be "rithmes." Perhaps the texts that would be more "poesie" than "rithme" are those for which silent attentive reading would be required—for example, the poems with anagrams of Maurice Scève's name.[19] This title change sets the tone for the work and marks an important difference from the prior editions.

There are a variety of poetic forms in Du Guillet's œuvre. As Antoine du Moulin writes in the prefatory letter, "avons trouvé Epygrammes, Chansons, et autres matieres de divers lieux … " ("[we] found Epigrams, Songs, and other sundry writings in various places," Du Guillet, 111). In Du Guillet's verse, there are épigrammes, *chansons,* élégies, épîtres *marotiques,* and other forms, including one *coq-à-l'âne.* The two Tournes editions do not distinguish among all of the different forms within the text other than this mention in the preface.[20] Marnef, on the other hand, classified the different poetic forms through the use of titles specific to their forms. Marnef titled many of the poems "Chanson," "Chant," and "Huitain." Poems by these titles are often followed by another poem of the same form with the title "Un autre" (see Fig. 2). By titling some of the poems "Chanson" and "Chant," Marnef draws attention to their musicality. The words *chanson* and *chant* are polyvalent in the sixteenth century—they can refer either to a poem or a song—but in either case, they are related to music. In *Art poetique françois* (1548), Thomas Sébillet defines *chant lyrique* in this way:

> Le chant Lyrique, ou Ode (car autant vaut a dire), se façonne ne plus ne moins que le Cantique, c'est a dire, autant variablement et inconstamment: sauf que lés plus cours et petis vers y sont plus souvent usités et mieus séans a cause du Luth ou autre instrument semblable sur lequel l'Ode se doit chanter.[21]

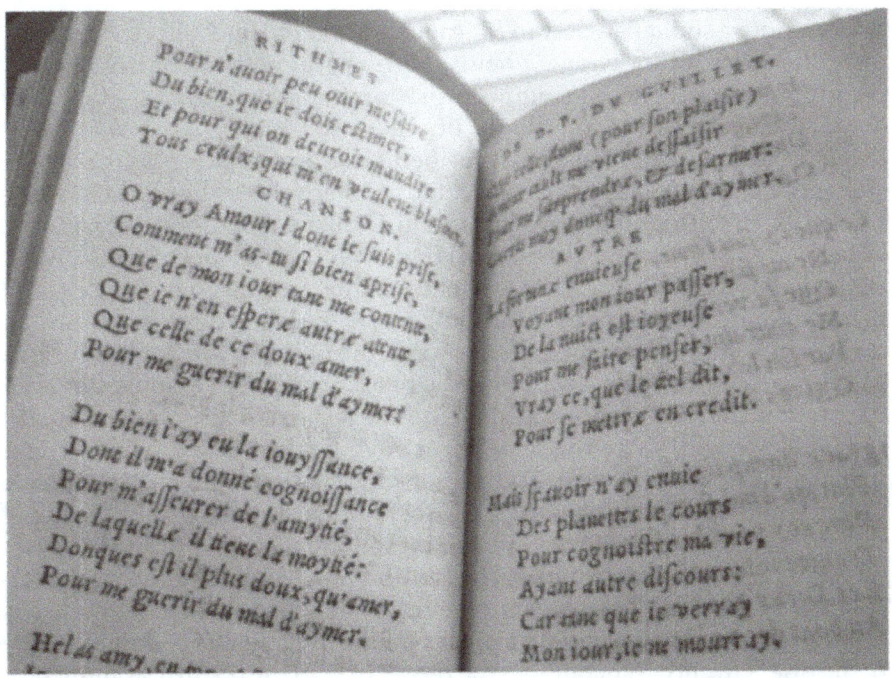

Figure 2. *Les Rithmes et poesies…*, ed. Jeanne de Marnef, 1546. Bibliothèque Nationale de France (Arsenal, cote 8-BL-8767).

A *chant* is not a poem to be read silently, but rather must be sung with an accompanying instrument. Sébillet then makes clear that the *chanson* is able to be sung: "Car encor que nous appelions bien en François, Chanson, tout ce que se peut chanter" ("Because still we call anything that can be sung a Song in French," Sébillet, 127). By adding titles like "Chanson" and "Chant" to Du Guillet's poems, Marnef assigns musicality to Du Guillet's verse.

Jan Miernowski makes a similar observation in a recent essay about Marguerite de Navarre's *Chansons spirituelles*. He notes that in Jean de Tournes's 1547 edition of the *Marguerites de la Marguerite*, Tournes titles certain poems "Chanson," reiterating their genre for the reader. Miernowski remarks:

> Such insistence on labeling as *chansons* the texts which follow the initial "Pensées" and the *rondeau* seems to indicate some kind of anxiety on the part of the author or publisher in regards to the generic and compositional coherence of the *Chansons spirituelles* section of the book.[22]

We can note a similar anxiety in Marnef's edition of Du Guillet's work—by inserting titles for individual poems, Marnef attempts to control readers' reception of the work. The editor insists on the poems' genre—that they are *chansons* and *chants* and should be read accordingly.

In Marnef's edition, many of the poems that are not titled "Chanson" or "Chant" can also be linked to music due to their prior publication in songbooks. The majority of the poems in Du Guillet's *Rymes* are épigrammes, either *huitains* (twenty-eight poems) or *dizains* (twenty-one poems). Most of the *huitains* follow the rhyme scheme ababbcbc. The poems xii, xiv, and lii in the Moderne songbook ("Le corps ravy," "Le grand desir," and "En lieu du bien") follow this rhyme scheme, while the other *huitain* set to music in Moderne's edition, xlii ("Je n'oserois le penser veritable"[I would not even dare to think it real]) follows ababbaab. The fact that many of the poems in Du Guillet's work share the same form, rhyme scheme, and syllable count means that it would have been easy for musicians and singers to use one piece of music for multiple songs. Different poems could be sung to one of the pieces in the Moderne or Attaingnant songbooks, substituting the lyrics but maintaining the same musical notation. The titles that Marnef added encourage this reading. The reader immediately understands that if the poem is a *huitain*, it might pair well with a piece of music for another *huitain*. The use of the title "Un autre" encourages the reader to read the poem in conjunction with or in reference to the one that precedes it. In this way, Marnef's *Rithmes* may have functioned more as a repertory of song lyrics than as a work to be read silently and solitarily.

Several other paratextual elements support this reading. The size of the Marnef edition (duodecimo) is small compared to the Tournes edition (octavo). The Marnef edition could have been slipped into a pocket, or even easily held in a hand, and carried to a gathering where there might be musicians playing from one of the songbooks in circulation at the time. No musical notation is in the Marnef edition, but this would not mean that its contents could not be interpreted as songs to be performed orally. Often, a standard musical mold would be used for many pieces of verse. One *air* or *timbre* would be used for many songs. We can consider the common practice of *contrafactum*, where bawdy words are sung to the tune of a spiritual song, or vice versa.[23] Sixteenth-century audiences would have known the tunes to popular songs and would have been accustomed to the practice of plugging new lyrics into standard *airs*.[24] Poems with repeating lines are common in Du Guillet's *chansons*, making them easy to sing. One of many examples is poem lvii:

> C'est un grand mal se sentir offensé,
> Et ne s'oser, ou sçavoir à qui plaindre:
> C'est un grand mal, voire trop incensé,
> Que d'aspirer, où l'on ne peut attaindre :
> C'est un grand mal que de son cueur contraindre,
> Oultre son gré, et à subjection :
> C'est un grand mal, qu'ardente affection
> Sans esperer de son mal allegeance :
> Mais c'est grand bien, quand à sa passion
> Un doux languir sert d'honnête vengeance.[25]

The phrase "C'est un grand mal" [It's terrible] and its counterpart "Mais c'est grand bien" [But it's wonderful] anchor the poem rhythmically, making it an appropriate choice for a composer or a singer. Indeed, this very poem was set to music in 1561 by Jean Maillard and published in *Quart livre de chansons nouvellement composé en musique* à *quatre parts*. Where would Maillard have come across this poem? Perhaps he found it in Marnef's edition, or perhaps it was one of Du Guillet's poems that were still circulating orally. This 1561 publication shows that Du Guillet's verse was known through music.

Another element that might be a sign that Marnef published her edition with orality and musicality in mind is the indication of the *e muet*, known in the sixteenth century as the *e féminin*, *synaléphe*, or *coupe féminine* (Sébillet, 42). Since before Du Guillet's time, when reading French poetry aloud, the speaker or singer must not pronounce a final *e* if the next word begins with a vowel or a non-aspirated *h*. In this way, the scansion of a verse can remain intact. Sébillet described the practice of drawing a line through silent e's to remind the reader not to pronounce them when reading aloud (Sébillet, 55–56). Indeed, we find just this practice in Marnef's edition of the *Rithmes* (see examples from Marnef's edition in Fig. 3).

The book instructs the reader on pronunciation and encourages an oral reading or singing. The physical features of the book, its size, and the typographical choices Marnef made show that Marnef designed it to be used in an oral, musical setting.

The poems that Marnef appended to Du Guillet's poetry also seem to have been chosen based on their oral, musical qualities. This is yet another sign that a sixteenth-century reader might receive the text as a book of songs. The "Triumphe des Muses sur Amour: Et autres nouvelles composicions" consists of ten poems that appear after Du Guillet's verse in the Marnef edition. Four of the ten poems had previously been printed in a 1545 Jean de Tournes imprint, *Panegyric des damoyselles de Paris sur les neuf muses*. This Tournes edition contained seven poems: a preliminary *huitain* by Jean de Tournes, and six anonymous works.[26] Marnef included four of these poems in her edition of the *Rithmes et poesies* and added six others: another

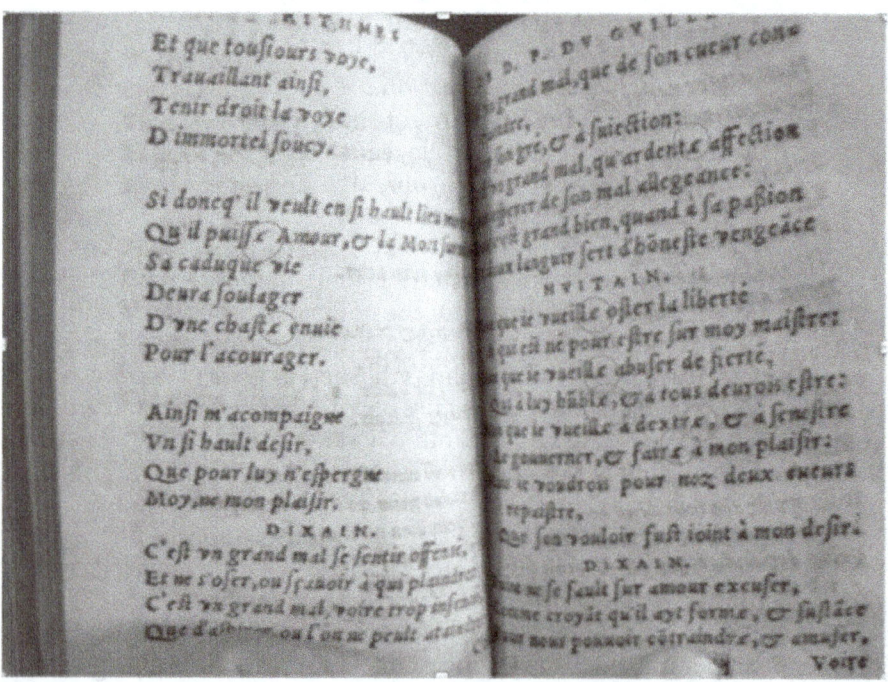

Figure 3. *Les Rithmes et poesies…*, ed. Jeanne de Marnef, 1546. Bibliothèque Nationale de France (Arsenal, cote 8-BL-8767).

anonymous poem, "Complainte," and five poems signed with initials.[27] Chang and the Beeches have hypothesized that Marnef's editorial choice to print these poems alongside Du Guillet's may have been a protofeminist one. Chang writes, for example, "the originality of the *Rithmes* ... lies principally in the way in which the entire volume acquires a gendered governing vision, from the title page, to the printer's notice, to the poetry authored by Du Guillet, to the poems compiled as the 'Nouvelles composicions.'"[28] I argue that music is the governing vision in Marnef's edition and that the poems she appended to Du Guillet's work are evidence of this vision. The poems from Tournes's *Panegyric* that Marnef excluded from her edition are the ones that describe composing poetry as writing instead of singing. Meanwhile, the four poems Marnef includes from the *Panegyric* all describe poetic composition in oral and musical terms. The "Panegyric," one of the poems that appeared in the Tournes edition but that was not included in Marnef's edition, begins:

> Je veulx par escript mettre
> En quelque petit metre
> La louange & honneur,
>   Qu'ont de Paris les Dames
> Vivantes sans diffames,
> Sans estre blasonneur (Panegyric, 3).[29]

The poet puts his praises of these ladies down "par escript." The reference to a text-based, written culture is clear. The physical book, Tournes's *Panegyric*, is that desire brought to fruition. Similarly, the preliminary *huitain* by Antoine du Moulin, also not included in Marnef's edition, is about the physical book meant to be read:

> Ce livre que lon peult nommer
> Romant des Dames vertueuses,
> Se veult faire en brief renommer
> Pour ses graces tant precieuses,
> Et pour ses veines copieuses.
> Lecteur, si l'Autheur tu ignores (*Panegyric*, 1).[30]

In the first line, the poet defines the work as a "livre," referring to the physical object to be read. The poet then uses the word "lecteur" instead of "auditeur" to signal to his audience how the book should be consumed. The poems that Marnef excluded are those that refer to poetry as written verses to be read.

In contrast, the poems from the *Panegyric* that Marnef printed in her edition refer explicitly to singing and oral performance. "Triumphe des muses, contre Amour" begins with the following lines:

> J'ay paour d'estre desdict,
> Ou n'avoir le credit,
> O Muses gracieuses,
> De pouvoir repeter,
> Et icy reciter Voz forces vertueuses (*Panegyric*, 17).[31]

The word "reciter" in line 5 refers to oral practices, rather than written ones. The other verb, "repeter," in line 4, could also refer to oral production. While these verbs could also indicate spoken verse, other poems point directly to singing. For example, the poem "Les obseques d'Amour," also in Marnef's edition, begins in this way:

> Phebus Amy chantez,
> En chantant escoutez:
> Vostre Muse Thalie
> Qui vous veult reciter,
> Et en beaulx vers compter
> D'Amour la grand folie
>
> Orpheus gracieux,
> En chantz melodieux,
> Terpsichore vous mande,
> De Cupido la mort,
> Son dangereux effort,
> Et temerité grande.[32]

Here, references to singing abound. Three words that have "chant" as their root appear in the first eight lines of the poem ("chantez," line 1; "chantant," line 2; "chantz," line 8). The first stanza begins with Phoebus, god of poetry, while the second begins with Orpheus, an accomplished musician in Greek mythology. Both of these refer to an oral, musical culture. The first lines of another poem Marnef culled from Tourne's *Panegyric* for inclusion in her edition, "Complainte d'une damoyselle fugitive," are as follows:

> Si lon peult ouyr ma complainte,
> Et le mal dont je suis atainte
> Je vous pouvois bien reciter,
> Mon dieu je serois heureuse,
> Si en voix forte & doloreuse
> Je sçavois le tout racompter![33]

Once again, rather than evoking written verses, the "Complainte" is about an oral recitation. The verbs "ouyr" and "reciter" in lines 1 and 3, respectively, as well as the reference to the speaker's "voix forte & douloreuse" in line 5 all indicate this oral framework. We can see Marnef carefully compiling the poetry that suits her musical vision of the work.

Jeanne de Marnef presented a new, more musically inclined Pernette du Guillet to her readers and created a different authorial space from the one provided by Jean de Tournes and Antoine du Moulin in the Lyonnais editions. Marnef manipulated the text and the paratext to change the appearance of the words on the page and, therefore, their reception. She interpreted Tournes's paratext and Du Guillet's poetry in order to present the product to waiting readers and singers. Marnef underscored the musical nature of the poetry, and these qualities shine through in her edition. In a culture still so attuned to the oral, musical quality of lyric poetry, Marnef sought to make an edition appealing to readers eager to use this slim edition as a repertory of more lyrics to put to *airs* they already knew.

It seems that her vision proved a profitable one, as she reprinted it the following year. At this time in France, reprinting a book involved a complete resetting, so this reprint shows that it must have been economically viable.[34] This musically inclined edition provides a secure place for Du Guillet as a female author. As we noted both in Castiglione and in Antoine du Moulin's preface, *Aux Dames Lyonnoises*, music was an accepted and encouraged pastime for women in the sixteenth century. The musical qualities of Du Guillet's work would have made sixteenth-century audiences more willing to read—and sing—Pernette du Guillet's verse.

Randolph-Macon College

NOTES

1. Pernette du Guillet, *Rymes de gentile, et vertueuse dame D. Pernette Du Guillet, lyonnoise* (Lyon: Jean de Tournes, 1545).
2. Pernette du Guillet, *Les rithmes et poesies de gentile et vertueuse Dame D. Pernette du Guillet, Lyonnoise. Avecq' le triomphe des Muses sur Amour et autres nouvelles composicions* (Paris, Jeanne de Marnef, 1545) ; Pernette Du Guillet, *Rymes de gentile, et vertueuse dame D. Pernette Du Guillet, lyonnoise de nouveau augmentees* (Lyon: Jean de Tournes, 1552).
3. *Second livre contenant XXVII chansons nouvelles à quatre parties en ung volume* (Paris: Pierre Attaignant and Hubert Jullet, 1540); *Parangon des chansons: neufvieme livre contenant XXXI chansons nouvelles* (Lyon: Jacques Moderne, 1541); *Quart livre de chansons nouvellement composé en musique à quatre parties* (Paris: Le Roy et Ballard, 1561).
4. Pernette du Guillet, *Poésies de Pernette Du Guillet, lyonnaise* (Lyon: Perrin, 1830); Pernette du Guillet, *Rymes De Gentile Et Vertueuse Dame D. Pernette Du Guillet lyonnoise* (Lyon: Perrin, 1856); Pernette Du Guillet. *Rymes De Gentile Et Vertueuse Dame D. Pernette Du Guillet lyonnoise,* (Lyon: Scheuring and Perrin, 1864). The first twentieth-century edition appeared in 1953: Pernette du Guillet, *Rymes de gentile et vertueuse Dame D. Pernette Du Guillet Lyonnoise* in *Poésies du XVIe siècle,* ed. Albert-Marie Schmidt (Paris: Bibliothèque de la Pléiade, Gallimard, 1953), 227–268. Schmidt does not include the two Italian epigrams.
5. Jean Vignes, "De Ronsard à Louise Labé: Les Amours de poésie et de musique," in *Poésie et musique à la Renaissance,* eds. O. Millet and A. Tacaille (Paris: Presses de l'université Paris-Sorbonne, 2015), 45; "But does not the acceptance of this meaning in the modern critical language lead to diminish what these Renaissance poets still owe to the traditional (that is to say, musical) conception of lyric verse, geared towards musical performance, the only meaning of the term that was used in the sixteenth century? In Ronsard's time, a collection of lyric verse gathers pieces according to their strophic form meant to be sung, with instrumental accompaniment" (All English translations are mine unless otherwise noted).
6. For a complete study of Denis Janot's activity that includes some references to Marnef's printing, see Stephen Rawles, *Denis Janot, Parisian Printer and Bookseller (fl. 1529–1544): A Bibliographical Study in Two Volumes* (Warwick: University of Warwick, 1976). For more on Janot, Marnef and their contemporary printers in Paris, see Lynden Warner, "Booksellers and the Market to the 1550s," in *The Ideas of Man and Woman in Renaissance France: Print, Rhetoric, and Law* (Burlington: Ashgate, 2011), especially 33–34.

7. The previous year, Jean de Tournes published four of the ten poems in a collection of seven anonymous poems *Le Panegyric des Damoyselles de Paris sur les neuf Muses*.

8. Leah Chang, "The Gender of the Book: Jeanne de Marnef Edits Pernette du Guillet," in *Early Modern Women and Transnational Communities of Letters*, eds. Julie D. Campbell and Anne R. Larsen (Aldershot: Ashgate, 2009), 97–120.

9. Beatrice H. Beech and George T. Beech, "A Painting, a Poem, and a Controversy about Women and Love in Paris in the 1530s" (*The Sixteenth Century Journal* 34. 3, 2003), 635–652; "'Les Obsèques D'Amour,' un poème de 1546 et une controverse parisienne sur les femmes et l'amour" (*Seizième siècle* 1, 2005), 237–256.

10. This *affaire* began with an anonymous satirical poem, "Les gracieux adieux faitz aux Dames de Paris," which circulated in manuscript form in 1529. In this poem, the anonymous author names sixteen Parisian ladies in order to disparage their bodies and supposedly loose morals. When it was rumored that Clément Marot penned the poem, other writings began to appear criticizing him. Marot then responded with his *Epitre des excuses de Marot faulsement accuse d'avoir faict certains Adieux au desadvantage des prinicpales Dame de Paris*. This incited several other responses in what came to be known as the *affaire des Dames de Paris*. According to the Beeches, "Les obsèques d'amour" was part of this exchange.

11. As Chang points out, it is not clear if Marnef was both editor and printer, or if an anonymous editor in fact prepared this edition. The Beeches assume Marnef acted as editor, see Beech and Beech, "Obsèques," 246–247. In his edition, Victor Graham assumes that Marnef would have approved of the choices made by an anonymous editor; see *Rymes*, ed. Graham, vii. Both of these situations are possible. For the purposes of this essay, I will assume that if Marnef did not edit the work herself, she would have still been involved in some way in the editing process, and I will therefore refer to her as both editor and printer until more precision becomes available.

12. Pernette du Guillet, *Rymes (1545)*, ed. Elise Rajchenbach (Paris: Droz, 2006), 111. All textual citations from du Guillet's works come from Rajchenbach's edition unless otherwise noted; "Seeing the short time that the Heavens allowed her to remain among us, it is almost impossible to believe that she was able to find the time, not only to become such an accomplished player of all musical instruments, including the Lute, Spinet, and others, which by themselves require a long life at which to become as perfectly proficient as she was (so much so that her quick aptitude for them astonsihed the most experienced of musicians) (translation by Marta Rijn Finch, *Complete Poems, a Bilingual Edition*, ed. Karen

Simroth James (Iter, Toronto, 2010), 83; all translations from Du Guillet's *Rymes* are Finch's).

13. "[H]er devoted husband found in rather poor order among her scattered papers, as of one who did not yet consider her work to be worthy of publication, until time and frequent study would have expanded and polished it. And because he and I, in the same manner, found Epigrams, Songs, and other sundry writings in various places, and numerous pages pulled together haphazardly, we have put them forth here, almost as a copy. We have done so as much to satisfy those to whom she recited them whenever the occasion arose in many a private gathering of good company (for which purpose most were composed), as from a desire not to lose the eternal silence of oblivion something that could not only delight you, but also honor you, Ladies of Lyon," (*Complete Poems*, 85).

14. Kate van Orden uses the words "scattered rhymes" to describe the works of poets Mellin de Saint-Gelais and Clément Marot while their works were being performed orally and before their verse was bound and printed. Van Orden reminds us that Clément Marot would have his lyric poetry printed, "only after it had enjoyed some success in musical performances." Kate Van Orden, *Music, Authorship, and the Book in the First Century of Print* (Berkeley and Los Angeles: University of California Press, 2013), 73.

15. See, for example, Carla Zecher, *Sounding Objects: Musical Instruments, Poetry, and Art in Renaissance France* (University of Toronto Press, 2007), 4–6.

16. Pierre de Ronsard, Œuvres *complètes*, vol IV, ed. Paul Laumonier (Paris: Nizet, 1982), 189.

17. Zecher, 8–10.

18. Baldassarre Castiglione, *The Book of the Courtier*, trans. George Bull (London: Penguin, 2004), 94.

19. Poem V's anagram of Maurice Scève's name is often cited as evidence of du Guillet's relationship with Scève.

20. Only six of the poems in Tournes's editions have titles, and only one of these titles, "Coq a lasne," refers to the poem's form. The five other titled poems in de Tournes's editions are "Parfacite amytié," "Conde claros de Adonis," "La nuict," "Desespoir traduict de la prose du Parangon Italien," and "Confort."

21. "The lyric song, or Ode (as they mean the same), is neither more or less crafted than the Hymn, that is to say, just as variably and inconsistently: except that the shortest and smallest verses are used more often in them and are better fitting because of the Lute or another similar instrument on which the Ode must be sung," Thomas Sébillet, *Art poétique français* in *Traités de poétique et de rhétorique à la Renaissance*, ed. Francis Goyet (Paris: Livre de poche, 2001), 127.

22. Jan Miernowski, "Chansons Spirituelles—Songs for a 'Delightful Transformation'" in *A Companion to Marguerite de Navarre,* eds. Gary Ferguson and Mary B. McKinley (Leiden: Brill, 2013), 237–279.

23. See, for example, Miernowski on Clément Marot and Marguerite de Navarre's two versions of "Jouyissance vous donnerai," 248.

24. Jan Miernowski suggests that the practice of using one tune for many texts may have been the case for Marguerite de Navarre's *Chansons spirituelles* at the compositional level. (Miernowski 246). He also notes that many of the poems in *Chansons spirituelles* "are built on repetitive structures which lend themselves to rhythmical and melodic arrangements. In many cases, the incipit or a portion of it is repeated throughout the text" (Miernowski 246).

25.   It's terrible to feel such an offense
     And not to dare nor know where to complain;
     It's terrible—surely, it makes no sense
     To long for something one cannot attain:
     It's terrible—the way one's heart must strain
     To serve against one's will in full defeat;
     It's terrible—affection's ardent heat,
     Bereft of hope of pain's alleviation;
              But it's wonderful, indeed, when a sweet
     Langour serves passion in true vindication, (Du Guillet, 167–168).

26. "Panegyric des damoyselles de Paris sur les neuf muses," "A celles qui se sont plaintes," "Le triumphe des muses, contre amour," "Les obseques d'Amour," "Complainte d'une damoyselle fugitive," and "L'amante loyale qui Depuis ha esté variable."

27. "Autre epistre a une dame qui se plaignoit de n'avoir esté assez louee par M. D. S. G," "Autre epistre a une noble et illustre dame, par C. G. P," "Autre epistre a une dame, par le dit C. G. P," "Response de la dame a l'amy dissimulé, L. P. A," and "Elegie du semi-dieu faunus demandant aux nymphes pourquoy elles ne le vouloient aimer par V. B." Graham has assigned the initials to the following poets: "M. D. S. G." (Mellin de Saint-Gelais); "C. G. P." (Claude Gruget, Parisien); "L. P. A." (Jean Maugin, known as Le petit Angevin)·, "V. B." (Victor Brodeau, fils). See notes in Graham's edition of Du Guillet.

28. Chang, "Gender," 99.

29.   I want to put down in writing
     In a few little verses
     The praise and honor
              That women of Paris have
     Living without infamy
     Without being a detractor

30.   This book that one can call
        Romant of virtuous Ladies,
        Is meant to be renowned shortly
        For its excellent graces,
        And for its copious styles.
        Reader, if you do not know the Author…

31.   I am afraid of being forbidden,
        or of not having the reputation,
        O gracious Muses,
        to be able to repeat
        And here recite Your virtuous powers.

32.   Phoebus friend, sing,
        In singing listen:
        Your Muse Thalia
        Who wants to recite for you
        And in beautiful lines tell
        of Love the great madness
        Gracious Orpheus.
        In melodious songs,
        Terpsichore calls to you,
        of Cupid's death
        His dangerous effort,
        and great Temerity.

33.   If one can hear my complaint,
        And the pain by which I am struck
        I could well recite to you,
        My god I would be happy,
        If with a strong and painful voice
        I knew how to tell it all !

34. See Lucien Febvre and Henri-Jean Martin, *L'Apparition du livre* (Paris: Les Éditions Albin Michel, 1958), 167.

WORKS CITED

Beech, Beatrice H. and George T. Beech. "A Painting, a Poem, and a Controversy about Women and Love in Paris in the 1530s." *The Sixteenth Century Journal* 34. 3 (2003): 635–652.

————. "'Les Obsèques D'Amour,' un poème de 1546 et une controverse parisienne sur les femmes et l'amour." *Seizième siècle* 1 (2005): 237–256.

Castiglione, Baldassarre. *The Book of the Courtier.* Translated by George Bull. London: Penguin, 2004.

Chang, Leah. "The Gender of the Book: Jeanne de Marnef Edits Pernette du Guillet." In *Early Modern Women and Transnational Communities of Letters*. Edited by Julie D. Campbell and Anne R. Larsen. Aldershot: Ashgate, 2009. 97–120.

Dejean, Joan. *Fictions of Sappho: 1546–1937*. Chicago: University of Chicago Press, 1989.

Du Guillet, Pernette. *Complete Poems: A Bilingual Edition*. Translated by Marta Rijn Finch. Edited by Karen Simroth James. Toronto: Iter, 2010.

———. *Poésies de Pernette Du Guillet, Lyonnaise*. Lyon: Louis Perrin, 1830.

———. *Les rithmes et poesies de gentile et vertueuse Dame D. Pernette du Guillet, Lyonnoise. Avecq' le triomphe des Muses sur Amour et autres nouvelles composicions*. Paris, Jeanne de Marnef, 1546.

———. *Les rithmes et poesies de gentile et vertueuse Dame D. Pernette du Guillet, Lyonnoise. Avecq' le triomphe des Muses sur Amour et autres nouvelles composicions*. Paris, Jeanne de Marnef, 1547.

———. *Rymes (1545)*. Edited by Elise Rajchenbach. Geneva: Droz, 2006.

———. *Rymes*. Edited by Victor E. Graham. Geneva : Droz, 1968.

———. *Rymes de gentile, et vertueuse dame D. Pernette Du Guillet, lyonnoise*. Lyon: Jean de Tournes, 1545.

———. *Rymes de gentile, et vertueuse dame D. Pernette Du Guillet, lyonnoise de nouveau augmentees*. Lyon: Jean de Tournes, 1552.

———. *Rymes de gentile et vertueuse Dame D. Pernette Du Guillet lyonnoise*. Lyon: Louis Perrin, 1856.

———. *Rymes de gentile et vertueuse Dame D. Pernette Du Guillet lyonnoise*. Lyon: Nicolas Scheuring and Louis Perrin, 1864.

———. *Rymes de gentile et vertueuse Dame D. Pernette Du Guillet Lyonnoise*. In *Poésies du XVIe siècle*, edited by Albert-Marie Schmidt. Paris: Bibliothèque de la Pléiade, Gallimard, 1953.

Heartz, Daniel. *Pierre Attaignant, Royal Printer of Music: A Historical Study and Bibliographical Catalogue*. Berkeley and Los Angeles: University of California Press, 1969.

Febvre, Lucien and Henri-Jean Martin. *L'Apparition du livre*. Paris: Les Éditions Albin Michel, 1971.

Marguerite de Navarre. *Chansons spirituelles*. Edited by Georges Dottin. Paris: Droz, 1971.

Miernowski, Jan. "Chansons Spirituelles—Songs for a 'Delightful Transformation'" in *A Companion to Marguerite de Navarre*. Edited by Gary Ferguson and Mary B. McKinley. Leiden: Brill, 2013. 237–279.

Parangon des chansons—neufvieme livre contenant XXXI chansons nouvelles. Lyon: Jacques Moderne, 1541.

Pogue, Samuel F. *Jacques Moderne: Lyons Music Printer of the Sixteenth Century*. Geneva: Droz, 1969.

Quart livre de chansons nouvellement composé en musique à quatre parties. Paris: Le Roy et Ballard, 1541.

Rawles, Stephen. *Denis Janot, Parisian Printer and Bookseller (fl. 1529–1544): A Bibliographical Study in Two Volumes.* Coventry: University of Warwick, September 1976.

Ronsard, Pierre de. Œuvres complètes. Edited by Paul Laumonier. Paris : Nizet, 1982.

Sébillet, Thomas. *Art poétique français* in *Traités de poétique et de rhétorique à la Renaissance.* Edited by Francis Goyet. Paris: Librairie générale française, 1990. 429–453

Second livre contenant XXVII chansons nouvelles à quatre parties en ung volume. Paris: Pierre Attaignant et Hubert Jullet, 1540.

Taruskin, Richard. *Music from the Earliest Notations to the Sixteenth Century: The Oxford History of Western Music, volume I.* Oxford: Oxford University Press, 2009.

Van Orden, Kate. *Music, Authorship, and the Book in the First Century of Print.* Berkeley and Los Angeles: University of California Press, 2013.

Vignes, Jean. "De Ronsard à Louise Labé: Les Amours de poésie et de musique," in *Poésie et musique à la Renaissance.* Edited by O. Millet and A. Tacaille. Paris: Presses de l'université Paris-Sorbonne, 2015. 45–65.

Zecher, Carla. *Sounding Objects: Musical Instruments, Poetry, and Art in Renaissance France.* Toronto: University of Toronto Press, 2007.

Balancing Form, Function, and Aesthetic: A Study of Ruling Patterns for Zodiac Men in Astro-Medical Manuscripts of Late Medieval England

SIAN WITHERDEN

Introduction

In studies of medieval literature, it has increasingly been emphasized that the *mise-en-page* has a fundamental impact on the reader's engagement with the text, and a growing amount of attention is thus being given to the semantics and pragmatics of organizational features such as rubrication, punctuation, and verse layout.[1] Recent examples concerning the late medieval period include Jessica Brantley's analysis of the presentation of tail-rhyme in Chaucer's *Sir Thopas*, Aditi Nafde's comparison of page layout in autograph and non-autograph manuscripts of Hoccleve's poetry, and the study of the *Polychronicon* by Ruth Carroll, et al., which highlights that paraphs were used as a "visual structuring device."[2] However, in discussions of medieval page design, the ruling patterns have received relatively little attention in comparison with other features. Matti Peikola has laid important foundations by arguing that ruling patterns shed valuable light upon the "communicative purpose of a text," but he nevertheless observes that "the research potential of this codicological feature remains largely underutilised."[3] The present article seeks to expose some of this potential by exploring how form, function, and aesthetic are balanced in the ruling patterns of Zodiac Men diagrams and their accompanying text.

The Zodiac Man is a representation of a man marked with astrologi-cal signs in verbal or pictorial form according to the parts of the body over which those particular signs were thought to have influence.[4] It is found in several forms in medieval culture, with and without supplementary text; for example, the iconography of the Zodiac Man features on items including a medieval quadrant and can also be found in Books of Hours.[5] In late medieval England, the Zodiac Man occurs commonly in astro-medical texts written in Latin and Middle English, including John Somer's *Kalendarium*, Nicholas of Lynn's *Kalendarium*, and astro-medical miscellanies.[6] In this context, the Zodiac Man is typically accompanied by a text explaining that operating on any of these body parts is unwise when the moon is in that particular sign. Although it is likely that some of these manuscripts were used by medical practitioners, such texts probably circulated among a wider audience than physicians alone.[7]

The ruling patterns for Zodiac Men offer a useful case study for un-derstandings of the *mise-en-page,* not least because of the need to accom-modate the awkwardly shaped diagram, which can take forms such as an arrow, a rectangle, or even a cross. As this diagram is typically encircled by text, the ruling patterns also shed light upon the imperative to balance word and image on the page. Furthermore, manuscripts featuring Zodiac Men often had to be ruled to accommodate various different kinds of informa-tion, which offers an insight into the functional priorities of page design in astro-medical manuscripts. For example, in addition to medical guidance, the medieval *Kalendarium* typically contained a variety of other types of in-formation including a chart of moveable feasts as well as specific dates for solar and lunar eclipses.[8]

This article commences with a brief descriptive survey of the ruling pat-terns found in a selection of manuscripts containing Zodiac Men in order to contextualize the extent of variation arising from these organizational challenges. Most attention is given to Somer's *Kalendarium,* especially a recurring arrow-shaped model found in a significant number of witnesses. Zodiac Men in other astro-medical texts, including Lynn's *Kalendarium,* will then be introduced for comparative purposes. Throughout, it is assumed that the scribe was responsible for creating the ruling patterns and copying out the text, while a separate individual completed the diagrams. These as-sumptions about ruling are impossible to confirm but reflect the most likely situation and are in line with common critical consensus.[9]

Subsequently, the implications of these ruling patterns are discussed. Although it has long been recognized that ruling patterns take into consid-eration form, function, and aesthetic, a close examination of Zodiac Men suggests these aspects can be more closely interwoven than previously rec-ognized.[10] Firstly, in several cases the desire for the Zodiac Man text and image to be tightly integrated on one page maximizes the accessibility of the information but also has the benefit of satisfying what Albert Derolez refers to as "the Gothic predilection for closed areas."[11] Similarly, the desire for balance within such ruling patterns allows an efficient reading process yet is also aesthetically harmonious with the imperative for order and equilibrium in medieval medicine. Finally, when Zodiac Men feature in folded almanacs, i.e., portable manuscripts that seem to have been attached to the owner's belt, a study of ruling patterns suggests a symbiotic relationship between the physical form of the page, the intricacy and coherence of the aesthetics, and the practical use of manuscript. In particular, portable almanacs likely helped to reassure patients by lending the physician authority, a function that may have drawn on the complex aesthetic of ruling for diagrams including Zodiac Men. Taken together, these observations suggest that a study of ruling patterns allows for a more nuanced approach to the production and reception of medieval manuscripts in astro-medical literature and beyond.

Descriptive Survey of Ruling Patterns for Zodiac Men

For the purposes of this article I have consulted all thirty-six of the complete or mostly complete witnesses of Somer's *Kalendarium* that are currently known to survive.[12] Of these manuscripts, twenty-eight contain a Zodiac Man or at least designate a space for one, as recorded in the appendix.[13] Scribes of Somer's *Kalendarium* found a variety different ways to rule the page for this peculiar diagram, but the most common approach was undoubtedly the arrow-shaped model, which features in seventeen copies (approximately 61 percent).[14] The fact that so many witnesses of Somer's *Kalendarium* share this common arrow-shaped ruling pattern suggests a degree of layout standardization in the text's transmission history, though this is not the focus of the present study.[15]

Four manuscripts that typify this arrow-shaped model will now be introduced, which variously date to between c. 1392 and 1462:[16]

Oxford, Bodleian Library, MS Ashmole 391, Part V, folio 9r
Oxford, Bodleian Library, MS Ashmole 789, Part VIII, folio 363r
Oxford, Bodleian Library, MS Rawlinson D.928, folio 9r
Oxford, Bodleian Library, MS Savile 39, folio 7r

The salient features of this ruling pattern for the Zodiac Man are a three-column format, usually delineated by four sets of double vertical rulings, and a geometric arrow shape that is tightly integrated within these three columns.[17] The first and third columns feature horizontal rulings that accommodate the text, but horizontal ruling is typically suspended in the arrow space.[18] This model is represented in figures 1 and 2 by the image and diagram of MS Ashmole 391, Part V, folio 9r.[19] While the four examples discussed here all fall within Linne R. Mooney's second group of manuscript witnesses of

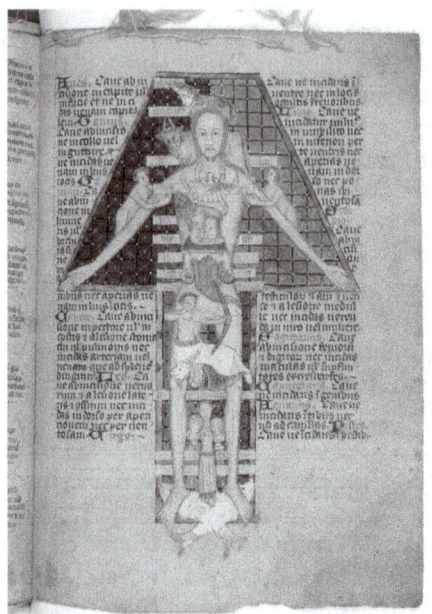

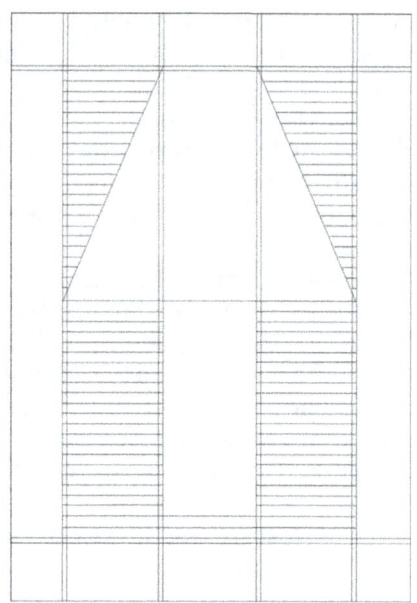

Figure 1. The Bodleian Libraries, The University of Oxford, MS Ashmole 391, Part V, folio 9r.

Figure 2. Diagram of the ruling pattern in Oxford, Bodleian Library, MS Ashmole 391, Part V, folio 9r.

Somer's *Kalendarium,* which are united by their common prologue, this conventional ruling pattern had wide purchase in the transmission history of Somer's *Kalendarium.*[20]

This recurring convention sustains some variation, which is unsurprising given that each manuscript has been individually crafted. Even the initial example from MS Ashmole 391 has its idiosyncrasies, in this case the two horizontal rulings that bisect the bottom of the arrow space. To outline some other areas of divergence, the ruling pattern in MS Rawlinson D.928 is notable because the two central sets of vertical rulings have been suspended in the top half of the diagram. Consequently, the arrow-shaped space is entirely free from ruling, which is particularly clear to a modern observer because the diagram has not actually been included (see Figs. 3 and 4). More obviously, in both MS Savile 39 and MS Ashmole 789, the arrow model takes up just half of the page, having been integrated into a more complex ruling pattern that enables a volvelle to appear on the same page, i.e., a moveable set of discs that can be used to calculate the sign the moon is in on a particular day (see Fig. 5).[21]

Figure 3. The Bodleian Libraries, The University of Oxford, MS Rawlinson D.928, folio 9r.

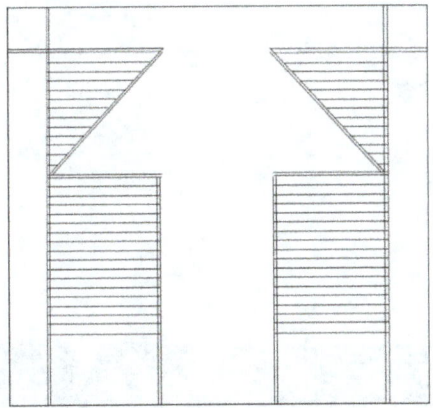

Figure 4. Diagram of the ruling pattern in Oxford, Bodleian Library, MS Rawlinson D.928, folio 9r.

Figure 5. The Bodleian Libraries, The University of Oxford, MS Savile 39, folio 7r.

Setting aside these differences, a key feature that unites these examples is the fact that the Zodiac Man requires a unique ruling pattern within the wider text of Somer's *Kalendarium*. Although the surrounding folios typically exhibit equally complex ruling patterns, they each cater to the particular task at hand. Returning to MS Savile 39, the Zodiac Man has a very different ruling pattern from, for example, the folio that accommodates the Tables of Bisextiles and Moveable Feasts at the top, and the Table of the Planets with its canon at the bottom (fol. 4r; see Figs. 6 and 7). Unlike the arrow-shaped Zodiac Man, the ruling pattern for this folio demands many vertical lines to accommodate the tabular nature of the information. Yet another different ruling pattern is necessary for the two folios representing eclipses (fol. 8v-9r). These folios have both been ruled to create forty-two uniform squares, one to enclose each eclipse of the moon and the sun.

On the surface, the *mise-en-page* for the Zodiac Man in London, British Library, MS Harley 5311 appears very similar to the examples that have been seen thus far: an arrow-shaped Zodiac Man occupies a central position in a three-column ruling pattern (fol. 5v; see Fig. 8). However, where previous examples of Somer's *Kalendarium* created a bespoke ruling pattern for the Zodiac Man and each surrounding folio, contrastingly this folded almanac,

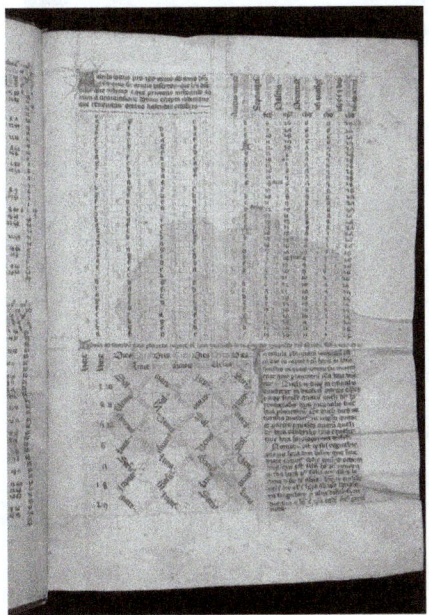

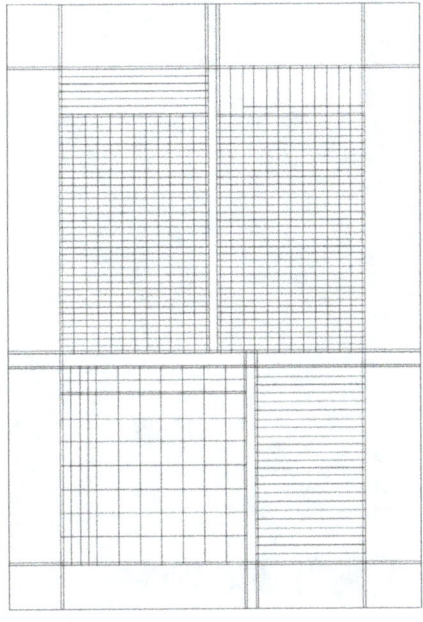

Figure 6. The Bodleian Libraries, The University of Oxford, MS Savile 39, folio 4r.

Figure 7. Diagram of the ruling pattern in Oxford, Bodleian Library, MS Savile 39, folio 4r.

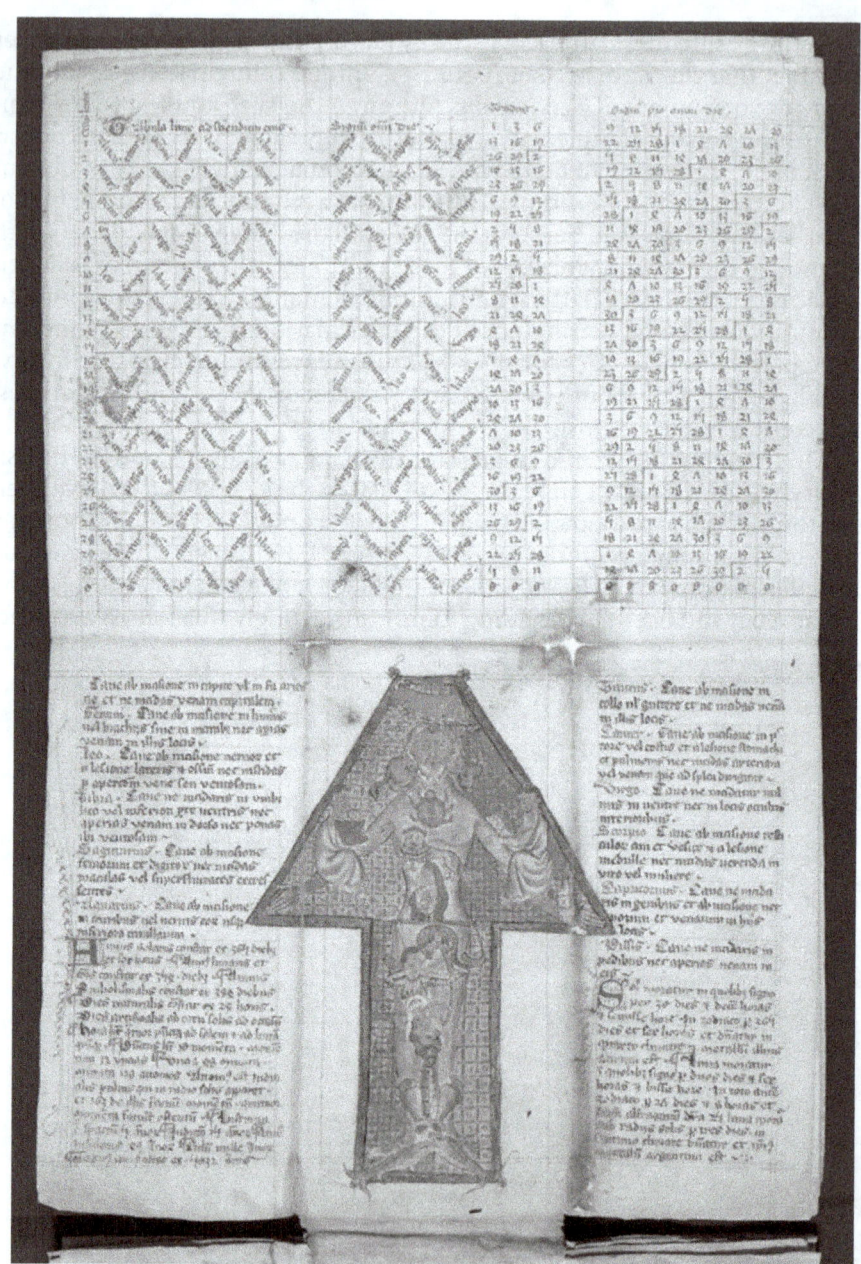

Figure 8. © British Library Board Harley 5311 folio 5v.

made circa 1398–1406, employs an identical three-columned ruling pattern as a starting point for *every* writing space.[22] This base ruling pattern has evidently been elaborated as required. For example, all of the columns on the top half of folio 5v feature extra horizontal and vertical rulings in order to accommodate the Tables to Know the Sign of the Moon and the Angle of the Moon. By contrast, only the outermost columns have been augmented on the bottom half of the same folio, in this case with horizontal rulings for the text of the Zodiac Man. As a consequence, the arrow-shaped Zodiac Man is not as tightly integrated within the ruling pattern as it is in the previous examples. The red ink of the vertical rulings remains visible through the arrow-shaped diagram, which adds credence to the theory that the tripartite column structure was ruled first and the accommodations for the Zodiac Man text and diagram considered later.

While the ruling pattern in MS Harley 5311 differs only slightly from the common model discussed above, other witnesses of Somer's *Kalendarium* preserve very different ruling patterns. For example, three manuscripts accommodate a rectangular space within their ruling pattern for the Zodiac Man page, each allowing for text to encircle the diagram.[23] Another manuscript features a ruling pattern that allows for a cross-shaped Zodiac Man, flanked by text at all four corners of the page.[24] Nevertheless, not all ruling patterns for Zodiac Men in Somer's *Kalendarium* accommodated for the diagram in advance. For example, in MS Ashmole 391, Part II, a Middle English version of the text copied *c.* 1433–1440, no attempt has been made to purposefully accommodate the Zodiac Man within the ruling pattern (fol. 3r).[25] Instead, the diagram has simply been inserted on top of the typical ruling pattern used for folios 1r-4v, which comprises a rectangular frame with horizontal rulings for the text in addition to some through lines (see figures 9 and 10). Close inspection confirms that no effort has been made to suspend the ruling for the diagram in question, as the horizontal rulings remain visible through the image.[26] The kind of abstract shape that the Zodiac Man takes here is described in this article as "body contour."[27]

To give a sense of the wider context, it is useful to introduce some different approaches to ruling Zodiac Men found in texts other than Somer's *Kalendarium*. Part I of Oxford, Bodleian Library, MS Ashmole 210 is a late-fourteenth-century astro-medical miscellany whose contents include the *Kalendarium* of Richard Thorpe and the *Middle English Verse Compendium of Astrological Medicine*.[28] The latter text synthesizes the influences of the signs of the zodiac over man's body with information on the four elements and four humors, thus complementing the Zodiac Man diagram it encircles on fol. 9r. Once again, this manuscript features a three-column format, with the Zodiac Man occupying the central space. However, the ruling is a simpler affair, comprising a frame with two additional vertical lines to subdivide the

Figure 9. The Bodleian Libraries, The University of Oxford, MS Ashmole 391, Part II, folio 3r.

Figure 10. Diagram of the ruling pattern in Oxford, Bodleian Library, MS Ashmole 391, Part II, folio 3r.

space (see Fig. 11). Some issues have evidently been encountered when trying to squeeze the text into the limited space afforded by this design. Many words stray beyond the ruled columns, which is especially noticeable at the right hand of the Zodiac Man, where image and text actually overlap.

Intriguingly, there is no ruling at all for the Zodiac Man in Oxford, Bodleian Library, MS Ashmole 370, Part I, a manuscript of Nicholas of Lynn's *Kalendarium* containing a vernacular Zodiac Man text and diagram from the early sixteenth century (fol. 27v).[29] The rectangular-shaped Zodiac Man does not appear to be superimposed on any existing ruled outline, and has been enclosed on all four sides by unruled text in an early Tudor secretary hand (see Fig. 12).[30] While this final example does not actually have any ruling, its page design does conform to the general trend that has been seen thus far: the Zodiac Man diagram occupies a central position with text encircling it.[31] Nevertheless, at the close of this descriptive survey, the strikingly different appearance of MS Ashmole 370 serves as a reminder that it is not possible to generalize too broadly about page design, even within a small subgenre of late medieval literature.

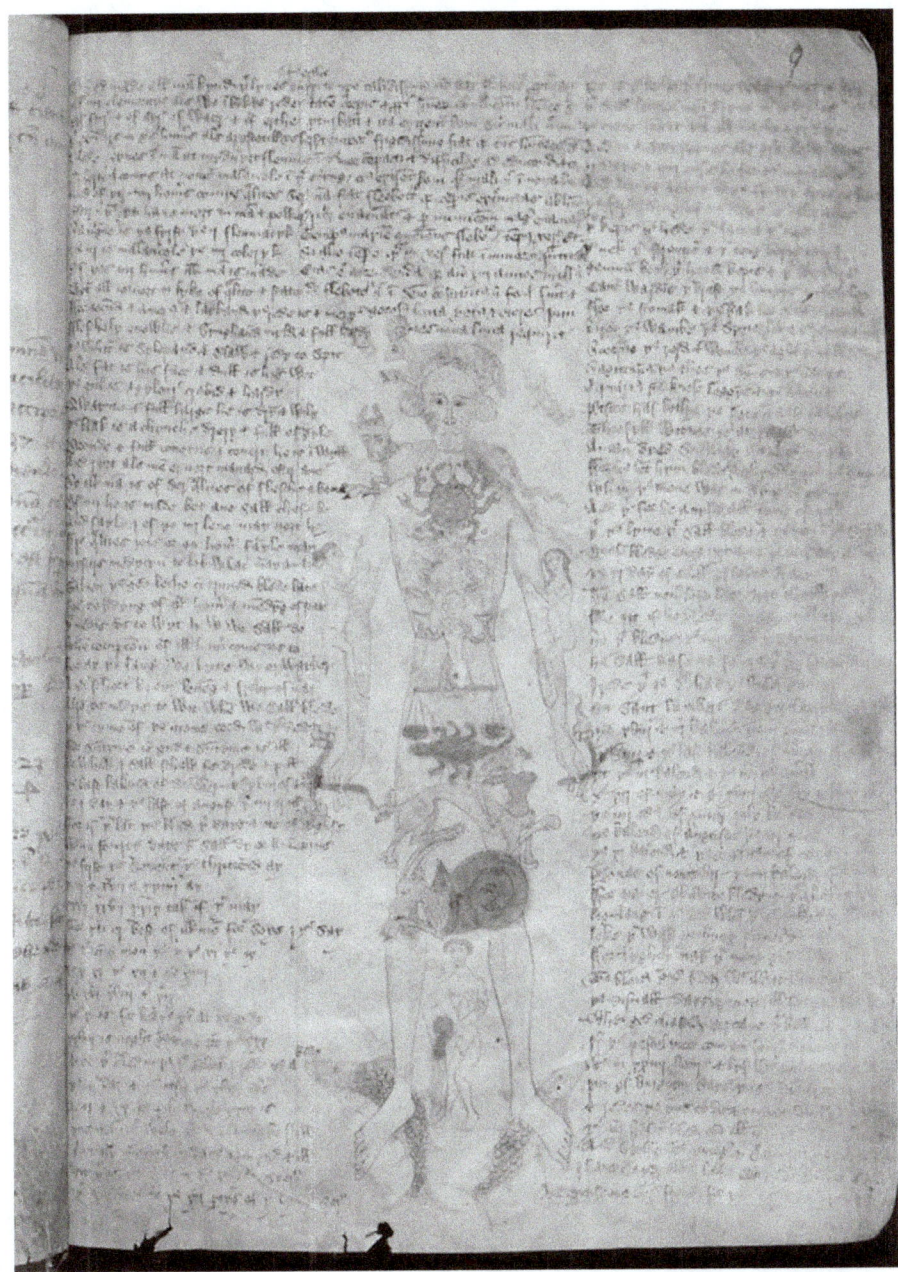

Figure 11. The Bodleian Libraries, The University of Oxford, MS Ashmole 210, Part I, folio 9r.

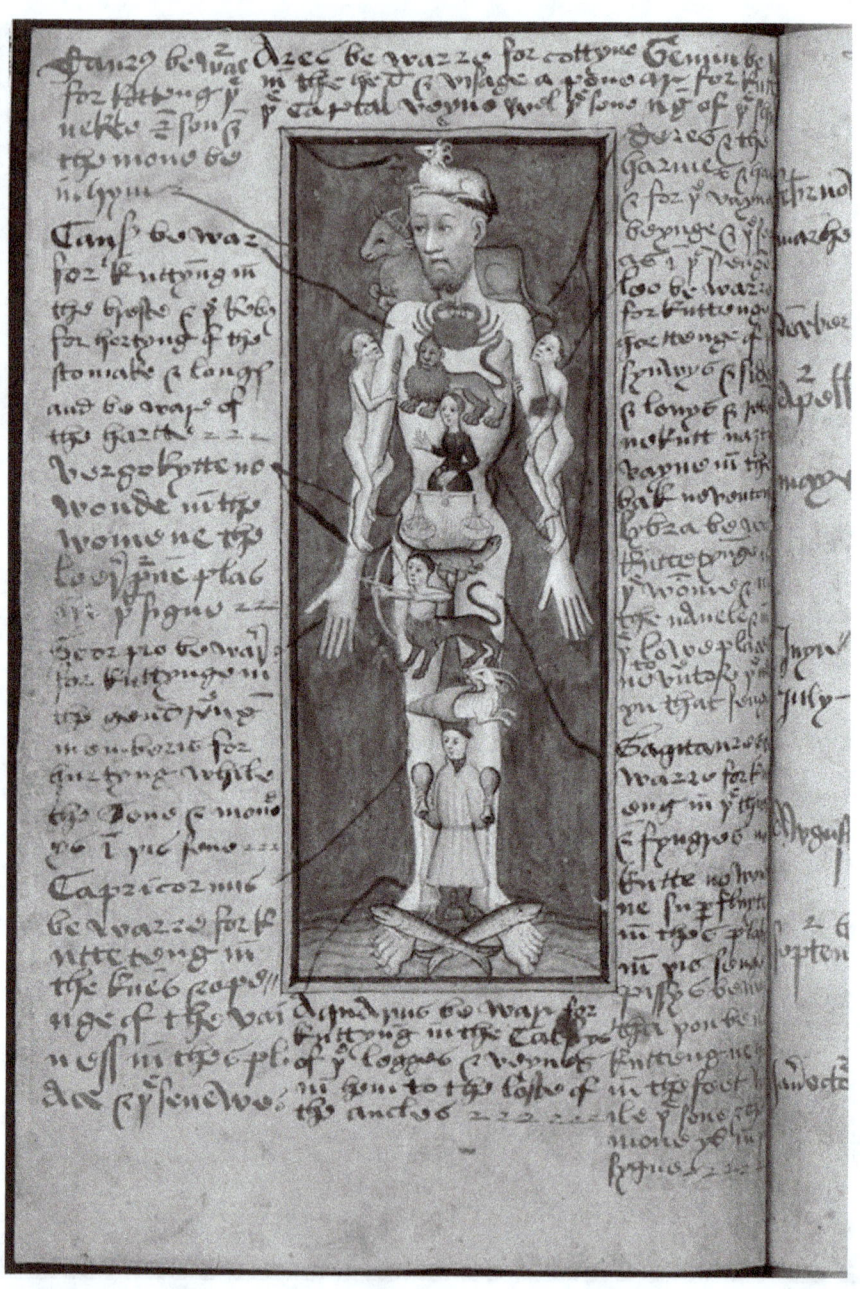

Figure 12. The Bodleian Libraries, The University of Oxford, MS Ashmole 370, Part I, folio 27v.

Discussion of Implications: Ruling Patterns with Function, Beauty, and Social Impact

The first question that arises from this survey is a practical one, pertaining to the relationship between conventional ruling patterns for the Zodiac Man and the form of the folded almanac.

Six folded almanacs of Somer's *Kalendarium* provide ruling for a Zodiac Man, and in each one the central vertical rulings coincide closely with the folds of the page.[32] This is well demonstrated by MS Rawlinson D.928 in figure 3. The ruling pattern therefore structures text and image in a way that complements and cooperates with the material form. This has the effect of lending the Zodiac Man a kind of visual coherence when the folded almanac is opened up, making it easy to use while simultaneously rendering it aesthetically pleasing.

One issue at stake is how far this effect was intentionally produced or was merely serendipitous. Even with a wider survey, this question would be impossible to resolve, as the motivations and human interactions behind production remain inaccessible. In particular, it is unclear how far the person responsible for the ruling pattern had influence over the folds of the pages. Furthermore, other factors likely played a role when the folds of the almanac were first created, including the size, quality, and dimensions of the membrane available. Ultimately, the most likely answer is that the relationship between form and ruling varies depending on the individual case.

However, it is worth noting that folded almanacs do not always utilize two folds to create three columns. For example, Oxford, Bodleian Library, MS Ashmole Rolls 6 is a fragmentary copy of Somer's *Kalendarium* from *c.* 1462 that does not actually include the Zodiac Man, and its pages have three folds, creating *four* columns.[33] Given that the form of the folded almanac is not fixed, yet there is evidently some correspondence between folded almanacs of two folds (i.e., three columns) and those containing the three-columned Zodiac Man, it remains plausible that conventional ruling patterns were one factor influencing the form of the almanac.[34] If there is potentially a relationship between ruling pattern and form, this adds a layer of complexity to the nuanced processes of manuscript production.

MS Rawlinson D.928 gives an insight into a second practical issue, namely the relative timescale of manuscript production. Notably, this folded almanac has been assembled even though the Zodiac Man diagram has not been included in the space demarcated for this purpose within the ruling pattern.[35] There are many possible reasons why such an image was not included: perhaps an illuminator with the requisite skills and knowledge could not be found, or there may have been insufficient funds to complete the project. It is also possible that the manuscript was bound with the idea that the illustration could be added at a later date, though the unwieldy form of the folded almanac would have made this challenging.

Regardless of whether the Zodiac Man image was intended to be supplied at a later stage, MS Rawlinson D.928 is still useful in several respects even without this diagram. Most obviously, other sections of the manuscript would still be valuable, including the table outlining good and evil days for bloodletting (fol. 8v). Despite the fact that the ruling pattern is unfulfilled, the Zodiac Man folio itself is still useful too, as even without the diagram one can glean from the text that Aries governs the head, and so on. This begs the question of the relative importance of text and image in this work. In an assessment of medical illustrations of this nature, Peter Murray Jones argues that "the text acts as a commentary on the illustration rather than *vice versa*—it explains the workings of the figure or provides additional information necessary to make use of it."[36] Murray Jones thus implies that text and image work together, with both media being necessary in order for the manuscript to be used. While this may have been the ideal situation, it is notable that the Zodiac Man folio in MS Rawlinson D.928 still works to a certain extent even without its diagram. Of course, the Zodiac Man diagram serves secondary functions that MS Rawlinson D.928 cannot fulfill in its current state, as will become apparent in the course of this article. Nevertheless, the unfulfilled ruling pattern in this manuscript alerts one to the possibility that there were contexts for use in which the text could be productively employed without the diagram.

The blank space in the ruling pattern of MS Rawlinson D.928 can also be approached from a different angle. In her study of the Middle English narrative texts in the Thornton manuscripts, Phillipa Hardman has argued that "pictorial intentions" can be just as meaningful as the actualization of these intentions, with an empty space drawing attention to itself in a way that marks divisions in the text "just as effectively" as the intended picture or initial.[37] In a similar vein, the ruling pattern of MS Rawlinson D.928 draws attention to itself precisely because something is missing.[38] Moreover, as it has been established that this folio utilizes a highly conventionalized ruling pattern, a reader familiar with the tradition might even impose the missing Zodiac Man onto the space in their mind. This conventional ruling pattern might, therefore, have the potential to be a form of visual synecdoche: an integral part of the diagram that actually has the power to recall the whole image.

Even if the Zodiac Man text can work in these ways without the accompanying image, it is worth elaborating the functional benefits of the ideal situation encouraged by the integrated arrow-shaped ruling pattern in which image and text work together. In particular, when the disposition of material orchestrated by the ruling pattern is executed, the ability to access text and diagram on a single folio increases the speed at which the reader can take in the material presented. The diagram takes on the function of a quick reference tool, condensing the information enclosed within the text into a visually efficient format. The reader can then, if necessary, look to the text for more detail. For example, in a manuscript like MS Ashmole 391, Part V (see Figs. 1 and 2), the Zodiac Man diagram quickly informs or reminds the reader that Cancer generally controls the region of the chest, but the text elaborates upon this situation, explaining the implications in more detail:

> Cancer. Cave ab inscisione in pectore vel costis et a lesione stomachi et pulmonis nec inscindas artheriam vel venam que ad splen dirigitur.

> Cancer. Beware of cutting in the chest or sides and of any lesion of the stomach and lungs, and do not cut into the artery or vein which leads to the spleen.[39]

This type of reading method, in which text and image are utilized simultaneously, is optimized by an integrated ruling pattern. Functional efficiency is even greater when the ruling pattern enables the reader to consult a volvelle on the same folio as the Zodiac Man image and text, as in MS Savile 39 (see Fig. 5). The ruling patterns in such manuscripts enable the physician or other user to work out the current astrological situation from the volvelle before glancing down to the Zodiac Man to establish the implications of the moon's position for surgery. By minimizing the number of eye movements, this ruling pattern increases the efficiency of the prognostic procedure, and reduces the chance of error.

If manuscripts like MS Savile 39 populate the top end of a scale of functionality, at the other extreme are manuscripts such as MS Ashmole 391, Part II (see Fig. 9). As outlined previously, in this manuscript no special attempt has been made to accommodate the Zodiac Man diagram within the ruling, as an image has simply been added on top of the typical pattern. As a consequence, the relationship between text and image becomes unbalanced. For example, it is possible to learn that Cancer governs the region of the chest from the diagram on the recto side (fol. 3r), but it is necessary to turn to the verso side (fol. 3v) to find the corresponding explanation that one should "bewar of kutting in þe breste" or "of hurtyng of þe stomake and artirs."[40] In terms of utility, the lack of an integrated ruling pattern makes a significant difference: not only is the speed at which the necessary information can be gleaned from the folio reduced, but the symbiotic relationship of text and image is undercut. In a different way, the balance of text and image has been destabilized in the astro-medical miscellany MS Ashmole 210, as the effort to squeeze too much text within the columns of the ruling pattern makes gleaning information a cumbersome task (see Fig. 11).

While integrated ruling patterns have considerable functional benefits, on the other hand the skillful integration of text and image in manuscripts like MS Ashmole 391, Part V also suggests a concern for aesthetics. In particular, it reflects what Albert Derolez refers to as the "*horror vacui.*"[41] By carefully arranging the text around the image in the integrated arrow-shaped ruling pattern, it is possible to sustain the Gothic aesthetic of the tight text-block. By contrast, if one were to imagine that the Zodiac Man were separated from the text, it seems likely that there would be more intentional blank space on the folio due to its unusual shape. However, in the case of MS Ashmole 789 and MS Savile 39, this particular aesthetic motivation has been sacrificed to a certain extent in order to increase the functionality of the folio as a unit: the task of creating a text-block that incorporates an arrow shape *and* a volvelle would seem to be insurmountable (see Fig. 5).

The notion that functionality has a high priority in ruling patterns for some manuscripts containing Zodiac Men is reinforced by a comparison to Peikola's work on the ruling patterns used in religious miscellanies. Peikola ultimately argues the following: "[S]cribes/compilers of religious miscellanies were often in the habit of regularising the ruling pattern for the whole manuscript to emphasize the textual and thematic unity of the compilation."[42] In the present examination of a subgenre of astro-medical literature, exactly the opposite phenomenon has emerged. Even when just one text, Somer's *Kalendarium*, is isolated, it becomes clear that typically each individual folio requires a unique ruling pattern: a table of astrological data cannot share the same ruling pattern as a Zodiac Man. In other words, uniformity is not to be found in the ruling patterns of a single text, let alone across a compilation of different texts of the same genre. The notable exception is MS Harley 5311, in which each folio starts with a base ruling pattern that is subsequently modified to suit each text and/or diagram (see Fig. 8). However, even in MS Harley 5311, each folio ultimately ends up having its own unique ruling pattern. In this survey, MS Harley 5311 is therefore best regarded as the exception that proves the general rule: far from standardizing ruling across the manuscript, the conventions of this genre often require bespoke treatment on each folio.

Unlike Peikola's religious miscellanies, the need to succinctly and clearly display the information provided by the individual image and/or text in Somer's *Kalendarium* outweighs any desire for thematic unity in terms of ruling pattern. Conversely, the ruling *style* can take on function of creating thematic unity across the text, even if the ruling *pattern* does not. Returning to the example of MS Savile 39, a sense of unity is sustained across the manuscript by the consistent use of red ink and double parallel lines, two features that can be seen on both of the folios illustrated in figures 5 and 6. However, these features also lend the manuscript a coherent aesthetic. Moreover, the use of double rather than single lines is an element of superfluity that must to a certain extent be an aesthetic choice, even if it does serve the function of sustaining thematic unity between folios. Thus, aesthetic and functional motivations are, once again, difficult to separate.

Turning now to some further aesthetic motivations at play, the preoccupation of medieval medicine with balance and order is arguably mirrored—consciously or unconsciously—in the visual impact of certain ruling patterns. Medieval anatomy and physiognomy inherited from Greek medicine the notion that the proportions of the four humors established an individual's "complexion" or "temperament."[43] As Nancy Siraisi explains, the balance of blood, phlegm, black bile, and red/yellow bile was "held to be responsible for psychological as well as physical disposition," with the "ideal complexion" being "well balanced."[44] These ideas are enshrined in works such as John Trevisa's translation of Bartholomæus Anglicus's *De Proprietatibus Rerum,* a popular encyclopaedic text of the late Middle Ages. In book four, Trevisa explains that the "foure humours" must be kept "in euene proporcioun in quantite and qualite" if a "state of helþe" is to be maintained; conversely, if the humors are "vneuen in proporcioun," this can breed sickness.[45]

Returning to the Zodiac Men, the concern for order and balance in medieval medicine is arguably complemented aesthetically by the overall impression of the ruling pattern and *mise-en-page* of Zodiac Men in some manuscripts of Somer's *Kalendarium,* in which the meticulously designed ruling patterns represent a careful equilibrium of visual and verbal information. While no two ruling patterns capture this balance in quite the same way, the dimensions of the rulings in MS Savile 39 are particularly notable. The flanking columns for the zodiac text are identical in width to the lower space for the zodiac arrow, with all three columns measuring 43mm. In addition, the upper half of the arrow space is almost precisely the same height as the bottom half, measuring 58mm and 50mm respectively. The concern for balance and order in cases like MS Savile 39 can be seen to mirror the medieval physicians' imperative to maintain a careful balance in bodily humours, and to perform surgery with an eye to the bodily equilibrium determined by the signs of the zodiac. Of course, the extent to which scribes, illuminators, and physicians would have been alert to such parallels is ultimately unknowable and arguably unlikely. Nevertheless, it is striking that integrated ruling patterns of this kind are in visual harmony with the mentality of medieval medicine.

On the other hand, one could dispute this connection by highlighting that other medieval ruling patterns have a symmetrical, balanced aspect, with the double column format of some manuscripts of Gower's *Confessio Amantis* in Peikola's study being just one example.[46] However, the precision necessitated by the arrow-shaped zodiac pattern is a far more demanding and ultimately impressive task, as it demands that one maintain symmetry in vertical *and* diagonal axes. Furthermore, it is not being suggested that a complex pattern in medieval manuscripts necessarily relates to contemporary medicine; instead, it is being argued that in this particular genre, the aesthetic of some ruling patterns is remarkably appropriate given the medical context. Yet this rule is not universally applicable. For example, in the astro-medical miscellany MS Ashmole 210 (Fig. 11) and the copy of Nicholas Lynn's *Kalendarium* in MS Ashmole 370 (Fig. 12), the page design does not cultivate an aesthetic of balance in the same way.

The issue of balance in ruling patterns, which has just been discussed from an aesthetic viewpoint, emerged previously as a functional strength due to its benefits for ease of use. If aesthetic and functional motivations behind ruling patterns appear at first to be difficult to separate, then on closer inspection these two aspects actually form a symbiotic relationship, not unlike that which characterizes the relationship between the Zodiac Man text and image itself. This becomes particularly clear when considering the role of aesthetics within the possible function of the Zodiac Man as a badge of the medieval physician's authority.

Murray Jones comments that the information contained in folded almanacs could have been committed to memory without much effort, and that, moreover, these manuscripts often contain errors.[47] If the almanacs were not necessarily relied upon as a reference tool, Murray Jones proposes that "opening up the leaves" may in part have been "an impressive part of the ritual of medical consultation."[48] Of course, Hilary Carey rightly cautions that one should not "over-state the evidence for associating the folded almanac with medical practice," as such manuscripts "appear to have been used by people from a wide range of social backgrounds" that includes—but is not limited to—medical practitioners.[49] With this caveat in mind, it is nevertheless plausible that in a certain context folded almanacs containing Zodiac Men were opened up at a consultation with the intention of giving the patient confidence in the physician. In this situation an elaborate and carefully proportioned ruling pattern may have had the function of complementing the impression that the physician had access to a complex and authoritative set of information. In this vein, it is possible to detect utility *in* the aesthetic of the ruling patterns. While the lines on the page might primarily serve the function of organizing information, the complex and intricate aesthetic of the ruling pattern also has the potential to reinforce the authoritative position of the physician within society.

This assessment of the mutually beneficial relationship between aesthetics and functionality is consonant with the observations that are made throughout this article. Firstly, it becomes clear that when the folds on the portable almanacs coincide with the ruling patterns for Zodiac Men, this creates an aesthetically pleasing *mise-en-page,* and also makes sense functionally. Furthermore, where an aesthetic of balance in line with medieval medicine is detected, the equilibrium of the folio is also highly functional. Finally, if an integrated ruling pattern coheres to the Gothic aesthetic of the tight text-block, it also becomes apparent that this keeps all of the information neatly accessible on one folio. Thus, where aesthetic incentives are identified, functional benefits always exist in parallel.

In order to make sense of this symbiotic relationship between beauty and utility in ruling patterns, it is useful to make a comparison to medieval architecture. As Mary Carruthers highlights:

> [W]ork on the Divinity School of the University of Oxford was re-contracted in 1439, because of expense and delay, and the concerns of the university's donors and dons about the excessive and superfluous curiosity of the work (*supervacuas curiositas*), in the form of crockets, babewyns, niches and the like.[50]

Carruthers uses this example to suggest that elements of curiosity can be seen as distracting and unbeneficial in medieval architecture if they do not help to "mark the way(s) through a work."[51] In much the same way, elements of beauty and intricacy have been found in medieval ruling patterns, yet they appear to be permissible precisely because they help "mark the way(s)" through the literary work, just as functional structures within architecture help one to navigate through a building.

It is striking that comparisons between ruling patterns and architecture are not uncommon in medieval literary studies. For example, Bonnie Mak discusses how twelfth-century books used ruling patterns to create "units that were conceptually and graphically distinct" within a chapter entitled "Architectures of the Page," while Albert Derolez remarks that the through lines common in twelfth- and thirteenth-century manuscripts create "a complicated grid of horizontal and vertical lines, which evokes the buttresses, flying buttresses and pinnacles of Gothic architecture."[52] Taking a step back, it is clear why architectural design proves such a fruitful reference point for the construction of ruling patterns: both processes share the need to strike a balance between form and function, between aesthetic and utility, and between navigation and decoration. Ultimately, ruling patterns are important building blocks of the medieval page, but if aesthetic without function is inefficient and distracting, then likewise function without aesthetic is cold and uninviting.

Conclusion

Overall, a close examination of the ruling patterns for Zodiac Men sheds valuable light on the practical use of late medieval astro-medical manuscripts, exposing the diverse motivations at play when designing the page for works of this nature. In particular, the lines on the page hint at the capacity for scribal decisions made on a micro-level to affect the production, reception, and social function of the manuscripts concerned. Furthermore, the present survey discourages binary distinctions such as text versus image and aesthetics versus functionality; in many cases, a symbiotic relationship is a more fitting conceptualization. At the same time, this survey also suggests that it is impossible to generalize too broadly about ruling patterns, even within a sub-genre of literature. While several Latin versions of Somer's *Kalendarium* have yielded complex and nuanced ruling patterns for discussion, these Zodiac Men differ markedly from those found in the astro-medical miscellany MS Ashmole 210, or Nicholas of Lynn's *Kalendarium* in MS Ashmole 370.

To conclude, it is worth considering what ripples these ideas cause in the wider pool of late medieval literary studies. Though ruling patterns are a relatively understudied phenomenon, they evidently play a vital role in the *mise-en-page* and therefore warrant further study. Even an unfulfilled ruling pattern can be significant, as the conventional ways of arranging lines on the page can act as a synecdoche for missing information. Thus, this codicological feature has the capacity to inform our understanding of the relationship between scribe and reader, between text and image, and between the manuscript page and the society in which it is received. By recognizing these facts and exploring their ramifications, a more nuanced approach to manuscript production and literary reception becomes possible.

Oxford University

APPENDIX

The following table provides supplementary information regarding the twenty-eight complete (or mostly complete) manuscripts of John Somer's *Kalendarium* that cater for a Zodiac Man diagram within their *mise-en-page,* as discussed on page 81.[53] The first column gives the relevant folio reference. The second column indicates the general shape planned for the diagram within the page design, which can be "arrow," "rectangle," "cross," or "body contour." These shape designations should be seen as approximate categories, which can sustain variation as discussed in the article above. Where this variation is particularly extreme, a secondary classification is included in parenthesis, as in the case of "Arrow (Cruciform)" and "Arrow (Splayed)."[54] In these twenty-eight manuscripts as a whole, the shapes for

Zodiac Men have almost always been dictated by a bespoke ruling pattern. However, if the shape designation has a star beside it, then the Zodiac Man has not been specifically accommodated by the ruling pattern. Instead, the shape has been created simply by virtue of the arrangement of text and image relative to each other on the page. The third column indicates whether the Zodiac Man conforms to the conventional ruling model discussed on pages 81 to 82. Finally, the fourth column of this table indicates whether the Zodiac Man diagram was ultimately filled in within each manuscript.

MANUSCRIPT	ZODIAC MAN			
	Location	Shape	Conventional Model	State of Diagram
Cambridge, St John's College, MS K.26	fol. 41v	Arrow	Yes	Filled in
Cambridge, Magdalene College, MS Pepys 1662 (folded almanac)	fol. 7v	Arrow	Yes	Filled in
Cambridge, Trinity College, MS R. 15. 18, Part V	p. 18	Arrow	Yes	Filled in
London, British Library, MS Additional 10628	fol. 24v	Arrow	Yes	Space only[55]
London, British Library, MS Additional 17358 (folded almanac)	fol. 2r	Rectangle	No	Filled in
London, British Library, MS Cotton Faustina A.ii	fol. 10v	Arrow	Yes	Space only
London, British Library, MS Cotton Vespasian E.vii	fol. 17v	Body Contour*	No	Filled in
London, British Library, MS Cotton Vitellius A.i	fol. 18r	Rectangle*	No	Space only
London, British Library, MS Harley 1785	fol. 12v	Arrow (Splayed)	No	Space only
London, British Library, MS Harley 5311 (folded almanac)	fol. 5v	Arrow	No[56]	Filled in
London, British Library, MS Royal 2 B.viii	fol. 12r	Arrow	Yes	Space only
London, British Library, MS Royal 12 E.xvi	fol. 20r	Cross	No	Space only
London, British Library, MS Sloane 282	fol. 6r	Arrow	Yes	Space only

London, British Library, MS Sloane 2250 (folded almanac)	fol. 12r	Arrow	Yes	Filled in
London, British Library, MS Sloane 2465	fol. 10r	Arrow	Yes	Filled in
London, Wellcome Library, MS 8932 (folded almanac)	fol. 5v	Arrow	Yes	Filled in
New York, Columbia University, MS Plimpton 254	fol. 10r	Body Contour	No	Filled in
Oxford, Bodleian Library, MS Ashmole 191, Part IV	fol. 210v	Rectangle	No	Filled in (partially)
Oxford, Bodleian Library, MS Ashmole 391, Part II	fol. 3r	Body Contour*	No	Filled in
Oxford, Bodleian Library, MS Ashmole 391, Part V	fol. 9r	Arrow	Yes	Filled in
Oxford, Bodleian Library, MS Ashmole 789, Part VIII	fol. 363r	Arrow	Yes	Filled in
Oxford, Bodleian Library, MS Digby 5	fol. 87v	Arrow	Yes	Space only
Oxford, Bodleian Library, MS Digby 48	fol. 15v	Arrow	Yes	Filled in
Oxford, Bodleian Library, MS Rawlinson D.928 (folded almanac)	fol. 9r	Arrow	Yes	Space only
Oxford, Bodleian Library, MS Savile 39	fol. 7r	Arrow	Yes	Filled in
Oxford, Bodleian Library, MS Selden Supra 90, Part I	fol. 11v	Rectangle	No	Filled in
Oxford, Corpus Christi College, MS 123	fol. 29r	Arrow	Yes	Filled in
Rome, Vatican Library, Reg. lat. 155	fol. 15r	Arrow (Cruciform)	No	Filled in

Acknowledgments

This article is an expanded version of an essay I completed during my M.St. in Medieval Studies at the University of Oxford. I am extremely grateful to Linne Mooney for discussing Zodiac Men in Somer's *Kalendarium* with me and for providing feedback on this article. I am also thankful to Daniel Wakelin and Jane Griffiths for giving me comments on earlier drafts. In addition, I am thankful to Kathy Haas (The Rosenbach), Joshua O'Driscoll (The Morgan Library & Museum), and Catherine Sutherland (Magdalene College, Cambridge) for corresponding with me about Zodiac Men in particular manuscripts of Somer's *Kalendarium*. Finally, I would like to thank

Federica Orlando (Vatican Library), Harriet Patrick (Corpus Christi College, Oxford), and the special collections reading room staff in the British Library and the Bodleian Library for helping me to consult relevant manuscripts.

NOTES

1. For an overview of *mise-en-page*, see Stephen Partridge, "Designing the Page," in *The Production of Books in England, 1350–1500,* ed. Alexandra Gillespie and Daniel Wakelin (Cambridge: Cambridge University Press, 2011), 79–103.
2. Jessica Brantley, "Reading the Forms of *Sir Thopas*," *Chaucer Review* 47, no. 4 (2013): 416–438; Aditi Nafde, "Hoccleve's Hands: The *Mise-en-Page* of the Autograph and Non-Autograph Manuscripts," *Journal of the Early Book Society* 16 (2013): 55–83; Ruth Carroll et al., "Pragmatics on the Page: Visual Text in Late Medieval English Books," *European Journal of English Studies* 17, no. 1 (2013): 59.
3. Matti Peikola, "Guidelines for Consumption: Scribal Ruling Patterns and Designing the *Mise-en page* in Later Medieval England," in *Manuscripts and Printed Books in Europe 1350–1550: Packaging, Presentation and Consumption,* ed. Emma Cayley and Susan Powell (Liverpool: Liverpool University Press, 2013), 14. On *mise-en-page* and ruling patterns, see also Peikola, "Aspects of *Mise-en-page* in Manuscripts of the Wycliffite Bible," in *Medieval Texts in Context,* ed. Denis Renevey and Graham D. Caie (London: Routledge, 2008), 28–67 (especially 36–44, 55–58).
4. See Peter Murray Jones, *Medieval Medicine in Illuminated Manuscripts,* rev. ed. (London: British Library, 1998), 53–54.
5. For the wider context of the Zodiac Man in medieval culture see Harry Bober, "The Zodiacal Miniature of the Très Riches Heures of the Duke of Berry: Its Sources and Meaning," *Journal of the Warburg and Courtauld Institutes* 11 (1948): 1–34. For the medieval quadrant, see plate 7a.
6. See Linne R. Mooney, ed., *The Kalendarium of John Somer* (Athens, GA: University of Georgia Press, 1998); Sigmund Eisner, ed., *The Kalendarium of Nicholas of Lynn* (London: Scolar Press, 1980). Regarding these two writers and their works, see also Cornelius O'Boyle, "Astrology and Medicine in Later Medieval England: The Calendars of John Somer and Nicholas of Lynn," *Sudhoffs Archiv* 89, no. 1 (2005): 1–22 (especially 5–6 for the Zodiac Man).
7. On the questions of audience and contexts for use, particularly where folded almanacs are concerned, see Hilary Carey, "Astrological Medicine and the English Folded Almanac," *Social History of Medicine* 17, no. 3 (2004): 362–363; O'Boyle, "Astrology," 10–16.

8. Regarding the phenomenon of the *Kalendarium* in medieval Europe, see Eisner, *Kalendarium*, 5–9.
9. Peikola works under similar assumptions when he writes: "by ruling the page in a certain way scribes laid the foundation for the design of the *mise-en-page.*" Peikola, "Guidelines," 14.
10. For example, James Douglas Farquhar argues that "rulings have an important functional and aesthetic role," but he does not consider the ways in which these aspects are complementary. James Douglas Farquhar, "The Manuscript as Book," in Sandra Hindman and James Douglas Farquhar, *Pen to Press: Illustrated Manuscripts and Printed Books in the First Century of Printing* (Baltimore: College Park, University of Maryland, 1977), 53. Peikola touches upon the symbiotic relationship between aesthetics and function but overall focuses more on issues of genre and standardization. See Peikola, "Guidelines," 15–16.
11. Albert Derolez, "Observations on the Aesthetics of the Gothic Manuscript," *Scriptorium* 50 (1996): 6. Regarding how this Gothic aesthetic is fulfilled within ruling patterns, see also Derolez, *The Palaeography of Gothic Manuscript Books: From the Twelfth to the Early Sixteenth Century* (Cambridge: Cambridge University Press, 2003), 37–39.
12. These manuscripts were mostly consulted in person, but surrogate forms were used where necessary. The number of complete or mostly complete witnesses given here is correct to the best of my knowledge, and is informed largely by the enumeration of thirty-four such textual witnesses in Mooney, *Kalendarium*, 48–81. The thirty-fifth witness is Oxford, Bodleian Library, MS Digby 48, as identified by Kathleen Scott, *An Index of Images in English Manuscripts from the Time of Chaucer to Henry VIII, c. 1380–c. 1509, Bodleian Library, Oxford* (London: Harvey Miller, 2000), 1:87 (cat. no. 375). The thirty-sixth witness is London, Wellcome Library, MS 8932 (folded almanac). There were undoubtedly more copies of Somer's *Kalendarium* circulating during the late-medieval period. It is quite possible that there are additional surviving witnesses of this text which are not widely known at present, or have not yet been discovered.
13. The following manuscripts contain complete or mostly complete witnesses of Somer's *Kalendarium*, yet do not in their current state contain a Zodiac Man or a space for one: Cambridge, Trinity College, MS R. 15. 21; London, British Library, MS Harley 937 (folded almanac); London, British Library, MS Sloane 807 (folded almanac); London, British Library, MS Sloane 2397; New York, The Morgan Library & Museum, MS Bühler 12; Oxford, Bodleian Library, MS Digby 167; Oxford, Bodleian Library, MS Rawlinson D.238; Philadelphia, The Rosenbach, MS 1004/29 (folded almanac).

14. See the third column of the table in the appendix for a list of these seventeen manuscripts. As a caveat, the ruling pattern for the arrow-shaped Zodiac Man in London, British Library, MS Harley 5311, folio 5v does not conform to this conventional model, for reasons that will become clear on pages 85–87. Two further manuscripts also feature a type of arrow-shaped Zodiac Man, but their ruling patterns are once again significantly different from the conventional model, to the extent that these diagrams even warrant their own shape subcategories in the appendix table: "Arrow (Splayed)" and "Arrow (Cruciform)." To the former category belongs the Zodiac Man in London, British Library, MS Harley 1785, folio 12v. In this example, the bottom half of the arrow is splayed, and is not constrained by any central vertical rulings. To the latter category belongs Rome, Vatican Library, Reg. lat. 155, folio 15r. This ruling pattern features a cruciform shape with text at all four corners of the page (similar in effect to MS Royal 12 E.xvi, fol. 20r), but the crossbar is angular, which creates an arrow effect. For descriptions of these manuscripts see Mooney, *Kalendarium*, 63–66, 80–81.

15. Regarding standardization of the *mise-en-page* in late medieval manuscripts, see for example Peikola, "Guidelines," 19–22; Peikola, "Aspects," especially 31–32, 51; A. I. Doyle and M. B. Parkes, "The Production of Copies of the *Canterbury Tales* and the *Confessio Amantis* in the Early Fifteenth Century," in *Medieval Scribes, Manuscripts, and Libraries: Essays Presented to N. R. Ker*, ed. M. B. Parkes and Andrew G. Watson (London: Scolar Press, 1978), 163–210; Kathleen Scott, "The Illustration and Decoration of Manuscripts of Nicholas Love's *Mirror of the Blessed Life of Jesus Christ*," in *Nicholas Love at Waseda: Proceedings of the International Conference 20–22 July 1995*, ed. Shoichi Oguru, Richard Beadle, and Michael G. Sargent (Cambridge: D. S. Brewer, 1997), 61–86 (especially 70).

16. For descriptions of these four manuscripts and more detail on their individual dates, which can be established with some confidence due to the years for which astronomical data is provided, see Mooney, *Kalendarium*, 51, 74–75, 78–79.

17. Occasionally, the four vertical rulings are delineated by single rather than double lines, as can be seen for example in London, British Library, MS Sloane 282, folio 6r and Oxford, Corpus Christi College, MS 123, folio 29r. For descriptions of these manuscripts see ibid., 66–67, 80.

18. For an exception, see London, British Library, Cotton Faustina A.ii, folio 10v, in which horizontal rulings continue across the entirety of the arrow space. For a description of this manuscript, see ibid., 60.

19. All diagrams are the author's own. All images have been reproduced with the permission of The British Library and The Bodleian

Libraries, The University of Oxford. Note that in MS Ashmole 391, Part V, folio 9r (see figure 1), a piece of cloth has been attached to the top of the folio, which exposes the Zodiac Man when lifted. Its function remains unclear; perhaps it serves to cover the modesty of the naked man, to protect the image, or maybe even to let the reader test their knowledge of the information. On material in manuscripts see also Christine Sciacca, "Raising the Curtain on the Use of Textiles in Manuscripts," in *Weaving, Veiling, and Dressing: Textiles and their Metaphors in the Late Middle Ages*, ed. Kathryn M. Rudy and Barbara Baert (Turnhout: Brepols, 2007), 161–190.

20. For a list of the various manuscript groups, see Mooney, *Kalendarium*, 50–53. The conventional arrow-shaped Zodiac Man pattern features in all fifteen of the first- and second-group manuscripts except the following: Cambridge, Trinity College MS R. 15. 21; London, British Library, Cotton Vespasian E.vii; London, British Library, MS Harley 1785; Oxford, Bodleian Library, Selden Supra 90 (Part I); Rome, Vatican Library, Reg. lat. 155. Approximately one-third of the third-group manuscripts contain a conventional arrow-shaped Zodiac Man. See Cambridge, Magdalene College, MS Pepys 1662, folio 7v (folded almanac); Cambridge, Trinity College, MS R. 15. 18, Part V, p. 18; London, British Library, MS Sloane 2250, folio 12r (folded almanac); London, British Library, MS Sloane 2465, folio 10r. Finally, for an example of the conventional arrow-shaped Zodiac Man model in the fourth group with the abbreviated canon, see Oxford, Bodleian Library, MS Digby 5, folio 87v. Although it is beyond the scope of the present study, it would likely be rewarding to consider the relationship between this arrow-shaped ruling pattern and the manuscript groups of Somer's *Kalendarium* in more detail, especially since Matti Peikola has suggested that "the comparative study of *mise-en-page* may [...] present itself as a method analogous (or even complementary) to stemmatics." Peikola, "Aspects," 28.

21. Regarding volvelles, see Murray Jones, *Medieval Medicine*, 54–57.

22. For a description of this manuscript and information regarding its likely date, see Mooney, *Kalendarium*, 52, 64–65.

23. The first of these is Oxford, Bodleian Library, MS Selden Supra 90, Part I, folio 11v. In this witness, an external frame encloses horizontal rulings for the text, but a central blank rectangular space has been carefully incorporated within the ruling pattern. The second example is London, British Library, MS Additional 17358, folio 2r. This three-columned folded almanac features two columns of text flanking a central rectangle for the Zodiac Man. In both of these examples, it is possible to infer that no horizontal lines feature within the rectangular outline because the skin of the Zodiac Man has been created by leaving the

membrane unadorned, which exposes—and takes advantage of—the unruled space beneath. The third example, Oxford, Bodleian Library, MS Ashmole 191, Part IV, folio 210v, is far simpler in design, featuring just frame ruling and a central rectangular ruled space for the diagram. For descriptions of these manuscripts see ibid., 59–60, 72–73, 79–80. Note that although the appendix lists four rectangular shaped Zodiac Men, the diagram in London, British Library, MS Cotton Vitellius A.i is not specifically accommodated by the ruling pattern and hence has a star beside the shape designation. Regarding the Zodiac Man in this manuscript, see note 26.

24. London, British Library, MS Royal 12 E.xvi, folio 20r. For a description of this manuscript, see ibid., 66.

25. For a description of this manuscript and information regarding its likely date, see ibid., 53, 73–74.

26. Two other manuscripts of Somer's *Kalendarium* do not feature a bespoke ruling pattern for the Zodiac Man. These are London, British Library, MS Cotton Vespasian E.vii, folio 17v and London, British Library, MS Cotton Vitellius A.i, folio 18r. In the former, a Zodiac Man has been neatly drawn on top of horizontal rulings, and this body contour is surrounded by text. No attempt has been made to enclose the body contour within a geometric shape. In the latter, the scribe has taken care not to write on parts of certain horizontal rulings in order to leave a rectangular shape free from text in the bottom-left corner for what is presumably the Zodiac Man diagram. For descriptions of these manuscripts, see ibid., 60–62.

27. Further examples of "body contour" Zodiac Men in Somer's *Kalendarium* (with and without bespoke ruling) are listed in the appendix.

28. For the original identification of this text and an edited version, see Linne R. Mooney, "A Middle English Verse Compendium of Astrological Medicine," *Medical History* 28, no. 4 (1984): 406–419. See 407–408 for a description of the manuscript.

29. For a description of this manuscript, see Eisner, *Kalendarium*, 42–43.

30. The hand is in keeping with Anthony G. Petti's description of early Tudor secretary as "broad, fairly open and somewhat splayed," and exhibits characteristic features including looped links on letters such as **h** (e.g. "the," l. 8). Anthony G. Petti, *English Literary Hands from Chaucer to Dryden* (London: Edward Arnold, 1977), 16.

31. This trend is not without exception. See the discussion of London, British Library, MS Cotton Vitellius A.i, folio 18r in note 26.

32. These six folded almanacs are listed in the appendix. In five of the six, the vertical rulings coincide almost exactly with the folds, but in MS Harley 5311, folio 5v, there is a small gap.

33. See also London, British Library, MS Sloane 807, an almost complete witness of Somer's *Kalendarium* that lacks a Zodiac Man and has four columns. For descriptions of these two manuscripts and information regarding their likely dates, see Mooney, *Kalendarium*, 53, 68, 84.
34. This pattern is not universally true, as demonstrated by New York, The Morgan Library & Museum, MS Glazier 47. This folded almanac has three folds to create four columns, but it features an arrow-shaped Zodiac Man diagram and text taking up just three of the four columns (fol. 6r). For a description of the manuscript, see John Plummer, *The Glazier Collection of Illuminated Manuscripts* (New York: The Morgan Library & Museum, 1968), 37. See also Martha W. Driver and Michael T. Orr, *An Index of Images in English Manuscripts From the Time of Chaucer to Henry VIII, c. 1380–1509* (London: Harvey Miller, 2007), 38–39.
35. It was not unusual for manuscripts of Somer's *Kalendarium* to leave a space for the Zodiac Man diagram that was not ultimately filled in. The appendix lists a total of nine examples of this phenomenon.
36. Peter Murray Jones, "'*Sicut hic depingitur . . .*': John of Arderne and English Medical Illustration in the 14th and 15th Centuries," in *Die Kunst und das Studium der Natur vom 14. zum 16. Jahrhundert*, ed. Wolfram Prinz and Andreas Beyer (Cologne: Acta Humaniora, 1987), 106.
37. Phillipa Hardman, "Reading the Spaces: Pictorial Intentions in the Thornton MSS, Lincoln Cathedral MS 91, and BL MS Add. 31042," *Medium Ævum* 63, no. 2 (1994): 258.
38. For a discussion of the attention that gaps can draw in a textual rather than a visual context, see Daniel Wakelin, "When Scribes Won't Write: Gaps in Middle English Books," *Studies in the Age of Chaucer* 36 (2014): 249–278.
39. This quotation and translation, a representative example of the text at this point in Somer's *Kalendarium*, derives from Mooney, *Kalendarium*, 148–149.
40. Transcribed from MS Ashmole 391, Part II, folio 3v. For an edited version of the entire Middle English Canon in this manuscript see ibid., 196–203.
41. Derolez, "Observations," 7.
42. Peikola, "Guidelines," 26.
43. Regarding the medieval theory of "complexion," particularly its debt to Galen, see Nancy G. Siraisi, *Medieval and Early Renaissance Medicine: An Introduction to Knowledge and Practice* (Chicago: University of Chicago Press, 1990), 101–104.
44. Ibid., 103–106.
45. M. C. Seymour et al., eds., *On the Properties of Things: John Trevisa's*

Translation of Bartholomæus Anglicus De Proprietatibus Rerum (Oxford: Clarendon Press, 1975–1988), 1:148.

46. See the diagrams in Peikola, "Guidelines," 16, 18, 20–21.
47. Peter Murray Jones, "Image, Word, and Medicine in the Middle Ages," in *Visualizing Medieval Medicine and Natural History, 1200–1550,* ed. Jean A. Givens, Karen M. Reeds, and Alain Touwaide (Aldershot: Ashgate, 2006), 10.
48. Ibid., 11.
49. See respectively Hilary Carey, "What is the Folded Almanac? The Form and Function of a Key Manuscript Source for Astro-medical Practice in Later Medieval England," *Social History of Medicine* 16, no. 3 (2003): 503; Carey, "Astrological Medicine," 363.
50. Mary Carruthers, *The Experience of Beauty in the Middle Ages* (Oxford: Oxford University Press, 2014), 150.
51. Ibid.
52. Bonnie Mak, *How the Page Matters* (Toronto: University of Toronto Press, 2011), 16; Derolez, *Palaeography,* 38.
53. For a discussion of the enumeration of manuscript witnesses, see note 12.
54. See note 14 for a discussion of these shape subcategories.
55. A Zodiac Man diagram does follow immediately afterwards on folio 25r. Folio 25 is a separate, significantly smaller leaf, and the verso is blank.
56. See pages 85–87 for a discussion of why this arrow-shaped diagram does not conform to the conventional ruling model.

WORKS CITED

Primary Sources

Eisner, Sigmund, ed. *The Kalendarium of Nicholas of Lynn.* London: Scolar Press, 1980.

Mooney, Linne R., ed. *The Kalendarium of John Somer.* Athens, GA: University of Georgia Press, 1998.

Seymour, M. C. et al. eds. *On the Properties of Things: John Trevisa's Translation of Bartholomæus Anglicus De Proprietatibus Rerum.* 3 vols. Oxford: Clarendon Press, 1975–1988.

Secondary Sources

Bober, Harry. "The Zodiacal Miniature of the Très Riches Heures of the Duke of Berry: Its Sources and Meaning." *Journal of the Warburg and Courtauld Institutes* 11 (1948): 1–34.

Brantley, Jessica. "Reading the Forms of *Sir Thopas.*" *Chaucer Review* 47, no 4 (2013): 416–438.

Carey, Hilary M. "Astrological Medicine and the English Folded Almanac." *Social History of Medicine* 17, no. 3 (2004): 345–363.

———— . "What is the Folded Almanac? The Form and Function of a Key Manuscript Source for Astro-medical Practice in Later Medieval England." *Social History of Medicine* 16, no. 3 (2003): 481–509.

Carroll, Ruth et al. "Pragmatics on the Page: Visual Text in Late Medieval English Books." *European Journal of English Studies* 17, no. 1 (2013): 54–71.

Carruthers, Mary. *The Experience of Beauty in the Middle Ages.* Oxford: Oxford University Press, 2014.

Derolez, Albert. "Observations on the Aesthetics of the Gothic Manuscript." *Scriptorium* 50 (1996): 3–12.

———— . *The Palaeography of Gothic Manuscript Books: From the Twelfth to the Early Sixteenth Century.* Cambridge: Cambridge University Press, 2003.

Doyle, A. I. and M. B. Parkes. "The Production of Copies of the *Canterbury Tales* and the *Confessio Amantis* in the Early Fifteenth Century." In *Medieval Scribes, Manuscripts, and Libraries: Essays Presented to N. R. Ker,* edited by M. B. Parkes and Andrew G. Watson, 163–210. London: Scolar Press, 1978.

Driver, Martha W. and Michael T. Orr. *An Index of Images in English Manuscripts From the Time of Chaucer to Henry VIII, c. 1380–1509.* London: Harvey Miller, 2007.

Farquhar, James Douglas. "The Manuscript as Book." In Sandra Hindman and James Douglas Farquhar, *Pen to Press: Illustrated Manuscripts and Printed Books in the First Century of Printing,* 11–99. Baltimore: College Park, University of Maryland, 1977.

Hardman, Phillipa. "Reading the Spaces: Pictorial Intentions in the Thornton MSS, Lincoln Cathedral MS 91, and BL MS Add. 31042." *Medium Ævum* 63, no. 2 (1994): 250–274.

Mak, Bonnie. *How the Page Matters.* Toronto: University of Toronto Press, 2011.

Mooney, Linne R. "A Middle English Verse Compendium of Astrological Medicine." *Medical History* 28, no. 4 (1984): 406–419.

Murray Jones, Peter. "Image, Word, and Medicine in the Middle Ages." In *Visualizing Medieval Medicine and Natural History, 1200–1550,* edited by Jean A. Givens, Karen M. Reeds, and Alain Touwaide, 1–24. Aldershot: Ashgate, 2006.

———— . *Medieval Medicine in Illuminated Manuscripts,* rev. ed. London: British Library, 1998.

———— . "'*Sicut hic depingitur . . .*': John of Arderne and English Medical Illustration in the 14th and 15th Centuries." In *Die Kunst und das*

Studium der Natur vom 14. zum 16. Jahrhundert, edited by Wolfram Prinz and Andreas Beyer, 103–126. Weinheim: VCH, 1987.

Nafde, Aditi. "Hoccleve's Hands: The *Mise-en-Page* of the Autograph and Non-Autograph Manuscripts." *Journal of the Early Book Society* 16 (2013): 55–83.

O'Boyle, Cornelius. "Astrology and Medicine in Later Medieval England: The Calendars of John Somer and Nicholas of Lynn." *Sudhoffs Archiv* 89, no. 1 (2005): 1–22.

Partridge, Stephen. "Designing the Page." In *The Production of Books in England, 1350–1500,* edited by Alexandra Gillespie and Daniel Wakelin, 79–103. Cambridge: Cambridge University Press, 2011.

Peikola, Matti. "Aspects of *Mise-en-page* in Manuscripts of the Wycliffite Bible." In *Medieval Texts in Context,* edited by Denis Renevey and Graham D. Caie, 28–67. London: Routledge, 2008.

———. "Guidelines for Consumption: Scribal Ruling Patterns and Designing the *Mise-en page* in Later Medieval England." In *Manuscripts and Printed Books in Europe 1350–1550: Packaging, Presentation and Consumption,* edited by Emma Cayley and Susan Powell, 14–31. Liverpool: Liverpool University Press, 2013.

Petti, Anthony G. *English Literary Hands from Chaucer to Dryden.* London: Edward Arnold, 1977.

Plummer, John. *The Glazier Collection of Illuminated Manuscripts.* New York: The Morgan Library & Museum, 1968.

Sciacca, Christine. "Raising the Curtain on the Use of Textiles in Manuscripts." In *Weaving, Veiling, and Dressing: Textiles and their Metaphors in the Late Middle Ages,* edited by Kathryn M. Rudy and Barbara Baert, 161–190. Turnhout: Brepols, 2007.

Scott, Kathleen. "The Illustration and Decoration of Manuscripts of Nicholas Love's *Mirror of the Blessed Life of Jesus Christ.*" In *Nicholas Love at Waseda: Proceedings of the International Conference 20–22 July 1995,* edited by Shoichi Oguru, Richard Beadle, and Michael G. Sargent, 61–86. Cambridge: D. S. Brewer, 1997.

———. *An Index of Images in English Manuscripts from the Time of Chaucer to Henry VIII, c. 1380–c. 1509, Bodleian Library, Oxford.* 3 vols. London: Harvey Miller, 2000–2002.

Siraisi, Nancy G. *Medieval and Early Renaissance Medicine: An Introduction to Knowledge and Practice.* Chicago: University of Chicago Press, 1990.

Wakelin, Daniel. "When Scribes Won't Write: Gaps in Middle English Books." *Studies in the Age of Chaucer* 36 (2014), 249–278.

Did the Scribe Draw the Miniatures in British Library, MS Cotton Nero A.x (The Pearl-Gawain Manuscript)?[1]

MAIDIE HILMO

I. The Miniatures in Context

New scientific analyses of the pigments and images, fresh paleographic evidence, and the resultant iconographic and thematic significance of what has been uncovered, strongly suggest that the scribe of the Pearl-Gawain manuscript, British Library, MS Cotton Nero A.x (art.3) and the person who made the underdrawings of the miniatures (as distinct from their coloring) could have been one and the same person. The implications of the new scientific data, which Paul Garside, the Conservation Scientist at the British Library, provided in answer to my queries regarding the pigments, will be examined here. One of the major discoveries is that the ink of the underdrawings and the text, as I had anticipated, is the same. Further, in the scientifically enhanced images, it is now possible to see how the added paint of the miniatures obscured visual information not previously apprehended. Working independently and simultaneously, paleographer Jane Roberts has also asked, "What if the drawings were made by the scribe?"[2] Her research corroborates the scientific evidence. In addition to this new scientific and paleographic information, my study considers how some of the missed or misconstrued details subsequently obscured by paint are important in extending the iconographic and interpretive range of the miniatures and, reflexively, of the poems—all supporting the likelihood that the scribe was also the thoughtful draftsperson of the underdrawings.

Favorably ranked with Chaucer's *Canterbury Tales*, for example, there is no question about the poetic excellence of Cotton Nero's four poems—*Pearl, Cleanness, Patience*, and *Sir Gawain and the Green Knight*. In contrast to what we know about Chaucer and the illustrated and decorated manuscripts of his work, however, we know almost nothing about the poet and the actual makers of the Pearl-Gawain manuscript. In some modest manuscripts, also of vernacular English poems—such as the Oxford, Bodleian Library, MS Douce 104 manuscript of *Piers Plowman*,[3] or even Oxford, Corpus Christi College, MS 201 of the same poem, and the *Prick of Conscience* in Durham, Ushaw College, MS 5[4]—the scribe appears to have provided the illustrations as well. In these examples, the illustrations are not always visual translations of the text, but sometimes involve a re-conceptualization of it, or as Kathryn Smith observes with respect to the Anglo-Norman *La Vie seint Edmund*, an enhancement of the text.[5] The Pearl-Gawain manuscript fits nicely into this company of manuscripts in which the scribe was also the artist—in this case, of the underdrawings of the miniatures.

While the inclusion of images prefacing texts was unusual for English vernacular manuscripts, they had been employed since the late Anglo-Saxon period for scriptural works, especially for psalters like the late eleventh-century Tiberius C VI Psalter, the twelfth-century St. Albans Psalter, and the early fourteenth-century Queen Mary Psalter.[6] Such a program was also utilized by James le Palmer for his fourteenth-century *Omne Bonum* as a replacement for "the opening chapters of non-alphabetical medieval ency-clopedias," as observed by Lucy Freeman Sandler.[7] This suggests the kind of material that may have informed the choice to include twelve miniatures in Cotton Nero A.x. They serve as the audience's first means of entry to the poems and introduce, at a glance, what subjects to anticipate and weight with meaning. In the case of the visual epilogue that follows *Sir Gawain and the Green Knight*, the last miniature sums up the impressions not only of that poem, but of the manuscript as a whole. They offer "a space," as Kathryn Smith puts it (though she refers to marginal images), "to reflect on their spiritual, social, moral, and ethical relevance."[8]

Yet the Pearl-Gawain miniatures have been dismissed as of little ac-count. With only a few exceptions, critics have conservatively tended to echo and even elaborate upon the disparaging remarks by Sir Frederic Madden. The first to publish *Syr Gawayne and the Grene Knyʒt* (his title) as part of an anthology in 1839, Madden describes the illustrations as being "coarse-ly executed."[9] Nevertheless, he includes four lithographic outlines of the *Gawain* miniatures inserted into the text where he thought they should go, each inscribed by the lithographer: "Madeley lith 3 Wellington St Strand." Because they were modeled on the manuscript before it had deteriorated further, they are of value for our present purposes.

Even a century after Madden's remarks, Roger Sherman Loomis and Laura Hibbard Loomis charged that this illustrator reached "the nadir of English illustrative art."[10] It is little wonder that such attitudes prevailed "because of their crude appearance and muddy colors," as Jennifer A. Lee described the way the miniatures now appear.[11] Since not only the plainness, but also the apparent "crudeness" of the Pearl-Gawain images has deterred some critics from taking them seriously (although Kathleen Scott considered them important enough to include in her survey[12]), it is worth noting that this assessment can be somewhat mitigated by a look at specific details indicating that the painting, which often seems "to defeat the objectives of the drawings," as observed by Lee, was likely done by a secondary hand,[13] and possibly even by more than one, as I shall suggest.

The plainness of style of the Pearl-Gawain miniatures might be a reflection of the religious milieu of the times in which some iconophobic reformers railed against any but simple images that did not idolatrously portray the deity, the saints, or the Blessed Virgin Mary. This reticence may even have factored into the decision not to portray Gawain's shield since, from an artistic point of view, the image of the Virgin Mary on the inside would have been a much more interesting subject than the pentangle on the front. It is likely that such an iconoclastic mindset might also account for the rubbing out of the Dreamer's face in the second *Pearl* miniature because the spiky circlet of branches behind his head might have been subsequently mistaken by a later viewer as the suggestion of a radiating halo (Fig. 1). That there may have been a consciousness of potential iconoclasm is further indicated by the choice to illustrate the scene of Belshazzar's feast in which Daniel interprets the handwriting on the wall as a prediction of the consequences of idolatry (Fig. 2). What new insights can be gleaned from a study of the pigments, the underdrawings, the script, and the content of selected miniatures in which important details have obscured by paint?

II. The Evidence of Pigments, Underdrawings, and Script
It was the dark aquamarine color of the wavy spot beneath the sleeping Dreamer in the first *Pearl* miniature (Fig. 3) that initially drew my attention to the pigments and the outlines as I examined this manuscript in the Manuscripts Reading Room located, at that time, in the British Museum. When I asked if it was possible to learn more about what was under this dark pigment defining the wavy spot paralleling the body of the Pearl Dreamer, the librarian helpfully contacted Anthony Parker, the Senior Conservation Officer. By applying what was then the newest technology, he was able to show what appeared to be under the spot; in this case, there was just a continuation of the flowery, grassy meadow (Fig. 4).[14]

Figure 1. The Dreamer walks through a forest. *Pearl* (2nd miniature), London, British Library, MS Cotton Nero A.x (art. 3), folio 37/41v. © The British Library Board.

Figure 2. The Handwriting on the Wall at Belshazzar's Feast. *Cleanness*, London, British Library, MS Cotton Nero A.x (art. 3), folio 56/60v. © The British Library Board.

Figure 3. The Dreamer falls asleep. *Pearl* (1st miniature), London, British Library, MS Cotton Nero A.x (art. 3), folio 37/41r. © The British Library Board.

More recently, I had occasion once again to request a more detailed scientific analysis of various elements concerning the miniatures, including simulated recovery of more of the outlines of the underdrawings beneath the paint layers and an examination of the chemistry of the pigments and inks on the illustrated folios[15] and on a facing text. Dr. Paul Garside, the Conservation Scientist at the British Library, responded to my queries in his report, "Analysis of Pigments found in Cotton Nero A.x" (see Appendix), stating that the pigments "were analyzed using a combination of multispectral imaging (employing the resultant data to derive visible reflectance spectra) and X-ray fluorescence (XRF)."[16] The different wavelengths revealed more clearly the outlines of the drawings, making it appear as if the paint had been removed, and the pigment analysis revealed the chemical composition of the various pigments used.

The pigment analysis was useful in determining the composition, for example, of the green colors, which were, as I suspected, various mixtures of the blues and yellows (see Appendix). The different shades of green, as Dr. Garside states, were due to the various proportions of indigo blue and yellow (likely ochre).[17] For the wavy spot below the Dreamer, the thick dark green paint appears to have been applied on top of a yellow ochre pigment

Figure 4. Under the dark spot (detail, enhanced). *Pearl* (1st miniature), London, British Library, MS Cotton Nero A.x (art. 3), folio 37/41r. © The British Library Board.

that gradually transitions into the paler green at the top and bottom of the surrounding meadow (Fig. 3). This yellow color is still faintly visible at the bottom of the spot and at its extremities, where the top layer of paint has partially worn off. Since the plants underneath this wavy spot are the same as those that appear in the rest of the meadow, as shown in the enhanced image (Fig. 4), it is unlikely that this definition of the spot was originally intended to be part of the scene as conceived by the scribal draftsperson. Whether the heavy outline around this spot was added to serve as a perimeter for the paint, or whether it was added afterward to highlight it, is a moot point.

Then, evidently at a further stage, highlighting strokes and dots, including white and red, similar to those in the rest of the flowery meadow, appear to have been painted on top of the wavy spot itself. This added complexity suggests that, in the coloring process, there might have been an intervention to emphasize the spot as an important interpretive focus, and then a return insistence on the flowery meadow (generically representing the plants summarized in *Pearl*[18]). It would appear that the rendition of this charged area of the field involved some controversy and creative engagement by the colorist(s) or some other person. In the poem, the spot where the "pearl" dropped has multivalent associations,[19] which may have occasioned some division of opinion about the best means of representing its literal and metaphoric significance visually.

In answer to my question asking if the ink of the text is the same as that of the underdrawings, Dr. Garside found "The ink of the text shows a typical VRS response for iron gall ink, becoming transparent in the infrared" and that "where the lines of the underdrawings can be observed, these show the same VRS response as the ink of the text, suggesting that they were also drawn out in iron gall ink" (see Appendix). This answer scientifically confirmed my visual observation about the similarity of the pigment of the underdrawings and of the text in this manuscript, but was that enough to indicate that the scribe also made the initial drawings for the miniatures? Further support for the increasing likelihood that the scribe drew the underdrawings of the miniatures, since both text and drawings were done in iron gall ink, was provided by Mark Clarke, who has published extensively on painters' techniques and on medieval recipes for pigments. He thought my conclusions about the identity of the scribe and person who made the underdrawing were justified: "[I]ndeed, English drawings were often (perhaps mostly) done in non-iron-gall ink, i.e., different from the text."[20]

Convincing evidence that would appear to resolve the issue further can be found in the *Cleanness* miniature of the Handwriting on the Wall at Belshazzar's Feast, in which text appears within the miniature to spell out in graphic terms God's divine retribution that will be visited upon the kingdom of Babylon (Fig. 2). In the miniature, "this central scene," as Paul Reichardt points out, "suggests the role of reading and writing in guiding the human soul on its journey from the earthly city to a heavenly one."[21] Because of the predominance of bare parchment in this miniature, it is possible to see the layered stages of composition, from the initial sketch of the scroll to its more prominent corrected drawing and the script of the words.

It is, however, the script of the handwriting on the wall that corroborates the likelihood that it is the scribe who also drew the underdrawings of the miniatures. In addition to noting the similarities of ink, Jane Roberts observed that the "lettering of the prophecy on the scroll, f. 56v, 'mane : techal: phares' looks similar" to the enlarged display script used for words like "Amen" at the end of each poem (folios 55/59v, 82/85r, 90/94r, and 124/128v).[22] This important paleographic evidence confirms the scientific evidence that the same ink was used for both the text and the underdrawings, and relates to Mark Clarke's observation that this was not usual practice, all indicating that the scribe and the conceptual artist who made the underdrawings was one and the same.

Recently, Kathryn Smith drew attention to the practice, "common in the 13th and 14th centuries, but not much studied ... termed scribal illustration or scribal art."[23] Her example is that of *La Vie Seint Edmund le Rei* in Rylands French MS 142. In one of the marginal illustrations, the scribe wrote the first verse of Psalm 1 in the book held by Edmund showing the saint learning his psalter (folio 15v). There and in the *Cleanness* miniature, the scribal text is very like an identifiable personal signature.

III. Divergent Priorities of the Draftsperson and the Colorist(s)

The colorist(s) of the miniatures did not attend to all the outlines of the underdrawings, nor did they understand the intent (or they disagreed with) the original draftsperson, as shown, for example, with respect to the overpainting of the tips of fingers, the sea creatures in the streams, the details of Jonah and the Whale, and certain features of the portraits of the Green Knight and Gawain. In doing so, the colorist(s) effectively covered over or censored some important interpretive features that serve to amplify the meaning of the poems and to connect some of them to each other.

Hands are important in the dynamic of a number of miniatures, as exemplified in the *Pearl* miniatures.[24] In the second miniature (Fig. 1), the Dreamer's left hand, slightly obscured by greenish paint, points down to the stream, while his right hand, partially rubbed out, points up to the sky above. There may have been an element of censorship in the rubbing out of his face, since this configuration might have derived from a common ancestor to that of the depiction of a haloed God pointing up to a stylized apple tree, as seen, for instance, in a manuscript now in the New York Public Library.[25] In the *Pearl* miniature, the directional opposition of the Dreamer's two gestures intensifies and echoes the inversions of his visionary landscape and his alternations in mood between ecstatic joy and fear of danger (lines 97–156). In the third *Pearl* miniature, the Dreamer points up across the stream to the Pearl Maiden with his right hand (amusingly, a fish exhibits interest in his finger, thereby also calling the viewer's attention to it) and at the stream with his left (Fig. 5). The colorist using indigo blue, however, has entirely painted over the pointing finger and nipped the tip of a couple of fingers of the other hand—yet the Dreamer's gestures again indicate the dichotomy of his state, caught between his desire to reach his daughter, toward whom he points, and his fear of the inhabited stream separating them (her gestures warn him to back off). In the last *Pearl* miniature, the Maiden touchingly puts her right hand over her heart and reaches out to him with her left hand (Fig. 6). This

Figure 5. The Dreamer points to the Pearl Maiden, who preaches to him and warns him not to cross the stream. *Pearl* (3rd miniature), London, British Library, MS Cotton Nero A.x (art. 3), folio 38/42r. © The British Library Board.

time, it is the green coloring of the vegetation (in differing shades of mixed indigo blue and yellow) that obscures the tips of their hands as they gesture toward each other in oblique alignment across the page, indicating a closer connection between them. Nevertheless, he is still stranded on the other side and is looking off into the distance as if the vision he sees in his dream is not on the same plane, but it is pictured for the viewer's gaze. The lines of the hands, faces, and plants have been somewhat recovered in the enhanced version of this miniature (Fig. 7).

The heavily overpainted pond-like spot of the first *Pearl* miniature seems to anticipate this symbolic stream, depicted in an ever more ominous fashion in succeeding miniatures. The flowing stream (cf. Revelations 22:1) is inhabited by disturbingly large fish-like creatures, innocuous enough in the second and third *Pearl* miniatures (Figs. 1 and 5), but a little more aggressive in the last one, in which a large beak-shaped fish is about to swallow an eel-like creature (Figs. 6 and 7). Then, in the *Cleanness* miniature of Noah, a fish with an inordinately large head carnivorously swallows a smaller one, while another fish appears to take issue with the oar stirring the waves

Figure 6. The Dreamer sees the Pearl Maiden within the New Jerusalem. *Pearl* (4th miniature), London, British Library, MS Cotton Nero A.x (art. 3), folio 38/42v. © The British Library Board.

Figure 7. The Dreamer sees the Pearl Maiden within the New Jerusalem (enhanced). *Pearl* (4th miniature), London, British Library, MS Cotton Nero A.x (art. 3), folio 38/42v. © The British Library Board.

(Fig. 8). In all these cases, indigo blue has muddied the outlines of the various sea monsters as they progressively increase in menace, anticipating the portrayal of the whale in the first *Patience* miniature.

There, in the dramatically conceived miniature of Jonah and the Whale, the indigo blue colorist painted over some of the most important features (Figs. 9 and 10). In a climactic moment, the huge whale, having arisen from the abyss, seizes Jonah, thereby encapsulating and echoing the lusty poetic description (lines 247–260). Conventional iconographic representations of Jonah and the Whale are based on the words of Christ himself: "For as Jonas was in the whale's belly three days and three nights: so shall the Son of man be in the heart of the earth three days and three nights" (Matt. 12.40), a passage not mentioned in *Patience*. There are numerous versions of the popular iconography of Jonah and the Whale showing Jonah being thrown into the whale's mouth and/or being rescued.[26] Offering hope of life after death for humankind, these images prefigure Christ's triumph over evil and death.

In the *Patience* miniature, however, not only is part of Jonah's head obscured, but so is a portion of the two-pronged harpoon with which one of

Figure 8. Noah in the ark. *Cleanness*, London, British Library, MS Cotton Nero A.x (art. 3), folio 56/60r. © The British Library Board.

Figure 9. Jonah and the Whale. *Patience*, London, British Library, MS Cotton Nero A.x (art. 3), folio 82/86r. © The British Library Board.

the sailors spears or hooks the whale through his nostril as it glances by his teeth (the Noah miniature shows only a paddle; see Fig. 8). These features, not mentioned in the poem, are important in that they signal a particular typological interpretation of the event, strengthening the case that the drafts-person knew the Christological symbolism of the Jonah story and wished to enhance the poetic text by means of a visual commentary alluding to its larger meaning in terms of salvation history.

This is explicated, for example, by Phillipus Presbyter, whose work was known to Bede.[27] Presbyter refers to the "hook" (see Job 40:19–20) by which Christ disguised his divinity in taking on the flesh of humanity, thereby fooling the devil who thought to swallow the man; instead, the devil was conquered or "hooked" through his nostrils, teeth, throat, or eyes. Presby-ter refers this conquest to various events, including the Passion, and says further that it is also prophetic of the Lord when, through the saints, the devil is smashed through the wood of the cross.[28] At the beginning of an il-lustrated manuscript of Presbyter's *Commentary on Job* (Fig. 11), made in an Anglo-Saxon center on the Continent, a figure initial shows a man pierc-ing a monster with a harpoon-like stake (one side of the curved tip of the

Figure 11. Figure initial beginning Phillipus Presbyter's *Commentary on Job*. Médiathèque d'Agglomération de Cambrai, Ms. B 470, folio 2r (cliché CNRS/IRHT).

Figure 10. Jonah and the Whale. *Patience* (enhanced), London, British Library, MS Cotton Nero A.x (art. 3), folio 82/86r. © The British Library Board.

hook pierces the monster below its eye, while the man's foot treads on its head and the other is positioned in its open jaw). The view that Christ deceived the satanic monster and rescued mankind survived into medieval exegesis,[29] was dramatized in the popular Harrowing of Hell plays,[30] and was visualized in art since late Anglo-Saxon times, when the classical image of a Hades head was converted into that of a bestial Hellmouth with an open jaw.[31] That the whale in the *Patience* miniature alludes to this infernal monster is visually implied by its prominent fangs, a common feature of early Hellmouths, but not of real whales, whether of the toothed or baleen variety. The draftsperson of the *Patience* miniature features the typological significance of the story of Jonah and the Whale, not much evident in this context in the poem, which presents such subjects more literally.[32]

That the colorist(s) of the miniatures carelessly ignored some of the outlines of the underdrawings, or misunderstood the intent (or disagreed with) the original draftsperson, is perhaps most strikingly demonstrated by a detail in the first *Gawain* miniature, "The Green Knight decapitated at the Yuletide feast" (Fig. 12a), as revealed in Edward Madeley's lithograph (Fig. 12b). Madden had the image placed not at the beginning of this romance, as in the manuscript, but facing the actual text describing the beheading. The poem tells us that the Green Knight laid his "longe louelych lokkez" ("long, lovely locks," line 419) over his head to expose

Figure 12a. The Green Knight decapitated (detail). *Gawain and the Green Knight*, London, British Library, MS Cotton Nero A.x (art. 3), folio 90/94v. © The British Library Board.

Figure 12b. The Green Knight decapitated (detail). Lithograph by Madeley, reproduced in Frederic Madden, *Syr Gawayne* (London: Richard and John Taylor (1839).

his neck for the decapitating blow by Gawain. The miniature does indeed show his locks, painted in yellow to indicate blond hair (all the illustrated figures in this manuscript have blond hair). What the colorist evidently did not pick up on, as shown more clearly in the lithograph (Fig. 12b), is that the Green Knight appears to be crowned with a leafy garland or fillet that goes around to the back of his head. It is partially obscured by the indigo blue of Arthur's robe. That the underdrawing of the Green Knight shows that he "was originally wearing a chaplet with two knobs, to suggest a garland" is observed by Sarah Horrall,[33] although she does not pursue the implications. If the drawings were initially meant to be painted, this garland should have been painted green to distinguish it from his blond locks and so would have envisioned the Green Knight as being definitely identified with the "grene" man (lines 464 and 2239), the Green Man of popular folklore! It is true that the clothing and the entire horse are painted in green, but that is not quite the same thing. It is the leafy foliage that makes all the difference, and it is this interpretive thrust by the person who conceived the initial underdrawing that was missed or ignored by the colorist. It is, however, the sort of re-reading or emphasis the scribe-artist might have highlighted to make this figure relevant to an audience familiar with the foliate head of the Green Man sculptures in

Figure 12c. Gawain seeks the Green Chapel, detail. *Gawain and the Green Knight*, London, British Library, MS Cotton Nero A.x (art. 3), folio 125/129v. © The British Library Board.

Figure 12d. Gawain welcomed back to Camelot, detail. *Gawain and the Green Knight* (enhanced), London, British Library, MS Cotton Nero A.x (art. 3), folio 126/130r. © The British Library Board.

medieval churches,[34] perhaps even a specific church in the immediate vicinity of where this manuscript was made. "Despite elements of paganism," as Kossick asserts with respect to this scene, "the poem is deeply religious in import."[35]

Further, a shape-shifting relationship between Gawain and the Green Knight seems to be implied by their transposition in this miniature (Fig. 12a) and that in which Gawain seeks the Green Chapel (Fig. 12c). In the first, the Green Knight is seated astride his horse while Gawain holds an axe; in the second, this configuration is reversed, and it is Gawain astride his horse while the Green Knight holds the axe, imaging a kind of mysterious identification of the two in person as well as in the roles they play in the beheading game. Each horse is equipped with a typical medieval saddle snugly seating the rider, with a high horn in front and cantle in the back. Along with all that he started out with and still wears in the last miniature in which he is welcomed back to Camelot, Gawain's armor includes his surcoat, steel shoes, greaves, polished knee pieces, and gloves of plate (lines 567–583), as well as his "high helmet" (line 607), all seen most clearly in the enhanced version (Fig. 12d).

The drafting of such precise details, excepting ornamentation, indicates familiarity with the text and a desire to broaden its interpretive scope for an audience familiar with related narratives and iconographies.

IV. Sequence of Execution of the Visual Elements

For these miniatures, the sequence of execution might have been something like this: after the text was written on the ruled lines, the scribal draftsperson sketched the outlines of the underdrawings. Whether shortly thereafter or at a later stage (if the drawings were not originally meant to be colored), one or more painters, with different skill levels and priorities, applied the colors, by which time the text had already been folded into booklets (indicated by the scalloped holes at the edge of the Jonah miniature being painted over on top of the folio that begins *Patience*; see folio 83/87r). Highlighting outlines and finishing touches were added (e.g., the red and white strokes on top of the wavy spot in the first miniature).

At what stage the large flourished capitals at the beginning of each poem, for which space was left by the scribe, were made is not certain since, as Joel Fredell notes, "penwork flourishing in this period often is conducted separately from text production."[36] This decorative flourishing, as well as the even application of color, is quite different aesthetically from the style of the plain miniatures. Further, as I had surmised, the blue pigment of the large capital beginning *Patience* is not the same as the blue used in the miniatures; instead of indigo, it is azurite blue (see Appendix). In addition to the scribal draftsperson and the colorist(s), it may be that another person, possibly an itinerant professional who had azurite pigments, was involved in the making of these flourished capitals; whether this occurred before or after the miniatures were painted is uncertain. Further research might help to refine and date these activities more precisely.

V. Concluding Thoughts

As in the Douce 104 manuscript of *Piers Plowman*, where the annotator, who was also the corrector, occasionally disagreed with the scribe-illustrator,[37] so in the Pearl-Gawain miniatures, the colorist(s) ignored some of the details of the underdrawings, either deliberately or in haste, or due to amateurish coloring skills. Further, from the various interventions in the coloring process, more than one colorist seems to have been involved, sometimes with conflicting results, as in the first miniature. The primary focus, however, would have been formulated by the conceptual underdrawings of the scribe-artist.

As Elizabeth Saxon points out, and this applies as well to the Pearl-Gawain series, visual images "contribute to the way experience, religious and secular, is shaped, framed and absorbed," and sometimes they are "sufficiently ambiguous to convey several ideas at once, increasing their 'imaginative reach', making the relationship of images to scripture and creeds 'not casual but dialogic'."[38] This appears to have been the case not only during the production process of the miniatures, when the Pearl-Gawain manuscript was the site of engaged involvement for some time, but it is still true for today's literary and artistic audience prepared to re-view the miniatures, especially now that there is clear scientific, paleographic, and interpretive evidence that the underdrawings, at least, were thoughtfully conceived by a scribe-artist as a gateway to the poems.

University of Victoria

APPENDIX

This is the first part of the report by Dr. Paul Garside, the Conservation Scientist at the British Library, in response to my request for a scientific analysis of MS Cotton Nero A.x, the Pearl-Gawain manuscript. The purpose was to determine what pigments were used in specific areas of the illustrations, in the text, and in a flourished initial to help determine how many stages and people might have been involved in the execution of the underdrawings, the paintings, and the script, and in what sequence and time frame these tasks might have been accomplished. My questions on these aspects of the manuscript led to the very generous report by Dr. Garside and started a whole new line of enquiry about the illustrations formerly described as crude. (This report was sent to me by Dr. Garside on July 8, 2015, after I sent my original queries to the Cotton Nero A.x Project on January 12, 2014, revised from July 5, 2013.)

Analysis of Pigments found in *Cotton Nero A.x*
Pigments from nine folios (41v, 85r, 86r, 86v, 87r, 128v, 129r, 129v, 130r)[39] from Cotton Nero A.x were analyzed using a combination of multispectral imaging (employing the resultant data to derive visible reflectance spectra) and X-ray fluorescence (XRF). There appeared to be seven distinct colors used in the illustrations in the manuscript, some of which appear in various different shades: red, yellow, blue, ochre/brown, white, purple, and green. In addition, there are the black lines used to create the underdrawings.

Method
Instrumental Analysis
Multispectral images were recorded using a *Forth Photonics "MuSIS"* system. This records 30 separate 8-bit monochrome images (each 1600 × 1200 pixels; i.e., approximately 2 megapixel), over the wavelength range

420–1000 nm, with a separation of 20 nm between images. Visible reflectance spectra (VRS) were derived from these image sets by measuring the intensity response of specific individual pixels across the full set of wavelengths; first derivatives of these spectra were also calculated to aid identification (this highlights points of inflexion in the spectra—minima, maxima and shoulders—and therefore emphasizes peak positions and other more subtle spectral features that may not be immediately obvious from the raw data).

X-ray fluorescence data was recorded using a Bruker Tracer-III SD portable device, and the resulting data were assessed with Bruker Artax software. The composition of the substrate was also assessed, and this datum was used as a background in order that its influence could be removed from the results.

Pigments were then identified by comparing the VRS and XRF data with appropriate reference libraries, in combination with a knowledge of pigments likely to be available at the time and location of creation of the manuscript (i.e., Western Europe in the late fourteenth century).

Pigment Characterization

Red

The presence of mercury in the XRF data associated with areas of red pigments in the illustration strongly suggests that it is vermilion (HgS). Although the VRS data is less conclusive in allowing a positive identification (the VRS spectra of the red pigments considered are broadly similar; Fig. 1), it does not contradict this result. The red capital found on folio 87r also shows a significant presence of mercury, suggesting that it too is vermilion.

Yellow

This pigment is more difficult to categorically identify, but the presence of iron in the XRF spectra of all of the examples of yellow pigment that were assessed suggests that it is a yellow earth pigment, such as yellow ochre ($FeO_2H \cdot nH_2O$). The VRS data are ambiguous, but the spectra possess a secondary peak at about 700 nm, as well as the primary peak at about 580 nm, which is typical of yellow earth pigments.

Blue

There are three likely candidates for blue pigments available at the appropriate time and location: indigo (probably from woad or a similar source), azurite, and lapis lazuli. If the VRS data is considered, in all the examples of blue pigments in the manuscript, by far the best spectral match is observed with indigo (see Fig. 2). Furthermore, azurite and lapis lazuli are both mineral pigments [$Cu_3(CO_3)_2(OH)_2$ and $Na_8Ca_8Al_6Si_6O_{34}S_4Cl_2$, respectively]; therefore, if the former was present, copper would be expected to be observed in the XRF data, and, for the latter, aluminum, silicon, and chlorine should be observed. In the painted images in the manuscript, no heavier elements are found associated with blue pigments, suggesting that the blue is an organic pigment—i.e., indigo.

There is, however, one exception to this finding, although this is not observed in the illustrations: the blue capital found on folio 87r uses azurite. This is identified through the visible reflectance spectrum (see Fig. 2) and through the presence of copper, detected through X-ray fluorescence.

Ochre/Brown

The strong presence of iron (detected by XRF) in the ochre/brown areas of the illustrations suggest an earth pigment. Examination of the VRS data gives the closest correlation as sienna $[FeO(OH)]$, which supports this conclusion.

Green

By examining the data, it is apparent that the green pigment is not derived from a single source, but is instead formed of a mixture of blue and yellow pigments. Thorough examination of the data in the manner employed above, it is possible to determine that these are the same blue and yellow pigments used elsewhere in the illustrations (i.e., indigo and what is likely to be an earth pigment yellow). Furthermore, the differing mixtures used to achieve the varying shades of the colour can be investigated by comparing the visually different green pigments found in various folios:

Table 1: Observed location of blue, yellow and various (nominal) shades of green pigments

Color	Folio
Blue	41v, 86r, 86v, 129r, 130r
Dark Green	41v, 86r, 129r, 129v
Mid Green	86v
Pale Green	41v, 129v
Green-Yellow	86r, 86v, 129r
Yellow	86r, 86v, 129r

If the VRS spectra for these various colors are considered, it can be seen that there is a fairly smooth transition from blue to yellow through the intermediate shades of green (Fig. 3), suggesting that the relative proportions of these two pigments were simply varied to achieve the desired tone.

White

This pigment is problematic. There are no significant elemental differences between the areas of white pigment and the underlying parchment when assessed by XRF. Importantly no significant contribution from lead is observed, so the material is not lead white. As with all white pigments, the VRS data shows a more or less uniform intensity across the whole spectral range, and therefore in this case cannot be used as a useful diagnostic tool.

Purple

The purple pigment is also problematic. As with the white pigments, there are no significant elemental differences between the areas of white pigment and the underlying parchment when assessed by XRF. The VRS suggests that the pigment bears similarities to organic red pigments such as kermes or possibly madder, but this is not conclusive. The VRS spectra do not, however, possess a peak at approximately 720 nm, which suggests the pigment is not a blend with indigo.

Ink

The ink of the text shows a typical VRS response for iron gall ink, becoming transparent in the infrared.

Underdrawings

Where the lines of the underdrawings can be observed, these show the same VRS response as the ink of the text, suggesting that they were also drawn out in iron gall ink.

Conclusion

The results of these analyses suggest a fairly limited pallet of six basic pigments, of which three (red, yellow, and blue) predominate. A further color, green, is achieved in various shades through differing combinations of the blue and yellow pigments (see Table 2).

Table 2: Range of pigments found in Cotton Nero A10

Color	Pigment
Red	Vermilion
Yellow	Iron-based earth pigment (such as yellow ochre)
Blue	Indigo*
Ochre/Brown	Iron-based earth pigment (possibly sienna)
White	Unknown
Purple	Unknown (possibly organic red/purple)
Green	Indigo + earth pigment yellow

*There is also one use of azurite, found in the capital on folio 87r.

NOTES

1. I dedicate this paper to the memory of artist Carle Hessay (1911–1978), who studied the chemistry of color during his art training in Paris and Dresden. I remember him in his studio mixing pigments for use in some of his small abstract paintings, many of which appeared in *For Kelly, With Love: Paintings on the Abstracts of Carle Hessay* (Treeline, 2014). I thank the following for their help and insightful comments during various stages of this study: Kathryn Kerby-Fulton, Nicole Eddy, Corinna Gilliland, Linda Olson, Mark Clarke, Wayne Hilmo, and my reader. I am grateful to Jane Roberts for permission to quote from the draft copy of her study. For permission to reproduce his "Analysis of Pigments found in Cotton Nero A.x," I am grateful to Dr. Paul Garside; I also thank Dr. Christina Duffy and all those whose interest and expertise facilitated the technological examination of this manuscript at the British Library following my initial queries about the pigments and underdrawings. I thank the British Library for permission to reproduce the original and enhanced images of MS Cotton Nero A.x. A full set of the latter is expected to become available online at the Cotton Nero A.x Project at http://www.gawain-MS.ca; for a digital facsimile of this manuscript see http://contentdm.ucalgary.ca/cdm/search/collection/gawain.
2. Jane Roberts, "The Hand and Script," 2, forthcoming on the Cotton Nero A.x Project. I am grateful to Jane Roberts for sharing her draft with me and for our email correspondence regarding this manuscript.

3. Kathryn Kerby-Fulton and Denise L. Despres, *Iconography and the Professional Reader: The Politics of Book Production in the Douce Piers Plowman* (Minneapolis: University of Minnesota Press, 1999).
4. Maidie Hilmo, "The Power of Images in the Auchinleck, Vernon, *Pearl*, and Two *Piers Plowman* Manuscripts," in *Opening Up Middle English Manuscripts: Literary and Visual Approaches* (Ithaca: Cornell University Press, 2012), 195–204.
5. Kathryn A. Smith, "The Drawings of Rylands French 142: Techniques, Creator, Date, Iconography and Relationship to the Text," in Denis Piramus, *La Vie seint Edmund le rei*, ed. by D. W. Russell (Oxford: Anglo-Norman Text Society, 2013–2014), 64.
6. British Library, MS Tiberius C VI; online: http://www.bl.uk/manuscripts/FullDisplay.aspx?ref=Cotton_MS_Tiberius_C_VI; The St. Albans Psalter, St Godehard, Hildesheim, deposited in the Dombibliothek Hs. 1, at Hildesheim, Germany; online: https://www.abdn.ac.uk/stalbanspsalter/english/; The Queen Mary Psalter, British Library, MS Royal 2 B VII; online: http://www.bl.uk/catalogues/illuminatedmanuscripts/record.asp?MSID=6467&CollID=16&NStart=20207.
7. Lucy Freeman Sandler, *Omne Bonum: A Fourteenth-Century Encyclopedia of Universal Knowledge, British Library MSS Royal 6 E VI–6 E VII*, vol. 1 (London: Harvey Miller, 1996), 92.
8. Kathryn A. Smith, "Margin," *Studies in Iconography* 33 (2012): 33.
9. Sir Frederic Madden, introduction to *Syr Gawayne: A Collection of Ancient Romance Poems, By Scottish and English Authors* (London: Rand J.E. Taylor, 1839), xlvii.
10. Roger Sherman Loomis and Laura Hibbard Loomis, *Arthurian Legends in Medieval Art*, MLS Monograph Series 9 (1938; New York, 1966), 138–139.
11. Jennifer A. Lee, "The Illuminating Critic: The Illustrator of Cotton Nero A.x," *Studies in Iconography* 3 (1977): 17.
12. Kathleen L. Scott, *Later Gothic Manuscripts 1390–1490*, vol. 2 (London, Harvey Miller, 1996), 66–68.
13. Lee, "The Illuminating Critic," 23 and 19.
14. Maidie Hilmo, "The Image Controversies in Late Medieval England and the Visual Prefaces and Epilogues in the *Pearl* Manuscript: Creating a Meta-Narrative of the Journey to the New Jerusalem," *Studies in Medieval and Renaissance History*, third series, vol. 1, ed. Kathryn Kerby-Fulton and Maidie Hilmo (New York: AMS Press, 2001), 11–17.
15. Since scholars vary in their use of folio numbers and for ease of reference, both the original folio number in ink and then the later number in pencil are mentioned here, following the example of many recent scholars. For example, the first illustration is on folio 37/41r.

16. Paul Garside, "Analysis of Pigments in Cotton Nero A.x." I thank Dr. Garside for permission to reproduce his report, which he sent to me on July 8, 2015.
17. Garside, "Analysis." This and other results mentioned in relation to the pigments are from this source.
18. *Pearl*, lines 42–45. All quotations and line references from the Cotton Nero A.x (art. 3) poems, mentioned in my text, are from Malcolm Andrew and Ronald Waldron, eds. *The Poems of the Pearl Manuscript*: Pearl, Cleanness, Patience, Sir Gawain and the Green Knight, 5th ed. (Exeter: University of Exeter Press, 2007). Translations, intended to be fairly literal, are my own.
19. In the *Pearl* poem, the "spot" operates on several levels; see Maidie Hilmo, *Medieval Images, Icons, and English Literary Texts: From the Ruthwell Cross to the Ellesmere Chaucer* (Aldershot: Ashgate, 2004), 148–149.
20. Mark Clarke, email to me on September 23, 2015.
21. Paul F. Reichardt, " 'Several Illuminations, Coarsely Executed': The Illustrations of the *Pearl* Manuscript," *Studies in Iconography* 18 (1997): 127.
22. Jane Roberts, "The Hand and Script," 4.
23. Smith, "The Drawings of Rylands French 142," 44 and 57.
24. Robert J. Blanch and Julian N. Wasserman, *From Pearl to Gawain: Forme to Fynisment* (Gainesville: University Press of Florida, 1995), 65–110; and also, throughout, Reichardt, " 'Several Illuminations'."
25. Full-page miniature of God pointing out the apple tree to Adam and Eve, 1445. New York Public Library Digital Collections. See https://digitalcollections.nypl.org/search/index?utf8=&keywords=Full+page+miniature+of+God+pointing+out+the+Apple+to+Adam+and+Eve.
26. The Queen Mary Psalter, British Library, MS Royal 2 B VII, folio 168v; see also British Library, MS Kings 5, folio 20r, and *Speculum humanae salvationis* manuscripts, such as British Library, MS Sloane 346, folio 22v.
27. Faith Wallis, *Bede, The Reckoning of Time* (Liverpool: Liverpool University Press, 1999), lxxxiv and 308. On references to the "hook of divinity," see also Gregory the Great, *Morals on the Book of Job by S. Gregory the Great*, col. 3 of A Library of the Catholic Fathers of the Church Anterior to the Division of East and West (Oxford: John Parker, 1844), 572–573. Gregory of Nyssa and Rufinus likewise refer to it; see Hilmo, *Medieval Images*, 50–54.
28. Phillipus Presbyter, *In Historiam Iob Commentariorum Libri Tres* (Basileae: Per Adamum Petrum, 1527), 195–203. I am grateful to Janie C. Morris, Research Services Librarian in the Rare Book, Manuscript, and Special Collections Library at Duke University for sending me a photocopy of the relevant pages.

29. C. L. Snow, *Job 1–21: Interpretation and Commentary* (Grand Rapids, MI: William B. Eerdmans, 2013), 211–213.
30. John Parker, *The Aesthetics of Anti-Christ: From Christian Drama to Christopher Marlowe* (Ithaca and London: Cornell University Press, 2007), 173–178.
31. For example, the leonine hell mouths in British Library, MS Tiberius, CVI, folio 14r; online (see note 6); or in Oxford, Bodleian Library, MS Junius 11, page 3; online: http://image.ox.ac.uk/show?collection=bodleian&manuscript=msjunius11; or the dragonesque version in British Library, MS Claudius B IV, folio 2r; online: http://www.bl.uk/manuscripts/Viewer.aspx?ref=cotton_ms_claudius_b_iv_f002r.
32. R.H. Bowers, in *The Legend of Jonah* (The Hague: Martinus Nijhoff, 1971), 61.
33. Sarah M. Horrall, "Notes on British Library, MS Cotton Nero A x," *Manuscripta* 30 (1986): 197.
34. See Tina Negus, "Medieval Foliate Heads: A Photographic Study of the Green Men and Green Beasts in Britain," *Folklore* 114 (2003): 247–270.
35. Shirley Kossick, "The Illustrations of the *Gawain Manuscript*," *de arte* (1990): 21.
36. Joel Fredell, "The *Pearl*-Poet in York," *Studies in the Age of Chaucer* 36 (2014): 21n52.
37. Maidie Hilmo, "Retributive Violence and the Reformist Agenda in the Illustrated Douce 104 MS of *Piers Plowman*," *Fifteenth-Century Studies* 23 (1997): 13–48.
38. Elizabeth Saxon, "Art and the Eucharist: Early Christian Art to *ca.* 800," in *A Companion to the Eucharist in the Middle Ages*, ed. Ian Christopher Levy, Gary Macy, and Kristen Van Ausdall (Leiden and Boston: Brill, 2012), 95.
39. To clarify, the ink and pencil foliation numbers are as follows: 37/41v, 81/85r, 82/86r, 82/86v, 83/87r, 124/128v, 125/129r, 125/129v, 126/130r.

WORKS CITED

Andrew, Malcolm and Ronald Waldron, eds. *The Poems of the Pearl Manuscript:* Pearl, Cleanness, Patience, Sir Gawain and the Green Knight. 5th ed. Exeter: University of Exeter Press, 2007.
Bede, the Venerable. *Bede, The Reckoning of* Time. Translated with an Introduction, Notes and Commentary by Faith Wallis. Liverpool: Liverpool University Press, 1999.
Blanch. Robert J. and Julian N. Wasserman. *From Pearl to Gawain: Forme to Fynisment.* Gainesville: University Press of Florida, 1995.

Bowers, R.H. *The Legend of Jonah.* The Hague: Martinus Nijhoff, 1971.

Fredell, Joel. "The *Pearl*-Poet in York." *Studies in the Age of Chaucer* 36 (2014): 1–39.

Garside, Paul. "Analysis of Pigments in Cotton Nero A.x" (by permission).

Gregory the Great. *Morals on the Book of Job by S. Gregory the Great.* A Library of the Catholic Fathers of the Church Anterior to the Division of East and West. Oxford: John Parker, 1844.

Hilmo, Maidie. "The Image Controversies in Late Medieval England and the Visual Prefaces and Epilogues in the *Pearl* Manuscript: Creating a Meta-Narrative of the Journey to the New Jerusalem." *Studies in Medieval and Renaissance History*, 3rd series, 1, ed. Kathryn Kerby-Fulton and Maidie Hilmo. New York: AMS Press, 2001: 1–40.

———. *Medieval Images, Icons, and English Literary Texts: From the Ruthwell Cross to the Ellesmere Chaucer.* Aldershot: Ashgate, 2004.

———. "The Power of Images in the Auchinleck, Vernon, *Pearl,* and Two *Piers Plowman* Manuscripts." *In Opening Up Middle English Manuscripts: Literary and Visual Approaches.* Ithaca: Cornell University Press: 195–204.

———. "Retributive Violence and the Reformist Agenda in the Illustrated Douce 104 MS of *Piers Plowman.*" *Fifteenth-Century Studies* 23 (1997): 13–48.

Horrall, Sarah M. "Notes on British Library, MS Cotton Nero A x." *Manuscripta* 30 (1986): 191–198.

Kerby-Fulton, Kathryn and Denise L. Despres. *Iconography and the Professional Reader: The Politics of Book Production in the Douce Piers Plowman.* Minneapolis: University of Minnesota Press, 1999.

Kossick, Shirley. "The Illustrations of the *Gawain* Manuscript." *de arte* (1990): 21–37.

Lee, Jennifer A. "The Illuminating Critic: The Illustrator of Cotton Nero A.x." *Studies in Iconography* 3 (1977): 17–46.

Loomis, Roger Sherman and Laura Hibbard Loomis. *Arthurian Legends in Medieval Art.* MLS Monograph Series 9. 1938. Reprint. New York, 1966.

Madden, Sir Frederic. Introduction, Notes and Glossary. *Syr Gawayne: A Collection of Ancient Romance Poems, By Scottish and English Authors.* London: Rand J.E. Taylor, 1839.

Negus, Tina. "Medieval Foliate Heads: A Photographic Study of the Green Men and Green Beasts in Britain." *Folklore* 114 (2003): 247–270.

Parker, John. *The Aesthetics of Anti-Christ: From Christian Drama to Christopher Marlowe.* Ithaca and London: Cornell University Press, 2007.

Presbyter, Phillipus. In *Historiam Iob Commentariorum Libri Tres.* Basileae: Per Adamum Petrum, 1527.

Reichardt, Paul F. "'Several Illuminations, Coarsely Executed': The Illustrations of the *Pearl* Manuscript," *Studies in Iconography* 18 (1997), 119–142.

Roberts, Jane. "The Hand and Script" (by permission).

Sandler, Lucy Freeman. *Omne Bonum: A Fourteenth-Century Encyclopedia of Universal Knowledge, British Library MSS Royal 6 E VI–6 E VII.* 2 vols. London: Harvey Miller, 1996.

Saxon, Elizabeth. "Art and the Eucharist: Early Christian Art to *ca.* 800." In *A Companion to the Eucharist in the Middle Ages.* Edited by Ian Christopher Levy, Gary Macy, and Kristen Van Ausdall, 93–159. Leiden and Boston: Brill, 2012.

Scott, Kathleen L. *Later Gothic Manuscripts: 1390–1490.* 2 vols. London, Harvey Miller, 1996.

Smith, Kathryn A. "The Drawings of Rylands French 142: Techniques, Creator Date, Iconography and Relationship to the Text." In Denis Piramus, *La Vie seint Edmund le rei.* Edited by D. W. Russell, 41–64. Oxford: Anglo-Norman Text Society, 2013–2014.

———. "Margin." *Studies in Iconography* 33 (2012): 29–44.

Snow, C. L. *Job 1–21: Interpretation and Commentary.* Grand Rapids, MI: William B. Eerdmans, 2013.

An Introduction to Oxford, Bodleian Library, MS Don. e. 247

MARLEEN CRÉ AND RAPHAELA ROHRHOFER[1]

On Wednesday, May 21, 2014, a newly discovered manuscript of *The Chastising of God's Children* that was part of the Marquess of Londonderry's art collection (in its turn auctioned on May 22 and 23, 2014)[2] was sold at Christie's in London. Lot 11, "The Chastysing of Godde's [sic] Children, and other mystical treatises, in Middle English,"[3] was acquired by the Bodleian Library. In this essay, the manuscript, which is now Oxford, Bodleian Library, MS Don. e. 247, is described in detail, the "other mystical treatises" are investigated, and the text of *The Chastising* in this newly discovered attestation is compared to the versions in the eleven known manuscripts and in Wynkyn de Worde's printed edition.

Description of Oxford, Bodleian Library, MS Don. e. 247

Oxford, Bodleian Library, MS Don. e. 247 (henceforth D), written on vellum and in a nineteenth-century brown calf-leather binding, measures 170 millimeters by 125 millimeters, with a writing area of 130 millimeters by 80 to 85 millimeters and twenty-three lines to the page in one column.[4] The pages have been cropped, as can be seen in the loss of some letters in marginal annotations and the loss of some complete annotations of which traces remain in the upper margins of folios 71r, 86r, and 98r. Strips of vellum have been cut away from folios 21, 93, 94, and 95. There is a hole in the vellum in the lower-right corner of folio 1, and on folio 32 the text is written around a hole in the page. Holes in the vellum were sewn up on folios 9, 13, 14, 71, and 90, probably before the text was written on them.

In each of these cases the thread has gone, but the tears and needle marks around them remain. Folio 61 has a cut running down the outer edge of the text from line 13 to line 22. This cut seems to have been made at a later stage, possibly during the rebinding process.

D is written in what looks like one hand, in Textura rotunda. The scribe varies spellings throughout the manuscript, but consistently remains within a limited range of varied spellings. The pages have been ruled, and prickings are visible (e.g. on fol. 22), though often they have been cropped. D can be roughly dated to the first half of the fifteenth century. It does not have any internal dates in the text nor medieval ownership marks that would help the exact dating process.[5] D is written in a southeast Midlands dialect, but some of the rarer forms in the text also occur in the North. The most likely placings of the text are west Norfolk or east Suffolk.

D divides into two units. Unit 1, folios 1 to 14v, presents part of a compilation made up of the final section of the Middle English *IX Poyntes* (a text that incorporates translated passages of James of Milan's *Stimulus amoris*), a passion meditation sequence that also derives from *Stimulus amoris*, and an excerpt of Richard Rolle's *Form of Living*, lines 267–486 in S. J. Ogilvie-Thomson's edition. These borrowings are followed by a hortatory conclusion. The compilation lacks its opening, and it is difficult to tell how much of *IX Poyntes* it originally included. Unit 1 at present collates as 1^8 [lacks 1, 2] 2^8 and has regular catchwords. Signatures were most likely lost through cropping. The text is divided by infrequent red paraphs and red-slashed capitals and looks plainer than unit 2.

Unit 2 contains *The Chastising of God's Children*,[6] which through loss of a quire after folio 70 lacks the passage from Chapter 18 at 169/21 to Chapter 20 at 180/19 and breaks off incompletely in Chapter 27 (the final recapitulatory chapter) at 223/6.[7] This unit collates as signatures 3–9^8 [missing quire] 10–13^8. As in many professionally produced copies of *The Chastising*, the text is written in black ink, divided by red paraphs, with chapter headings and two-line initials in red, and biblical and patristic citations underlined in red, yet D lacks the use of blue ink for some paraph marks and lombards embellished with red penwork common in many of the other manuscripts in which the text survives. Again, regular catchwords remain, and signatures are absent, probably through cropping at the rebinding stage. In its southeast Midlands dialect, D resembles the majority of *Chastising* manuscripts.[8]

It is hard to tell whether the units were presented in this order before D's nineteenth-century rebinding, and whether the loss of the quire between the ninth and tenth quires of D happened at the rebinding stage or before it. The darkening of the vellum on folios 101v to 102v suggests that the closing quire (and most likely part of the binding of the manuscript) had been lost for some time before it was rebound.

D has some drawings, which, apart from the trefoils on folios 3r, 8v, 13v, 54v, 62r, 85r, 87v, and 88r, do not seem to have been used to mark meaningful passages and seem to be random scribbles rather than intentional drawings of recognizable objects.[9] All but two of the trefoils are medieval; on folio 54v two trefoils are added in a later hand, that is, the hand of postmedieval annotator 1 (see below).

At various stages in D, annotations are written in a sixteenth- or seventeenth-century hand in black ink and with a pen that results in a thickly set script. This first hand (postmedieval annotator 1) leaves a first quatrain on folio 14v. The third line of this annotation is hard to read, but this represents what can be deciphered:

> The time of youthe sore
> yere spent membringe home
> y ?? it so spente gere
> my lorde god omnypotent.

On folio 25v, in the lower margin, the same hand writes: "The vi condycion / Of this obligacyon." This annotation is boxed, in hastily drawn lines. On folio 43v, in the lower margin, the annotator writes: "The condiecyon." On folio 47v, the phrase written on folio 25v and—in part—on folio 43v is repeated, "The condiecyone of thes obliegacion of," with a flourish underneath the phrase. In these cases the annotator closed the volume before the ink of the inscription had dried properly, as traces of ink can be found on the facing pages (see fols. 48r and 55v). On the basis of script and the traces of ink on the opposite page, Cré believes that this annotator is also responsible for the marginal annotation on folio 26v:

> is in gost
> li leuynge
> he schal
> with alle
> mekenes
> and glad
> nes of spirit

Though at first this annotation seems contemporary with the scribe, none of the medieval annotations in this manuscript are this long. Moreover, this annotation is not cropped but seems to have been written after the manuscript was cropped. Also, the form of t at the end of the word "spirit" closely resembles the t-form of postmedieval annotator 1, who may here have been imitating medieval script (and doing a good job).

The annotation "Cudes god" in the lower margin of folio 34r also seems to have been made by this annotator, as do the annotations on folio 54v, underneath the trefoils that we will argue later are added in this hand. The same hand also seems responsible for three words—also on folio 54v—that are hard to read ("per me nes?"), followed by Psalm 50 (51):17:

> Domine la
> bia mea a
> peries
> et os
> me meum

This is written next to "þat ferst amendith a man and purgith hym here be scharp chastisyng...from euerlastyng turment" (cf. Bazire-Colledge 148/12–14). Again, it is striking that this annotation has not been cropped, so it must have been made after the manuscript was cropped, and some centuries before it was rebound in the nineteenth century.

On folio 46v, again in the lower margin, we find the phrase "The time of ?an" followed by flourishes or initials ("IN"?). Though this annotator (post-medieval annotator 2) forms the letter t in the same way as postmedieval annotator 1, this might be another annotator altogether. The phrase seems written with a different pen (one with a fine nib), and in different ink. Whoever wrote this phrase may also have written the pen trials in the lower margin of folio 7r. Yet this hand seems different still from a third sixteenth- or seventeenth-century annotator who identifies himself as "Anthonye Trolloppe."

The following annotations all seem to be written by this third hand (postmedieval annotator 3), who writes a neat and careful script and uses ink that has faded to brown (or brown ink) and a pen with a fine nib. This hand seems responsible for the name "Sampson" written in capital letters in the lower margin of folio 31r. The name written underneath (possibly "Trallop") has been lost in cropping. On folio 50v, written across in the left-hand margin, the same hand has entered a four-line prayer of which the first line has been cropped, followed by an ownership inscription placed to the right of the prayer written in tercet form, which seems complete:

> to speicke to the o lord vouchsayf
> to heare my dolefull voice ~~with~~
> with vniforme accorde
>
> Anthonye Trallopp
> ys my naime and with my hand
> I wrote this saime

On folio 53v, in the lower margin, "Anthonye Trolloppe" signs his name again. The quatrain written at the page foot of folio 55v seems in the same hand:

When hope and healthe and lyfe
and welthe ar heyeste
Then woe and wracke diseace
and lacke ar neyeste

The first line of this poem on the fickleness of Fortune is repeated at the foot of folio 56r: "When hope and health and lyf."

Ralph Hanna and Vincent Gillespie have suggested that D came to the Marquesses of Londonderry through Anne Vane-Tempest (1800–1865). A descendant of the recusant Tempest family,[10] she was the second wife of Charles William Stewart (1778–1854), the third Marquess of Londonderry, whom she married on April 3, 1819. It is unclear what the relationship of the Trolloppe gentleman was to the Tempest family and if or when D came to be owned by the Tempest family. It is a plausible scenario, however, that a manuscript like D came to be owned by a recusant family after the Act of Supremacy and Dissolution of the Monasteries in Henry VIII's reign or slightly later under Elizabeth I. Though any links between the Tempest family and a man called Anthony Trolloppe or Trallopp would need to be investigated further, the annotations betray religious interests on the part of the annotators.

D's Envisioned Audience

In its present form, D provides no explicit links to a specific medieval religious house or contemporary individual, nor are there any comments by the scribe or compiler explaining the choice of material. The absence of any concrete evidence concerning the manuscript's place of origin (beyond the results of the dialectal analysis), and the anonymity of the guiding hand(s), commissioner(s), scribe, and target audience requires the consideration of relevant clues in the texts themselves.

The Chastising is the only text in D that is not acephalous, and it retains its address to a "[r]eligiouse sustir" (fol. 18r, ll. 1–2; cf. Bazire-Colledge 95/1), which would support the hypothesis that the manuscript was originally written as a work of spiritual guidance for a single religious or for a convent. *The Chastising* circulated widely in religious houses in the fifteenth century. While the "schort pistil" (fol. 18r, l. 2; cf. 95/1) enjoyed great popularity among a female readership, it also achieved great success in male monasteries and with lay readers, facilitated by the reference to either men or men *and* women throughout the treatise. All but one of the copies discussed in the Bazire-Colledge edition retain the address to a "sister."[11] Even manuscripts owned by houses of male religious kept these references, such as Oxford, Bodleian Library, MS Rawlinson C57, which was given to the Sheen Carthusians,[12] and Oxford, Bodleian Library, MS Bodley 505, which belonged to the London Charterhouse of the Salutation of St. Mary the Virgin[13]—although it has to be taken into consideration that these manuscripts' known provenance does not necessarily have to coincide with their initial audience. Not every readership approved of the female form of address, as customization in the copy of *The Chastising* in Cambridge, Magdalene College, MS Pepys 2125 exemplifies. In this manuscript, "f(r)end"[14] replaced the original address, which was scraped off.[15]

We may conclude from these manuscript witnesses that in many cases the address to a religious sister at the beginning of *The Chastising* came to accommodate any of its readers' gender identities and thus functioned as a catchall term that was not perceived as inappropriate enough to warrant contemporary or later modification. At the same time, the female appellation was not treated as sacrosanct and could be adjusted to oblige the preferences of a different audience, as MS Pepys 2125 demonstrates. Finally, as Joyce Bazire and Edmund Colledge point out, the religious sister to whom *The Chastising* appeals may have been nothing but a literary invention allowing its author to frame the text on other devotional treatises that depicted the spiritual advisor's enlightening of his charge.[16] D's early readership does not seem to have perceived the gendered dedication as a hindrance to their engagement with the text.

Four further pieces of internal evidence contribute to the illumination of the manuscript's target audience. A segment from *The Form of Living* quoted in Ogilvie-Thomson's edition reads "Men þat comen to þe, praise þe, for þei see þi gret abstinence, and for þay se þe enclosed" (14, ll. 460–461), and Hereford, Cathedral Library, MS P. I. 9 (henceforth Hf),[17] whose close textual connections to D are explored below,[18] renders this phrase: "þei preisen þe for þei seen þe enclosed" (fol. 146r, l. 34).[19] However, D records: "men and women parauenture preiseth þe for þou hast y bounde þe to religion" (fol. 13r, l. 323). This denotes an alteration of Margaret Kirkby's state of living—she was the epistle's original recipient, and her enclosure in the anchorhold of Richmond occasioned Rolle to compose *The Form*.[20] D's modification extends the intended audience to individuals in religious orders eager to adhere to monastic laws and devote their lives to their faith, but not necessarily living in enclosure. This phrasing could also suggest that the manuscript may have been intended to address a vowess or a community of vowesses.

As discussed below, the major part of D's hortatory conclusion that is appended to its first part is unique to the manuscript. In it, the narrative voice as the spiritual guide refers to the reader as "my leue frende" (fol. 14r, ll. 346–347) and "dere frende" (fol. 14v, l. 358). Even though the latter appears in the passage that agrees with the final part of *The Form* in Hf (D, fol. 14v, ll. 358–361; Hf, fol. 150v, ll. 34–38; discussed below), "dere frende" is only recorded in D. These forms of address, embedded in passages that were either explicitly written for the original audience or copied from preexisting material directly to appeal to the reader's consciousness, may not shed light on the initial audience's gender, but they do testify to the discourse of spiritual friendship that D's scribe or compiler was trying to establish. When he counsels that his audience not forget the lessons imparted to them, he is reacting to the preceding collection of contemplative material's concern with introducing a beginner on the spiritual path to the contemplative life. The hortatory conclusion gives evidence that the arrangement of texts was presented in this form with the aim of edifying a spiritual beginner who was not yet perceived as stable in his or her faith: "for diu*er*se occupacions and lettyngs þat þou hast in þe worlde, þou fyndest no gret sauoure þ*er* in atte þe begynnyng" (fol. 14r, ll. 348–349; note that the reference to "þe worlde" may denote the secular world or the present life in contrast to the next, and does as such not necessarily narrow down the target audience beyond the already stated).

Neither do the "spouse" references in the hortatory conclusion limit the original audience, because they could both allude to female religious or to the neutral soul spiritually married to God or Christ. In the absence of further evidence that would reveal their intended referential meaning, they remain gender-neutral expressions of love, such as when the audience is cautioned to give up "unclene loue" (fol. 14v, l. 356) to be granted intimate sponsal bliss: "*And* þanne schalt þou ben his spouse, dwellyng *with* hym in þe blisse of heuen endlich" (fol. 14r, ll. 356–357). Another reference to spiritual wedlock establishes that the addressee has already chosen God or Christ as a "spouse þat þou hast take þe to" (fol. 14v, l. 361), but future spiritual growth relies solely on the "grace of god," "þ*at* is verrai loue *and* comfort of his loueris," and may thus "kepe þe fro euyl, and bryng þe to þi spouse . . . þe wich is eu*er*lastyng god" (fol. 14v, ll. 359–361).

A further noteworthy piece of internal evidence pertaining to the envisioned readership is a variation in the *Stimulus* passage. While the corresponding segment in the Peltier edition[21] appeals to the readers to direct their prayers to God the Father, Christ, the Virgin Mary, "et beati Francisci, et omnium sanctorum merita" (Pt. I, ch. 2), D replaces any reference to Saint Francis with "þe meritis of alle holy seintes" (fol. 6v, l. 148). The significance of this omission is, however, contestable, because, as mentioned above, there are numerous omissions and several additions throughout the text that are witnesses to the *Stimulus*'s fluid nature of circulation. Hf does not contain a reference to Saint Francis either, even though it is of Franciscan origin. The omission of Saint Francis as an intercessor in D, therefore, does not exclude Franciscan houses from the intended audience altogether.

While the only available evidence for D's target audience is written into the text, the frame of reference is not defined enough to allow conclusions that would locate D in a specific religious house or in the hands of a particular individual, and it would be unwise to suggest anything more definite at this point. The results of the dialectal analysis may invite further research, but they are not diagnostically conclusive at the moment. What can be posited when weighing the probabilities is that D was intended for circulation in religious houses or for personal use of a religious not leading an enclosed life.

D's First Unit and Its Relationship to the Second Unit
The following is a list of the texts in D:[22]

Unit 1
[**Text 1**] fols. 1r–1v: final section of *IX Poyntes* [IPMEP 11;[23] Jolliffe I.26];[24] D most probably contained a full copy of *IX Poyntes*, but the manuscript as it stands lacks the first two folios; the full text is printed in Horstmann 375–377.[25] *IX Poyntes*[26] translates and expands passages from the *Stimulus amoris maior*, Part II, chapter 1[27] (but will henceforth still be referred to as *IX Poyntes* and *IX Poyntis* in D and Hf respectively).
[**Text 2**] fols. 1v–6v: excerpts from the *Stimulus amoris maior* Part II, chapter 8 and Part I, chapter 1.[28]
[**Text 3**] fols. 6v–14r: Richard Rolle, *The Form of Living*, an excerpt corresponding to 9–15, ll. 267–486 in Ogilvie-Thomson's edition.[29]

Unit 2
[**Text 4**]: D's second part contains *The Chastising of God's Children* (fols. 18r–102v), preceded on fols. 15r–17v by a table of chapters.

A single scribe[30] wrote D's two units in a hand of great regularity, but the absence of a linking catchword raises the question of whether they were intended to circulate together or whether they were joined at a later date. An accidental combination seems unlikely for the following reasons: they share the same master plan—the same script, scale of the writing area, size of ruling, and a regular collation. The units' mise-en-page displays a substantial degree of similarity, and, therefore, formal relations compensate for the missing catchword. The sequence of the units' production, however, cannot readily be established: they were most likely written over a relatively narrow period of time with the intention to complement one another. However, the lack of consecutive quiring could also indicate separate campaigns of copying.

On a textual level, the two units are related as well. Literary analysis[31] demonstrates that the segments forming D's first part were combined to reinforce each other. The first unit's omission of the emotive and imaginary apexes of contemplative longing (expounded in the excluded parts of the *Stimulus* and *The Form*'s "Amore langueo" section) established a shared argumentative foundation between the first part and the more self-disciplined and austere *Chastising*, creating fluid connections between texts whose argumentation would otherwise at times run the risk of reversing each another. Thus there is compelling reason to suggest that the two parts of the manuscript were always intended to circulate together in their time.

Quite apart from shared formal features, it is D's thematic consistency that distinguishes the codex from a haphazard and more randomly organized miscellany[32] and identifies it as a carefully selected and purposefully coordinated collection of contemplative material.[33]

In terms of taxonomy, the first part of the codex therefore classifies as a compilation: a quarrying of texts from unacknowledged authors, with only minimal distinctions between them, which form a new text and condition a different reading experience.[34] The categorization of the whole manuscript, however, is far from a simple issue, especially because the missing folios at the beginning may have comprised an index, a table of contents, or an attribution to authors: indeed, these missing pages may have given some information on the guiding principle behind D.

A Comparison of D's First Unit with the Text in Hereford, Cathedral Library, MS P. I. 9

D's first part is intimately connected to the second manuscript bound into Hf. The *Linguistic Atlas of Late Medieval English* (LALME) locates the latter's dialect to Worcestershire,[35] and it is written in Anglicana formata, in contrast to D's southeast Midlands dialect and Textura rotunda script.

Hf was owned by the Franciscan brethren of Oxford and has variously been dated to the second half of the fourteenth[36] or to the fifteenth century.[37] It is the only other known manuscript that contains the same texts as D's first unit, albeit in a different *ordinatio*, and with complete copies of *The Form* and *IX Poyntis* where D has extracts.

The following list summarizes the contents of Hf:

[**Text 1**] fols. 141r–150v: ***The Form of Living***, complete copy.
[**Text 2**] fols. 150v–151v: ***IX Poyntis***, complete copy.
[**Text 3**] fols. 151v–153r: excerpts from the ***Stimulus amoris maior*** Part II, chapter 8 and Part I, chapter 1.

Previous scholarship maintained that Hf's as yet unassigned excerpts on folios 151v to 153r were a single treatise unique to the manuscript.[38] These passages, however, were actually quarried from the *Stimulus amoris*, a highly influential guide to the contemplative life.[39]

An important witness to D's textual transmission history, Hf may be the older manuscript according to paleographical analysis, but cannot have been D's direct source. Although much of the evidence (including the temporal sequence, Hf's inclusion of complete texts where D has extracts or acephalous texts, and the fact that the same combination of texts is found in both manuscripts and nowhere else) seem to suggest that Hf is D's direct ancestor, the pattern of variants[40] reveals a more complicated history of transmission.

The most significant evidence that irrevocably refutes the possibility of D directly deriving from Hf is found in D's *IX Poyntes*, which in addition to Hf is also recorded in complete copies in British Library, MS Harley 1706 (henceforth Har)[41] and Cambridge, Trinity College, MS B.15.39 (henceforth Tr).[42] D's *IX Poyntes* contains a passage that Hf omits but Har and Tr retain (fol. 153r, col. 1, l. 14–col. 2, l. 6, and fol. 171v, ll. 12–15, respectively):

> For godis loue take hede. ȝif þou art aschamid for to do a dedly synne be fore thyn euencristen, þe wich is frele and sinful as þou art *and* may noȝt greue but þi bodi, moche more scholdest þou be agast to synne bi fore thi god þat neuere trespased and schal be þi domesman at þe dai of dome. (fol. 1r, ll. 4–7)[43]

The analysis of the variants reveals neither Har nor Tr to be direct derivatives of D or Hf, and indicates that the opposite is unlikely too.[44] Har and Tr are closer to each other than to the latter two manuscripts. For example, they omit "and how he hath taken thi kynde and suffred for thi loue despites deth," which D (fol. 1r, ll. 11–12) and Hf (fol. 152v, ll. 21–22—minor variations) record (see Appendix B). Where D reads "he lieth on the aut*er* atte masse" (fol. 1v, l. 19, also present in Hf, fol. 152v, ll. 29–30), Har's rendering is "þou seeste þe holy sacramente of Crystys body at þe masse or on þe aut*er*" (fol. 154r, col. 1, l. 17–col. 2, l. 1), and Tr's version is "þou seest þe holy sacrament of cristis bodi at masse or on þe autir" (fol. 171v, ll. 26–27). On the basis of these data, the following hypotheses can be proposed:

1. There is no direct lineage from Hf to D.
2. The manuscripts were copied from a close ancestor or ancestors, no longer extant.
3. D and Hf must be cognate copies. They are horizontally related at some degree.
4. There must also have been separate and more complicated strands of transmission for *IX Poyntes*, which strongly indicates the existence of more than the four surviving copies.

While D and Hf are undoubtedly related at some remove, D's erroneous readings in the form of omissions of letters (and confusion of letters with ascenders), words, and phrases result in several deficiencies in the first part (see Appendix A), in contrast with Hf's more accurate text, most of whose very few errors have been corrected. Examples of these patterns are when D reads "whom" (fol. 6r, l. 132) instead of "wisdom" (Hf, fol. 153r, l. 18), or when D records "and þe mende for hym euermore he dwellyng fresch in my herte" (fol. 6v, l. 156) instead of Hf's "*and* þe munde of ham euer be dwelling freschliche in myn herte" (fol. 153r, ll. 43–44). Moreover, D breaks off the following sentence "And forþermore hit schal quike þi saule þe more able to parfeccion and trauail and make þe holde litel be þi self, and in thynkyng worchyng schal make þe parfit in þe loue of" (fol. 9r, ll. 84–87; Hf lets it end with "god" (fol. 152v, l. 13). Erroneous readings in Hf are few, and the scribe supplied missing letters, short words (such as þat, ʒif, in, or þe), and phrases from above the line or in the manuscript's margin (e.g., "ʒif," fol. 144r, l. 11, "sorewe," fol. 145v, l. 7, or "mete *and* drinke," fol. 146r, l. 15).

Moreover, Hf's *Stimulus* extract is closer to the Latin because it contains material that D omits, as discussed below. Further points at which the two manuscripts diverge are the transposition of phrases and doublets, the addition of material in both manuscripts (and additions in D not attested elsewhere), the substitution of some items in *The Form*'s lists, and D's occasional use of the singular in instances where Hf uses plural variants. The sum of these features leaves no doubt as to the derivative character of the texts assembled in D, and the fact that most of these idiolectal scribal features in D's first unit are similar to those found in the second unit strongly suggests that they were introduced by the scribe at the time of copying. The somewhat less convincing counterhypothesis one could entertain would be that in addition to *IX Poyntes*, the *Stimulus* extracts, and *The Form*, D's lost exemplar could also have contained *The Chastising*, whereby D's scribe copied his exemplar somewhat faithfully.

In addition to issues of scribal competence, D invites questions of intention and accident. Uncorrected errors constitute only one aspect of its first unit, and its pertinently inserted additions, which are not found in Hf, could have been introduced as editorial playing on its ancestor at the time of copying—penned by the scribe or compiler or borrowed from other sources—or may have already existed in the parent manuscript.

In terms of *ordinatio*, the placement of red paraphs, red-slashed capitals, and two-line unflourished lombards of the same color that divide D's first unit into parts does not correspond in most instances to Hf's division of the text through its program of decoration. In the segment in Hf corresponding to D's text, the decoration consists of blue initials with red flourishings and paraphs alternating in red and blue. D's two-line red lombards are the only features of design that indicate the beginnings of the segments that were quarried from different sources (and various parts of the *Stimulus*). Conversely, Hf refers to the (supposed) authors at the beginning of the texts ascribed to them: *The Form* is glossed as "informacio sancti ricardi de hampull scripta margarete incluse de hampull" (fol. 141r),[45] and an inscription next to a manicule that signals the beginning of *IX Poyntis* announces: "hic incipit doctrina ffratris henrici Chambernoun magistri in uiam perfeccionis" (fol. 150v). Henry Chambernoun was a Franciscan, "associated with Oxford in 1382";[46] six of his sermons are extant in other manuscripts.[47] Reflecting upon the addition of references to Chambernoun (as evidence for his alleged authorship) in the context of other manuscripts, Wenzel suggests that he was "a well-known preacher whose name became easily attached to sermons of different origin."[48] The fact that the *Stimulus* was a Franciscan text may have caused the attribution to Chambernoun. Little more than this speculative hypothesis can be proposed as to why Hf ascribed *IX Poyntis* to him.

Applying Ralph Hanna's suggestion that the inscription mentioning Chambernoun in Hf's second part is possibly in the same hand as a table of St. Francis's miracles on folio 140v, the last folio of the first part,[49] all indications are that the pseudo-Bonaventuran *Meditatio vitae Christi* on folios 1r to 93r and Bonaventura's *Vita et miracula Francisci (legenda maior)* on folios 93v to 140v[50] were read alongside Hf's complete copy of *The Form* (including the "Amore langueo" passage), *IX Poyntis*, and the *Stimulus* excerpts from the time of annotation.

There remains the possibility that the wanting pages at D's beginning contained a reference to authors and sources too, or offered a rationale for the selection and arrangement of the material. As the only formal divisions in D's first unit, the two-line red lombards mark the beginning of the sections that originated from various source texts, and the constituent parts were thus combined to form a single text whose composite origins were obscured. The need to introduce and distinguish the segments could have diminished if the manuscript were intended for circulation within a restricted milieu that would have been able to offer oral instruction as to the codex's perusal (see "D's Envisioned Audience" above).[51]

Marginal finding aids and annotations in English and Latin appear as structuring and mnemonic devices in Hf, as do the numbers added next to *The Form*'s comprehensive lists to promote memorization of their various items (see Appendix B). Folio 145r, for example, contains the following marginal annotations that correspond to *The Form*'s structure: "synnes of mouþ" (l. 8) "synnes of dede" (l. 22), and "synnes of omission" (l. 37). These finding aids display an eagerness to render the text more accessible, facilitate quick reference, and help readers to learn its contents by rote. Annotations of this kind can also be read as the report of the text's close analysis and projected readerly engagement, whereby the internalization of the sins and their parent categories qualifies the readers to discern their transgressions.

In its present state, there is no evidence that D's first unit was furnished with annotations comparable to those in Hf, but it is possible that they were cut off when the pages were trimmed from their original size. The first part of D as it now stands contains a nota on folio 3r and two short marginal annotations that insert missing text on folio 10r, one of which is partially cut off (see Appendix A, note 10, and "Signposting, Corrections and Annotations in D"), and a later annotation on folio 14v (see "Description of Oxford, Bodleian Library, MS Don. e. 247").

In what follows below, the individual segments that make up D's first unit are discussed in further depth, exploring the significance of its variations when compared to other witnesses.

The IX Poyntes Segment

The Middle English text known as *IX Poyntes* is actually a reworking of selected passages from Part II, chapter 1 of the *Stimulus amoris* (All references to the *Stimulus* in the *IX Poyntes* segment refer to Part II, chapter 1). *IX Poyntes* expands on the Latin extracts, and instead of the Latin third-person present subjunctive employs a second-person present indicative. Coupled with the addition of second-person personal and possessive pronouns (so highly recurrent that they will not be enumerated in the list below), this alteration integrates the reader more fully into the text and heightens the text's subjective immediacy.

As it now stands, D opens halfway through the eighth of the nine points with an elaboration on the *Stimulus* that is also attested, with minor modifications, in Hf, Har, and Tr (fol. 151v, ll. 13–16; fol. 153v, col. 1, ll. 4–14, and fol. 171v, ll. 9–12 respectively):

> For godisseruant scholde neuer more thenke, ne speke, ne do bote as he wolde in þe *presence* of his lorde. For certenli al þat þou spekest and dost god seye as ueralich as þou wer in his presence þer oure ladi sit in heue[n]. (fol. 1r, ll. 1–4).

> Cf. The *Stimulus*: Deum tamen semper actu in corde habeat, et nihil aliud quam honorem suum in omnibus actualiter, seu habitualiter intendat: ac ad hoc præcipue nitatur, ut sic semper præsentem Deum intelligat, ac si ipsum qui ubique est praesens in sua videret substantia et essentia.

D elaborates on the *Stimulus*'s "actu," "actualiter," and "habitualiter" with "thenke," "speke," and "do," and also introduces the image of the Virgin.

This is followed by the passage "For godis loue," which in addition to D and the *Stimulus* is attested only in Har and Tr (quoted in full on p. 146). Intriguingly, D reinterprets the *Stimulus*'s "eum [Deum] timeat, et revereatur, et immenso amore in ipsum feratur," which is an exhortation to relate to God with a combination of reverent dread and boundless love, as "For godis loue take hede," and in the ensuing lines recasts love and holy dread as profound terror and shame to be experienced if sinning against the fellow faithful, but, most significantly, against God—to whom the reader will be held accountable on Judgement Day (fol. 1r, ll. 4–7).

IX Poyntes's ninth point translates the *Stimulus*'s tenth, with the following pertinent variations and additions:

> fol. 1r, ll. 7–8: D's "in cas þat þou myȝt come to þe *parfeccion* of þis poyntes" rewrites the *Stimulus*'s "ut si praedicta assequi potest"; Hf speaks of perfection as well (fol. 151v, ll. 16–17).

> fol. 1r, ll. 8–10: D expands on the *Stimulus*'s "esse magna Dei beneficia recognoscat" with another reference to perfection that is achieved through the *donum gratia gratis data*: "þou knowlech þat hit is a grete grace of godis goudnesse þat he wil woch saue to ȝeue þe so muche grace of *parfeccion*"; also recorded, with minor modifications, in Hf (fol. 151v, l. 18).

> fol. 1r, l. 10: D's "oft be thenke þe" (cf. Hf, fol. 151v, l. 19) exhorts the reader to call to mind divine grace repeatedly, while the *Stimulus*'s "secundum quod potest reminisci" is more vague.

> fol. 1r, ll. 10–11: Where the *Stimulus* reads "quod sua eum voluit imagine insigniri," D gives weight to God's love for the soul by rendering "voluit" as "worschiped þi soule": "how [he] hath worschiped þi soule be enpreyntyng of his owene ymage"; cf. Hf (fol. 151v, ll. 20–21).

> fol. 1r, l. 12: Compared to the *Stimulus*'s "et se pro ipso morti tradere," D's "suffred for thi loue despites deth" again appends a reference to love and further emphasizes Christ's sacrifice by adding "despites"; Hf speaks of "despitous deþ" (fol. 151v, l. 22).

> fol. 1r, l. 13: D's "wil be þi ioie and thi blisse in an oþer lif" emphasizes future gifts, whereas the Latin model references Christ's self-sacrifice: "[voluit] in gloria in praemium tribuere semetipsum"; Hf expands on the Latin (fol. 151v, l. 23).

> fols. 1r–1v, ll. 14–15: "þat þou myȝt not [MS: "now," see discussion below] sen hem in his godhed whiles þou art in þis worlde" rewrites the *Stimulus*'s "Et quia nondum assecutus est eum in praemium" to

ensure consistency with the arguments made before about divine grace bestowed freely; Hf advances the same argument in another phrasing (fol. 151v, ll. 24–25).

fol. 1v, l. 15: D adds "hongyng for þe" to the *Stimulus*'s "aspiciat eum in patibulo," which identifies the reader as the cause for Christ's agony; Hf reads "honging in þe cros" (fol. 151v, ll. 25–26).

fol. 1v, ll. 16–21: D's "haue sorwe and conpassion" expands on the *Stimulus*'s "compatiatur," and several lines down another doubling, "fede me and fulfille me with þe," further develops the *Stimulus*'s "ita me de te satiare dignare" (Hf, fol. 151v, ll. 26–32).

fol. 1v, ll. 16–17: D's appeal to feel "his [Cristes] wondes and his paynes in þi bodi" (cf. Hf, fol. 151v, l. 27) centers on physical pain where the *Stimulus* privileges spiritual agony as a result of compassion: "omnia ejus vulnera in suo corde sustineret."

fol. 1v, ll. 17–18: D references the sinner's individual interior sorrow— "be inward sori þat þou miȝt not fele in þe be þe paynes þat he suffred for þe, synful wrecche" (cf. Hf, fol. 151v, ll. 27–29—with minor variations), but the *Stimulus* posits the reader's distress as a result of seeing his fellows being deprived of God's grace: "praecipue dolere debet, quod tot videt frustrari beneficio tam immense."

fol. 1v, l. 18: D prepends "Þe thoghtes ofte haue in mynde" to "Cernat eum denique," thereby endorsing continual reaccessing of the exhortations to come; so does Hf (fol. 151v, l. 29).

fol. 1v, l. 19: D adds "atte masse" to the *Stimulus*'s "Cernat eum denique in altari exhibitum"; so does Hf (fol. 151v, l. 30).

fol. 1v, l. 19: D streamlines "in ipso toto affectu delectatus clamet, et dicat" as "say to hym in this manere"; cf. Hf (fol. 151v, l. 30).

fol. 1v, l. 20: to the *Stimulus*'s "qui es panis vitae" D appends "þat cometh out of heuene"; see Hf (fol. 151v, l. 31).

fol. 1v, l. 22: D adds "with þi bloude and of thi loue" to the *Stimulus*'s "ita me de te inebriare digneris"; see Hf (fol. 151v, l. 33).

fol. 1v, ll. 22–24: The final lines of D's *IX Poyntes* segment condense its message: "Lorde hold so faste my soule *and* my loue to þe þat for non oþere loue ne for synne ne be neuere departid fro me"—cf. the *Stimulus*'s "Tene, Domine, mentem meam, ne interveniente umbra terrae."

Fittingly, the substitution of "soule *and* my loue" for the *Stimulus*'s "mentem" as well as the concrete menace of a rivaling love and spiritually destructive sins—which are the ultimate failure to love—replace the poetically threatening (but vague) "umbra terrae"; see Hf (fol. 151v, ll. 33–35).

Leading right into beatific-vision territory, what can be classified as one of the most blatant errors in D's first unit occurs on folios 1r–1v (ll. 14–15 in Appendix A): "And for encheison þat þou myȝt now sen hem in his godhed whiles þou art in þis worlde." Both Har and Tr record "no" instead of "now," and Hf negates the possibility of direct perception of God in this life too (fol. 154r, col. 1, l. 3; fol. 171v, l. 21; and fol. 151v, l. 24 respectively; cf. the *Stimulus*: "nondum," Part II, chapter 1). Such a grave mistake in D was no doubt caused by an innocent memorial slip, but it is an exemplary case for the first unit in that it is not only evidence of haste in production but also illustrative of a lack of recension. Much like the occasional confusion of s/l and h/b respectively, such an obvious error betrays the fact that there was a lack of time, care, or expertise in production, since otherwise these mis-spellings could have been spotted easily and corrected or would not have occurred in the first place. Some further conspicuous errors in D's first part include "For encheson þat loue may alle do with any mysdo" (fol. 1v, ll. 25–26, which Hf renders as "withoute," fol. 151v, l. 36) or "ȝif þou loue many metys þat men vsen ... þou dost wel" (fol. 12v, l. 308; Hf reads "leue" instead of "loue," fol. 146r, l. 17). D's "Allas þe folly of men þat cheseþ for to dwel in þe worde, in þe flesch, and in þe places þat ben vnclene" (fol. 6r, ll. 135–136) is recorded as "in þe world" in Hf (fol. 153r, l. 22). Apart from two further problematic renderings on folio 4v (l. 101) and fol 12r (l. 300), other errors in D's first part are restricted to grammar and spelling and stay clear of doctrinal controversies.

The *Stimulus amoris* Segment

Falk Eisermann's comprehensive study of the *Stimulus* draws on Claire Kirchberger's and Ian Doyle's previous scholarship to elucidate the ways in which restructuring, extraction, abridgement, addition of further material, and vernacular translations shaped the *Stimulus* in fourteenth- and fifteenth-century England.[52] The extracts in D do not derive from *The Prickynge of Love*, a Middle English translation of the *Stimulus*, but from an independent translation of extracts from the *Stimulus amoris maior*'s Part II, chapter 8 and Part I, chapter 1. Some pertinent longer discrepancies between D and Hf include:

> fol. 2r, l. 32: Where D gives "Loue makeþ man, for he maketh frende and þe seruant child," Hf presents the following addition after D's "man": "god and god man. Þe heiȝest he makiþ lowist and þe lowest heiȝest" (fol. 151v, l. 43–fol. 152r, l. 1). Omitted in D, Hf's lines are a direct translation of the *Stimulus*'s "Deum facit hominem, et hominem facit Deum ... et imum excelsum constituit" (Pt, II, ch. 8).
>
> fol. 4r, ll. 86–87: D's "in thynkyng worchyng schal make þe parfit in þe

loue of" rewrites "affectus tuos tam in cogitatione, quam in locutione, ac etiam operatione regulabit" (Pt. I, ch. 1). Thus, whereas the *Stimulus* speaks of regulating the *affectus*, D posits the perfection of love as the final goal. Hf's reading is again closer to the Latin. It adds "*and* spekynge and" after "þenkinge" (fol. 152v, ll. 12–13).

fol. 5r, ll. 114–116: D appends "*and* speke" to a list of activities performed when in communion with God: "Þere I wil reste, and slepe, and ete, and drinke, rede, and synge, and praye, and alle my nedes tret *and* speke." "*And* speke" is probably a slip that occurred by jumping ahead to the next sentence, which begins with "Þere I schal speke" (l. 116). Compare the Latin "ubi volo quiescere, dormire, videre, bibere, comedere, legere, orare, et omnia mea negotia pertractare. Ibi loquar," which contains a reference to seeing but omits singing (Pt. I, ch. 1). Note also the change from "negotia" (matters, troubles) to "nedes," which is more in tune with the series of preceding infinitives. Hf alters the Latin text by adding "*and* speke" and "singe," while omitting "videre," too (see fol. 152v, ll. 44–45), which means that these alterations must have been present in D and Hf's exemplar(s).

fol. 5r, l. 116: D modifies the *Stimulus's* reference to speaking to Christ's heart ("Ibi loquar ad cor ejus," Pt. I, ch. 1) as the narrative voice speaking "wi*th* swete hert"; Hf, on the other hand, stays faithful to the Latin (fol. 152v, l. 45).

fol. 5v, ll. 121–122: It is a short omission, but when D fails to record "non"/"nouȝht," Hf is again closer to the Latin: while the text in D reads "onlich I wil apeere I crucified with hir son," Hf gives it as "nouȝht onli I wol apeer" (fol. 153r, ll. 5–6); cf. the *Stimulus's*: "Et non solum apparebo" (Pt. I, ch. 1).

fol. 5v, l. 122: D's, "I wil go to chirche" is more removed from the *Stimulus's* "ad praesepe [crib] rediens" (Pt. I, ch. 1) than Hf's "I wol gon to þe crache" (fol. 153r, l. 6).

Additional examples of how D's text is further detached from the Latin *Stimulus* than Hf: where the *Stimulus* reads: "passio ignominiosa glorificat," Hf retains "þe passion schameful makeþ vs gloriouse" (fol. 152v, ll. 18–19), whereas D stops after "passion" (fol. 4v, l. 92). The *Stimulus's* "et mihi faciam unam dulcissimam potionem" is present in Hf's "*and* make me a noble drinke" (fol. 153r, l. 8) but not in D (f. 5v, l. 124; references to the *Stimulus* are to Pt. I, ch. 1).

There is a curious case of translation in D and Hf where the two manuscripts reference different parts of the *Stimulus*, which is another indication that D cannot derive from Hf directly: D rephrases the *Stimulus's* "tamen hoc lenius, suavius, delectabilius, seu opportunius" as "þe wiche were more bettre *and* more delettable" (fol. 3v, l. 78), whereas Hf records: "albehit þat þis wer liȝter *and* esier"; see Hf (fol. 152v, ll. 3–4).

Some longer additions and alterations in D when compared to the *Stimulus* include:

fols. 1v–2r, ll. 25–29: D adds:

> For encheson þat loue may alle do *with* any mysdo, and loue is þe rote of *p*arfeccion of alle vertues, and þe more þou hast of god loue, þe betre þou art, and þe more liche to god, and nere to blisse. For all þe mesure of goud loue schalle ȝeue þe mesure of blisse in heuen, and þere fore þer is non bettre to man oþer woman þan for to studie how he may in god loue.

Also found in Hf (fol. 151v, ll. 36–41), with the addition of "and fruit and þe" after "rote." (The following references to the *Stimulus* pertain to Pt. II, ch. 8 until indicated otherwise.)

fol. 2r, l. 33: An addition in D reads: "and þe sori ioious"; also attested in Hf (fol. 152r, ll. 2–3).

fol. 2r, ll. 35–36: D adds: "As witnesseth þe deuout saule in þe boke of loue spekyng to god in þis manere"; also attested in Hf (fol. 152r, ll. 3–4). Where the *Stimulus* in the following gives "anima mea liquefacta est, etc," D and Hf supply the full quotation from the *Song of Songs*: "An[y] saule meltiþ atte þe speche of hym þat I loue" (D, fol. 2r, l. 36; Hf, fol. 152r, l. 5).

fol. 2r, l. 38: D's "how am y so muche loued of þe" (see also Hf, fol. 152r, l. 7) modifies the *Stimulus*'s "tibi tantae charitatis vinculo colligatus" and thereby emphasizes the narrative voice's amazement caused by the fortunate bestowal of divine love.

fols. 2v–2r, l. 39: "O brennyng of trewe loue, moche is þi miȝth," also recorded in Hf (fol. 152r, l. 8), alters the *Stimulus*'s "O ardor amoris, qui intima mentis in Deum infundis," again prioritizing affective wonder.

fol. 2v, ll. 40–41: "O goud loue, what may I ȝeue the þat þou woldest euere more dwelle with me?" (see also Hf, fol. 152r, ll. 10–11) renders the *Stimulus*'s "O amor, quid tibi tribuam, qui me fecisti divinum?" with a stress on the process- and future-oriented character of the bond with divine love.

fol. 2v, ll. 41–42: D's "Ffor wondurful is þi uertu þat turnest me in to god and god in to me," also found in Hf (fol. 152r, ll. 11–12), appends five words to the *Stimulus*'s "Inenarrabilis est virtus tua, o amor, qui lutum in Deum transfiguras!" The change from "lutum" [dirt, mud] to "me" makes the addition possible and emphasizes the reciprocal nature of love.

fol. 2v, ll. 43–48: D adds:

> Certis no thyng. Þou bindest god to þe piler. Þou puttest þe croune of thorne vp on his hede. Þou heng hym opon þe crois and nailedest hym þer to. Þou opinidest his blissed hert with þe scharpe spere, out of þe wich com water and bloude in remission of mannys trespas. Wasch wel thi saule in þat bathe and þanne schalt þou haue with þe vertu of brennyng loue.

This is not attested in Hf, nor in the *Stimulus*, though Hf retains "Certis noþing" (fol. 152r, l. 13.)

folio 2v, l. 51: D adds: "For at a louelich worde of þe my saule is molt in me" to the *Stimulus*; also attested in Hf (fol. 152r, ll. 15–16).

folios 2v–3r, ll. 53–62: A longer extract is added in D that urges the reader to cultivate the fire of love by thinking about the Passion of Christ, divine love, and human malice:

> Certes no tonge may telle, and þere fore, ʒif þou wilt be parfite, lerne for þe quike to feer in thyn herte, and ther fore thou schalt vnderstonde þat aman þat is colde becomyth hoot in diuers maneris: be clothyng of many clothis, be goyng to þe fier, be trauaillyng of body, hoot spices, and strong drynke. So gostlich, ʒif þou wilt wer hoot in þe loue of god, do on many clothes of vertu, for vertu is clothes to mannys saule. Ho so lakkeþ o vertu, his saule is naked in o partie, and þer fore ʒif þou wilt be hoot, alle a boute clothe thi saule with many vertues, so þat non lakke to þe. And sit ofte bi þe brennyng fier of loue þat crist aqueked in his brennynge and betir passion, and thenke ofte on þe loue of god and charite toward man, and of blyndnesse and þe malice of man toward god.

Also attested in Hf (fol. 152r, ll. 18–29). This addition seems to have been inspired by two passages in D's *Stimulus* segment on folio 4v: "he naked cloþed vs with vertues" (l. 93; see also Hf, fol. 152v, l. 20), which loosely translates the *Stimulus*'s "nudens existens virtutum vestimentis ornat" (Pt. I, ch. 1) and "He desireth to hange naked on þe croce *with* his lorde, and in þat he is clothed *with* clothyng of vertues" (ll. 102–103; see also Hf, fol. 152v, ll. 30–31), which rephrases "Vult secum in ligno sine vestimentis frigescere; et nimio amoris ardore accenditur" (quotations from the *Stimulus* henceforth refer to Pt. I, ch. 1).

folio 3v, ll. 67–69: "What wodnesse is in þat man þat makeþ hym cloose his herte to god, and openeth hit to wrecchidnesse, likyng to þe deuille, to þe worlde, and to þe flesch" (cf. Hf, fol. 152r, ll. 33–36) adds to the *Stimulus*'s "Quae vesania animae, quod hoc negligit et potius vult stercoribus adhaerere," by expounding "vesania" (madness, frenzy) and "stercoribus" (filth, manure) and paraphrasing the latter.

folio 3v, l. 73: D's "euere haue his saule to god bi loue and contemplacion" is a rendering of the *Stimulus*'s "et semper se exigat ad divina" that localizes the place of human love in the soul and elucidates the methods of communion with the divine; Hf records this phrase with minor modifications (fol. 152r, ll. 38–39).

folios 3v–4r, l. 79: D's "Certes þey a saule were worse þanne a best" (see also Hf, fol. 152v, ll. 4–5) modifies the *Stimulus*'s "Certe si anima non esset pejor omni animali" and thus paints the human soul in a more negative light. D's sentence continues in much the same tone: "ȝit he scholde loue god to whom he is liche, for eche thyng loueþ kendlich þat is liche to hym" (fol. 4r, ll. 79–80; cf. Hf, fol. 152v, ll. 5–6) and slightly reworks the *Stimulus*'s "Deum, cui similis est, deberet super omnia diligere." In D and Hf's version, the soul is ennobled through divine love and love that it directs towards the divine.

folio 4r, l. 82: D adds "and payned *with*oute mesure greuouslich"; cf. Hf (fol. 152v, l. 8).

folio 4r, ll. 83–84: D records "for þe meditacion of cristes passion rerith manys saule and his mende to heuene, and techiþ what he schal do, and he schal þenke, and speke" (see also Hf, fol. 152v, ll. 9–11), adding "saule and his mende to heuene" and substituting "speke" for the *Stimulus*'s "sciendum et sentiendum."

folio 4r, l. 85: D's "quike þi saule þe more able to p*ar*feccion and trauail," also given, with variations, in Hf (fol. 152v, ll. 11–12), renders the *Stimulus*'s "te demum ad ardua inflammabit" with an emphasis on the soul as the place from which love springs and pertinently paraphrases "ardua" as "p*ar*feccion and trauail."

folio 4r, ll. 85–86: "make þe holde litel be þi self" (see Hf, fol. 152v, l. 12) is a shortening of the *Stimulus*'s "te vilificari, et contemni, et affligi faciet" that lessens the demand to debase onself.

folio 4r, ll. 89–90: D adds: "sorwe þat gladeþ"; also found in Hf (fol. 152v, l. 16).

folio 4r, l. 90: As a fine example of the affective heightening that the translation of the *Stimulus* effects, D's "Þe openynge of his syde heuyth oure herte to his hert" (cf. Hf, fol. 152v, l. 16) adds possessive pronouns to "apertio lateris cor cordi conjugat."

folios 4r–4v, l. 92: D adds "þe well dried more welleth þe passion"; also found in Hf (fol. 152v, l. 18).

folio 4v, l. 95: D adds "to hym. Be þe way of loue and goude werkes *and*"; also recorded in Hf (fol. 152v, ll. 22–23).

folio 4v, ll. 95–96: D's "he enspireth gostli lif in to oure soule" (cf. Hf, fol. 152v, ll. 22–23) emphasizes the soul yet another time when compared to the *Stimulus*'s "emittens spiritum vitam inspirat."

folio 4v, ll. 97–98: After "O passion meruaillous þat makest hym þat thenkyþ oft on þe noȝt onlich euen *with* angeles," which corresponds to the *Stimulus*, D adds "bot passe angeles," thereby augmenting the meditant's kinetic energy; see also Hf (fol. 152v, l. 25).

folio 4v, ll. 100ff.: A string of alterations and additions accentuates Christ as the reader's envisioned target of love: D reads "*with* his lorde" (l. 100) instead of the *Stimulus*'s "secum," adds "as his lorde" (l. 101), appends the adjective "endless" to the phrase "ioie endless" (l. 102), adds "*with* his lorde" (l. 103), "*with* crist" (ll. 103–104), "and crist" (l. 104); these insertions are also found with minor variations in Hf (fol. 152v, ll. 27–31).

folio 4v, l. 103: D's "he is clothed *with* clothyng of vertues" (see Hf, fol. 152v, l. 31) refers to clothing imagery, where the *Stimulus* reads "et nimio amoris ardore ascenditur." This potent change reflects the first part of the sentence, which illustrates the desire of the individual who meditates on Christ's Passion to "hange naked" (l. 102; see also Hf, l. 30) with him, where the *Stimulus* records "frigescere" instead. Moreover, this alteration provides a link to D's previous addition, which compares virtues to clothing for the faithfuls' souls (fols. 2v–3r, ll. 53–62, quoted above).

folio 5r, ll. 106–107: D adds "The sorwe of cristes in man other woman torneth hym to gladnesse and þe payne to ese"; also found with slight alterations in Hf (fol. 152v, ll. 34–35).

folio 5r, l. 108: An addition in D reads "and suffre þat he suffred"; see also Hf (fol. 152v, ll. 36–37).

folio 5r, l. 109: D adds "and clippeth [MS: clipprth] as his owene brother and childe"; Hf adds these lines, too (fol. 152v, ll. 37–38).

folio 5r, l. 111: D's text excises reference to "Joseph ab Arimathia" and privileges the relationship between the narrative voice and Christ: "Þanne miȝt I haue deyd with hym"; see also Hf (fol. 152v, ll. 40–41).

folio 5r, l. 113: D adds "and entre in to hym"; cf. Hf (fol. 152v, l. 42).

folio 5r, l. 114: to better anchor the affective stirrings it tries to elicit, D's text alters the *Stimulus*'s reference to Christ's side ("latere") and substitutes "hert" instead; Hf adapts the *Stimulus* in the same way (fol. 152v, l. 43).

folio 5r, l. 115: D's list of activities performed when contemplating Christ's Passion transposes two items and adds the reference to singing: "reste, and slepe, and ete, and drinke, rede, and synge, and praye." The *Stimulus* reads: "quiescere, dormire, videre, bibere, comedere, legere, orare; see also Hf (fol. 152v, l. 44).

folio 5r, ll. 116–117: D represents a more pragmatic viewpoint when it reads "alle þat me nediþ" (cf. also Hf, fol. 153r, l. 1) instead of the *Stimulus*'s "quod voluero." D furthermore appends "alone" to the end of the sentence, which now reads "y schal purchace of hym alone"; see Hf (fol. 153r, l. 1).

folios 5r–5v, ll. 117–118: D adds "Þer may non enemy me greue ne disese, and þer fore wil I abide and dwelle for euer more" to the *Stimulus*. This is an addition also found in Hf (fol. 153r, ll. 1–2).

folio 5v, l. 123: D adds "meke and innocent as a lombe," as does Hf (fol. 153r, l. 7).

folio 6r, l. 130: "*and in frut*" is another addition to the *Stimulus* that D shares with Hf (fol. 153r, l. 16).

folio 6r, ll. 135–136: "Allas þe folly of men þat cheseþ for to dwel in þe wor[l]de, in þe flesch, and in þe places þat ben vnclene, wrecchid, and sinful" is a less poetic but more theologically precise paraphrase of "O stulti et tardi corde, qui ad possidendum aliquod vanum per incerta foramina introitis"; this corresponds to Hf (fol. 153r, ll. 21–23).

folio 6r, l. 138: D's addition "hauyngge inwardlich mende þere on" to the text of the *Stimulus* is not attested in Hf (fol. 153r, l. 25).

folios 6r–6v, ll. 142–145: D adds the following passage to the *Stimulus*:

> Be holde þe wondes of hym þat hangyth, þe bloude of þe innocent, þe pris of þe diggere. His hed he hath enclined þe for to kysse, his armes he hath spred þe for to clippe, his syde he opened þe for to loue, and alle þis for to drawe mannys saule for to loue hym.

Also attested in Hf, though instead of the last part of the second sentence in D (from "and alle" to "hym"), Hf records: "so þat he al be fichid faste in þin herte þat for þe was nayled to þe cros" (fol. 153r, l. 31).

folio 6v, l. 146: D adds "And for to come to þi desire" to the *Stimulus's* text; also found in Hf (fol. 153r, l. 32).

folio 6v, ll. 149–150: the phrase "myn hert be euermore brennyng in þe fuer of loue" adds "myn hert" to the *Stimulus* and modifies "tuo amore semper sitiam," presumably to follow the recurrent previous references to the conceptualization and experience of divine love as fire and burning; this quote is also attested in Hf (fol. 153r, ll. 36–37).

folio 6v, l. 150: D adds "in alle þyng and alle my workes desire þi worschippe" to the *Stimulus*; see also Hf (fol. 153r, ll. 37–38).

folio 6v, ll. 152–153: Another addition in D is "In nothyng be my ioie bot in þe and for þe, and with alle myn herte I beseche þe"; see also Hf (fol. 153r, ll. 39–50).

folio 6v, ll. 153–156: The following passage was added to the *Stimulus*: "ffor þe wich þe sonne suffred painful deth and despitous. Louelich lorde and spouse ihesu crist, write in myn hert so þat I mowe rede þi loue towar[d] me and þi sorwe for me, and þe mende for hym euermore he dwellyng fresch in my herte"; see also Hf (fol. 153r, ll. 41–44).

The above list demonstrates that an accurate and faithful translation of extracts from the *Stimulus* was coupled with pertinent additions in D. Some of these must have already been present in D's ancestor, because they agree with Hf (more on this below). The *modus agendi* of the additions to the *Stimulus* is one of adaptation of the Latin text, and many of the alterations are evidence of an affective heightening that prioritizes meditation on the Passion. In their effective operation, the modifications evoke the reciprocal love between the reader and God.

The Form of Living *Segment*

Most variations between D's first unit and Hf occur in the *Form* segment, and they are all listed in Appendix B, so a few examples quoted here should suffice. D, for instance, reads: "ffor þai schul be breþeren and felawes in his maieste" (fol. 8r, l. 186), whereas Hf adds after "felawes": "wiþ angeles and holi men, preising, seinge and hauyng þe kyng of ioye in his fairhede and schinyng" (fol. 144v, ll. 4–5). Where D reads "werinesse and sorynesse of lif" (fol. 7r, ll. 165–166), the doublet in Hf is reversed: "sorynesse and werynes of þi lif" (fol. 144r, l. 22). A similar transposition occurs between D's "vncertayne and vnknowe" (fol. 7v, l. 174) and Hf's "vnknowe *and* vncerteyn" (fol. 144r, l. 30). Not only does the length of the *Form* extract give rise to most additions, transposition of words, and omissions, but the text's lists of sins repeatedly lend themselves to adaptation and are as such particularly malleable[53]—see, for instance, D's "for pride, for aray of oure body, oþer for any oþer vanite" (fol. 10r, l. 244), which Hf omits.

Concrete textual evidence demonstrates that D's target audience was either a house of religious or an individual not living an enclosed life. The text consequently ensures that the sins on which the *Form* extract elaborates are compatible with the daily practices and needs of this spiritual milieu, while at the same time exhibiting great caution not to overwhelm its audience by engaging them in matters evidently considered too worldly and unfitting. An example of such processes of thought is D's (or its parent manuscript's) omission (fol. 10r, l. 237) of "defendyng of synne, creiyng in lauȝtre, mowe makyng on any man, to singe seculer songes *and* loue ham," found in Hf (fol. 145r, ll. 19–21), which is also recorded in Ogilvie-Thomson's edition (12, ll. 361–362). More conspicuous still is Hf's "to hurte any man in his bodi, or in his good . . . , þefte, rauyn, vsur, deseyt . . . , ȝiue to harlotes" (fol. 145r, ll. 25–27, also recorded by Ogilvie-Thomson, 12, ll. 367–369), which is not mentioned in D (fol. 10r, ll. 242–244). Processes of careful adaptation to the audience's needs and/or requests may have governed the choice of material in this section—assuming the selection was not already predefined in D's exemplar.

The final part of D rises to a hortatory conclusion that is attested neither in Hf nor in Ogilvie-Thomson:

> and as saith seynt James, "hit were bettre noȝth for to knowe þe lawe of god þenne knowe hit and do noȝt þere after." And þer fore, my leue frende, y consaille þe þat þou forsake noȝth and dispise liȝtlich þis lore and doctrine, alle be hit þat parauenture for diuerse occupacions and lettyngs þat þou hast in þe worlde, þou fyndest no gret sauoure þer in atte þe begynnyng. For as ich haue saide afore, hertlich loue of god and goudnesse of lif wil noȝt be geten with oute grete trauail and long continuaunce, bot whanne hit is hadde, hit is ful of lykyng of swetnesse. And þere fore, whanne þe holi gost sendeþ þe eny sauour to loue god, forsake hit noȝt, bot kepe hit stille. And after þe grace þat he ȝeueþ þe, parforme hit and encrece hit, *and* ȝif þou dost þus, I drede noȝt þat þou schalt forsake alle unclene loue þat

> is noȝth to his worschippe for his loue. *And* þanne
> schalt þou ben his spouse, dwellyng *with* hym in
> þe blisse of heuen endlich. (fol. 14r, ll. 345–357)

However, the final lines of the added hortatory conclusion to the *Form* extract in D also largely correspond to the closing lines added to the complete version of *The Form* in Hf:

> And if hit be so, dere frende, þat þis schort lesson
> do þe goud, þanke god þere of and pray for me.
> The grace of god almyȝtti, ih*e*su verrai god and man
> þat is verrai loue *and* comfort of his loueris be *with*
> þe, and kepe þe fro euyl, and bryng þe to þi spouse
> þat þou hast take þe to, þe wich is eu*er*lastyng god.
> Amen. (D, fol. 14v, ll. 358–361; see also Hf, fol.
> 150v, ll. 34–38)

Conclusions

Based on the preceding comparison between D's first unit and Hf, the following hypotheses can be proposed:

1. The longer sections in D that do not correspond to Hf either could have been added by D's scribe or compiler (penned by him or sourced from elsewhere) or may have been inherited from D's exemplar.
2. If these passages were already present in D's parent manuscript, this would indicate that either:
    a) D and Hf did not share the same source but are related at some remove; or
    b) Hf excised these passages.

The variations in D exemplify the ways in which the scribe (or his model) altered the text creatively. A genuine interest in catering to the needs of audience members who were at the beginning of their spiritual careers and eager to intensify their relationship to the divine underlies the longer added passages that are unique to D (the graphic Passion meditation on fol. 2v [ll. 43–48] and the conclusion on fol. 14r [ll. 345–357]), as well as the omissions in *The Form*'s list of sins. See, for example, the narrative voice's adoption of a spiritual advisor's earnest tone of exhortation in the conclusion: "hertlich loue of god and goudnesse of lif wil noȝt be geten *with* oute grete trauail and long continuaunce, bot whanne hit is hadde, hit is ful of lykyng of swetnesse" (fol. 14r, ll. 350–352).

The guiding hand(s) behind D's production seem(s) to have had a fairly clear idea of the kind of work they wanted. Complementing *IX Poyntes*, the passages from *The Stimulus*, and the extract from *The Form*, the longer additions in the manuscript's first part oscillate between the poles that these texts embrace: they instruct the readers in God's love and the love of God and to this end provide a template on how to cultivate meekness and extensive scrutiny of the self in the face of their sinful past, present inadequacy, and inevitable inclination to sin again.

The hortatory conclusion references the scope of D's entire first part and expresses a carefully considered commentary on the ensuing spiritual efforts expected of its audience. As an exhortation appended to the other texts, it betrays a deliberate effort to produce a more accessible and effective work.

D's Second Unit: A New Copy of *The Chastising of God's Children*

The Chastising of God's Children is a treatise in twenty-seven chapters on how to deal with temptations in the advanced religious life, most likely written between 1391 and 1408.[54] The text is a devotional compilation: it is composed by the placing together of fragments from existing texts, including *Quandoque tribularis*, a Latin compilation of material from *Ancrene Wisse*, Henry Suso's *Horologium sapientiae*, John Ruusbroec's *Spiritual Espousals*, James of Milan's *Stimulus amoris*, and Alphonse of Pecha's *Epistola solitarii ad reges*, which are interspersed with the compiler's own comments and biblical and patristic references.[55] The *Chastising* compiler translates his sources from Latin source texts and addresses the treatise, which he calls "a short pistle," to a "religious sister" (Bazire-Colledge 95/1), who is presented in the text as a woman responsible for her own spiritual life and that of others. It is a remarkably cerebral text that places great stress on knowing and knowledge, teaching the sister about the various guises in which temptations can manifest themselves so that she can recognize and remedy them in herself and others. This instruction is combined with performative passages and occasional, quite beautifully translated descriptions of the joys experienced when the contemplative feels God's presence in the soul.

The manuscripts and an early printed edition in which *The Chastising of God's Children* survives are the following:

> **A:** Oxford, Bodleian Library, MS Ashmole 41 (second half fifteenth century)
> **Add:** London, British Library, MS Additional 33971 (middle or second half fifteenth century)
> **B:** Oxford, Bodleian Library, MS Bodley 505 (Sheen Charterhouse, first half fifteenth century)
> **D:** Oxford, Bodleian Library, MS Don. e. 247 (first half fifteenth century)

H: London, British Library, MS Harley 6615 (second half fifteenth century)

Ha: London, British Library, MS Harley 2218 (middle or second half fifteenth century; chapters 24 and 25)

He: Yale, Beinecke Library, MS Osborn fa46 (*olim* Taunton, Somerset Record Office, MS Heneage 3084; first half fifteenth century)

J: Cambridge, St. John's College, MS E.25 (fifteenth century, probably not before 1450)

L: Liverpool, University Library, MS folio 4.10 (second half fifteenth century)

P: Cambridge, Magdalene College, MS Pepys 2125 (first half fifteenth century)

R: Oxford, Bodleian Library, MS Rawlinson C. 57 (given to Sheen Charterhouse by John Kingslow, the first Sheen recluse, early fifteenth century)

T: Cambridge, Trinity College, MS B.14.19 (first unit first quarter fifteenth century)

W: Wynkyn de Worde's printed edition (*ca.* 1493)

Sixteen of *The Chastising*'s twenty-seven chapters have been borrowed in the compilation *Disce mori*, which survives in two manuscripts:[56]

Je: Oxford, Jesus College, MS 39 (between 1453 and 1464)

La: Oxford, Bodleian Library, MS Laud. Misc. 99 (after 1470, around 1500?)

Disce mori, in its turn, was one of the sources for the compilation known as *Ignorancia sacerdotum*, extant in one manuscript:

E: Oxford, Bodleian Library, MS Eng. th. c. 57 (between 1453 and 1464)

Though all manuscripts but one keep the address to the religious sister,[57] the text also seems to have been read in houses of male religious—B, He, R, and T have links to the Carthusians. On the whole, the instruction in the text is not gendered, as its advice is relevant to both male and female religious and laypeople who want to devote their lives to God. It is unknown who wrote the text and for whom. Though Oxford, Bodleian Library, MS Bodley 923, a manuscript owned by Sibilla de Felton, abbess of Barking from 1394 to 1419, mentions *The Chastising* as a text known at Barking, none of the manuscripts in which *The Chastising* survives has been linked to the abbey.[58]

D's Place in the Manuscript Tradition of *The Chastising*

D has been compared against the text and variants offered in Bazire and Colledge's edition as well as the variants of He, a manuscript unknown at the time of the Bazire-Colledge edition.[59] In addition to variant readings occurring in the manuscripts and early printed edition listed above, variants by the correctors of He (Hec), P (Pc) and T (Tc) have also at times been recorded.[60] Rather than readings from Bazire-Colledge, which was based on a manuscript in a different group (BHeJeLaTc) from the one D belongs to, the variants were transcribed from D, with the corresponding reading from the edition given between brackets.[61] Readings from the BHeJeLaTc group occur only occasionally in what follows, as D only occasionally shares variant readings with them.

In the *stemma codicum* offered by Bazire and Colledge, D belongs in the group AddJP. Whenever Add, J, and P (J and P in the chapters that Add lacks at its beginning)[62] share the same reading, D coincides with these readings. In forty-one instances, Add, J, D, and P (J, D, and P where Add lacks the beginning) agree against all other manuscripts. In a first group of variant readings, the AddDJP manuscripts lack words or phrases present in the other manuscripts, but without greatly affecting the meaning:

> **DJP:** is more delitable to the soule (cf. Bazire-Colledge 102/22–23: is more delitable to *þe body and* þe soule);
> **AddDJP:** þei be most traueylid þat do her besynes (cf. 117/17: þei bien most traueiled þat *most* do her besynes)
> **AddDJP:** so it semyth whan a man wielfulli gruchchiþ (cf. 118/23: so it semeþ *wele þat* whan a man wilfulli gruccheþ)
> **AddDJP:** his gostli childryn whiche haue forsaken hem self (cf. 122/14–15: his goostli children whiche *vttirly* han forsaken hem self)
> **AddDJP:** of eche leuyng *and* comyne of eche matier (cf. 126/13–14: of eche lyueng; *þei wol* comune of eche matier)
> **AddDJP:** sche ȝaf holli to hym þat alle goudnes sent (cf. 137/16: she ȝaf *al* hooli to hym þat al goodenesse sent)
> **AddDJP:** he berith hom his sceip þat first was lost (cf. 151/19–20: he beriþ hom *aȝen* his shep, þat first was lost)
> **AddDJP:** owre tyme of turnyng.' for yn þe lest moment of an howre (cf. 152/11–12: oure tyme of tournyng, *neiþer long ne short*, for in þe leest moment of an hour)
> **AddDJP:** or to one or twei oþer to gostli lyuers (cf. 155/17–18: *or ellis* to one or tweyne oþer gostli lyuers)
> **AddDJP:** as owre holi fadris saide (cf. 166/18: as oure hooli fadirs *in oold tyme* seiden)

AddDJP: for þei fiende nat grace or ellis þowh þai fiend grace (cf. 188/1–2: for þei fynde nat grace *or see it nat,* or ellis, þouȝ þei fynde grace)

AddDJP: whan a man felith eny steryng (cf. 204/24–25: whan a man *or womman* feeliþ ony stirynge)

AddDJP: ensawmple of manye which nyed nat to reherse here (cf. 222/7–8: ensample of many *seintis,* which neden nat to reherse)

In two instances, the omissions are longer and are arguably the result of eyeskip in a common source for AddDJP:

AddDJP: for þei thyng wilfulli be her owne worchynge (cf. 140/3–4: for þei *þenke if þei diden any* þing wilfulli bi her owne wirchyng)

AddDJP: yn reisyng of dede men, speche to dombe men (cf. 181/6–8: in reisyng of deede men, *in ȝeuynge siȝt to blynde men, heeryng to deef men,* speche to domb men)

In the same vein as the shorter omissions, the AddDJP manuscripts have words or phrases not present in the other manuscripts:

DJP: þat hit semyth *to* a man ynwardli (cf. Bazire-Colledge 102/20–21: þat it semeþ a man inwardli)

DJP: receiuyng of his *graciouse* ȝiftes (cf. 105/6–7: receyuenge of his ȝiftes)

AddDJP: þis rest men mowe fynde *and haue* be verray kynde (cf. 131/2–3: þis rest men mowen fynde bi verrei kynde)

AddDJP: and þat þei haue god *yn* her spiriet (cf. 141/9–10: and þat þei haue god þeir spirit);

AddDJP: and þei had *gret* plente of water (cf. 185/4: and þei had plente of watir)

AddDJP: with *smytyng on þe brest* and crossing þe forhed (cf. 202/13–14: wiþ crossing on þe forhed *and brest*)

AddDJP: and such *oþer* passyng thynges (cf. 209/12: and suche passyng þinges)

Other readings in AddDJP substitute one word for another, in some cases synonymously:

DJP: *suche* gostli science (cf. Bazire-Colledge 95/18–19: *that* goostli science)

DJP: alle *maner* knowlechyng (cf. 110/13–14: al *oþer* knowlechynge)

AddDJP: Bot as of power of *wicked* spiritis (cf. 162/11–12: But as of power of *yuel* spirites)

AddDJP: a *goud* spede (cf. 164/22: a *grete* spede)

AddDJP: þat ȝe wil nat *say* ȝowre psawter (cf. 221/23–24: þat ȝe wil not *use* ȝoure sautier)

In some instances, the substitutions change the meaning of the sentence but still make sense. When DJP read "for what euere he *desire*" in comparison to "for what euere he *deserue*" (105/19) in the other manuscripts, both readings are meaningful in context: contemplatives will receive plentiful gifts from God and have to respond to them with meekness. These gifts can be desired as well as deserved. The AddDJP sentence "And greteli it is to drede: *y vnderstonde* þei be messageris of antecrist" works as well as "and greteli it is to drede þat *in auenture* þei be messangiers of antecrist" (144/9–10), though AddDJP assert more strongly that the people described are the heralds of Antichrist, whereas the other manuscripts posit this as a possibility to be feared.

The substitution of "neydful" for "profitable" in the following variant reading reflects the exchange between "nedeful/neydful" and "medeful" (here rendered as "profitable") that repeatedly occurs in the manuscript tradition of *The Chastising*, as shown below:

AddDJP: and suche chastisynges be *neydful* as y saide be fore (cf. Bazire-Colledge 151/11–12: and such chastisynges bien *profitable,* as I seide bifore)

These meanings also seem closely connected. In order to be rewarding, the chastising of God's children is indeed necessary, so even though the error is letter- or word-based, the erroneous reading sticks because it not without its merits.

Small, momentary shifts in the understanding of how the spiritual life is lived occur when AddDJP has "to vse *beides and* mekenes" instead of "to use *deedis of* mekenesse" (Bazire-Colledge 207/5), adding the saying of prayers as a remedy against pride to the deeds of meekness described in the text. Even though the AddDJP reading here is not the better one, it does not jar with the rest of the text. When AddDJP has "as fer forth as y *knowe*" instead of "as ferforth as I *feele*" (Bazire-Colledge 220/27) in a comment on the necessity of saying the prayers of the office attentively, this may not be the better reading to be followed by "and as I haue lierned"—logically it makes more sense for a feeling to be confirmed by what one has learnt. Yet the speaker's assertion of "knowing" the importance of saying the prayer attentively does not jar with the phrase that follows, and "y knowe" comes across as decisive and confident. In addition, it is in keeping with the text's repeated stress on knowledge.[63]

In one instance we can see how a variant reading was caused by the misreading of a word (either turning one word in two, or the opposite):

AddDJP: withoute eny desire or *besechynge* to god (cf. Bazire-Colledge 134/14–15: wiþout any desire or *besi seekyng* to god);

In two instances the AddDJP reading is grammatically slightly different from the reading found in the other manuscripts. In the first an indicative verb is rewritten as a past participle, and in the second a different modal auxiliary is used. Again, both versions work without a major shift in meaning:

AddDJP: be amendid and *profitid* yn vertw (cf. Bazire-Colledge 123/20: and bien amendid and *profiten* in uertu);
AddDJP: þat ladi *wil* nat put me awei (cf. 159/22–23: þat ladi *may* not putt me awey)

This cannot be said of the instances in which AddDJP readings are clearly erroneous:

AddDJP: and sey with þe *mowth* (cf. 158/19: and seie wiþ þe *herte*)
AddDJP: bot his power is *euer* riȝthful (cf. 160/23: but his power is *neuer* riȝthful)
AddDJP: Also ȝif a man or woman louyth his neyhbor (cf. 201/16–17: Also if a man or woman loueþ *nat* his neiȝbor);
AddDJP: þowh he be riȝth *stable* of conplexion (cf. 213/6: þouȝ he be *fieble* of complexion)

In two instances the AddDJP manuscripts coincide with W, the early printed edition placed in relation to the same group by Bazire and Colledge, but neither of these is significant.[64] Similarly, in the six instances in which the members of the group AddDJP do not agree, the differences are minor (omissions, minimally varying vocabulary) and do not affect the meaning of the text.[65] In all the instances in which Add and J present unique readings, D agrees with all the other MS, including P, against AddJ.[66]

The complex manuscript tradition of *The Chastising* shows in the many instances in which members of the group AddJDP share readings with manuscripts from other groups. These readings, often as a result of minor changes and thus not significantly different, seem to occur across groups without any clear pattern emerging.[67] More significant overlap might be concluded from the instances in which manuscripts from group AddJDP share readings with manuscripts from the group ALRT. As is the case with most of the variant readings between attestations of *The Chastising*, the changes are minor and as such testify to a faithful and mostly uniform transmission of this text.[68]

Some of these variants, however, result in interesting readings. In the refrain at the end of each chapter, the ADJLPRT manuscripts have "wakith and praith þat ʒe *falle* nat in to temptacion" rather than "wakeþ and preieþ, þat ʒe *entre* nat into temptacion" (Bazire-Colledge 96/12–13), which renders the Latin "ut non intretis in temptacionem" more closely. In ADJeHPRTW the four erroneous opinions and their resulting heretical and sinful behavior described in chapters 9 to 12 are announced as "fowre maner sektis," whereas the other manuscripts describe them as "foure maner sikenessis" (130/2–3), a choice of word still deriving from the preceding descriptions, in chapters 7 and 8, of the dropsy and the four fevers befalling those who "vnskillfulli and vnresonabli bien enclyned to lustes and eesis of þe bodi" (126/7–8). The "sektis" reading, on the other hand, is forward-looking and the better reading. Indeed, in chapter 10 the word is used in all manuscripts to refer to types of erroneous living.[69]

Another substitution we have come across earlier is AAddDJLRT's "þe werkis whiche god werkith *be hem* be more noble and *neydful*" for "þe werkis þat god worchiþ bien more noble and *medeful*" (142/21). In addition to the added emphasis on the person in which God works his good works, the AAddDJLRT manuscripts stress the necessity of the works in order to be deserving of the reward rather than the reward they bring.

The AddDJPRTW sources stress the readers' capability for discernment when they have "But for as mych as ʒe se euyrmore þat many perelis fallith to gostli lyuers be þei neuer so holi" instead of "But for as moche as *I see*" (187/5–6), which favors the authoritative position of the compiler. Another pronoun shift occurs when the AddDHHeJJeLPW sources have "Clepe me yn þe day of tribulacion: for y schal delyuere þe and *y* schal worschipe *þe*" when the last phrase should read "and þou schalt worship me" (203/14) in the translation of Palm 49:15 ("Et inuoca me in die tribulationis, eruam te et honorificabis me"). Obviously caused by repetition of the sequence "y—þe" in the preceding phrase, the shift has the effect of switching speakers. As the phrase "and y schal worschipe þe" needs to be spoken by the reader to "our lorde" (203/11), the psalm verse becomes a short dialogue between the reader and God, rather than a speech by God to the reader by way of the psalmist—an unintended but intriguing momentary effect of a copying error.

The shared readings between members of the groups AddDJP and ALRT might be significant in particular because it might be enlightening with regard to the quality of the text version and the superiority of the readings members of these two groups share over other readings, even when the variations are only minor. It is outside the scope of this essay to reassess

Bazire and Colledge's editorial decisions—in particular their decision to choose B as their base manuscript, which seems an odd choice given the many instances in which B disagrees with all other manuscripts.[70] Yet it would be worthwhile to check whether the readings the AddDJP manuscripts have in common with RT especially (two manuscripts that, like B and He, have a Carthusian connection and hence have been subject to correction in keeping with the Carthusian preoccupation with good-quality texts),[71] do not present a better reading (i.e., possibly closer to the *Chastising* compiler's) than the equivalent readings in B.

Within the group AddDJP, D is closest to P and diverges from Add and J, as pointed out above. D and P share unique readings in nineteen instances, of which some are significant in that they are not just omissions of words, the use of synonyms, or small grammatical alterations. D and P have "þat askid not to be forsake *oueral*" when all other manuscripts have "þat asked nat to be forsake *at al tymes*" (Colledge-Bazire 99/1–2), stressing place rather than time, and read "þus fel adam *owt of* paradise" when all other manuscripts have "þus fel adam *in* paradise" (136/19), with D and P presenting the more accurate reading. When D and P read "and to fowre maner sieknes" rather than "and to foure maner sectis" (187/4), they repeat the word "sieknes" from the earlier "to þe gostli seiknes" (cf. 187/3) but lose the distinction made earlier between the dropsy and fevers discussed in chapters 7 and 8 and the four sects of men discussed in chapters 9 to 12. In this case, D and P do not make the distinction, making this reading the poorer one.

D's and P's distance from Add and J also shows in that D shares twenty-five readings with P and other manuscripts but not with Add and J.[72] However, the fact that D, as is the case with all extant copies of *The Chastising*,[73] is an independent copy the immediate model of which does not survive is shown by the instances in which D differs from P and agrees with all other manuscripts against P, often because of omissions in P, as in the following examples of omission through eyeskip:

D: whan þei fiel hem not tempted (**P** omits) (cf. Bazire-Colledge 97/21)

D: ȝeuyng obedience to no man neiþir to pope (**P**: omits "to no man neiþir") (cf. 140/20–21)

D: Also it is a grete fredom and liberte whan a man is delyuered of þe seruage of þe deyuyl (**P** omits) (cf. 153/23–24)

D: to þis me thenkith eche man may se and feile þat he schal thynke hym self able to receyue mercy (**P** omits) (cf. 154/16–17)

That D cannot have been the direct ancestor of P or another manuscript in the AddDJP group is shown by omissions as a result of eyeskip unique to D:

> **D:** þis men yn her own siȝth þei be* verrei futyuys be cawse þei haue
> rwn away and fled far fram god / and as þai be fled. from god :
> so hit is neydful þat alle men fle away from hem as from a gostly
> enemy. (*left out: ful contemplatif, but in goddis siȝth þei bien;
> cf. Bazire-Colledge 139/5–9. This is also an omission in **HeJeLa**,
> otherwise unrelated to **D**)
> **D:** For þai be passid þe trauayl* for to be dischargid of vertwis þan for
> to gete hem. (*left out: of excercises, as þei seien, and dischargid
> of alle vertuse. Alsswa þai say þat a man nediþ more to traueile; cf.
> 140/16–19)
> **D:** þer fore þei trowe þat þei mowe no more encrece yn vertwis.* and.
> þat þei mowe no more synne yn as myche as to her own siȝt (*left
> out: and þat þei mowe disserue no more mede; cf. 141/6–8)
> **D:** ȝif we turne to hym* cleirli: and with a symple meke hert (*left out:
> he takeþ us into grace. Þe pite of god is so grete þat he dispiseþ
> neuer penaunce where it is offrid up to hym; cf. 152/12–15)
> **D:** owr lorde gladli takiþ hym and louyngli beclippith hym* aȝen
> to his first state (*left out: and bi his mercy reformeþ hym; cf.
> 152/16–18)
> **D:** and for we be bownde be þe precept of* god we schul loue owre
> neyhbor (*left out: god to loue oure euencristen. We shuln also
> loue hym þat is nat oure enemy bi kynde, for he is a man, and bi
> þe precept of; cf. 196/9–12)

In addition, D has a large number of unique readings, most of which are too minor to discuss here. The scribe does have a tendency to intensify the text with small additions that could be interpreted as adding emphasis:

> **D:** take hym *yn* to mercie (cf. Bazire-Colledge 154/25: take hym to
> mercy)
> **D:** how*euer* hit schall falle of me (cf. 159/12: what shal fal of me)
> **D:** what *euyr* thei wil (cf. 190/24: what þei woln)
> **D:** myche more *þanne* þat noble and soothfast fadir (cf. 207/24–
> 208/1: moche more þat noble and soþfast fadir)
> **D:** bodeli penawnce *owtward* with preier (cf. 218/2: bodili penance
> wiþ preier)

Another group of unique readings testify to the scribe's deliberate or, rather, intelligent interaction with the spiritual content of the text. Thus, asking advice is understood as a way to humble oneself, and meekness is seen as a means to purify rather than prove a person—a subtle qualification:

> **D:** aske oft *consail to meke* hym (cf. Bazire-Colledge 155/18–19: and aske oft *conseil, and to meke* him)
> **D:** bot man ys *purid* be meyknesse (cf. 164/12: but man is *preued* bi mekenesse)

The text as rendered in D also distinguishes between the cause of an action and its aim where the other manuscripts do not, and characterizes fasting and keeping vigils as physical works:

> **D:** for þe loue and to þe worschip of god (cf. Bazire-Colledge 191/22: for þe loue and worship of god)
> **D:** sum oþir bodeli traueyle (cf. 213/1: sum oþer traueile)

The substitution "medeful"/"nedeful" is revisited here as well, though here D focuses on the spiritual reward brought by affliction rather than on the necessity of affliction for the purity of the soul and on the rewards of mortification rather than its needs:[74]

> **D:** and oþir gostli meide (cf. Bazire-Colledge 214/10: and oþer gostli nede)
> **D:** it is a meydful riwle (cf. 214/17: it is a nedeful rule)
> **D:** it is only meydful to refreyne (cf. 215/1: it is nat oonli nedeful to refreyne)

The scribe's occasional lapses in concentration show in D's second unit in forty-odd erroneous readings, some of which are obviously nonsensical, and all of which remain uncorrected.[75] Whether the scribe of D uses different words or phrases with the same meaning as the other text versions, whether he chooses different pronouns, puts singular nouns in the plural or vice versa, or repeats articles after "and" or "or," whether he more significantly adds words for extra emphasis or introduces variants that change or intensify the spiritual content or import of a passage, the unique readings he brings to D illustrate his active engagement with the text. He does not just copy his model passively, or not always, at any rate. Thoughtful attention while copying, either by the scribe of D, or by the scribe of his model copy,[76] also shows in the playful transpositions of sentence elements and in doublets, which are frequent enough to be significant.[77]

Signposting, Corrections, and Marginal Annotations in D

Some of the marginal annotations in D, written in red ink in the same hand as the main text and the rubrics, signpost dropsy in chapter 7,[78] the four fevers in chapter 8[79] and the seven deadly sins in chapter 25,[80] as well as—somewhat randomly—the names of Heliseus and Balthasar in chapter 18.[81] The structural signposting of the illness, fevers, and seven deadly sins also occurs in other *Chastising* manuscripts. The Add manuscript signposts the seven deadly sins in Latin from folio 50v to 54r,[82] R marks them in English (fols. 45r–47r). B (fols. 23r–25v and fols. 76v–81r) and P (fols. 6v–7v and fols. 23v–25r) signpost both the illnesses and the seven sins in the same way as D. Though structural signposting may have been a scribal decision independent of the exemplar used, it seems likely that these marginalia were deemed integral to the text and were passed on from one copy to the other. D shares this form of signposting with P, the manuscript it is closest to, and with Add, another member of its group. Through shared ancestors, this type of signposting also links D to R and B, manuscripts outside its group, which might again be taken to show the complex textual relationships between the copies of *The Chastising*.

D has been little corrected. Erroneous readings mostly remain unspotted by the corrector (who was most likely the scribe)[83] and the annotator(s) contemporary with the scribe. Three marginal additions and one interlinear correction were made to the text.[84] In none of these instances is the resulting reading listed in Bazire and Colledge's apparatus of variants.

Marginal annotations contemporary with the work of the scribe and made by the scribe or, judging from the different color of ink, by subsequent readers, are relatively few:

> folio 10r: "of þy fle[sch] next to "The synnes beth þise: Glotonye. Lecherie. Symonie. Wichecraft."
>
> folio 37r: "[?] to þis" next to "Eche suche man þat hath þis perfeccion and come to þis lownesse and parfite sufferaunce is first schaprli thretnyd"

Five different shapes of *notae* can be distinguished. The first *nota* in the margin occurs on folio 8v; it is larger than all others in D and has been written in the same ink as the trefoils (see below), next to "þat þou be riȝt dispoused boþe for þi saule and for þi bodi, þou schalt vnderstande foure thynges" (fol. 8v, ll. 206–207.).

A second type of *"nota"* is made in a small script with a small circular-shaped abbreviation mark. This form of annotation marks occurs on folios 48r, 49v, 57r, 64r, 66v, and 101r, with the forms on folio 49v and folio 66v somewhat smaller and hence possibly by a different reader:

folio 48r, right-hand margin: "*nota hic*" next to "and alle owtward
vertwis" (cf. Bazire-Colledge 138/12).[85]

folio 49v, left-hand margin: "*nota*" next to "ʒif here bodeli kiend
coueytiþ or be sterid to eny lust or lykyng so ferforth þat þe sperit
hath not his fredom" (cf. 141/12–14).

folio 57r, right-hand margin: "*nota bene*" next to "þat a man
schulde neuyr mystrust þowh he be not turned to þe last ende"
(cf. 152/2–3).

folio 64r, right-hand margin: "*nota*" next to "þe wil of þe deiuele is
alwei wicked" (cf. 160/22–23).

folio 66v, left-hand margin: "*nota*" next to the opening of chapter 17,
"Ful holi men for liʒth defawtis haue be take bodeli to þe wicked
spiritis" (cf. 164/6–7).

folio 101r, right-hand margin: "*nota*" next to "Many men repryeue
it to haue þe psawter and matyns and gospels or þe bible in
englisch" (cf. 221/8–10).

A third form of "*nota*," with a distinct abbreviation mark (two linked
minims and an upward curving stroke), occurs only once, on folio 56r:

folio 56r, right-hand margin: "*nota*" next to "It is meydful to riʒthful
men and holi men" (cf. 150/13–15)

In two instances, the "*nota*" has a larger abbreviation mark. These
annotations may have been made by a fourth reader:

folio 68r, right-hand margin: "*nota*" next to "Of þis we mowe se ful
many of ensawmplis" (cf. 166/9–10).

folio 78r, right-hand margin: "*nota bene hic*" next to "þis men beth so
blendid yn here saule" (cf. 190/12–13).

In a fifth form, "*Nota*" is written with a capital N, which looks scribal:

folio 85r, right-hand margin: "*Nota*" next to "þer fore what euer
temptacion a man haue wheþir hit be of feith" (cf. 201/8–9).

If we can take these "*notae*" as signs of interest on the part of the readers and/or as pointers they left for future readers, it is interesting to note
that they express interest in the same themes. The first "*nota*" on folio 8v
marks a passage that teaches conversion from a sinful life in the world to the
conforming of the will to God's. The annotations to *The Chastising* mark
passages warning against spiritual error and giving messages of reassurance.

The second type of "*notae (bene)*" marks passages warning against spiritual error (fols. 48r, 49v, and 66v) but also passages of reassuring patristic teaching by Isidore of Seville (fol. 57r) and Gregory the Great (fol. 64r). In particular, the saying by Isidore, which teaches that it is never too late for a sinner to repent and be saved, represents the spiritual optimism that in spite of its stress on temptation and tribulation, is at the heart of *The Chastising*. Intriguingly, this annotator also marks a passage pointing to the objections many contemporaries had to the use of English for prayer and religious instruction (fol. 101r), showing the compiler's (and this annotator's) engagement with the controversies surrounding Wycliff's Bible translation, which led to Arundel's 1409 Constitutions.[86]

The third type of "*nota*" highlights a passage that details the necessity for righteous and holy people to learn from adversity (fol. 56r). The fourth type of "*notae*" (with the larger abbreviation mark) points to two passages in which models are held up to the reader. The first passage (fol. 68r) shows the devil at work when he torments people on their deathbed who have always led a good and religious life. The second passage (fol. 78r) discusses the people who hold the errors signaled in passages marked earlier (fols. 48r and 49v). The scribal "*Nota*" (fol. 85r), like the comforting messages marked by the first annotator, points to a passage that is reassuring and positive: when a man has doubts about points of the faith, he does not sin when he regrets his doubts.

Several trefoils serve the same highlighting function. In the right-hand margin on folio 3r, there is a trefoil next to "so gostlich, ȝif þou wilt wex hoot in þe loue of god, do on many clothes of vertu, for vertu is clothes to mannys saule" (fol. 3r, ll. 57–58), a passage in praise of a virtuous life. In the left-hand margin on folio 8v, a trefoil has been drawn next to a passage urging moderation in abstinence: "I holde þe neuer of þe lasse merite ȝif þou be noȝt in lo abstinence as were sum tyme holi men and women a fore vs" (fol. 8v, ll. 201–203). In the left-hand margin on folio 13v, a trefoil occurs next to "for only wrecchidnesse haþ non enemy in erthe. Ffor to drawe vs þat we conforme our wille to godis wille þar beþ þre thynges: on ensample of holi men and wommen" (fol. 13v, ll. 329–331), again, a passage that points to the necessity of conforming one's will to God's. On folio 54v in the left-hand margin, three trefoils occur in descending order of size and each of them drawn closer to the text. The two lower trefoils, drawn in black ink, and with a pen that results in a thickly-set line, seem to have been added by postmedieval annotator 1. Marking "ffor eþyr . . . hym be his mercy" (cf. Bazire-Colledge 148/6–11) and reinforcing the passage underlined in red "ffor eþyr . . . of holi chirche" (cf. 148/8–10), they draw attention to a passage commenting on the way a sinner may be punished for his misdeeds. God may punish the sinner in this life or, everlastingly, in the next. The sinner may also punish himself through his own devotion or because the Church tells him to do penance, and in these cases God will withdraw his rod.

In the right-hand margin on folio 62r, a trefoil marks a passage that announces a prayer that can be used to chase the devil away: "to his confusyon for he . . . . and set at nawth" (cf. Bazire-Colledge 158/19–21). The trefoil next to "Also yn eche temptacion or tribulacion bodili or gostli it is ful cownfortable to thynke on þe wordis þat god saith be þe prophete" (cf. 200/21–23) in the right-hand margin on folio 85r serves the same function, as do the ones in the left-hand margin on folio 87v, next to "Also I rede how owre ladi tawht seynt Bride" (cf. 204/17–18), and in the right-hand margin on folio 88r, next to "þat þe dyeuele may knowe what a man saith to his schame and confusion yn þis manere. Almiȝthti god fadre yn heuene" (cf. 204/26–28). Thus the trefoils signpost the reader to themes ranging from virtue, moderation, conforming one's will to God, and remedies against sin to effective shaming of the devil.

D illustrates both scribes' and readers' creative interaction with texts in Unit I, which reorders, deletes from, and adds to material grouped together in Hf, and scribes' and readers' reverence for the integrity of texts such as *The Chastising*, copied in its entirety without deliberate or major alterations in Unit II. With the Bodleian Library's acquisition of D, the scholarly community has access to yet another fine and unique example of the devotional books that proliferated in the late fourteenth and fifteenth century in England, an anthology of thematically similar texts aimed at helping their audience shape and live a life of prayer and contemplation.

Acknowledgments
The authors are grateful to Vincent Gillespie, Ralph Hanna, Michael Sargent, Jeremy Smith, Elizabeth Solopova, and Daniel Wakelin for sharing their knowledge and their research of this manuscript, and to Martin Kauffmann of the Bodleian Library for allowing them to work with the manuscript. The sections "Description of Oxford, Bodleian Library, MS Don. e. 247," "D's Second Unit: A New Copy of *The Chastising of God's Children*," "D's Place in the Manuscript Tradition of *The Chastising*," and "Signposting, Corrections, and Marginal Annotations in D" were written by Cré as part of the Swiss National Science Foundation project, "Late Medieval Religiosity in England: The Evidence of Late Fourteenth- and Fifteenth-Century Devotional Compilations," carried out at the University of Lausanne. The research of this new manuscript was made possible by a Cost-Action Short Term Scientific Mission Grant, awarded to Cré by Cost-Action IS-1301, "New Communities of Interpretation: Contexts, Strategies and Processes of Religious Transformation in Late Medieval and Early Modern Europe," coordinated by Profesor Sabrina Corbellini at the University of Groningen, The Netherlands.

NOTES

1. Marleen Cré wrote the sections "Description of Oxford, Bodleian Library, MS Don. e. 247," "D's Second Unit: A New Copy of *The Chastising of God's Children*," "D's Place in the Manuscript Tradition of The Chastising," and "Signposting, Corrections, and Marginal Annotations in D" of this essay. Raphaela Rohrhofer wrote the sections "D's Envisioned Audience," "D's First Unit and Its Relationship to the Second Unit," and "A Comparison of D's First Unit with the Text in Hereford, Cathedral Library, MS P. I. 9." Rohrhofer also provided the transcription and variants of D's first unit in Appendices A and B of this essay.

2. An article on the sale appeared in the *Telegraph* on March 30, 2014. It does not mention the manuscript. See "Sale of the Century as Aristocrats Auction Heirlooms," *Telegraph,* March 30, 2014, http://www. telegraph.co.uk/culture/art/artsales/10732013/Sale-of-the-century-as-aristocrats-auction-heirlooms.html.

3. A reference to the sale can still be found on Christie's website; see "Sale 1550/London: Valuable Manuscripts and Printed Books, 21 May 2014," Christie's, http://www.christies.com/lotfinder/print_sale. aspx?saleid=24630&lid=1.

4. The description of the manuscript is based on the description by Ralph Hanna and Vincent Gillespie. The authors are grateful that Gillespie and Hanna made their description available to them (in private correspondence).

5. Hanna dates D to the mid-fifteenth-century, though both Gillespie and Daniel Wakelin suggest—on the basis of its resemblance to early *Pore Caitif* manuscripts as regards size and layout—that it might well be an early fifteenth-century book (in private conversation). Both hypotheses will have to be tested in further research of the volume.

6. For the edition of the text see Joyce Bazire and Eric Colledge, eds., *The Chastising of God's Children and The Treatise of Perfection of the Sons of God* (Oxford: Basil Blackwell, 1957).

7. Quotation from *The Chastising* is by folio and line numbers in D, followed by reference to page and line numbers in the Bazire-Colledge edition.

8. To briefly summarize the evidence, nine of the twelve *Chastising* manuscripts have been located to the southeast Midlands: L (Soke of Peterborough, eLALME, unnumbered Linguistic Profile (LP) for *The Scale of Perfection* in this manuscript), R (Norfolk, eLALME, LP 4648), T (Suffolk, eLALME, LP 8420), P (southeast Midlands, Bazire 1957), D (west Norfolk or east Suffolk), B (Cambridgeshire, eLALME, LP 4773), He (southeast Midlands, Sargent 1977), H (southeast Midlands, Bazire

1957), and Ha (Lincolnshire, eLALME, unnumbered LP for Hand B). A is written in a west Midlands dialect (Staffordshire, eLALME, LP 243 for *The Prick of Conscience* in this manuscript). Add and J are northern copies: Add (northern, Bazire 1957) and J (Yorkshire, North Riding, eLALME, LP 203). This suggests that *The Chastising* had a strong early circulation in the southeast Midlands and traveled further afield (to the north and west) in the second half of the fifteenth century. Je is written in a southeast/central Midlands dialect, and both La and E may have a London/Middlesex basis. (See below for the identification of the sigla used here.) Joyce Bazire, "The Dialects of the Manuscripts of *The Chastising of God's Children*," *English and Germanic Studies* 6 (1957):64–78; and Michael G. Sargent, "A New Manuscript of *The Chastising of God's Children* with an Ascription to Walter Hilton," *Medium Aevum* 46 (1977):49–65, at 57. On L, also see Michael G. Sargent, "Bishops, Patrons, Mystics and Manuscripts: Walter Hilton, Nicholas Love and the Arundel and Holland Connections," in *Middle English Texts in Transition: A Festschrift Dedicated to Toshiyuki Takamiya on his 70th Birthday*, ed. Simon Horobin and Linne Mooney (York, UK: York Medieval Press, 2014), 159–177, at 168. On Je, La, and E, see E. A. Jones, ed., *The "Exhortacion" from Disce mori: Edited from Oxford, Jesus College, MS 39* (Heidelberg, Germany: Universitätsverlag Winter, 2006), xxvi–xxvii.

9. On folio 18v lower margin, left-hand corner: a drawing of what looks like a purse or jug, with letters (four minims) written inside it. On folio 35r right-hand margin: vague drawings or pen trials. On folio 37v lower margin: a drawing of two parallel horizontal lines connected by four lines curving inward to the center (two from the left, two from the right). On folio 80v lower margin: scribble (unintended?).

10. See A. G. Dickens, *Reformation Studies* (London: Hambledon Press, 1982), 176ff.

11. Bazire and Colledge, *Chastising*, 95, l. 1.

12. Ibid., 8; Catherine Innes-Parker, "The Legacy of *Ancrene Wisse*: Translations, Adaptations, Influences and Audience, with Special Attention to Women Readers," in *A Companion to Ancrene Wisse*, ed. Yoko Wada (Cambridge: D.S. Brewer, 2003), 164.

13. Bazire and Colledge, *Chastising*, 4.

14. Ibid., 95. Contemporary modifications in this manuscript appropriated the text to a male audience (7–8).

15. Ibid., 95.

16. Ibid., 41.

17. Hf also contains a manuscript that consists of the pseudo-Bonaventuran *Meditatio vitae Christi* on folios 1r–93r and Bonaventura's *Vita et miracula*

Francisci (*legenda maior*) on folios 93v–140v; R. A. B. Mynors and R. Thomson, *Catalogue of the Manuscripts of Hereford Cathedral Library* (Cambridge, UK: D.S. Brewer, 1993), 69. In the following, reference to Hf pertains to the second manuscript bound into Hf (fols. 141r–153r).

18. In the Christie's sales catalogue, Emilio Donadoni first posited a link between D and Hf on the basis of the shared presence of a "Treatise on Love" (which is actually an excerpt from the *Stimulus*); Emilio Donadoni, "The Chastysing of Godde's Children," *Valuable Manuscripts and Printed Books: Sale 1550; 21 May 2014* (London: Christie's, 2014).

19. Ogilvie-Thomson gives the following variant for "enclosed" in MS Pepys 2125: "holdeþ þe holy and hyʒe and þat passyng oþer and preyseþ þe and wurshepiþ þe þerof"; Richard Rolle, *Richard Rolle: Prose and Verse*, ed. S. J. Ogilvie-Thomson, EETS (o.s.) 293 (Oxford: Oxford University Press, 1988), 111, l. 461.

20. For more information on Margaret Kirkby, see Hope Emily Allen, ed. *English Writings of Richard Rolle, Hermit of Hampole* (Oxford: Oxford University Press, 1963), 82–83.

21. Saint Bonaventura, *S.R.E. Cardinalis S. Bonaventurae ex ordine minorum episcopi Albanensis, eximii ecclesiae doctoris, opera omnia*, vol. 12, ed. by Adolphe Charles Peltier (Paris: Vivès, 1868).

22. This is an expansion of the list containing the manuscript's source texts written by Vincent Gillespie and Ralph Hanna and kindly made accessible to Rohrhofer and Cré, who have made additions.

23. Robert E. Lewis, Norman Francis Blake, and A. S. G. Edwards, *Index of Printed Middle English Prose* (New York: Garland, 1985).

24. P. S. Jolliffe, *A Check-List of Middle English Prose Writings of Spiritual Guidance* (Toronto: Pontifical Institute of Medieval Studies, 1974).

25. Carl Horstmann, *Yorkshire Writers: Richard Rolle of Hampole: An English Father of the Church and His Followers*, vol. 2 (London: Sonnenschein, 1895–1896).

26. In addition to D and Hf, *IX Poyntes* occurs in London, British Library, MS Harley 1706 (henceforth Har; the text printed in Horstmann) and in Cambridge, Trinity College, MS B.15.39 (henceforth Tr): see Jolliffe, *Check-List*, 111. For references to other texts using the nine-points scheme, see Valerie Edden, *Index of Middle English Prose. Handlist XV: Manuscripts in Midland Libraries* (Cambridge, UK: D.S. Brewer, 2000), 27.

27. See note 21.

28. Following a hint from Vincent Gillespie, Ralph Hanna, and Michael Sargent, Rohrhofer identified this passage in D as a translation from the *Stimulus amoris*.

29. Rolle, *Prose and Verse*.
30. The authors are grateful to Vincent Gillespie and Ralph Hanna for this information.
31. As the present essay defines itself as an introduction to D, Rohrhofer plans to publish in-depth results of the literary analysis in the future.
32. For discussions on miscellanies and anthologies, see, e.g., Julia Boffey and John S. Thompson, "Anthologies and Miscellanies: Production and Choice of Texts," in *Book Production and Publishing in Britain 1375–1475*, ed. Jeremy Griffiths and Derek Pearsall (Cambridge, UK: Cambridge University Press, 1989), 279–316; Stephen G. Nichols and Siegfried Wenzel, eds., *The Whole Book: Cultural Perspectives on the Medieval Miscellany* (Ann Arbor: University of Michigan Press, 1996).
33. See Julia Boffey, "Short Texts in Manuscript Anthologies: The Minor Poems of John Lydgate in Two Fifteenth-Century Collections," in *The Whole Book: Cultural Perspectives on the Medieval Miscellany*, ed. Stephen G. Nichols and Siegfried Wenzel (Ann Arbor: University of Michigan Press, 1999), 73–74; see also the other essays in the same volume; Boffey and Thompson, "Anthologies and Miscellanies," 279–316.
34. See, e.g., Elizabeth Dutton, *Julian of Norwich: The Influence of Late-Medieval Devotional Compilations* (Cambridge, UK: D. S. Brewer, 2008), 3.
35. Angus McIntosh, Michael Benskin, and M. L. Samuels, *A Linguistic Atlas of Late Medieval English: County Dictionary*, vol. 4 (Aberdeen, Scotland: Aberdeen University Press, 1986), 250.
36. Mynors and Thomson, *Catalogue of the Manuscripts*, 69; Edden, *Index of Middle English Prose*, 28; Ralph Hanna, *The English Manuscripts of Richard Rolle: A Descriptive Catalogue*, Exeter Medieval Texts and Studies (Exeter, UK: Exeter University Press, 2010), 66.
37. Hope Emily Allen, *Writings Ascribed to Richard Rolle, Hermit of Hampole, and Materials for His Biography* (New York and London: D. C. Heath and Oxford University Press, 1927), 261.
38. Ibid., 261. See also Edden, *Index of Middle English Prose*, 28; Hanna, *English Manuscripts*, 66; Mynors and Thomson, *Catalogue of the Manuscripts*, 69; Siegfried Wenzel, *Latin Sermon Collections from Later Medieval England* (Cambridge, UK: Cambridge University Press, 2005), 131.
39. The *Stimulus amoris* circulated in several versions, and the *Stimulus amoris minor*, the Latin urtext composed by the Franciscan James of Milan at the end of the thirteenth century, received considerable expansion, forming the *Stimulus amoris maior I and II*, in Eisermann's terminology: Falk Eisermann, *Stimulus amoris: Inhalt, lateinische Überlieferung, deutsche Übersetzung, Rezeption* (Tübingen, Germany: Max Niemeyer Verlag, 2001), 4–5. Michael Sargent counts 130 manuscripts of the

Stimulus amoris maior, ninety containing the *Stimulus amoris minor*, and a further 150 codices incorporating fragments, in Michael Sargent, "Bonaventura English: A Survey of the Middle English Prose Translations of Early Franciscan Literature," in *Spätmittelalterliche geistliche Literatur in der Nationalsprache*, vol. 2, *Analecta Cartusiana* 106, ed. James Hogg (Salzburg, Austria: Institut für Anglistik und Amerikanistik, 1983–1984), 159. Eisermann increases the number of complete and fragmentary *Stimulus* witnesses to five hundred, of which thirty were circulating in England. The work's reception history in England included its circulation in Latin versions, Walter Hilton's translation into the vernacular, and its incorporation into new contexts; Eisermann, *Stimulus amoris*, 227–229, 521.

40. See Appendix B.
41. Ralph Hanna dates this part of Harley 1706 to the second half of the fifteenth century; Hanna, *English Manuscripts*, 98.
42. James dates Tr to the early fifteenth century; M. R. James, *The Western Manuscripts in the Library of Trinity College, Cambridge: A Descriptive Catalogue*, vol. 1 (Cambridge, UK: Cambridge University Press, 1900), 233.
43. Line numbers in D refer to the transcription in Appendix A.
44. The fact that Tr and Har contain full copies of *IX Poyntes* is not part of the argument on lineage, because the date when D lost its first pages remains elusive.
45. Mynors and Thomson, *Catalogue of the Manuscripts*, 69, attribute this Latin ascription to the hand of John Foxholes OFM, archbishop of Armagh in the first half of the 1470s, who is referenced on 154r.
46. Hanna, *English Manuscripts*, 67–68; see also Wenzel, *Latin Sermon Collections*, 125–131; and Richard Sharpe, *A Handlist of the Latin Writers of Great Britain and Ireland before 1540* (Turnhout, Belgium: Brepols, 1997), 165.
47. Wenzel, *Latin Sermon Collections*, 125.
48. Ibid., 131.
49. Hanna, *English Manuscripts*, 66.
50. See note 17.
51. See Vincent Gillespie, "'Lukynge in haly bukes': Lectio in Some Late Medieval Miscellanies," in *Looking in Holy Books: Essays on Late Medieval Religious Writing in England*, Brepols Collected Essays in European Culture 3 (Turnhout, Belgium: Brepols, 2011), 136; Ralph Hanna, "Miscellaneity and Vernacularity: Conditions of Literary Production in Late Medieval England," in *The Whole Book: Cultural Perspectives on the Medieval Miscellany*, ed. Stephen G. Nichols and Siegfried Wenzel (Ann Arbor: University of Michigan Press, 1999), 37; Marleen Cré,

Vernacular Mysticism in the Charterhouse: A Study of London, British Library, MS Additional 37790, Medieval Translator 9 (Turnhout, Belgium: Brepols, 2006), 20.

52. Eisermann, *Stimulus amoris*, 236–238; see also Ian Doyle, "A Survey of the Origins and Circulation of Theological Writings in English in the Fourteenth and Fifteenth Centuries" (PhD thesis, Cambridge University, 1954), 207; Claire Kirchberger, ed. *Introduction to* The Goad of Love, *attributed to Walter Hilton* (London: Faber and Faber, 1952), 13–46.

53. See the variant readings Ogilvie-Thomson provides for ll. 329–484; Rolle, *Prose and Verse*, 104–113. Rolle builds on Hugh of Strasbourg's *Compendium theologicae veritatis* in this section; see Allen, *Writings Ascribed*, 265; and Claire Elizabeth McIlroy, *The English Prose Treatises of Richard Rolle*, Studies in Medieval Mysticism (Cambridge, UK: D.S. Brewer, 2004), 142.

54. See Annie Sutherland, "*The Chastising of God's Children*: A Neglected Text," in *Text and Controversy from Wyclif to Bale: Essays in Honour of Anne Hudson*, ed. Helen Barr and Ann M. Hutchison, Medieval Church Studies 4 (Turnhout, Belgium: Brepols, 2005), 353–373, at 354–358.

55. On *The Chastising* as a devotional compilation and contemplative text, see Rosalynn Voaden, "Rewriting the Letter: Variations in the Middle English Translation of the *Epistola solitarii ad reges* of Alphonso of Jaén," in *The Translation of the Works of Saint Birgitta of Sweden into the Medieval European Vernaculars*, ed. Bridget Morris and Veronica O'Mara, The Medieval Translator 7 (Turnhout, Belgium: Brepols, 2000), 170–185; see also Marleen Cré, "'We Are United with God (and God with Us?)': Adapting Ruusbroec in *The Treatise of Perfection of the Sons of God* and *The Chastising of God's Children*," in *The Medieval Mystical Tradition in England VII*, ed. E. A. Jones (Cambridge: Brewer, 2004), 21–36; and Marleen Cré, "Take a Walk on the Safe Side: Reading the Fragments from Ruusbroec's *Die geestelike brulocht* in *The Chastising of God's Children*," in *De letter levend maken: Opstellen aangeboden aan Guido de Baere bij zijn zeventigste verjaardag*, ed. Frans Hendrickx, and Kees Schepers, Miscellanea Neerlandica 39 (Leuven, Belgium: Peeters, 2010), 233–246. Also see Marleen Cré, "'Ʒe han desired to knowe in comfort of ʒoure soule': Female Agency in *The Chastising of God's Children*," *Journal of Medieval Religious Cultures* 42.2 (2016):164–180; and Marleen Cré, "Spiritual Comfort and Reasonable Feeling: Annotating *The Chastising of God's Children* in Oxford, Bodleian Library, MS Rawlinson C 57," in *Emotion and Medieval Textual Media*, ed. Mary C. Flannery (Turnhout, Belgium: Brepols, forthcoming).

56. On the manuscripts of *Disce mori* and *Ignorancia sacerdotum*, see Jones, "Exhortacion," xv–xxiii. For a list of the chapters from *The Chastising* that occur in *Disce mori*, see ibid., xl.

57. As pointed out above, P addresses the text to a "dere f(r)end" (over an erasure; see the variants listed in footnote in Bazire-Colledge, p. 95), and Bazire and Colledge point out that the work of the corrector of P "consists not so much of textual improvements and emendations as of manipulations of the text to make it appropriate for reading in a house of male religious"; Bazire and Colledge, *Chastising*, 7–8.

58. Ibid., 36; and Sutherland, "*Chastising*," 356–357.

59. These variants are listed in Sargent, "New Manuscript."

60. Cré follows Michael Sargent in the naming of the correctors, deviating from Bazire and Colledge's practice of referring to them using Greek letters. See Sargent, "New Manuscript," 62, n. 49.

61. Abbreviations have been silently expanded, and all italics in the analysis of the variants listed below are Cré's. For the groups of manuscripts that Bazire and Colledge distinguish, see Bazire and Colledge, *Chastising*, 32.

62. The text in Add starts halfway through ch. 4, at Bazire-Colledge 110/17.

63. Cré, "ʒe han desired to knowe.'"

64. The AddDJPW sources have "yn to mynystracion" instead of the erroneous "into my mynistracion" (Bazire-Colledge 197/15)—caused by repetition of the initial letters of "mynistracion"—found in the other manuscripts. They also read "and accusith *his* riʒthwisnes," an abbreviation of the longer "accusiþ þe riʒtwisnesse *of god*" (199/13). Yet D agrees with all manuscripts against AddBJPW when it has "and aboue al *vertwis* werkis" (cf. 139/16) rather than "aboue all *uertus* werkis."

65. DJP against Add: in alle þyng *mot* be fulfilled (cf. Bazire-Colledge 112/17: in al þinge *euer mote* be fulfilled; Add has "myght"); DJP: þat *blissidful* ladi fond grace aʒenst pride (cf. 137/9: þat *blissful* ladi fonde grace aʒens pride); ADHLRTW against AddJP: also *y* trowe not ʒe desire as for ʒowre self (cf. 152/19: also *I suppose* ʒe desiren it nat as for ʒoureself; Add omits "I suppose"); DJP against Add: *þat* we leue owre goude wurchyng (cf. 157/7–8: *þat if* we leeue oure goode worchyng; Add omits "þat if"); DEJeLa: erroneous "a priuat *a* temperal ioye" against AddJPW: a *priue* temperal ioye (cf. 183/17–18: a *priuat* temperal ioie); DJP against Add: for as saith seynt augstyn þere ech synne is not wilful is no synne. but þan it be wilful þat is to saye no deidly synne (cf. 201/19–21: for as seiþ seint austyn, þat eche synne þat is nat wilful is no dedeli synne; there is eyeskip here in Add, which omits "is no dedeli synne. But al be it suche temptacions bien no synne þat bien nat wilful"). That this was a difficult sentence with which many scribes had problems can be seen in the many variant readings (cf. Bazire-Colledge 201, n. 20).

66. All these instances are recorded in Bazire and Colledge, *Chastising*. D agrees with the majority of manuscripts whenever they disagree with the BHeJeLa group and whenever they disagree with a unique reading in another manuscript or W, unless listed in the variants in this essay.

67. The only variant reading that is not the omission or substitution of an article, demonstrative or possessive, is the following: AddDHaJPW: þat is trauelid with eny *spice* of pride (cf. Bazire-Colledge 207/4–5: þat is trauelid with ony *spirit* of pride). The AddDHaJPW sources have the more common reading here, but when "spirit of pride" means "the urge to pride" (see *Middle English Dictionary*, s.v. spirit (n.), meaning 4c(b)), the text also makes sense.

68. The differences are of the same kind as the ones discussed earlier between AddDJP and the other manuscripts: omissions and additions of single words, use of synonymous words, and small grammatical changes such as the use of singular or plural forms of nouns and pronouns and the use of different verb forms. On the significance of the uniform transmission of texts, see Daniel Wakelin, *Scribal Correction and Literary Craft: English Manuscripts 1375–1510* (Cambridge, UK: Cambridge University Press, 2014), 3–10 and 43–53.

69. The phrase "the secwnde sekt of contrarios leuyng" (cf. Bazire-Colledge 134/10) is the one instance in which the word returns. The other three chapters simply speak of people who live contrary to virtuous living: "which lyue contrariousli to all maner vertwis" (cf. 130/11); "he leuyth yn al maner contrariete to haue þe loue of god" (cf. 138/17); "Oþir men þer be of contrarious leuyng" (cf. 142/14).

70. Bazire and Colledge choose B on the basis of its superior readings—of which they give three examples (Bazire and Colledge, 33)—and because it is a copy "for which it can be justly claimed that it is physically perfect, whereas other good and careful manuscripts, such as A, Add and J are not"; ibid., 33. Thus, rather than editing T as corrected by corrector Tc on the basis of He, they choose to "present readers with the most nearly perfect manuscript, and to emend that where emendation seemed necessary and warrantable"; ibid., 34. Bazire and Colledge do not always emend the B reading when it disagrees with all other manuscripts, probably because they do not consider the variations significant enough.

71. Wakelin, *Scribal Correction*, 78–81. Also see Michael G. Sargent, *James Grenehalgh as Textual Critic*, Analecta Cartusiana 85.1–2 (Salzburg, Austria: Institut für Anglistik und Amerikanistik, 1984).

72. Of these twenty-five, the following are the most significant: ADJeLaPR: *Now we schul knowe* þe presence of owre lorde ihesu (cf. Bazire-Colledge 105/5: *How mowen we haue* þe presence of oure lord iesu crist); DPRW: whan þere *was but litil eny congregacioun of* monkis (cf. 162/15: whanne

þer *were but fewe* monkes); DLPRT: to *vexe* hem soor (cf. 163/15: to *trauele* hem soore); DHLPRTW: bot be *stereyng* of anoþer (cf. 164/14: but be *strengþe* of anoþer); DHLPRTW: for brekyng of behest of *deedli* thyng (cf. 89/12: for brekyng of biheeste of *an erþli* þing).

73. A direct link between two *Chastising* manuscript is lateral, as T and He were corrected against each other. All corrections by Tc derive from He, and He has indeed been corrected against a manuscript from the LRT group. Hec also left corrective notes in T. See Sargent, "New Manuscript," 59.

74. Indeed, in this passage, the opening of chapter 26, D shares readings with all other manuscripts against P, which has clearly erroneous readings:

D: þat þat is leifful (P: "vnleful," with "vn" erased) (cf. Bazire-
    Colledge 214/19)
D: þat þat is leifful (P: "vnlieful") (cf. 214/22)
D: þynges þat beþ leifful (P: "vnlieful") (cf. 215/2)

It is a *meydful* riwle in general ordir of louyng to a man or woman which hath do vnleiffulli: þat he refrayne hym self / from þat / þat is *leifful* ❡ In þis refreynyng we most holde twe þyngis / þat is to seie: þe maner of satisfaccion / and þe neyd of purgacion ❡ þe maner of satisfaccion is : þat after þe trespas refreynyng of þat þat is *leifful* / be mesurid be auctorite of holy churche / þat aftir þe wordis of seynt John: we mowe do worthi fruytis of penawnce / bot þis maner of satisfaccion longith to hym to knowe þat hath cure of saule / as it is write yn holi chirche lawe / to ʒow it nedith nat to knowe þer fore y passe ouyr of satisfaccion. ❡ Bot now to schewe ʒow of þe nyed of purgacion of þe saule: ʒe schul vndirstonde þat it is onli *meydful* to re-freyne fram þynges þat beþ *leifful* for satisfaccion bot also to vse afflic-cions or trauayl in gostli werkyng owtward to put a wai possessions or make hem lasse which we haue yn custom / for y trowe eche man and woman hath som traueyl with oo þyng more þan with an oþir/ and þat traueyl we clepe a passyon. (D, fols. 95v–96r)

cf. Bazire-Colledge 214/17–215/7:
It is a *nedeful* rule in general ordre of livyng to a man or womman which haþ do vnlieffuli, þat he refreyne hymself for þat whiche is *leeful*. In this refreyneng we musten holde twei þinges: þat is to seie, þe maner of satisfaccion, and nede of purgacion. The maner of sat-isfaccion is þat aftir the trespas, þe refreyneng of þat þat is *leeful* be

mesured bi auctorite of holi chirche, þat aftir þe wordis of seint joon, we mowe do worþi fruytes of penaunce; but þis maner of satisfaccion longiþ to hym to knowe þat haþ cure of soule, as it is writen in holi chirche lawe. To ȝou it nediþ nat to knowe: þerfor I passe ouer of satisfaccion. But now to shewe ȝou of þe nede of purgacion of þe soule: ȝe shul vndirstonde þat it is nat oonli *nedeful* to refreyne of þinges þat bien *lieful* for satisfaccion, but also to use affliccions or trauaile in goostli werkyng outward to put awei passions, or make hem lasse, which we han in custom; for I trowe eche man and womman haþ sum trauaile wiþ oon þing more þan anoþer, and þat trauel we clepen a passion.

75. The two most obviously nonsensical errors are D: to his *costly* fadre (cf. Bazire-Colledge 111/8: to his *goostli* fadir); and D: to mennys *cwoieng* (cf. 119/15: to mennys *knowynge*). In two instances, the scribe ends copying in mid-word: D: aȝens such *tempta* (cf. 151/15–16: aȝens suche *temptacions*); and D: þe *chasti* þat he sufferith (cf. 199/6–7: þe *chastisynge* þat he suffriþ).

76. On scribes' making and thinking, see Wakelin, *Scribal Correction*, 3–10.

77. Some examples should suffice: D: I haue rehersid schortli here (cf. Bazire-Colledge 99/15: I haue rehersid heere schortli); D: þat fulli he is beclupid (cf. 102/21: þat he is fulli beclipped); D: yn his blisse be his merci (cf. 148/22: bi his merci in his blisse); D: cownseile and cownfort oþir (cf. 150/11: counceil oþer and comforten); D: god hath ȝif me and put in me (cf. 155/3–4: god haþ put in me and ȝoue me); D: al ordynaunce and obseruawnce (cf. 192/11–12: alle þe obseruaunces and ordenauncis); D: myekli to suffre with wte eny gruchchyng (cf. 199/14–15: mekeli wiþout grucchynge to suffre); D: remedies aȝenst dredful goostli temptacions (cf. 205/12–13: remedies aȝens goostli dredful temptacions).

78. Folio 38v, left-hand margin, bracketed, in red: "of þe dro/pesie" next to "wexe seke for colde þanne þai falle yn to þe dropsie" (cf. Bazire-Colledge 125/16–17).

79. Folio 39v, left-hand margin, cropped, bracketed, in red: "[þis i]s þe coti/[di]ane fe/[u]yr" next to "This is a cotidian fyuere" (cf. Bazire-Colledge 126/20), and "[?] þe feuyr / [ter]cian þat co/[my]th of an /[h]ete" next to "þe secunde feuyr is clepid a tercia" (cf. 127/3); fol. 40v, left-hand margin, cropped, bracketed, in red: "[?] þe tercian / [fy]euer þat is / [ca]wsid of colde" next to "þe secunde fieuer of vnstabilnes is cawsid of colde" (cf. 128/12); fol. 41r, right-hand margin, cropped, bracketed, in red: "Of þe quar[t]/yn fyeu[er]" next to "In some men þe quarteyn fyeuyr is cawsid of þis vnstabilnesse" (cf. 129/10–11).

80. Folio 89r, right-hand margin, cropped, in red: "Pri[de]" next to "aȝenst

Pride" (cf. Bazire-Colledge 206/12); folio 89v, left-hand margin, cropped, in red: "[C]oueytise" next to "Aʒenst coueytise" (cf. 207/11); folio 90v, left-hand margin, cropped, in red: "[W]rathe" next to "Aʒenst wrathe" (cf. 208/20); folio 91r, right-hand margin, cropped, in red: "Enuy[e]" next to "Aʒenst enuye" (cf. 209/10); folio 92r, right-hand margin, cropped, in red: "Slewt[h]" next to "Aʒenst slewth" (cf. 210/12); folio 93r, right-hand margin, cropped, in red: "Gloteny[e]" next to "Aʒenst glotonye" (cf. 211/15); folio 93v, left-hand margin, in red: "Lecherie" next to "Aʒenst lecherie" (cf. 212/11).

81. Folio 70v, left-hand margin: "helyseus" next to "helyseus" (cf. Bazire-Colledge 169/16) and "balthasar" next to "balthasar" (cf. 169/17–18).

82. Folio 50v: contra superbiam; folio 51r: contra auariciam; folio 52r: contra iram; folio 52v: contra inuidiam; folio 53r: contra accidiam; folio 53v: contra gulam; folio 54r: contra luxuriam.

83. This often seems to have been the case. In Wakelin's survey of the corrections in manuscripts from the Huntington Library, "the overall results show a clear tendency for correcting to be done by the people who do the copying itself." Wakelin, *Scribal Correction*, 72ff.

84. Folio 10r: marginal correction "wych" to be inserted instead of the crossed-out words in "takyng away any mannys name or fame ʒif ʒe spekyng oþer"; folio 18r: marginal correction "þe tym" and caret (at *) in the text in "in to * þat hit pleise god for his grete pite to cownfort hym be grace"; folio 68r: marginal correction "many," and caret (at *) in the text in "Of þis we mowe se ful * of ensawmplis" (cf. Bazire-Colledge 166/9–10); folio 72r: interlinear correction "man and woman" in "euery * scholde mekeli drede visions" (cf. 182/11–12); folio 90r: marginal addition "X ihu" and caret (at *) in the text in "for eiþer he wil ordeyne for hem þat * neydith (cf. 208/3–4); folio 99r: marginal correction "ʒe" and caret (at *) in the text in "þat * falle not yn to temptacion" (cf. 219/18–19).

85. Next to the chapter opening, another hand has erroneously written "ca xij."

86. See Sutherland, "*Chastising*," 355–357.

WORKS CITED

Manuscripts

Cambridge, Magdalene College, MS Pepys 2125.
Cambridge, St. John's College, MS E.25.
Cambridge, Trinity College, MS B.14.19.
Cambridge, Trinity College, MS B.15.39.
Hereford, Cathedral Library, MS P. I. 9.
Liverpool, University Library, MS F.40.10.

London, British Library, MS Additional 33971.
London, British Library, MS Harley 1706.
London, British Library, MS Harley 2218.
London, British Library, MS Harley 6615.
Oxford, Bodleian Library, MS Ashmole 41.
Oxford, Bodleian Library, MS Bodley 505.
Oxford, Bodleian Library, MS Bodley 923.
Oxford, Bodleian Library, MS Don. e. 247.
Oxford, Bodleian Library, MS Eng. th. c. 57.
Oxford, Bodleian Library, MS Laud. Misc. 99.
Oxford, Bodleian Library, MS Rawlinson C57.
Oxford, Jesus College, MS 39.
Wynkyn de Worde's printed edition of *The Chastising of God's Children.*
Yale, Beinecke Library, MS Osborn fa46 (olim Taunton, Somerset Record Office, MS Heneage 3084).

Primary Texts

Bazire, Joyce, and Eric Colledge, eds. *The Chastising of God's Children and The Treatise of Perfection of the Sons of God.* Oxford: Basil Blackwell, 1957.

Saint Bonaventura. *S.R.E. Cardinalis S. Bonaventurae ex ordine minorum episcopi Albanensis, eximii ecclesiae doctoris, opera omnia.* Vol. 12, ed. Adolphe Charles Peltier. Paris: Vivès, 1868.

Horstmann, Carl. *Yorkshire Writers: Richard Rolle of Hampole, an English Father of the Church, and His Followers.* Vol. 2. London: Sonnenschein, 1895–1896.

Rolle, Richard. *Richard Rolle: Prose and Verse,* ed. S. J. Ogilvie-Thomson. EETS 293. Oxford: Oxford University Press, 1988.

Secondary Texts

Allen, Hope Emily, ed. *English Writings of Richard Rolle, Hermit of Hampole,* Oxford: Oxford University Press, 1963.

———. *Writings Ascribed to Richard Rolle, Hermit of Hampole, and Materials for His Biography.* New York and London: D.C. Heath and Oxford University Press, 1927.

Bazire, Joyce. "The Dialects of the Manuscripts of *The Chastising of God's Children."* *English and Germanic Studies* 6 (1957): 64–78.

Boffey, Julia. "Short Texts in Manuscript Anthologies: The Minor Poems of John Lydgate in Two Fifteenth-Century Collections." In *The Whole Book: Cultural Perspectives on the Medieval Miscellany,* ed. Stephen G. Nichols and Siegfried Wenzel, 69–82. Ann Arbor: University of Michigan Press, 1999.

——— and John S. Thompson. "Anthologies and Miscellanies: Production and Choice of Texts." In *Book Production and Publishing in Britain 1375–1475*, ed. Jeremy Griffiths and Derek Pearsall, 279–316. Cambridge, UK: Cambridge University Press, 1989.

Cré, Marleen. "Spiritual Comfort and Reasonable Feeling: Annotating *The Chastising of God's Children* in Oxford, Bodleian Library, MS Rawlinson C 57." In *Emotion and Medieval Textual Media*, ed. Mary C. Flannery. Turnhout, Belgium: Brepols, forthcoming.

———. "'3e han desired to knowe in comfort of 3oure soule': Female Agency in *The Chastising of God's Children." Journal of Medieval Religious Cultures* 42.2 (2016):164–180.

———. "Take a Walk on the Safe Side: Reading the Fragments from Ruusbroec's *Die geestelike brulocht in The Chastising of God's Children."* In *De letter levend maken: Opstellen aangeboden aan Guido de Baere bij zijn zeventigste verjaardag*, ed. Frans Hendrickx and Kees Schepers, 233–246. Miscellanea Neerlandica 39. Leuven, Belgium: Peeters, 2010.

———. *Vernacular Mysticism in the Charterhouse: A Study of London, British Library, MS Additional 37790*. Medieval Translator 9. Turnhout, Belgium: Brepols, 2006.

———. "'We Are United with God (and God with Us?)': Adapting Ruusbroec in *The Treatise of Perfection of the Sons of God and The Chastising of God's Children." In The Medieval Mystical Tradition in England VII*, ed. E. A. Jones, 21–36. Cambridge, UK: Brewer, 2004.

Dickens, A. G. *Reformation Studies*. London: Hambledon Press, 1982.

Donadoni, Emilio. "The Chastysing of Godde's Children." In *Valuable Manuscripts and Printed Books: Sale 1550; 21 May 2014*. London: Christie's, 2014.

Doyle, Ian. "A Survey of the Origins and Circulation of Theological Writings in English in the Fourteenth and Fifteenth Centuries." PhD thesis, Cambridge University, 1954.

Dutton, Elizabeth. *Julian of Norwich: The Influence of Late-Medieval Devotional Compilations*. Cambridge, UK: D.S. Brewer, 2008.

Edden, Valerie. *Index of Middle English Prose. Handlist XV: Manuscripts in Midland Libraries*. Cambridge, UK: D.S. Brewer, 2000.

Eisermann, Falk. *Stimulus amoris: Inhalt, lateinische Überlieferung, deutsche Übersetzung, Rezeption*. Tübingen, Germany: Max Niemeyer Verlag, 2001.

Gillespie, Vincent. "'Lukynge in haly bukes': Lectio in Some Late Medieval Miscellanies." In *Looking in Holy Books: Essays on Late Medieval Religious Writing in England*. Brepols Collected Essays in European Culture 3. Turnhout, Belgium: Brepols, 2011. 113–144.

Hanna, Ralph. *The English Manuscripts of Richard Rolle: A Descriptive*

Catalogue. Exeter Medieval Texts and Studies. Exeter, UK: Exeter University Press, 2010.

————. "Miscellaneity and Vernacularity: Conditions of Literary Production in Late Medieval England." In *The Whole Book: Cultural Perspectives on the Medieval Miscellany*, ed. Stephen G. Nichols and Siegfried Wenzel, 37–52. Ann Arbor: University of Michigan Press, 1999.

Innes-Parker, Catherine. "The Legacy of *Ancrene Wisse*: Translations, Adaptations, Influences and Audience, with Special Attention to Women Readers." In *A Companion to* Ancrene Wisse, ed. Yoko Wada, 145–173. Cambridge, UK: D.S. Brewer, 2003.

James, M. R. *The Western Manuscripts in the Library of Trinity College, Cambridge: A Descriptive Catalogue*. Vol. 1. Cambridge, UK: Cambridge University Press, 1900.

Jolliffe, P. S. *A Check-List of Middle English Prose Writings of Spiritual Guidance*. Toronto: Pontifical Institute of Medieval Studies, 1974.

Jones, E. A., ed. *The "Exhortacion" from* Disce mori: *Edited from Oxford, Jesus College, MS 39*. Heidelberg, Germany: Universitätsverlag Winter, 2006.

Kirchberger, Claire, ed. *Introduction to* The Goad of Love, *attributed to Walter Hilton*. London: Faber and Faber, 1952.

Lewis, Robert E., Norman Francis Blake, and A. S. G. Edwards. *Index of Printed Middle English Prose*. New York: Garland, 1985.

McIlroy, Claire Elizabeth. *The English Prose Treatises of Richard Rolle*. Studies in Medieval Mysticism. Cambridge, UK: D.S. Brewer, 2004.

McIntosh, Angus, Michael Benskin, and M. L. Samuels. *A Linguistic Atlas of Late Medieval English: County Dictionary*. Vol. 4. Aberdeen, Scotland: Aberdeen University Press, 1986.

Mynors, R. A. B., and R. Thomson. *Catalogue of the Manuscripts of Hereford Cathedral Library*. Cambridge, UK: D.S. Brewer, 1993.

Nichols, Stephen G., and Siegfried Wenzel, eds. *The Whole Book: Cultural Perspectives on the Medieval Miscellany*. Ann Arbor: University of Michigan Press, 1996.

Sargent, Michael G. "Bishops, Patrons, Mystics and Manuscripts: Walter Hilton, Nicholas Love and the Arundel and Holland Connections." *In Middle English Texts in Transition: A Festschrift Dedicated to Toshiyuki Takamiya on his 70th Birthday*, ed. Simon Horobin and Linne Mooney, 159–177. York, UK: York Medieval Press, 2014.

————. *James Grenehalgh as Textual Critic. Analecta Cartusiana* 85.1–2 (Salzburg, Austria: Institut für Anglistik und Amerikanistik, 1984).

————. "Bonaventura English: A Survey of the Middle English Prose Translations of Early Franciscan Literature." In *Spätmittelalterliche geistliche Literatur in der Nationalsprache*. Vol 2. *Analecta Cartusiana*

106, ed. James Hogg, 145–176. Salzburg, Austria: Institut für Anglistik und Amerikanistik, 1983–1984.

———. "A New Manuscript of *The Chastising of God's Children* with an Ascription to Walter Hilton." *Medium Aevum* 46 (1977):49–65.

Sharpe, Richard. *A Handlist of the Latin Writers of Great Britain and Ireland before 1540*. Turnhout, Belgium: Brepols, 1997.

Sutherland, Annie. "*The Chastising of God's Children*: A Neglected Text." In *Text and Controversy from Wyclif to Bale: Essays in Honour of Anne Hudson*, ed. Helen Barr and Ann M. Hutchison, 353–373. Medieval Church Studies 4. Turnhout, Belgium: Brepols, 2005.

Voaden, Rosalynn. "Rewriting the Letter: Variations in the Middle English Translation of the *Epistolasolitarii ad reges* of Alphonso of Jaén." In *The Translation of the Works of Saint Birgitta of Sweden into the Medieval European Vernaculars*, ed. Bridget Morris and Veronica O'Mara, 170–185. The Medieval Translator 7. Turnhout, Belgium: Brepols, 2000.

Wakelin, Daniel. *Scribal Correction and Literary Craft: English Manuscripts 1375–1510*. Cambridge, UK: Cambridge University Press, 2014.

Wenzel, Siegfried. *Latin Sermon Collections from Later Medieval England*. Cambridge, UK: Cambridge University Press, 2005.

APPENDIX A:

Transcription of the First Booklet of Oxford, Bodleian Library, MS Don. e. 247

Method of transcription: to replicate D's text as closely as possible, the original word division has been retained, which means that parts of compound words that have been written separately in the manuscript have not been joined in the transcription. Equally, forms that were written together have also been recorded as such.

D's scribe uses v in word-initial position in all but six cases, where he wrote u, and his spelling is reflected in the following pages. Abbreviations have been expanded in italics in accordance with the majority of unabbreviated forms, punctuation has been modernized to make the text more readable, and capitalization has been regularized to agree with the editorial decisions on punctuation.

Most of the incongruencies and omissions have not been corrected in the text, because the reader will be able to resolve these erroneous readings readily by referring to the variants in Appendix B. As a rule, notes are only used in cases where reference to the variants would not result in clarity, and editorial alterations to the text are marked with square brackets.

Only extant in four manuscripts, the *IX Poyntes* extract in D has been compared to London, British Library, MS Harley 1706 (Har, as printed in

Horstmann), Cambridge, Trinity College, MS B.15.39 (Tr), and Hereford, Cathedral Library, MS P. I. IX (Hf). From the start of the *Stimulus amoris* segment in line 25, the variants refer to Hf only. In the variants section (Appendix B), abbreviations have been expanded silently, and marginal additions have been identified with an asterisk.

[**fol. 1r**] [**extract *from IX Poyntes***] in thi li3t. ¶ For godisseruant scholde neuermore thenke, ne speke, ne do bote as he wolde in þe presence of his lorde. For certenli al þat þou spekest and dost god seye as ueralich as þou wer in his presence þer oure ladi sit in heue[n]. For godis loue take hede. 3if þou art aschamid for to do a
5 dedly synne be fore thyn euencristen, þe wich is frele and sinful as þou art *and* may no3t greue but þi bodi, moche more scholdest þou be agast to synne bi fore thi god þat neuere trespased and schal be þi domesman at þe dai of dome. ¶ The ix poynt is, in cas þat þou my3t come to þe parfeccion of þis poyntes, þat þou knowlech þat hit is a grete grace of godis goudnesse þat he wil woch saue to 3eue þe so muche grace of
10 parfeccion. Natheles oft be thenke þe of oþer many benfait3 of god how hath worschiped þi soule be enpreyntyng of his owene ymage, and how he hath taken thi kynde and suffred for thi loue despites deth, and how hath grauntes to be þi fode in þis lif and wil be þi ioie and thi blisse in an oþer lif.

And for encheison þat þou my3t [**fol. 1v**] now sen hem in his godhed whiles
15 þou art in þis worlde, oft þerfore beholde hym in his manhode hongyng for þe on the crois, and haue sorwe and conpassion hym, as þou haddest and suffredest alle his wondes and his paynes in þi bodi. *And* be inward sori þat þou mi3t not fele in þe be þe paynes þat he suffred for þe, synful wrecche. Þe thoghtes ofte haue in mynde and speciallich wanne he lieth on the auter atte masse, and say to hym in this manere:
20 'Lord ihesu crist, þou þat art bred of lif þat cometh out of heuene, so fede me and fulfille me *with* þe, so þat I haue non hongur after no thyng bot þe. And so make me drynke *with* þi bloude and of thi loue þat I be nou3t a þerst bot after þe. Lorde hold so faste my soule *and* my loue to þe þat for non oþere loue ne for synne ne be neuere departid fro me. Amen.'
25 [***Stimulus* extracts and additions**] For encheson þat loue may alle do *with* any mysdo, and loue is þe rote of parfeccion of alle vertues, and þe more þou hast of god loue, þe betre þou art, and þe more liche to god, and nere to blisse. For [**fol. 2r**] all þe mesure of goud loue schalle 3eue þe mesure of blisse in heuen, and þere fore þer is non bettre to man oþer woman þan for to studie how he may in god loue.
30 Certis wonderful is þe vertu of loue, for hit enclineth god to erthe and rereth[1] mannys saule to heuen, and god and þi saule knytteþ to gedre in ioie and *in* blisse. Loue makeþ man, for he maketh frende and þe seruant child. The abhominable he makeþ glorious and þe sori ioious. Þe colde he makeþ hoot, and þe derke he makiþ bri3th, and þe harde he makith nesche.
35 As witnesseth þe deuout saule in þe boke of loue spekyng to god in þis manere: An[y] saule meltiþ atte þe speche of hym þat I loue. O worde amable. O worde dilettable. I vnworthi wrecche þat am not worthi be clepid on of godes

creatures, bot how am y so muche loued of þe þat my hert meltith at þe speche of þe.
O brennyng of trewe loue, moche is þi miȝth. Ffor her to for myn herte was as drie and
40 as harde as [**fol. 2v**] ston. And now thorw þe uertu of my saule is multen in me. O
goud loue, what may I ȝeue the þat þou woldest euere more dwelle with me? Ffor
wondurful is þi uertu þat turnest me in to god and god in to me.

What is more myȝtti, or swettere, or gladdere, or noblere þan þou? Certis no
thyng. Þou bindest god to þe piler. Þou puttest þe croune of thorne vp on his hede.
45 Þou heng hym opon þe crois and nailedest hym þer to. Þou opinidest his blissed hert
with þe scharpe spere, out of þe wich com *water* and bloude in remission of mannys
trespas. Wasch wel thi saule *in* þat bathe, and þanne schalt þou haue *with* þe vertu of
brennyng loue.

O blissful loue, þou makest me morne, *and* loue lonynge *after* oure spouse
50 ihe*su* crist, and desire hym alone. O loue desirous þat fulfillest þe hongri of
soue*raigne* delites. For at a louelich worde of þe my saule is molt in me.
O þou swete saule, ȝif þou art milte at o swete worde of þi spouse, what likyng were
hit to þe ȝif he wolde klippe and kisse þe. Certes no tonge may telle, [**fol. 3r**] and þere
fore, ȝif þou wilt be pa*r*fite, lerne for þe quike to feer in thyn herte, and therfore thou
55 schalt vnderstonde þat a man þat is colde becomyth hoot in diuers maneris: be
clothyng of many clothis, be goyng to þe fier, be trauaillyng of body, hoot spices, and
strong drynke. So gostlich, ȝif þou wilt wer hoot in þe loue of god, do on many
clothes of vertu, for vertu is clothes to mannys saule. Ho so lakkeþ o vertu, his saule is
naked in o pa*r*tie, and þe*r* fore ȝif þou wilt be hoot, alle a boute clothe thi saule *with*
60 many vertues, so þat non lakke to þe. And sit ofte bi þe brennyng fier of loue þat crist
aqueked in his brennynge and betir passion, and thenke ofte on þe loue of god and
charite toward man, and of blyndnesse *and* þe malice of man toward god.

For ȝif hit is so þat godis sone wolde one[2] to hym mankynde *with*oute
depa*r*tyng, how muche more schulde oure saule one hym self to god, and euermore
65 cleue to hym *with*oute depa*r*tyng? Certes ȝif goddes sone wolde of so brennyng loue
one hym a sonys to mankynd, moche more schulde man [**fol. 3v**] open his hert for to
receyue hym to dwelle þere ynne. What wodnesse is in þat man þat makeþ hym
cloose his herte to god, and openeth hit to wrecchidnesse, likyng to þe deuille, to þe
worlde, and to þe flesch. For certis goddis sone toke noȝt mannis flesch for a man
70 scholde loue lykyng of his flesch, bot as he dwellyng and beyng in flesch punisched
and[3] painde his flesch, and left þe likynges of his flesch. And his saule was eu*er*
cleyuy*n*g to god be loue. So a man dwellyng *in* flesche scholde leue and destroie þe
likynges of his flesch and eu*er*e haue his saule to god bi loue and contemplacion.
¶ Allas muche his þe blyndnesse of man þat is made of bodi and saule. *And* þe
75 saule with oute compa*r*ison is bettre þanne þe bodie. Natheles, alle his tyme he
spendeþ aboute his likynges and thenges þat longeþ to þe bodi, and a boute his saule
hath he non besenesse for to fede hym, for to norische hym, ne for to resten hym in
god, þe wiche were more bettre *and* more delettable *with* outen compa*r*ison.
¶ Cer[**fol. 4r**]tes þey a saule were worse þanne a best, ȝit he scholde loue god

80 to whom he is liche, for eche thyng loueþ kendlich þat is liche to hym. And þere fore
my saule, ȝif þou wilt algate loue flesch, loue no flesch bot cristes flesch, þat for þe
and almankynde hangyd on tre and payned wiþoute mesure greuouslich. Here on
þenke continualli for þe meditacion of cristes passion rerith manys saule and his
mende to heuene, and techiþ what he schal do, and he schal þenke, and speke. And
85 forþermore hit schal quike þi saule þe more able to parfeccion and trauail and make
þe holde litel be þi self, and in thynkyng worchyng schal make þe parfit in þe loue
of.[4]

O passion desirous. O deth wonderful. What is more wonderful þan deth þat
quiketh, þan wondes þat helen, þan blod þat maketh whit and clenseth, þan sorwe þat
90 gladeþ? Þe openynge of his syde heuyth oure herte to his hert. Bot ȝit sese noȝt for to
wondre, for þe sonne wanne he was derke schyned more briȝth, þe fier aquaynt more
heteþ, þe well dried [**fol. 4v**] more welleth þe passion. And certes ouer wonderful hit
is þat crist in þe croce thurstyng made drynke, he naked cloþed vs with vertues, his
hondes nayled to þe tre vnbyndeþ oure hondes, his feet[5] nailid to þe croce makeþ vs
95 renne to hym. Be þe way of loue and goude werkes and out sendyng his saule, he
enspireth gostli lif in to oure soule.

O passion meruaillous þat makest hym þat thenkyþ oft on þe noȝt onlich euen
with angeles bot passe angeles to þe liknesse of almiȝtti god. Ffor he þat dwelleth in
meditacion be cristes turment and wondes takeþ non hede of hym self, bot his god
100 paynid for hym. He desireth [to] bere þe croce with his lorde, and in þat he berith
hym, he berith heuene and erthe. He desireth to be coronnyd with thornes as his lorde
was, and in þat he is coroned with hope of ioie endless. He desireth to hange naked on
þe croce with his lorde, and in þat he is clothed with clothyng of vertues. He wil with
crist drynke of his betir drinke, and crist hym drynkesse with soueraigne wyne of [**fol.
105 5r**] swetnesse. He wol be paynid with hym on þe croce, and in þat angeles hym
worschippith and oure ladi hym taketh as here owne sone. ¶ The sorwe of cristes in
man other woman torneth hym to gladnesse and þe payne to ese, and whanne a man
desireth to hange on þe croce with crist and suffre þat he suffred, criste hym takeþ,
kisseþ, and clippeth[6] as his owene brother and childe.

O passion amable and delectable. ¶ Allas, allas, whi naddy ben don on þe
110 croce with hym, and honde and foot nayled to hym? Þanne miȝt I haue deyd with hym
and be beried with hym, and neuere haue departid from hym. And þere fore certes ȝif
I ne may noȝt do þus bodelich, I will do thus gostlich and entre in to hym, and in hym
I wil me þre dwellynges. On is in hondes, on is in feet, þe þridde in hert. Þere I wil
115 reste, and slepe, and ete, and drinke, rede, and synge, and praye, and alle my nedes
tret and speke. Þere I schal speke with swete hert, and alle þat me nediþ y schal
purchace of hym alone. Þer may [**fol. 5v**] non enemy me greue ne disese, and þer fore
wil I abide and dwelle for euer more.

And in þis manere schal I folowe þe stappis of his swete modre, whas saule þe
120 swerd of sorwe parced in the tyme of his paynful passyon. To her I wil speke
sekerlich and to what thyng me likeþ I schal encline her, and onlich I wil apeere I

crucified with hir son, bot also I wil go to chirche and bicom a litil childe with my
lorde, meke and innocent as a lombe. I schal medle þe moderis milke with þe childes
bloude þat schal quenche al þe mislikyng of my flesch and of my saule.

125   O swete woundes of oure lord ihesu crist. O þe blyndnesse of man þat haþ no
mende ne no reward to his wondes þat beþ þe gates of paradis opend for I go in. Ne
knowe I now3t þat crist is þe ioie and þe delites of hem þat bein in blisse. Whi þanne
be þai slowe for to entre in to hym be þe opon gates of his wondes? Be holde how þe
gates of paradis beþ iopened with o scharp swerde. Be holde þe tre of lif boþe in
130   braunche [**fol. 6r**] and in frut, fulle of holis oueralle. In wiche holis bot þou sette þi
foot of þi loue, þou schalt neuer take þe fruyt of þe tre. Be holde now on is openyd þe
tresour of godis whom and of endeles delites. Of þat I ne hadde be in þe stede of þe
spere þat wente in to cristes syde and yn to hys herte. Certes I wolde neuer haue
comen out be my wille. Bot y wolde haue sayde: 'Here is my reste for euer more.
135   Here I wil dwelle, for I haue chosun þis place'. Allas þe folly of men þat cheseþ for to
dwel in þe worde, in þe flesch, and in þe places þat ben vnclene, wrecchid, and sinful,
and for to haue goddes sone þat is souereyn goudnesse, ioie and blisse, ne wil entre in
to hym be his open woundes, hauyngge inwardlich mende þere on.
           O my saule þou art maked to þe liknesse of god. Ho mute holde þe with þi
140   self. Lo how þi swete spouse is wonded for þe oueral and desireth for to clippe þe and
kysse þe. Be holde how for grete loue he hath opened his side to þe, and profered to
þe his hert. Be holde þe wondes of hym þat hangyth, þe bloude of þe innocent, þe pris
of þe diggere. His hed he hath enclined þe for to [**fol. 6v**] kysse, his armes he hath
spred þe for to clippe, his syde he opened þe for to loue, and alle þis for to drawe
145   mannys saule for to loue hym.
           And for to come to þi desire, say þis orison: 'Lorde almy3tti god, fadre of
heuene, for þat largesse and þi sonnesse passion and for me suffrede deth, and his ~~and
his~~[7] moder excellent holynesse and þe meritis of alle holy seintes, graunte me synful
and vnworthe creature for to loue þe alone, so þat myn hert be euermore brennyng in
150   þe fuer of loue, and þat I mowe in alle þyng and alle my workes desire þi worschippe,
and euer more haue þi passion in myn herte, and verray knowlechyng of my
wrechidnesse and vnworthinesse. In nothyng be my ioie bot in þe and for þe, and with
alle myn herte I beseche þe þat for no þynge be I disesed, ne sori bot for synne, ffor
þe wich þe sonne suffred painful deth and despitous. Louelich lorde and spouse ihesu
155   crist, write in myn hert so þat I mowe rede þi loue towar[d] me and þi sorwe for me,
and þe mende for hym euermore he dwellyng fresch in my herte. Amen.
           [**extract from *The Form of Living* begins**] Atte þe firste begynnynge torne
enterelich [**fol. 7r**] to þi lorde ihesu crist. Þis turnyng is now3t ellis bot þe turnyng
from alle coueytise and likyng and ocupacions, and besinesse of þis wordlich þynges,
160   and fleschlich lustes, and vayn loue. So þat þi thou3t þat was alway downward in to
þe erthe wiles þou wer in þe worlde now be vpward as fier sechys þe heest place of
heuene ri3t to þi spouse þere he sittiþ in his blisse. To hym þou art turnyd wanne his
grace ledeth þyn hert, and forsakest alle vices, and conformest hit to vertues, and to

goud þewys, and to alle manere bonerte and meknesse. And þou maist leste and wex
165 in goudnesse, for þou hast be gunne wiþ oute eny slownesse and werinesse and
sorynesse of lif.

¶ Ffoure thynges þou schalt haue in thi þou3t for to þou be in parfit loue. For
whanne þou art comen þer to, þi ioie and þi desir wil al wey be hyngyng in ihesu crist.
On is of þe mesure of þi lif her þat so schort is þat vnnethes hit is ou3t. Ffor we ne
170 leue bot in o poynt þat is þe lest thyng þat may be, and trewlich oure lif is [**fol. 7v**]
lasse þanne o poynt 3if we likne hit to þe lif þat lastiþ euere.

An oþer is an vncerteinesse of oure endyng, for we wetiþ neuere whanne we
schul dye, ne where, ne how, ne wheder whe schulle gone whanne we be ded. And god
wille þat þis be vncertayne and vnknowe for we scholde euere more be redi to dy and
175 go.

¶ The þridde is þat we schulle answere to fore þe ri3twis iuge of alle þe tyme
þat we han here ben: how we haue here lyued, what oure occupacions han here ben,
and what goud we my3t haue donne whanne we han here ben idel. For þe profit saith:
he þat clepeth þe tyme a3ens me þat euereche day he hath lent vs here for to spende
180 hit in godes seruise, and in penaunce, and in goud vse. 3if we lese hit and wast hit in
erthli loue and vanites, ful greuously schalle we be demed and punisched þer fore. Hit
is on of þe most sorwe þat may be, bot we enforce vs mi3thli in þe loue of god al þat
we may the while oure schort tyme lasteth. For þat we þenkeþ not on god we [**fol. 8r**]
may counte as þyng þat we haue lost.

185 ¶ The furthe is þat we þenke how moche is þe ioie þat þai hanne þat lastiþ in
godes loue in to here endyng, ffor þai schul be breþeren and felawes in his maieste, þe
whiche si3th schal be mede and mete, and alle delites þat any creature may thenke,
and more þan any man may telle to alle his louers wiþ outen ende. Hit is mochel to
cum to þat blis þanne to þenke hit oþer telle hit. Also þenke what sorwe and what
190 payne and what tornement þai schul haue þat loue nou3t god ouer alle oþer thengis
þat men seie in þis worlde bot feyneth here body and here saule in lust and in
vnclennesse of þis lif, in pride, and in coueytise, and in oþer synnes. Thay schul
brenne in þe fier of helle wiþ þe deuelis wham þai serue as long as god is in heuene
wiþ his seruantes, þat is euermore.

195 I wolde þat þou were clene brennyng al way to ihesu cristward, and
encressyng þi lif and þi seruise in hym no3th as foles doth, for þai begynyth in þe
hiest degre and [**fol. 8v**] cometh doune to þe lowest. I say no3t 3if þou haue be gunne
vnskilful abstinence þat þou holde on, bot for many þat were brennyng atte þe
begynnyng and able to þe loue of ihesu crist for ouer muche penaunce þai han lettid
200 þam self and made hem so feble þat þay mowe no3t loue god as thai schulde. In þe
wich loue þat þou be euermore and more is my desire and couaytise. I holde þe neuer
of þe lasse merite 3if þou be no3t in so abstinence as were sum tyme holi men and
women a fore vs. But souereynlich loke þou sette al þi þou3t how þou my3t loue þi
spouse ihesu crist more þanne þou hast doon.

205 And dar I lay þat þi mede waxing, where fore þat þou be ri3t dispoused boþe

for þi soule and for þi bodi, þou schalt vnderstande foure thynges. The first is what
fowleþ[8] a man. The secunde what makiþ hym clene. The thridde what holdith hym in
clennesse. The ferthe what thyng draweþ hym for to ordeyne his wille alto godis
wille.

210   Ffor the ferste wer þou wil þat we synne in þre thynges þat [**fol. 9r**] makeþ vs
fowle,[9] þat is with herte, mout, and dede. The synnes of hert beth thies: euyl thou3tes,
euyl delites, assent to synne, longe abydyng, and likyng, and vnclene þou3tes, desire
of werk, euyl suspecion. 3if þou let þyn hert any tyme idel withoute ocupacion of þe
loue and of þe preisyng of god, eny drede, euyl loue, errour, fleschlich affeccion to thi
215   frendes, ioie of eny mannis euil fare, wether thai be enmy oþer non, despit of poure
oþer synful men, honoure riche men for here richesse, sorwe of loste of thi wrecchid
catelle, dout what is to do and what for echemanne o way to be siker, and what he
schal do, and what he schall leue, obstinacion in euylle, anoi to do goude, anger to do
goude, sorwe þat he dede no more euyl, or he did no3t þe wille and þe lust of his
220   flesch, þe wich he my3t haue don, gladnesse in thenkyng in euyl þat þou hast [done],
vnstabilnesse of þou3t, pyne of penaunce, ypocrisie, loue to pleise men for hem selue,
schame of goude dedis, ioie of euil dedis. Singuler [**fol. 9v**] with, couaitise of honour,
or of dignite, or to better þanne oþer, or fairer, or to be more dred, vayn glorie of
goudis of kynde hope oþer of grace, schame of poure frendes, pride and bost and of
225   riche kyn or gentel. Ffor alle riche and poure we ben liche gentel and fre a for godis
face, bot of oure goud dedis make vs any bettre or worse þanne oþer, despite of goud
consail and goud techyng.

     ¶ The synnes of thi mouth beth þise: Ofte sweryng, forswere, sclaundre of crist
or of any of his halowen, nemne his name withoute reuerence, striwyng a3ens
230   soþnesse, grotchyng a3ens god for any anguische, or any tribulacion, or disese þat
may falle in erthe, to say godis office indeuoutable and with oute reuerence, flateryng,
cursyng, disesyng, bakbityng, chidyng, diffamyng, makyng discorde or debat, fals
witnesse, euyl consail, scornyng, vnbuxumnesse in worde to þi souerayn, turne goude
dede to euyl for to make hym be holde euyl þat doth hym noye, for we ben holde for
235   to tourne owre [**fol. 10r**] euencristen in to þe best, excityng any man to wreche to
vndernemen in any oþer þat he doth hym self, faynspeche, moche speche, idel speche,
oþer wordes þat beth needful. Preysyng or maymtenyng of euyl dedis, synge or prai
more for drede or for praysyng þanne for þe loue of god.

     The synnes[10] beth þise: glotonye, lecherie, symonye, wichecraft, brekyng of
240   the holidai, receyue godes bodi in dedli synne, brekyng of a vowe. Apostasie,
dissolucion in godis seruise, brekyng of licence many place þat is forbode, euyl
ensaumple 3euyng, takyng away any mannys name or fame, 3if 3e[11] spekyng oþer[12]
vnclennesse oþer blethlich heryng, custom ofte for to falle in to þe same synne be
sleuthe, desire more goud for pride, for aray of oure body, oþer for any oþer vanite
245   þanne we haue nede of, for to seme to vs self holier, cunnyng, wiser þanne we ben. To
desire any degre cunnyng oþer worschip þat we be no3t worthi to, to desire vertues
no3t for hym self bot for worschip þat comyþ þer of, and þanne þat scholde 3oure

principal cause of ȝoure loue and of ȝoure lowe[**fol. 10v**]nesse toward god [be][13]
cause of vnkyndenesse, hate, and vnbuxumnesse, rebelle to oure soueraynes,
250 dispisyng or noȝt charchynge þe lawes and þe hestes of oure religion, despisyng hem
þat ben lasse þenne we, mislokyng, euyl heryng, vnclene touchyng or handlyng.
And in alle synnes of dede ȝe most haue and charge þe circumstances, þe wich
beth thise: þe tyme of place, þe manere, þe noumbre, þe parsones, þe dwellyng, þe
cunnyng,[14] þe condicion, þe age. Þise makeþ þe synne more oþer lasse to conuert[15] to
255 synne or constrayne ony to synne.
Oþer many synnes þer beth of omission, þat ben leuyng goud un do þat
scholde be do: noȝt þenkyng on god, ne louyng, ne dredyng, ne preisyng hym, ne
þonkyng hym of þe benefices, do noȝt alle þat we schulde do for godes loue, be noȝt
sorie for synne as we schulde be, dispose vs noȝt to receyue grace, and, ȝif we haue
260 take grace, to vse hit noȝt as we owȝt to done, to turne noȝt to inspiracion of god, to
confourme noȝt þi wille to godis wille, to ȝeue noȝt thyn entent to þi preieres and to
þyn offys [**fol. 11r**] bot rebelle out faste and rekke neuere bot þat þai be sayd for to
do necligentlich þat we be holde to do be a vowe or heste, or eniunid[16] in penaunce,
haue no ioie of oure euencristen profit as of oure owen. Sorwe noȝt for here euyl fare,
265 stondyng noȝt aȝens temptacions, for ȝeuyng noȝt hym þat haþ don vs harme, pesyng
noȝt striues to hem þat beþ vnkunnyng, conforte noȝt þam þat ben in sorowe, oþer
sekenesse, oþer pouerte, penance, or any oþer disese. Thyse synnes and many mo
makyn men foule.
The þynges þat clensith vs beþ þre aȝens þis þre manere of synnyng. Þe ferst
270 is sorwe of herte aȝens þe synnes of þowȝt of hert, and þat þou most haue fulle wille
neuere to synne more, and þat þou haue sorwe of alle þi synnes, and alle þi ioie and
alle þi solace be on god, and yn god, þat he be noȝt put out of þyn herte. Þat oþer is
schrifte of mouþe aȝeyns þe synnes of mouthe, and þou schalt be hasted withoute
tareyng, open withoute excusing, and hole with oute departyng. As for to telle o
275 synne to o prest and an oþer to þe secunde, þou most telle alle þat þou hast in þy
mynde, or [**fol. 11v**] þou art þou noȝt schreuyn. The þridde is satisfaccion aȝens þe
synnes of dede. And he haþ þre parties: fastyng, praiere, and almosdede. Noȝt onlich
to ȝif mete and drynke to poure men, bot forto for ȝif hem þat doþ vs wrong and pray
for hem, and enforme hym how þai schuld do þat kenneþ noȝt so welle as we. Ffor þe
280 þridde thynge þou schalt wel weten þat clennesse be houeth be kepte in hert, in
mouth, and in warke. Clennesse of herte þre þynges kepen. On is wakir þogȝt and
stable in god. Anoþer is besynesse to kepe þi fyue wittes, so þat alle wikked steryng
of hem be kept and closed out of þi flesch. The þridde is honest ocupacion and
profitable.
285   Also þre thynges kepith clennesse of mouth. On is þat þou be þynke þe or þou
speke. An oþer is þat þou be noȝt muche of speche til þin hert be stabled in þe loue of
ihesu crist, so þat þe beseme þat þou lokest alway on hym wheþer þou speke or noȝt.
Bot suche a grace myȝt þou not haue in þe first dai, bot with grete trauail, and grete
besynesse to loue ihesu crist, and with custom þat þe eyȝe of þyn [**fol. 12r**] hert be

290   euermore vpwarde. And þus þou schalt com þer to. The þridde is þou schalt for
        nothyng ne for no meknesse lye in any manere, ffor ich lesyng is synne, and euyl, and
        displeisyng to god. Hit be houeþ noȝt þat þou say alle þe soþe, bot be no way sai non
        lesyng. Ȝif þou sayst o þinge of þi self þe semeþ þi praisyng and saist hit to þe
        praisyng of some and helpe of oþer, þou dost noȝt unwisli, for þou saist þe soþe. Bot
295   ȝif þou wilt haue eny thyng preue, telle hit to non bot to hym þat þou wost wel wille
        noȝt schewe hit bot onlich to þe praisyng of god, of whom is alle goudnesse. Ffor god
        ȝif hym o special grace noȝt onlich for hym self, bot also for hem þat willeþ do wel
        for here ensample.
                Clennesse of werke þre þynges kepeþ. On is continual þoȝt on deþ, for þe
300   wiseman seiþ: 'þynke on þyn endyng and þou schalt neuer dye'. Anoþer is þis: fle fro
        euyl þat ȝeueþ more ensaumple to loue þe worlde þanne god, þe lustes of body þanne
        clennesse of saule. Þe þridde is temperaunce and discrecion in mete and drynke, þat
        hit be noȝt to muche ne to litel for substance of þi body, for boþe [**fol. 12v**] comeþ to
        on endyng, outrage and of ouer moche abstinence, for noþer is godis wille, and þat
305   wil noȝt manye wene, for noȝt þat man can say. Ȝif þou wilt take þi substaunce of
        suche as god sendeth at tyme and stede what hit euer be, I take out no mete no drynke
        þat cristen men vsith with discrecion and mesure, þou dost wel, ffor so dede criste
        hym self and his apostelis. Ȝif þou loue many metys þat men vsen, noȝt dispysing þe
        mete þat god haþ maked to mans helpe, bot for þe þenkeþ þou hast no nede þere of,
310   þou dost wel. Ȝif þou se þat þou art strong to serue þi god, and þat hit breke noȝt þi
        stomak, for ȝif þou haue brokun hit with ouer muche abstinence, and þat hym lakke
        appetit to mete, oft schalt þou be faynt as þou schuldest ȝif vppe þi gost. And wete
        þou wel þat þou synnest in þat dede and for þat þou myȝt wete sone for þyng be aȝens
        þe or with þe. Þere fore while þou art ȝong, I rede þat þou ete þe betre and werte
315   as hit comeþ þat þou be noȝt be gylid, and after [**fol. 13r**] ward, whanne þou hast
        sayd manye þinges, and ouercome many temptacions, and knowest þi self and god
        betre þan þou dost now, þanne if þou seyst hit be to done, þan þou myȝt take þe to þe
        more abstinence. And þer whil be þou myȝt do preuy penaunce þat alle þer of noȝt
        weten.
320   Riȝtwynesse is noþer in fastyng ne in etyng, bot þou art riȝthwis ȝif hit alle
        yliche to þe: despite and praysyng, pouert and richesses, hongur and delites, nede
        and plente. Ȝif þou take þise with a þoȝt of god, I holde þe blissed and childe of ihesu.
        Meny men and women parauenture preiseth þe for þou hast y bounde þe to religion,
        bot no wisman wil noȝt prayse þe so liȝtlich, for oȝth þat þe seiȝt þe don withouten
325   forth. Bot ȝif þi wil be conformed enterlich to do gods wille, and recche noȝt of
        mannys praisyng no blaming, and take non hede ȝif þay speke lasse goud of þe þanne
        þay dede a fore, bot onlich þat þou be more brennyng in godes loue þanne þou were.
        Ffor o þyng [**fol. 13v**] werne I þe þat I trowe þat god hath non parfite seruant in erthe
        withoute enemye, for only wrecchidnesse haþ non enemy in erthe.
330   Ffor to drawe vs þat we conforme oure wille to godis wille þar beþ þre
        thynges: on ensample of holimen and wommen þe wich were bese nyȝt and day to

serue god and drede hym *and* loued hym. And we folowe hym *in* erthe, we schul be *with* hym in heuene. A no*þ*er is þe goudnesse of oure lorde þat desspiseth non bot gladlich receyue alle þo þat comyth to his mercy and is more homlich to hym þanne
335 his broþer, or suster, or eny frende þat þay most loue or tristen. The þridde is þe wondurful ioie of þe kyngd*om* of heuene þat is more þanne tong may telle. For ri3th as in helle no man leue may for muche payne, bot godis mi3t suffred hit no3t for to deye. So þe ioie of þe si3t of i*h*e*s*u *in* godhede is so muche þat þai most deie for ioie, 3if ne were his goudnesse þat he wil his loueres be eu*er* more leuynge in blisse, as
340 [**fol. 14r**] his ri3thwisnesse wille þat alle þat loueþ not hym be eu*er*more leuyng in fure þat is orible any man to þenke. Loke þanne what hit is to fele, bot for as moche as þai wil no3t þenke hit now ne drede hit, þay schulle suffre hit eu*er* more with outen ende.

Now hast þou harde how þou my3th dispose þi lif and rule hit to godes wille,
345 [**hortatory conclusion begins**] and as saith seynt James, 'hit were bettre no3th for to knowe þe lawe of god þe*nn*e knowe hit and do no3t þere after.' And þ*er*fore, my leue frende, y consaille þe þat þou forsake no3th and dispise li3tlich þis lore and doctrine, alle be hit þat p*ar*auenture for diu*er*se occupacions and lettyngs þat þou hast in þe worlde, þou fyndest no gret sauoure þ*er* in atte þe begynnyng. For as ich haue saide
350 afore, hertlich loue of god and goudnesse of lif wil no3t be geten *with* oute grete trauail and long continuaunce, bot whanne hit is hadde, hit is ful of lykyng of swetnesse.

And þere fore, whanne þe holi gost sendeþ þe eny sauour to loue [**fol. 14v**] god, forsake hit no3t, bot kepe hit stille. And after þe *grace* þat he 3eueþ þe, p*ar*forme
355 hit and encrece hit, *and* 3if þou dost þus, I drede no3t þat þou schalt forsake alle unclene loue þat is no3th to his worschippe for his loue. *And* þanne schalt þou ben his spouse, dwellyng *with* hym in þe blisse of heuen endlich.

And if hit be so, dere frende, þat þis schort lesson do þe goud, þanke god þere of and pray for me. The grace of god almy3tti, i*h*e*s*u verrai god and man þat is verrai
360 loue *and* comfort of his loueris be *with* þe, and kepe þe fro euyl, and bryng þe to þi spouse þat þou hast take þe to, þe wich is eu*er*lastyng god. Amen.

NOTES

1. MS: strereth.
2. "one" has been scraped off, but faint traces remain.
3. MS: and and.
4. Whereas in D this sentence is left incomplete, in Hf it ends with "god."
5. MS: fert.
6. MS: clipprth.
7. Crossed out.
8. MS: folweþ.
9. MS: folwe.

10. Inserted in the right margin: "of þi fle[sch]" (cut off).
11. Crossed out, "wyth" inserted in the right margin.
12. MS: written twice, abbreviated the second time.
13. MS: is.
14. MS: cumyng.
15. MS: couert.
16. MS: eininid.

APPENDIX B:

Variants

1 liȝt] syȝte Har, siȝt Tr, sight Hf   godisseruant] ne add. TrHf
2 bote] bote (te added above the line) Hf   wolde] do add. HarTr
his lorde] god Har
3 al] as HarTr   þat þou] þenkeste add. Har, þenkist add. Tr,
þenkest and add. Hf   and] or Har   seye] yt add. Har, it add.
Tr   as þou] as þouȝ þou HarTri
4 oure ladi sit in heue] as he syttyþ in heuene Har, as he sittiþ in heuene
Tr   For] and for HarTr
4–7 For…dome] om. Hf
5 is] ben Har
7 is] þat add. HarTrHf
8 þat] om. Har   þis poyntes] þese poins her bifor Hf   knowlech]
welle add. Har, weel add. Tr
9 grace] benefice Hf   he] om. Hf   woch saue] for add. Hf
of] and HarTrHf
10 benfaitȝ] benefices   Hf, benefetys Har, benefitis Tr   how] he add
HarTrHf
11–12 and how he hath taken thi kynde and suffred for thi loue despites
deth] om. HarTri
12 despites] despitous Hf   how] he add. Har   grauntes]
graunted HarTri, granted for add. Hf   þi] mede and þi add. Hf
13 and thi blisse] om. Hf   lif] þat haþ non ende add. Hf
14 þou] ne add. Hf   now] not HarTr, om. Hf   sen hem]
him se Hf
15 þis worlde] þe wei toward þi contrei Hf   oft þerfore] om. Hf,
þerfore oft Har   for þe] om. Hf.   on] vpon Har, in TrHf
16 conpassion] of add. HarHf, on add. Tr   as] þouȝ add.
HarTri   suffredest] feledest Hf
17 his] om. Har   þou] ne add. Hf   þe be] þi body TrHar, þi bodi
Hf
18 wrecche] wrche (crossed out in red ink) Tr   Þe] þese HarHf

thoghtes] poyntys Har   ofte haue] haue ofte Har   in] þi add. Har
19 he lieth on the auter atte masse] þou seeste þe holy sacramente of
Crystys body at þe masse or on þe auter Har, þou seest þe holy sacrament
of cristis bodi at masse or on þe autir Tr   and] þan add. Har, þanne add.
Tr   to hym] om. Har
20 þou] om. Har   so] to Har   and] to add. Har
21 so] graunte me add. Har   I haue non hongur] me ne hungre Hf
no] eny Har   bot] oonly after add. Har, aftir add. Tr
22 I be nouȝt a þerst bot after þe] me þirste noþing bote þe Hf   so] om.
Har
23 þat for] for om. Tr   ne be] y Har, I Tr   neuere]
be add. HarTr
24 me] þe Har, þee Tr
25 Line 25 marks the start of the *Stimulus amoris* segment. The variants
compared below refer to D and Hf.
25 with] withoute
26 rote of] rote and fruit and þe add.
28 schalle] be add.
29 oþer woman] om.   may] encrece add.
30 strereth] reryþ   * amor facit mirabilia hic (the asterisk
denotes a marginal addition)
31 and in] in om.
32 man] god and god man. Þe heiȝest he makiþ lowist and þe lowest
heiȝest add.   for] þe fo   seruant] he makiþ add.
33 he makiþ] om.
34 he makith] om.
36 an] ani
38 bot] om.   at þe] þe om.
40 harde as] a add.   of] þe add.
42 me in to god and god in to me] god in to me and me in to god
44–48 þou bindest … brennyng loue] om.
49 þou] þat   me] vs
52 O þou] þou om.
53 ȝif] and   klippe] þe add.   þe] om.
54 quike to feer] tende þe fur of loue
55 in] in (inserted above the line)
58 vertu is] vertues ben   to] of   to mannys saule] of mannis
soule and
59 alle a boute] om.
61 aqueked] atende
62 and of] þe add.
66 hym a sonys] himself to alles of mankind

68 likyng to þe deuille] and
69 goddissone] ne add.
70 and beyng] om.
71 and and] and   flesch, and] and om.
74 Allas] wondir add.
76 saule] ne add.
77 hym, for to] for to om.
78 þe wiche were more bettre] albehit þat þis wer liȝter and esier
82 and] for add.   on tre] was on þe cros
84 techiþ] him add.   do, and] what add.
85 quike] tende   þe more able to] to workis of   and trauail] and of
trauail add.
86 thynkyng] and spekynge and add.
87 of] god add.
90 heuyth] oneþ   hert] om.
91 wanne he was derke] derkid
92 passion] schameful makeþ vs gloriouse add.
92–93 hit is] om.
95 loue and] of add.
97 thenkyþ oft] ofte þenkiþ
99 be] in   turment] tormentes   takeþ non hede of hym self] ne
seȝet nouȝt himself
101 hym, he] hym þat
102 to] om.   on] in
103 croce with] cros as
104–105 drynkesse with soueraigne wyne of swetnesse] drynkeþ with
wyn of souereine swetnesse
105 paynid] and scornid add.   hym] crist   on] in
106 sone] child   cristes] passion add.   in] a add.
107 other woman] om.
108 desireth] for add.   on þe croce with crist] with crist in þe croce
109 kisseþ, and clipprth] clippiþ and kisseþ
110 passion] an deþ add.   and delectable] om.   Allas] O allas
on] in
112 þere fore] om.
114 wil] make to add.
116 with] to his
117 þer fore] þer add.
119 schal I] I schal
120 paynful] om.
121 her, and] nouȝht add.   apeere I] I om.
122 chirche] þe crache

123 childes] sonis
124 bloude] and make me a noble drinke add.
125 man] men   haþ] han
126 I] scholde add.
127 I] hei
129 gates] ʒate swerde] spere
130 braunche] braunches
131 schalt neuer] ne miʒht nouʒht
132 whom] wisdom   Of] O
136 worde] world   þe places] oþer places
137 wil] nouʒht add.
138 hauyngge inwardlich mende þere on] om.
139 mute] myʒhte
140 is wonded for þe] for þe is wondid ('is' inserted above the line)
141 kysse þe] þe om.
143 diggere] bugger   armes he hath] haþ om.
144 he] om.
144–145 and … hym] so þat he al be fichid faste in þin herte þat for þe was
nayled to þe cros
147 þat] þi   and for] þat for
147–148 and his ~~and his~~] ~~and his~~ om.
148 graunte] to add.
150 of] þi add.   þyng and alle] þynges and in alle
152 ioie] and in gladnes add.
153 þynge] ne add.
154 þe] om.   þe sonne] þi sone   deth and despitous] and despitous
deþ
156 euermore he] euer be
157 þe firste] om.   torne] þe add.
159 alle] þe add.   and] þe add.   and] þe add.   and] þe add.
wordlich] worldes
160 lustes, and] lustes and (d inserted above the line)   to] om.
161 þe worlde] þe (inserted above the line) world   sechys] seching   of] in
163 ledeth] lighteþ
164 manere] of add.   And] ʒif add. (inserted above the line)
165–166 werinesse and sorynesse of lif] sorynesse and werynes of þi lif
167 to] te   * nota quattuor meditanda
168 hyngyng] brenyng
169 is of] of om.   * ·1·
172 an] om.   * ·2·
174 vncertayne and vnknowe] vnknowe and vncerteyn   for we scholde
euere more be] to vs for he wole þat we be alwey

176 to fore] bifore   * ·3·
177 occupacions han here] here om.
178 here] om.
179 he þat] he haþ
180 hit and] hit or
181 loue and] in add.
182 miȝthli] nameli
184 counte] hit add.
185 is þe ioie] þat þe ioye is   * ·4·
186 felawes] wiþ angeles and holi men, preising, seinge, and hauyng þe kyng of ioye in his fairhede and schinyng add.
188 man] om.   mochel] lighter add.
190 tornement] þat add.
191 feyneth] fileþ
192 vnclennesse] lecherie   in coueytise] in om.   in oþer] in om.
193 deuelis] deiul
195 clene brennyng al way to ihesu cristward] alwey clymbing to ihesu ward
196 * ·contra indiscretam abstinenciam·
197 noȝt] for I wolde þat add.
198 on] hit add.   þe] om.
201 desire and couaytise] coueityng and myn amoneisting
202 so] muche add.
202–203 as were sum tyme holi men and women a fore vs] om.
203 souereynlich loke] om.
205 And] þanne   lay] sey   mede] is add.   waxyng] and nouȝt wanyng add.
206 * nota quattuor hic
207 folweþ] fileþ   The secunde what] Þat oþer what þing
207–208 * ·1·2··3·4·
210 wer] wyte   * ·1·
211 folwe] foule   herte] and add. * ·synnes of herte·   thouȝtes] þouȝht
212 longe abydyng, and likyng, and vnclene þouȝtes] om.
213 of] euil add.   werk] wikkid wille add.   suspecion] indeuocion add.
214 eny] euil   errour] and add.
215 frendes] oþer þat þou louest add.
216 richesse] vncouenable ioye of any worly vanites add.   thi wrecchid] þe worldes
217 dout what] noȝht add.   o way] oweþ   and] om.

218–219 anger to do goude] anger to serue god
219 wille and þe lust] lust or þe wil
220 gladnesse in thenkyng in euyl þat þou hast] om.
221 for hem selue] drede to displese ham
222 euil] ydul
223 dignite, or to] behold add.
224 kynde] or of add.   and bost and] om.
225 riche and poure] om.   gentel and] om.
226 bot of] bot ȝif
227 and] of add.
228 Ofte sweryng] swer oftesiþes   * ·synnes of mouþ·
229–230 striwyng aȝens soþnesse] aȝeyn seiȝenge and striuyng soþfastnes
230 or any] or noy or   or disese] om.
232 chidyng, diffamyng, makyng discorde or debat] defamyng, chiding,
sowing of discord, treson
233 to þi souerayn] om.
234 ben holde for] owe
235 euencristen] neyȝbur dedis   best] nouȝht in to þe worste add.
(r inserted)   excityng] of add.   wreche] wraþþe
236 idel] foul
237 oþer] ydul   wordes] or wordes add.   þat beth] nouȝht
add.   Preysyng] of glosinge wordes, defendyng of synne, creiyng in
lauȝtre, mowe makyng on any man, to singe seculer songes and loue ham
add.   or mayntenyng] om.   or prai] om.
238 drede or for] om.   praysyng] of men add.   for þe loue] om.
239 synnes] of dede add.   lecherie] drinkenes add.   * ·synnes
of dede·
240 holidai] sacrilegie add.   vowe] owes
241 brekyng of licence many place þat is forbode] om.
241–242 euyl ensaumple ȝeuyng] to ȝiue ensample of euil
242–244 takyng away any mannys name or fame … sleuthe] to hurte any
man in his bodi, or in his good, or in his fame, þefte, rauyn, vsur, deseyt,
sulle riȝhtwisnes, here euil, ȝiue to harlotes, wiþhold necessaries fro þi
bodi or to ȝiue hit outrage, to bigynne þink þat is ouer miȝht, custome to
synne or falling ofte in synne
244 for pride, for aray of oure body, oþer for any oþer vanite] om.
245 to vs self] om.   cunnyng] or connynger, or
245–249 To desire … rebelle] to holde þe office þat we suffise nouȝht
vnto, brynge vp newe gyses, to be rebel
250 dispisyng or noȝt charchynge þe lawes and þe hestes of oure religion]
om.   despisyng] defoule
251 we] in seyng, in hering, in smelling, in touching, in handling, in

swolewing, in wiʒtes, in weyes, in signes, to receyue þe circumstanses of synnes, þat is to sey add.

253 of place] þe stede   parsones] person

254 cumyng] cunyng   þe condicion] þe eelde   makeþ þe] þe om.   oþer] or

255 or] be temptid to add.

256 ben] is of   * synnes of omission

257 do] þat is add.   on] in   ne louyng] om.

258–259 be noʒt sorie for synne as we schulde be] to sorewe nouʒht for synne as he scholde do   vs] him

259 we] he

260 we owʒt to done] he ouʒte to done to kepe hit nouʒht   noʒt to] nouʒt atte

261–262 and to þyn offys] om.

262 þat] þat (inserted above the line)

263 we be] he is   be] þorow   heste] comandement   or] is add.   penaunce] to drawe along þat scholde be do sone add.

264 oure euencristen] his neiʒbur   oure] his   Sorwe] om. * sorewe   here] his

265 vs] him   harme] keping nouʒht trewe to his neiʒbor as he wolde þat he dude to him and ʒeldyng him nouʒht a good dede for an oþer ʒif he may, amending nouʒht him þat synneþ bifor his eyʒen

266 to hem] teaching hem nouʒht   oþer] or in

267 oþer] or in   pouerte] or in prison add.   penance, or any oþer disese] om.   mo] om.

269 * vs clenseþ þre þinges ·2·

270 of hert] om.

270–271 most haue fulle wille neuere to synne] haue in wille neuere to singe

271 þat] þat (inserted from above)   haue] haue (e inserted)

272 be] only add.   he] om. * the

273 þou schalt be hasted] þat schal be hasti

274 tareyng] delay   open] nakid

275 to þe secunde] synne to anoþer

275–276 þou most telle alle þat þou hast in þy mynde, or þou art þou noʒt schreuyn] om.

276 satisfaccion] þat add.

276–277 aʒens þe synnes of dede. And he] om.

278 to ʒif mete and drynke to poure men] ʒeue pore men mete and drinke doþ vs] don þe

279 hym] hem   kenneþ noʒt so welle as we] beþ in poynt to perische

281 kepen] kepiþ   * ·3· hou clennes schal be kepid·
282 in] of   alle] þe add.
283 kept and] om.
285 þre thynges kepith clennesse of mouth] clennes of mouþ kepiþ þre
þinges   be þynke þe or] pynke þe bifor ar
286 is] om.   til] bot of lytel semliche alwey forte
287 crist] om.   þe beseme] þou þenke
288 in] on   with grete] wiþ long
290 euermore] euer   is] þat
292 displeisyng to god. Hit be houeþ noзt þat þou say] nouзht at godis
wille. Þou þarst nouзht telle alwei   soþe] зif þou wilt add.
292–293 bot be no way sai non lesyng] bot alle lesinges hate
294 some] god   saist þe soþe] spekist soþfastnes
295 to hym] such on
295–296 wost wel wille noзt schewe hit] wer siker þat he scholde nouзht
be schewid
296 goudnesse] and þat to some bettr þan to oþer
296–297 Ffor god зif hym] and зeuiþ ham
297 hym] hem
299 continual] assiduel
300 endyng] endinges   dye] synne   þis] om.
301 god] erþe þan heuene add.   þe lustes] fulþe
303 noзt to muche ne] neyþer to outrage ne þat hit be   substance]
sustinance   þi] þe
304 of] om.   abstinence] fasting
305 wil noзt manye] manie wol nouзht   can] may   substaunce]
sustinance
306 at] þe add.   and] þe add.   euer] om.   mete no
drynke] no maner   * mete and drinke
308 loue] leue
309 þenkeþ] þat add.
310 strong] stalworthe   þi god] þi om.
311 þat hym lakke] þe is bynome
312 faynt] in quoþes   schuldest зif vppe] wer redi to зelde
313 for þat] þat om.   myзt] nouзht add.   for þyng] weþir
þin abstinence
314 ete] and drinke   werte] þe worse
317 seyst] see þat   done, þan] do   þe] om.
318 þer whilbe] þe while   myзt] maist   alle] men add.
þer of noзt] men parnouзht
320 hit] om.

321 yliche] be add.   hongur and] nede as add.
delites] and deinteþes add.
322 and plente] om.   þoȝt] þonkyng   childe of] heyed bi for
323–324 Meny…wil] Men þat comeþ to þe þei preisen þe for þei seen þe
enclosed, bot I ne may
324 be seiȝt] I see
325 forth] om.
326 no] ne of her   take] þou add.
327 a fore] om.   onlich] om.
329 enemye] enemys of some men   in erthe] om.
330 * ·4·
331 on] is add.   bese] and ententif add.   * ·1·
332 loued] loueden   folowe hym] folewe ham
333 hym] ham   * ·2·
334 þo] om.
335 loue or] most add.   * ·3·
336 For riȝt] Hit is so
337 no man leue may] miȝt noþing liue   bot] þat add.   for] om.
338 of] in   in] his add.
339 ne were] hit newer   wil] þat add.   euer more leuynge]
lyuyng euer
340 not] om.   hym] nouȝt add.   euermore] euere
341–342 as moche as] om.
342 now ne] and   drede hit] now add.
344 hast þou] hast ou
345–357 and…endlich] om.
358 And if hit be so, dere frende, þat þis schort lesson do þe goud] ȝif hit
do þe good and profit
358–359 þere of] om.
360 fro] al add.
361 euerlastyng god] euer lyuynge god wiþ oute ende

Nota Bene: Brief Notes on Manuscripts and Early Printed Books

Highlighting Little-Known or Recently Uncovered Items or Related Issues

Unnoticed and Unusual: An Illustration in a Manuscript of John Lydgate's *Fall of Princes*

SONJA DRIMMER

An historiated initial on the opening page to a manuscript of John Lydgate's *Fall of Princes* (Chicago, Newberry Library MS 33.3) has escaped notice and is not mentioned in any published descriptions of the manuscript (Fig. 1).[1] As A. S. G. Edwards's devoted scholarship shows, the manuscript history of Lydgate's verse is a long work in progress, which has been and continues to be written in increments as new fragments surface and important discoveries are made.[2] The purpose of this article is to supplement these labors by recording the presence of this historiated initial and by drawing attention to some of the larger issues regarding the illumination of Lydgate's works that this representation raises. This initial is the single surviving representation of a figure at a desk—whether reading or writing—at the beginning of any Lydgate manuscript, and as such is a remarkable addition to our knowledge of the visual apparatus that accompanied manuscripts of his works.[3]

The manuscript is an elegant mid-fifteenth-century volume that contains only John Lydgate's *Fall of Princes*. The decorative features of the manuscript localize it to London, and both these ornamental elements, which appear to have been executed by a single illuminator, and the hybrid anglicana and secretary hand of the single scribe who copied the text suggest a date close to 1450, but certainly within the third quarter of the fifteenth century. Throughout the manuscript, each stanza's rhyme scheme is denoted by red brackets, and apparently the same pigment used to create the brackets was also used to underline proper names and chapter summaries and to provide

Figure 1. Man at a Desk. John Lydgate, *Fall of Princes*, London, *c.* 1450–1475. Chicago, Newberry Library MS 33.3, folio 1r.

the sporadic chapter heads. Likewise, these chapter heads appear to have been written by the same scribe who copied the main text. With the exception of the explicit to the Prologue, explicits and incipits are written in large black letters throughout the manuscript, and where they do mention the author of the text, they refer to "Bochas" (i.e., Boccaccio) as opposed to John Lydgate. Overall, it is a well-organized, carefully written volume that confers prestige on the text by virtue of its careful apparatus and attractive—but not sumptuous—illumination.

At some unknown point, however, water beset the manuscript and obscured the historiated initial that adorns its opening page.[4] From a modest distance, the initial seems only to be decorated (as opposed to historiated), and only a tentative note in an internal file hazards that the letter might frame representational content.[5] Under close inspection, it is clear that the miniature shows a man bent over an open book upon a desk; it is no longer possible to discern whether he is engaged in writing or reading. What is easily discernible is the desk itself, which contains a cupboard filled with two books, the one red and the other blue. The figure at the desk wears a dark brown habit, but no other features of his attire or physiognomy are, in the miniature's present state, legible. No other manuscript of the *Fall of Princes* nor of any work by Lydgate features this kind of image at its opening.[6]

The five extant copies of the *Fall of Princes* with figural illumination vary considerably in their decorative programs, leading Lesley Lawton to remark that they "represent in microcosm the various interpretative and technical solutions available to producers of illustrated manuscripts in a late medieval English context."[7] The most lavish copy (San Marino, Huntington HM 268, along with the fragment from it that is now British Library, Sloane MS 2452) provides fifty-eight narrative illustrations, each in a framed column miniature.[8] The only miniature in this manuscript that portrays Lydgate shows him seated beside Boccaccio, receiving a book from his *auctor*.[9] Another deluxe copy, British Library, Harley MS 1766, contains 156 unframed marginal illustrations of the exempla in addition to a half-page prefatory miniature portraying two monks kneeling before St. Edmund enthroned.[10] If we can extrapolate something about the manuscript from which the Montréal, McGill University MS 143 fragment was excised, it seems to have flaunted a plentiful schedule of framed column miniatures that illustrate exempla: of the two surviving miniatures it contains, one represents the decapitation of Duke Gaultier, while the other includes an image of Lydgate kneeling before Humphrey, duke of Gloucester, before the work's envoy.[11] Philadelphia, Rosenbach Library MS 439/16, in contrast, has a more modest pictorial cycle that prefaces seven of the poem's books with a column miniature.[12] Most of these miniatures address the poem's frame and show Boccaccio seated at his desk and encountering characters whose tales are told in the book to follow.[13] And Oxford, Bodleian Library, MS Bodley 263 contains a single frontispiece miniature before Book I, which brings together a medley of twelve scenes, ten of which represent exempla recounted in the first book of the poem. In neither of these latter manuscripts (Rosenbach and Bodley) does a representation of Lydgate appear. In light of this variation, I would go further than Lawton's assessment quoted above and infer that manuscript producers were undecided as to the most appropriate illustrative apparatus for this, a monumental poem in English.[14]

Although the historiated initial in Newberry MS 33.3 is located in the space that one would associate with an author portrait, determining its subject is not so straightforward. The sober opening verses to the *Fall of Princes* record the name of its original Italian author, Boccaccio, and its French translator, Laurent de Premierfait. What is more, the first word to the poem, "He," refers to Laurent, and it is in the initial 'H' that we encounter the representation described above.[15] The question this historiated initial raises, then, is: Whom does it depict? Boccaccio? Laurent de Premierfait? John Lydgate? On the one hand, the logical answer would be Laurent, because he is the subject of the opening verse; and equally possible is Boccaccio, since he, too, is mentioned. On the other hand, the figure's attire—a dark (though not black) habit—might suggest Lydgate.

Whether or not the illuminator had a particular figure in mind, the fact that the portrait's identity is even open to debate is a signal symptom of the conditions of Middle English poetic production at this time. Specifically, in producing so much of his nondevotional work in translation, Lydgate left open to interpretation his authorial role, a topic that is explored at length by Alexandra Gillespie, with respect both to Lydgate's output at large and to his *Fall of Princes* in particular.[16] In the case of this manuscript, nothing of its paratext mentions Lydgate, and a reader might easily overlook or be unaware of the identity of the person who composed this English poem. What a fifteenth-century audience would have made of the person portrayed on the manuscript's first page cannot be determined, but the mere presence of a figure at a desk in the classic style of an *auctor* may not have had the same authorizing effect on the English language that such images are often thought to confer. Instead, a late-medieval audience may have perceived this figure as the French translator or even the Italian, Latin-language *auctor* whose name peppers the text. Because the absence of medieval ownership marks and heraldry leaves us ignorant of the manuscript's patron(s), I am reluctant to deduce anything about the interests of the reading community for which this copy was produced other than to say that they apparently saw an English version of Boccaccio's *De casibus virorum illustrium* as a worthy investment.[17] A final note about the production of this manuscript compounds the questions it raises about the illuminator's role in mediating the identity of the poem's author. In certain places in the manuscript, the ru-bricated brackets that highlight the rhyme scheme run over the decorative illumination (Fig. 2). As we know from numerous incomplete examples, manuscripts were typically copied first and then supplied with illumination. This standard order does indeed appear to have been the operating proce-dure for this manuscript as well, where, for example, on folio 41v, the frame for the large decorated initial breaks in order not to run over the 'f' in the verse that begins, "full wele" (Fig. 3). Yet, to reiterate, the red bracket lines run over both the text they bracket (naturally) and, at times, the illuminated ornamentation (unusually).

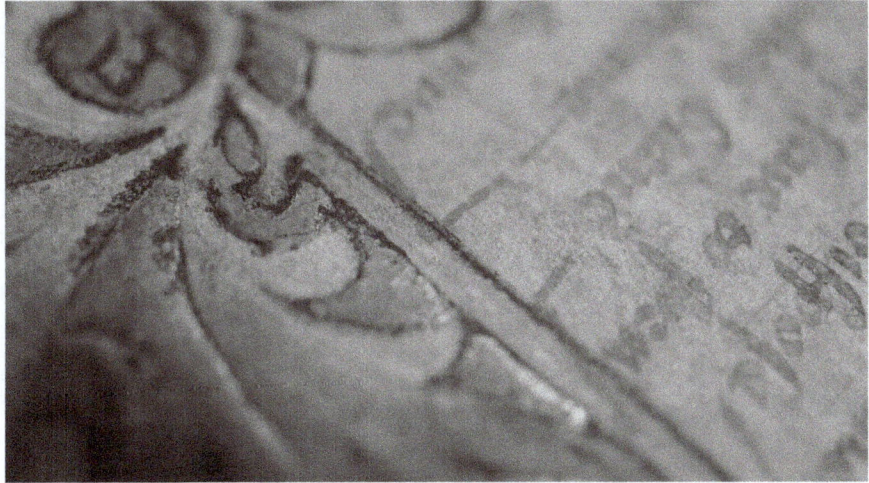

Figure 2. Rubrication over decorative border. John Lydgate, *Fall of Princes*, London, c. 1450–1475. Chicago, Newberry Library MS 33.3, folio 1r.

The following, then, is the order in which parts of the manuscript were created: first, the scribe laid out and copied the text; then an illuminator provided the illumination; and finally a figure supplied the red and blue paraph marks, brackets, and underlining throughout the text. If we assume that the scribe and illuminator were different individuals, this sequence would require the gatherings to originate with a scribe, be passed off to the illuminator, and then return to the scribe for rubricating. Alternatively, for this last phase, the illuminator might have been entrusted with the rubrica-tion. The potential movement back and forth between artisans strikes me as inconvenient, particularly in light of the small work spaces of London illuminators and stationers, which by no stretch of the imagination could accommodate multiple practitioners in the style of a scriptorium.[18] While it cannot be proved that the scribe and the illuminator were one and the same

Figure 3. Break in decorative illumination to accommodate letter. John Lydgate, *Fall of Princes*, London, *c.* 1450–1475. Chicago, Newberry Library MS 33.3, folio 41v.

individual, this manuscript provides grounds for considering the possibility. If the illuminator of this manuscript was also its scribe—a scribe who not only copied the text but was also sufficiently attentive to its form that he accentuated its rhyme scheme—then the unusual illumination at the opening to the manuscript may be the product of an attentiveness to the poem's formal and thematic properties, resulting in an image of authorship that equivocates on the identity of the man it portrays because the poem itself equivocates on its own authorial origins.

University of Massachusetts, Amherst

Acknowledgments
My thanks to A.S.G. Edwards for his feedback on a draft of this article. I am also grateful to the Andrew W. Mellon Foundation Fellowship of Scholars in Critical Bibliography for funding and facilitating my visit to the Newberry Library in Chicago.

NOTES

1. For a brief description of the manuscript, see Paul Saenger, *A Catalogue of the Pre-1500 Western Manuscript Books at the Newberry Library* (Chicago: University of Chicago Press, 1989), 60–61. This manuscript was unknown to Henry Bergen, Lydgate's modern editor. For descriptions of other *Fall of Princes* manuscripts, see Henry Bergen, *Lydgate's Troy Book*, Part IV, EETS, e.s. 126 (1935): 1–54. The copies of the *Fall of Princes* that contain figural illumination amount to a modest number (previously numbering only five, and now, including Newberry MS 33.3, numbering six) of the total number of extant copies (thirty-five), making this finding all the more significant. These manuscripts are: London, BL Harley MS 1766; Montréal, McGill University MS 143, a fragment comprising four leaves with two miniatures; Oxford, Bodleian Library, MS Bodley 263; Philadelphia, Rosenbach Library, MS 439/16; San Marino, Huntington HM 268 and a fragment from this same manuscript, now London, BL Sloane MS 2452.

2. A. S. G. Edwards, "Lydgate's *Fall of Princes*: Unrecorded Headings," *Notes & Queries* n.s. 16 (1969): 170–171; A. S. G. Edwards, "Lydgate's *Siege of Thebes*: A New Fragment," *Neuphilologische Mitteilungen* 71 (1970): 133–136; A. S. G. Edwards, "A Missing Leaf from the Plimpton *Fall of Princes*," *Manuscripta* 15 (1971): 29–31; A. S. G. Edwards, "Selections from Lydgate's *Fall of Princes*: A Checklist," *The Library*, 5th ser., 26 (1971): 337–342; A. S. G. Edwards (with A.W. Jenkins), "Lydgate's *Life of Our Lady*: An Unedited Manuscript of Part of Book III," *English Language Notes* 9 (1971): 1–3; A. S. G. Edwards, "The Huntington *Fall of Princes* and Sloane 2452," *Manuscripta* 16 (1972): 380–385; A. S. G. Edwards, "The McGill Fragment of Lydgate's *Fall of Princes*," *Scriptorium* 28 (1974): 75–77; A. S. G. Edwards, "Lydgate's *Fall of Princes*: A 'Lost' Manuscript Found," *Manuscripta* 22 (1978): 176–178; A. S. G. Edwards, "Lydgate Manuscripts: Some Directions for Future Research," in *Manuscripts and Readers in Fifteenth-Century England: The Literary Implications of Manuscript Study: Papers from the 1981 Conference at the University of York*, ed. Derek Pearsall (Cambridge, UK: Brewer, 1983), 15–26; A. S. G. Edwards, "An Unidentified Extract from Lydgate's *Troy Book*," *Notes & Queries*, n.s., 36 (1989): 307–308; A. S. G. Edwards, "Introduction," in *The Life of St Edmund, King and Martyr: John Lydgate's Illustrated Verse Life Presented to Henry VI: A Facsimile of British Library MS Harley 2278* (London: British Library, 2004), 1–18; A. S. G. Edwards, "Lydgate in Scotland," *Nottingham Medieval Studies* 54 (2010): 185–194; A. S. G. Edwards, "Lydgate's *Fall of Princes*: Translation, Retranslation and History," in *Renaissance Cultural Crossroads: Translation,*

Print and Culture in Britain, 1473–1640, ed. Brenda Hosington and S. K. Barker (Leiden, Netherlands: Brill, 2012), 21–33.

3. *Pace* Bale, there is no extant image of John Lydgate writing in his study, although one manuscript of the *Fall of Princes* (San Marino, Huntington Library HM 268, fol. 79v) does depict a "man" (not Lydgate) writing, and another manuscript of the *Lives of Saints Edmund and Fremund* (BL, Harley MS 2278, fol. 74r) depicts Burchard (not Lydgate), Fremund's secretary, writing. See Anthony Bale, "From Translator to Laureate: Imagining the Medieval Poet," *Literature Compass* 5 (2008): 918–934, 929.

4. While it is impossible to know for certain when this damage occurred, the manuscript's possible provenance includes its presence in a collection damaged by fire (and presumably by the water that quenched it). See J. R. Hall, "William G. Mendlicott (1816): An American Book Collector and His Collection," *Harvard Library Bulletin*, n.s., 1 (1990): 13–46, esp. 30, n. 58; and *Catalogue of a Collection of Books Formed by William Mendlicott of Longmeadow, Mass* (Boston: Rockwell and Churchill, 1878), no. 2715. The latter records that the manuscript was "defaced by the fire at Sotheby's in 1865." My thanks to Tony Edwards for these references and his suggestion that this refers to the George Offor sale at Sotheby's on June 27, 1865 (email correspondence, May 3, 2016).

5. "The initial 'h' at the beginning seems to have a portrait miniature in it." (Chicago, Newberry Library, MS 33.3, internal file).

6. For an overview of illuminations in manuscripts of the *Fall of Princes*, see Lesley Lawton, "'To Studie in Bookis of Antiquitie': The Illustrated Manuscripts of John Lydgate's *Fall of Princes* as Witnesses of Cultural Practice," *Anglophonia* 29 (2011): 61–77.

7. Ibid., 64.

8. Many leaves have been excised from this manuscript—their whereabouts are unknown, or they may simply have been destroyed—and Lawton estimates that the complete manuscript might have contained more than ninety miniatures (Lawton, "'To Studie in Bookis,'" 65). See Kathleen L. Scott, *Later Gothic Manuscripts, 1390–1490*, 2 vols., Survey of Manuscripts Illuminated in the British Isles 6 (London: H. Miller Publishers, 1996), II, no. 79.

9. San Marino, Huntington Library, HM 268, folio 18r. Although Seth Lerer assumes that the image imagines the moment when Lydgate presents his work to his "patron" (i.e., Boccaccio), logic suggests to me that the book is passing in the opposite direction: from the long-dead *auctor* to his follower to translate. See Seth Lerer, *Chaucer and His Readers: Imagining the Author in Late-Medieval England* (Princeton, NJ: Princeton University Press, 1993), 40–44.

10. On this manuscript, see Sarah Louise Pittaway, "The Political Appropriation of John Lydgate's *Fall of Princes*: A Manuscript Study of British Library, MS Harley 1766" (PhD diss., University of Birmingham, 2011); and Sarah Pittaway, "'In this signe thou shalt ouercome hem alle': Visual Rhetoric and Yorkist Propaganda in Lydgate's *Fall of Princes* (Harl. MS. 1766)," *British Library Journal* (2011): article 4. Each of these monks has a banderole hovering beside him, but these were left blank originally. On one of these banderoles a later reader wrote, "dan Iohn Lidgate." The added words are attributed to a sixteenth-century hand in Catherine Reynolds, "Illustrated Boccaccio Manuscripts in the British Library (London)," *Studi sul Boccaccio* 17 (1988): 113–183 (143), but they may be of the later fifteenth century.

11. The exemplum of Duke Gaultier and the envoy to Humphrey are *Troy Book*, IX: 2553–2804 and 3303–3540 respectively.

12. On this manuscript, see Victoria Kirkham, "Decoration and Iconography of Lydgate's *Fall of Princes* (*De casibus virorum illustrium*) at the Philadelphia Rosenbach," *Studi sul Boccaccio* 25 (1997): 297–310.

13. Before Book II there is a blank space for a miniature, which was never completed; and the first two leaves of Book VIII have been excised. See Scott, *Later Gothic Manuscripts,* II, no. 119.

14. For the tradition of illumination in the French copies, see Anne D. Hedeman, *Translating the Past: Laurent de Premierfait and Boccaccio's "De Casibus"* (Los Angeles: Getty, 2008).

15. "He that did som tyme his besi diligence / The boke of Bokas in frensh to translate owte of latin i called was laurence"; Newberry Library MS 33.3, folio 1r; I have silently expanded all abbreviations.

16. Alexandra Gillespie, "Framing Lydgate's Fall of Princes: The Evidence of Book History," *Mediaevalia* 20 (2001): 153–178; and Alexandra Gillespie, *Print Culture and the Medieval Author: Chaucer, Lydgate, and Their Books, 1473–1557* (Oxford: Oxford University Press, 2006).

17. The words "forget nott" appear in a *c.* 1500 hand on folio 45r, as well as the letters "FENRGET" along with a closed S. The manuscript also contains the bookplates of George E. Leighton of St. Louis, Missouri (b. 1835), with a monogram shield "Wrenwood," and his son George B. Leighton of Monadnock Farms, New Hampshire. Apparently, "a conspicuous feature of the Leighton home is an extensive library, which could hardly be duplicated in the West. The books have been collected in Europe and America with great judgment, and reflect the taste and studies of the collector"; *The National Cyclopaedia of American Biography,* 4 vols. (New York: White & Company, 1893), 4:361–362. Perhaps Leighton acquired the manuscript at the Offor sale or from George Mendlicott (see above, n. 4). The absence of medieval ownership marks and

heraldry are typical and should not be taken necessarily as evidence of nonarmigerous owners. See Kate Harris, "Patrons, Buyers and Owners: The Evidence for Ownership and the Role of Book Owners in Book Production and the Book Trade," in *Book Production and Publishing in Britain 1375–1475*, ed. Jeremy Griffiths and Derek Pearsall (Cambridge, UK: Cambridge University Press, 1989), 163–200.

18. C. Paul Christianson, "Evidence for the Study of London's Late Medieval Manuscript-Book Trade," in *Book Production and Publishing in Britain 1375–1475: Cambridge Studies in Publishing and Printing History*, ed. Jeremy Griffiths and Derek Pearsall (Cambridge, UK: Cambridge University Press, 1989), 87–108.

Raoul Lefèvre in Dutch: Two 1521 Editions of the Antwerp Printer Jan van Doesborch

BART BESAMUSCA

As far as we know, the Antwerp printer and publisher Jan van Doesborch started his career around 1501, when he took over the printing house of the widow of Rolant van den Dorpe, including her typographic material, woodcuts, and two printer's marks. Van Doesborch worked in Antwerp until his move to Utrecht around 1531. There, he continued his printing press until his death in 1536.[1] According to the Universal Short Title Catalogue, van Doesborch published sixty-one editions.[2] His printer's list shows that he focused on grammars, vocabularies, catechetic texts, medical texts, and prose romances. It is noteworthy that around one third of van Doesborch's books were printed in English. Producing books such as *A Gest of Robyn Hode* (*ca.* 1510, USTC 436806), *Mary of Nemmegen* (*ca.* 1518, USTC 437010), *Frederyke of Jennen* (1518, USTC 437023), and *Of the Newe Landes* (*ca.* 1520, USTC 410154), van Doesborch was responsible for almost 25 percent of all the books printed for the English market in Antwerp in the first half of the sixteenth century.[3] As is shown, for instance, by *The Fifteen Tokens* (*ca.* 1505, USTC 410043) and *Vijftheen vreesselijke tekenen* (*ca.* 1505, USTC 436709), he also printed texts in both an English and a Dutch edition.[4] These parallel productions testify to van Doesborch's strong market-driven printing strategy. Another, quite remarkable example of his commercial orientation is discussed in this article.

On November 8, 1521, van Doesborch published *Van Jason ende Hercules* [Of Jason and Hercules] (Fig. 1). In addition to the four images, to which I return below, the text on the title page attempts to attract potential readers. It states:

> Van Jason ende Hercules, die wonderlike, vreemde historien. Hoe dat die edel, vrome Jason ghewan dat gulden vlies ende van noch veel wonderlike avontueren die Jason met die schone Medea hadde. Ende voert vanden alder stercsten Hercules, die wonderlike feyten van wapenen in orloghen dede doe hi Troyen twee reysen destrueerde ende hoe hi vacht tegens vreemde wonderlike beesten, die hi al verwan. Ende tis genuechlick ende wonderlick om te horen lesen. (fol. A1r)[5]

> [Of Jason and Hercules, amazing, strange stories. How the noble and valiant Jason won the golden fleece, and of many more amazing adventures which Jason experienced with the beautiful Medea. And, in addition, of the mighty strong Hercules, who performed amazing feats of arms in times of war, destroying Troy twice under way, and how he fought against strange, amazing creatures, all of which he defeated. And it [the story] is pleasant and amazing to hear being read.][6]

Both the story as a whole and the individual adventures are called "wonderli(c)k(e)," amazing. The adjective is printed no less than five times to recommend the romance to potential buyers. Although present-day readers may share the opinion that van Doesborch is hammering his point home, he must have known that this adjective could increase sales figures.[7]

The source of van Doesborch's romance was a printed edition published by Jacob Bellaert, who had a printing house in Haarlem between December 1483 and August 1486.[8] Bellaert's printer's list shows that he attempted to interest a Dutch-speaking audience in texts that were part of the courtly culture of the dukes of Burgundy. Somewhere between 1483 and 1485, Bellaert printed a Dutch translation of Raoul Lefèvre's *Histoire de Jason*. The text is accompanied by striking illustrations, which were made by the so-called Master of Bellaert.[9]

Just one month after the publication of *Van Jason ende Hercules*, van Doesborch completed printing *Die historie vanden stercken Hercules* [The

Figure 1. Title page of *Van Jason ende Hercules*. Copy: London, British Library, C.97.d.13, folio A1r.

Story of the Strong Hercules] (Fig. 2).[10] The text on the title page of the book, which dates from December 12, 1521, reads:

> Die historie vanden stercken Hercules, die veel wonderlike dinghen in sijn leven heeft ghedaen. Sijn gheboerte was wonderlic ende sijn leven was avontuerlic, want hi menich vervaerlic beeste verslaghen heeft, ghelijc men in die historie hier na verclaren sal. Ende si is seer avontuerlic ende ghenuechlic om lesen. (fol. a1r)

> [The story of the strong Hercules, who did many amazing things in his lifetime. His birth was amazing, and his life was exciting, because he killed many dangerous creatures, as will be explained in the following story. And it is very exciting and pleasant to read.]

The source of this edition was again a book published by Bellaert. On May 5, 1485, the Haarlem printer completed a Dutch translation of Lefèvre's *Recueil des histoires de Troyes* under the title *Vergaderinge der historien van Troyen*.[11] This text was also illustrated by the Bellaert Master.[12] The part of the *Vergaderinge* that was concerned with the story of Hercules served as the source of van Doesborch's *Die historie vanden stercken Hercules*. Incidentally, in France the same phenomenon occurred: using Lefèvre's *Recueil*, the Parish printer Michel Le Noir published *Les prouesses et vaillances du preux Hercule* in 1500.[13]

Bellaert's editions were both similarly adapted by van Doesborch to suit the needs of the early sixteenth-century readers whom he had in mind. As I have shown elsewhere, van Doesborch heavily abbreviated his source texts. His adaptation resulted in texts that focused more on action and sensationalism than Bellaert's texts did.[14] Furthermore, both *Van Jason ende Hercules* and *Die historie vanden stercken Hercules* were provided with a more extensive illustration program. Some of van Doesborch's woodcuts are copies of the striking woodcuts of the Master of Bellaert. In both his editions, van Doesborch increased the number of illustrations by recycling woodblocks that had originally been cut for other texts.[15]

By designing alluring title pages, abbreviating his source texts, and adding illustrations, van Doesborch tried to make his books as attractive and thus as marketable as possible. In addition, his commercial strategy led to a sort of package deal. As is apparent from the title page of *Die historie vanden stercken Hercules*, this book was intended to be sold as a single edition. However, it

Figure 2. Title page of *Die historie vanden stercken Hercules*. Copy: London, British Library, C.97.d.13, folio a1r.

will become clear that van Doesborch stimulated and promoted in various ways the purchase of both *Van Jason ende Hercules* and *Die historie vanden stercken Hercules* together.

Three passages in *Van Jason ende Hercules* announce events featuring Hercules that would be related later on. The first reference is in the episode in which Jason and his companions are staying on the island of Lemnos. Hercules decides to go in search of adventures, and:

> Hi quam in eens conincs huys die hi eens verlost
> hadde van die van Ariens, also die historie noch
> verclaren sal. (*Van Jason ende Hercules*, fol. D4v,a)

> [He arrived at the dwelling of a king, whom he had
> delivered from those of Ariens, as the story will tell
> later on.]

This puzzling phrase turns out to be a bungled reference to Hercules' fight against the frightening Harpies, as is clear from Bellaert's wording in the *Historie van Jason*:

> Hi quam op een tijt in eens conincs huus ghenoemt
> Furius, die hy vanden arpien verloste ende jaechdese
> tot up de rivier van Sturphalen, also opt lange in sijn
> historie bet verclaert staet. (*Historie van Jason*, fol.
> E2v,a)

> [He arrived one time at the dwelling of a king called
> Furis, whom he delivered from the Harpies which
> he pursued until the river of Sturphalen, as is told
> extensively in his story.]

Both Bellaert's text and the French *Histoire de Jason* refer to a wide-ranging account of this event in Hercules' story, which may be, according to Gert Pinkernell, Boccaccio's *Genealogie deorum gentilium libri*.[16] Van Doesborch changed this reference to an independent work into an internal reference, falsely suggesting that the reader would eventually read about "those of Ariens."

The second announcement of Hercules' deeds in van Doesborch's *Van Jason ende Hercules* follows on the hero's return to Lemnos. The text reads:

> Ende hier en tusschen soe quam Hercules weder
> om in die stadt van Lennos uter bosschagien, daer hi
> in ghegaen was om vreemde avontuere te soecken,
> ghelijc hier voer verclaert staet. Ende hi hadde ooc
> int bossche veel avontueren, ghelijc noch hier na in
> sijn historie verclaert sal werden. (*Van Jason ende
> Hercules*, fol. E1v,b)

> [And meanwhile, Hercules returned to the city of
> Lemnos from the woods, which he had entered to
> search for strange adventures, as was stated earlier.
> And he experienced many adventures in the forest,
> as will be related in his story later on.]

This reference is missing in both Bellaert's *Historie van Jason* and the French *Histoire de Jason*.[17]

The third and last announcement of Hercules' great future exploits in van Doesborch's *Van Jason ende Hercules* is located right at the end of the text. The narrator tells us that Jason and Medea died when they were very old, after a happy and fertile life (fol. L4r,b). The narrator's final sentences read as follows:

> Ende hier mede is van Jason ghenoech. Nu willen wi
> voert bescrijven die historie ende dat leven vanden
> vromen Hercules. (*Van Jason ende Hercules*, fol.
> L4r,b)

> [And enough here (has been told) about Jason.
> Now we will describe the history and the life of the
> valiant Hercules.]

It is beyond doubt that these concluding sentences, which are absent in both Bellaert's *Historie van Jason* and the French *Histoire de Jason*,[18] establish a connection between *Van Jason ende Hercules* and *Die historie vanden stercken Hercules*. And even though the romance about Hercules has its own title page and was produced separately, as is shown by the numbering of the signatures, starting again with "a," its prologue's first sentences refer back to *Van Jason ende Hercules*. They read as follows:

Prologhe om voert tot onser materien te gaen die
wi begonnen hebben. Ende want die historie ende
dat leven van Jason nu bescreven ende voleyndt is,
so willen wi nu bescriven ende verclaren de gesten
ende wercken vanden stercken Hercules. (*Die
historie vanden stercken Hercules*, fol. a1v,a)

[Prologue in order to continue the matter that we
have started. And since the history and the life of
Jason have been described and finished now, we
will describe and elucidate the deeds and actions
of the strong Hercules.]

This explicit connection between *Van Jason ende Hercules* and *Die historie vanden stercken Hercules* is strongly reinforced by their title pages. The phrases on the title page of *Van Jason ende Hercules* promise feats of arms by Hercules that are, however, related only in the second romance, *Die historie vanden stercken Hercules*. This link between the two texts is visually confirmed by two of the four woodcuts (Fig. 1). The top-right image on the title page of *Van Jason ende Hercules* shows Hercules before the walls of Troy, defending King Laomedon's daughter against a terrible monster. The bottom-right woodcut illustrates Hercules' fight against the Hydra of Lerna. However, neither episode features in *Van Jason ende Hercules*; they are both part of the *Die historie vanden stercken Hercules*.[19]

These two images are repeated on the title page of *Die historie vanden stercken Hercules* (Fig. 2). Here, they function in two ways: they signal the beginning of a new romance, thus visualizing separation of the two texts, and at the same time they link *Die historie vanden stercken Hercules* through the repetition of the images to the preceding volume, *Van Jason ende Hercules*, thus creating unity between the two books.

Van Jason ende Hercules and *Die historie vanden stercken Hercules* could be bought separately, yet they were clearly designed for sale as a set of two single but related editions. This marketing strategy may be clever, but it does not allot van Doesborch a unique position in the early history of printing. Martha Driver shows, for example, that van Doesborch's contemporary Wynkyn de Worde applied a comparable scheme. In 1496, he printed the *Book of Hawking, Hunting and Heraldry*, which actually consists of four treatises, including a tract on fishing.[20] Although de Worde linked these parts together by means of cross references, he published the treatise on fishing in a single edition in 1533.[21] Another example of the pairing of books is provided by de Worde's 1498 edition of Chaucer's *Canterbury Tales* and Lydgate's *The Assembly of Gods*, printed by de Worde around the same time.[22] By using the same woodcut on the title page, illustrating the gathering of the pilgrims at the inn or the gods on Olympus, de Worde suggested that these editions belonged together, and indeed, a number of the surviving copies are found together.[23] One may wonder if van Doesborch, who stayed in London for quite some time, as witnessed by the tithes roll of the parish of St. Martin in the Fields for 1523, and who must have known de Worde personally, got his inspiration for his marketing tactics from his English colleague.[24]

Van Doesborch even included a third print in his sales strategy. Clearly aware of the literary taste of the potential buyers of his books, he reminds the readers in the prologue of *Die historie vanden stercken Hercules* of the existence of yet another, related romance:

> Die derde destructie die daer nae van den Griecxsschen heeren gheschyede, daer dye vrome Hector van Troyen verslaghen was, die historie is in een ander boeck gheprent, die geheten es "die destructie van Troyen ende vander amoruesheyt van Troylus ende Briseda." (*Die historie vanden stercken Hercules*, fol. a1v)

> [The history of the third destruction by the Greek army later on, in which the valiant Hector of Troy was killed, is printed in another book, entitled "The Destruction of Troy and about the love of Troilus and Cressida."]

This is a reference to an edition that was published by van Doesborch around 1508.[25] Its title page reads:

> Die distructie van Troyen die laetste. Ende die schoone ammoruesheyt van Troylus ende der schoonder Breseda, Calcas dochter, die een verrader was. (*Die distructie van Troyen*, fol. a1r)

> [The final destruction of Troy. And (about) the wonderful love of Troilus and the beautiful Cressida, daughter of Calchas, who was a traitor.]

On the last page of van Doesborch's *Die historie vanden stercken Hercules*, readers are again reminded of this third romance:

Hier eyndet die historie ende dat leven vanden
vromen Hercules, met die twee destructien van
Troyen, die doer Hercules gheschieden. Ende isser
yemant die de derde destructie van Troyen begheert
te weten, daer die vrome Hector verslaghen was,
dats gheprent in een ander boeck, geheten "Die
destructie van Troyen" (*Die historie vanden stercken
Hercules*, fol. m4r)

[Here ends the story and the life of the valiant
Hercules, including the two destructions of Troy
that were carried out by Hercules. And if someone
wants to know about the third destruction of Troy,
in which the valiant Hector was killed, that is
printed in another book, entitled "The destruction
of Troy."]

We will probably never know if van Doesborch really increased his sales
by linking his books. There are, however, four reasons to assume that his
1521 editions of *Van Jason ende Hercules* and *Die historie vanden stercken
Hercules* were definitely a commercial success. First, the only two extant
copies of these editions are indeed bound together in a single book, which
is nowadays part of the collection of the British Library.[26] Although it is
unknown when they were first united, their joint preservation could hint at
the successful sale of both books as a set.

The second clue is provided by a book that was bought by the Hen-
drik Conscience Heritage Library in Antwerp in the spring of 2016.[27] This
volume consists of new editions by van Doesborch of both romances, again
bound together. According to a note by their former owner and early-book
specialist Willy Braekman (d. 2006), these editions were published around
1525. Piet Franssen has suggested a date around 1530.[28] The short period
between the production of these 1525 to 1530 editions and the 1521 editions points at their being a joint bestseller.

The third indication for their commercial triumph is provided by the
title page of the 1525 to 1530 edition of *Van Jason ende Hercules*. Below
the woodcuts, which are, incidentally, printed in an order that differs from
the 1521 edition (here the images of Hercules's adventures are placed on
the left side), a phrase reads: "Dese boecken vintmen te coop bi Willem
Vorsterman" [These books can be found for sale at Willem Vorsterman].[29]
The plural "boecken" proves that the two editions could still be purchased
together around 1525 to 1530. And what is more, even though van Doesborch printed the books, as is shown by the colophon of *Die historie vanden*

stercken Hercules (fol. m3v), his Antwerp colleague Vorsterman, famous for his keen business sense,[30] expected to gain profit from selling them.[31]

The fourth indication for the commercial success of *Van Jason ende Hercules* and *Die historie vanden stercken Hercules* is provided by a book that was published by the Antwerp printer Symon Cock in 1556.[32] This time, the romances are not available in two stand-alone copies. The text of *Van Jason ende Hercules* ends on folio H4v, followed by the title and prologue of *Die historie vanden stercken Hercules* on signature J1. Instead of producing two books that could be purchased both individually and together, Cock took a financial risk by printing a single bulky book. He clearly believed, therefore, in the sales potential of this edition.[33]

In the printing business, books were not produced to customer's orders. As a result, printers had to develop a nose for the interests of the potential buyers of their editions. In addition, they tried to counterbalance the fact that books were produced speculatively by introducing various methods to attract readers. Alluring title pages and extensive illustration programs served this goal. In this respect, van Doesborch did not differ from his colleagues in the early period of print. However, he did not stop there. He attempted to increase his sales by producing Dutch-English parallel editions, and, as I show, by linking romances, which could be bought both as a set and separately. The printing history of *Van Jason ende Hercules* and *Die historie vanden stercken Hercules* indicates, I would argue, that van Doesborch had found a formula for success.

Utrecht Centre for Medieval Studies, Utrecht University

Acknowledgments

This article results from the Netherlands Organisation for Scientific Research (NWO) and Research Foundation Flanders (FWO) research project, "The Changing Face of Medieval Dutch Narrative Literature in the Early Period of Print (1477–c. 1540)" (http://changingface.eu/). I would like to thank Elisabeth de Bruijn and Rita Schlusemann for their comments on an earlier draft of this essay. A version of the text was read at the Fifteenth Triennial Congress of the International Courtly Literature Society in Lexington, KY, July 24–29, 2016.

NOTES

1. See Piet J. A. Franssen, *Tussen tekst en publiek: Jan van Doesborch, drukker-uitgever en literator te Antwerpen en Utrecht in de eerste helft van de zestiende eeuw* (Amsterdam: Rodopi, 1990), 12; Anne Rouzet, *Dictionnaire des imprimeurs, libraires et éditeurs des XVe et XVIe siècles dans les*

limites géographiques de la Belgique actuelle (Nieuwkoop, Netherlands: De Graaf, 1975), 56–57 (about van Doesborch), 57–58 (about van den Dorpe). See Piet J. A. Franssen, "Jan van Doesborch's Departure from Antwerp and His Influence on the Utrecht Printer Jan Berntsz," *Quaerendo* 18 (1988): 161–190, for van Doesborch's move to Utrecht.

2. See the Universal Short Title Catalogue (USTC), http://ustc.ac.uk/ index.php/search/cicero?tm_fulltext=&tm_field_allauthr=&tm_ translator=&tm_editor=&ts_field_short_title=&tm_field_ imprint=van+Doesborch&tm_field_place=&sm_field_year=&f_ sm_field_year=&t_sm_field_year=&sm_field_country=&sm_field_ lang=&sm_field_format=&sm_field_digital=&sm_field_class=&tm_ field_cit_name=&tm_field_cit_no=&order=year_asc&sm_field_ ty=true&start=0; .Franssen, *Tussen tekst*, 14–15, lists fifty-eight editions.

3. See Piet J. A. Franssen, "Jan van Doesborch (?–1536), Printer of English Texts," *Quaerendo*, 16 (1986): 259–280, 263; and Franssen, "Jan van Doesborch's Departure," 167.

4. Franssen, "Jan van Doesborch's Departure," 259.

5. I quote from the only extant copy of this edition: London, British Library, C.97.d.13. I have adapted the use of "u," "v," and "w," punctuation and capital letters to modern conventions. Abbreviations have been expanded without notice.

6. All translations of the Middle Dutch are my own.

7. For "wonderlijc," see Yves G. Vermeulen, *Tot profijt en genoegen: Motive-ringen voor de produktie van Nederlandstalige gedrukte teksten 1477–1540* (Groningen, Netherlands: Wolters-Noordhoff, 1986), 174–176, 251.

8. See the Incunabula Short Title Catalogue (ISTC), http://data.cerl.org/ istc/_search?query=Bellaert&from=0&size=10&mode=default&sort =default. For Bellaert, see Lotte Hellinga, *Texts in Transit: Manuscript to Proof and Print in the Fifteenth Century* (Leiden, Netherlands: Brill, 2014), 323–327.

9. ISTC il00111000. For the Master of Bellaert, see Rineke Nieuwstraten, "Overlevering en verandering: de pentekeningen van de Jasonmeester en de houtsneden van Meester van Bellaert in de *Historie van Jason*," in *Boeken in de late Middeleeuwen: Verslag van de Groningse Codicologenda-gen 1992*, ed. Jos M. M. Hermans and Klaas van der Hoek (Groningen, Netherlands: Forsten, 1994), 111–124; and Ina Kok, *Woodcuts in Incu-nabula Printed in the Low Countries*, 4 vols. (Houten, Netherlands: Hes & De Graaf, 2013), ser. 160.1–21. For digitized images of the illustra-tions, see the edition in the Library of Congress collection, which has been digitized and is available online at https://www.loc.gov/resource/ rbc0001.2014rosen0490/?sp=1.

10. The only extant copy is bound together with *Van Jason ende Hercules* in London, British Library, C.97.d.13.
11. ISTC il00116000. For digitized images, see https://www.loc.gov/resource/rbc0001.2014rosen0487/?sp=1.
12. See Kok, *Woodcuts,* ser. 162.1–25.
13. ISTC il00112400.
14. Bart Besamusca, "Tekst en beeld in twee drukken van Jan van Doesborch: *Van Jason ende Hercules en Die historie van den stercken Hercules,*" *Spiegel der Letteren,* 59 (2017): forthcoming.
15. Ibid.
16. Raoul Lefèvre, *L'Histoire de Jason. Ein Roman aus dem 15. Jahrhundert,* ed. Gert Pinkernell (Frankfurt am Main, Germany: Athenäum Verlag, 1971), 172, lines 27–29: "Et il lui advint qu'il se trouva un jour en la maison d'un roy nommé Fineus, qu'il delivra des Arpies, et les enchassa jusques ou fleuve de Stinphale, comme il est contenu es fais d'Herculés." For Boccaccio, see ibid., 251–252.
17. *Historie van Jason,* fol. E4r; Lefèvre, *L'Histoire,* 174, lines 13–14.
18. *Historie van Jason,* fol. L6r; Lefèvre, *L'Histoire,* 240.
19. *Die historie vanden stercken Hercules,* fol. c2r and h4r.
20. ISTC ib01031000.
21. Martha W. Driver, "Woodcuts and Decorative Techniques," in *A Companion to the Early Printed Book in Britain 1476–1558,* ed. Vincent Gillespie and Susan Powell (Cambridge, UK: Brewer, 2014), 95–123, 112–113.
22. *Canterbury Tales:* ISTC ic00434000; *Assembly of Gods:* ISTC il00404000.
23. Driver, "Woodcuts," 113–118.
24. For van Doesborch in London, see Franssen, "Jan van Doesborch (?–1536)," 263; and Franssen, *Tussen tekst,* 12.
25. USTC 436813, Franssen, *Tussen tekst,* 55, number 12.
26. London, British Library, C.97.d.13.
27. Bart Besamusca, "Van drie naar een: over *Van Jason ende Hercules (1556)* van Symon Cock," in *Schriftgeheimen. Bundel opstellen ter gelegenheid van het emeritaat van Jos Biemans,* ed. Lisa Kuitert, Paul Dijstelberge, and Marjolein Hogenbirk (Amsterdam, Netherlands: Amsterdam University Press, 2017), forthcoming.
28. Piet Franssen, *"Van Jason ende Hercules:* een onbekende editie," *Neerlandistiek* (http://www.neerlandistiek.nl/2016/09/van-jason-ende-hercules-een-onbekende-editie/)
29. For an image, see Rita Schlusemann, *Schöne Historien: Niederländische Romane im deutschen Spätmittelalter und in der frühen Neuzeit* (Berlin and Boston: De Gruyter, 2016), 301.

30. Vermeulen, *Tot profijt*, 129: "scherpe koopmansgeest."
31. For the cooperation between van Doesborch and Vorsterman, see Rita Schlusemann, "De uitwisseling van houtsneden tussen Willem Vorsterman en Jan van Doesborch," *Queeste* 4 (1994): 156–173; and Schluse-mann, *Schöne Historien*, 75–83.
32. USTC 407516.
33. Besamusca, "Van drie naar een."

Caxton and His Readers: Histories of Book Use in a Copy of *The Canterbury Tales* (c. 1483)

DEVANI SINGH

At the Fondation Martin Bodmer in Cologny, Switzerland, is a little-known annotated copy of Chaucer's *Canterbury Tales*, the first illustrated edition published by Caxton around 1483.[1] This copy, Inc. B. 70, bears the physical marks of a long history of use, and this essay accounts for what is known of the book's provenance between its origins in Westminster and its arrival in Switzerland in the early 1940s. Its marginalia, damages, repairs, signatures, and binding are the signs of the individuals and institutions that read, revered, rejected, and coveted it, and are rewarding subjects for the history of reading. From this copy's history it is also possible to deduce the shifting cultural value of incunabula and specifically of the Caxton imprimatur during the intervening centuries since publication. A book like the Bodmer Caxton reaffirms the ways in which early books were used as well as read, and permits consideration of how historical users variously determined the utility and value attached to old books—as texts for reading, blank spaces for writing, and objects for collecting.[2]

"moral tale[s] vertuous"

The earliest evidence for the reception of this copy of *The Canterbury Tales* is a set of annotations likely written in the sixteenth century. These notes are clustered in two of the tales regarded as Chaucer's most sententious. Throughout *The Tale of Melibee* and in the first part of *The Parson's Tale* ("prima pars penitencie"), this reader has marked the margins with annotations in coarse red pencil. His marginalia, with their abbreviated Latin and frequent *Nota* symbols, suggest a certain economy in the reading and recording process. Despite their reticence, however, these annotations shed some light on the reader's engagement with the *Tales*. While they occasionally highlight important plot points, such as Melibee's confrontation of his enemies near the tale's conclusion, the annotations chiefly reflect an interest in each text's religious and moral maxims. In reading *Melibee*, the red-pencil reader is most interested in Dame Prudence's counsel, marking *sententiae* such as "For the Poete sayth / That we oughten pacyently to taken the trybulacions that comen to vs" with a gloss, "pacie*n*cia," or her advice to "alleway haue thre thynges in your herte" with the marginal gloss "Nota iii."[3] This reader's choice to add marginal notes exclusively beside the two prose tales suggests a selective reading of the collection. The enthusiasm of Renaissance readers for *Melibee* is witnessed by the comparatively higher volume of marginal glosses in copies of the *Tales*, as Alison Wiggins has documented.[4] The evidence from the Bodmer Caxton affirms not only that tale's attractiveness as a site for marginal commentary, but also demonstrates that certain readers judiciously gravitated towards both of Chaucer's "moral tale[s] vertuous" in prose.[5]

A second, probably later, annotator of *The Parson's Tale* wrote in black ink, leaving systematic finding notes that record his reading. On one representative page, a series of marginalia tracks the Parson's catalogue of sin: "discorde," "betreyinge tru[st]," "Id[le] words," "Jangleinge," "geast[er]s," "ye remedy against ire."[6] Both of these annotators identified and extracted moral guidance from the text, engaging with the book as a source of instruction and a site of Chaucer's own *auctoritas*. This is a literary appraisal that they might share with Caxton himself, whose Proheyme to the second edition names Chaucer as "that noble & grete philosopher Gefferey Chaucer," author of "many a noble historye as wel in metre as in ryme and prose."[7] Chaucer was hailed as an "Antient and Learned English Poet" on title pages of his works around the turn of the sixteenth century, but the surviving marginalia suggest that some of his most vocal early annotators—those who read with pen or pencil in hand—were commonplacing consumers of his prose tales who extracted *sententiae* as they read.[8]

Names in the Margins

The most striking evidence of the Bodmer Caxton's reception is the total of thirty-one premodern names and signatures preserved in its margins.[9] As in other annotated books, the handwritten traces left in this copy can appear inscrutable, revealing less about readers' engagement with Chaucer than about the varied and idiosyncratic forms of book use that exist alongside and beyond reading. Precisely because of their incidental nature—their engagement with the book *qua* book—such annotations signal, too, the type of value and utility a Caxton volume held for its later owners.

The Bodmer Caxton came into the possession of an annotator named John Loskey around the middle of the seventeenth century.[10] Developing a rudimentary system of secret writing, Loskey marked the book in six places with ciphered words and messages. He appears to have practiced encoding his own name—"J4hS 64sk2y"—inscribing it into the margins of the book at three points.[11] In one case, he copied both the ciphered name and, directly underneath, its decoded counterpart, "John Loskey" (Fig. 1).[12] The persistent declarations of his name elsewhere in the volume cast doubt on the notion that he wished to mask his identity.[13] Instead, the copy of Chaucer seems to have been a place for him to elaborate and refine a skill that he could also use for playful or practical purposes beyond the book.

Loskey jotted down a partial key to his ciphers within the volume, and on the same page tested his system by enciphering some of the Middle English from "The Man of Law's Tale." This sample text appears on the same page as the key and comes from the first three lines of one stanza. When deciphered, it reads: "The fame anone thorough rome / how as a king shal come a pilg[...]/ By herbengers."[14] In Loskey's hands, the leaves of the Bodmer Caxton appear to have been a site for rehearsing a practice whose utility would extend beyond the covers of the book itself.[15]

Figure 1. John Loskey's signature, ciphered and regular (sig. r.2r, detail).

Another substantial set of Loskey's ciphers transliterates not into English, but into an imperfect Latin (Fig. 2, lines 1–4):

> est liber iste meus possum promutere [sic]
> si furatur Johannes sic nominitur [sic]
> qui scripsit scripsita dextra siua sit benedicti [sic]
> qui scripsit carmen Loskeus est sibi nomen[16]

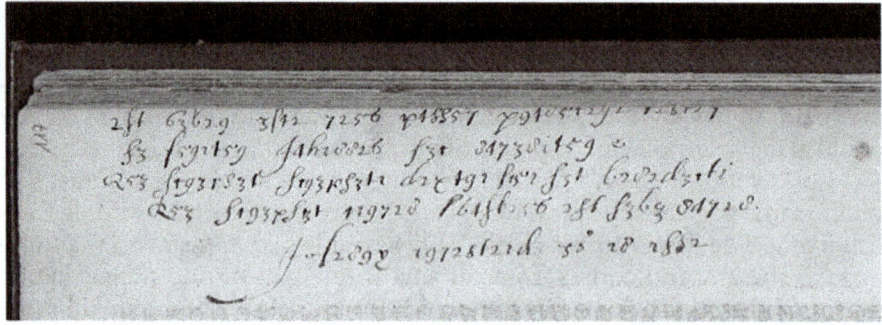

Figure 2. John Loskey's ciphered ownership note (lines 1–4) and insult "Josenry armestead is an asse" (line 5) (sig. p.5r, detail).

In its deciphered state, this inscription shares an important characteristic with some of the medieval ownership notes in manuscripts described by Daniel Wakelin, who proposes that "the very fact of addressing other readers of these books suggest[s] a rather public conception of private property."[17] As Nadine Akkerman has illustrated, the exchange of ciphered communication in the early modern period not only facilitated the passage of secret information but also forged social and political bonds within coteries of writers and recipients.[18] While we cannot know whether Loskey's cryptography in his Chaucer represents the wholly secret practice of an individual, what is certain is his wariness of circumstances and people who could undermine his assertion that the book was his personal property. In imagining a future in which his book is stolen (*"si furatur"*), Loskey resembles Wakelin's medieval annotators who "express some dislike of a world where the ownership of books is mobile and fragile."[19]

This Latin claim to ownership of the book is Loskey's most insistent, yet it is nearly impossible to work out without the key, making his encrypted self-naming (*"Johannes," "Loskeus"*) an illuminating exception to what Wakelin has summarized as the "public role and address […] implicit in their mere existence."[20] Rather than a potentially public record, Loskey's encoded ownership note is like a textual booby trap, hidden in plain sight, and only

requiring deciphering if the book should be stolen.[21] Impossible to understand without the key and almost playful in its execution in the form of
ciphers, the concealed ownership note seems to be created as much for
the writer himself as for any future readers. This note serves more than the
practical functions performed by conventional claims of ownership, and it
shares its enigmatic quality with other historical practices of customizing
one's books. Sir Hans Sloane (1660–1753) and Henry Yates Thomson
(1838–1928), for instance, both developed coded systems to record the details of their book buying, while Thomas Jefferson (1743–1826) customized
the relevant page signatures in many of his books so that they would spell
out his initials.[22] Writing of medieval manuscripts, Wakelin similarly invokes
the "knowing and playful comment" invited by more symbolic visual marks
of ownership, such as coats of arms and rebuses.[23] Like Loskey, another
early modern book owner wrote his ciphered ownership note—"Thomas
Ma[r?]k / his Book (1710)"—on the title page of his copy of Webster's
The principles of arithmetic (1634).[24] Such means of personalizing one's
library do more than protect its contents; these symbols of ownership also
seek to implicate owner and viewer alike in a discreet game of concealment
and recognition. The paradoxically secretive nature of Loskey's ownership
note in his Caxton is reinforced by another enciphered line underneath it,
which, when decoded, reads "Josenry armestead is an asse" (Fig. 2, line 5).
The name "Armestead" is familiar from elsewhere in the volume, where
another early modern annotation claims ownership for someone else: "Anthonie Armistead / Est verus possessor huius Libri."[25] Directly underneath
it is a competing charge in Loskey's familiar hand: "John Loskey Booke."

For all its engagement with people and purposes outside the book, however, Loskey's marginalia is noticeably bookish, concerned with his relation
to the volume itself and with his status as owner, if not reader, of this copy
of *The Canterbury Tales*. This bookishness is evident not only in Loskey's
rebuttal of Anthony Armistead's claim to the volume, or in the fear of theft
that his ciphers betray, but also in the persistent signatures, ciphered or not,
that he inscribed in ten places throughout the copy. He used the space of the
Caxton volume to cultivate a readerly persona, and it is precisely through the
praxis of writing (*"qui scripsit"*) that he articulates this identity. As Wakelin
observes of notes of ownership, "The people learning to read and write are
also learning to write about themselves as readers or owners of books."[26]
Similarly, Adam Smyth has argued that marginalia composed of "reiterated
signatures" might best be understood as a form of work in progress—of "an
identity in the process of being made, reformed, practised, tried out."[27] This
is demonstrably the case with Loskey where his ownership note—"John
Loskey Booke"—appears twice on the same page, not in a display hand nor
in a prominent place in the book, but tucked into a space in the lower left

margin of a verso leaf, where it is penned in very small letters.[28] This occurs as well on another leaf, where he wrote only "John Loskey B," before he trailed off into a series of six attempts at fashioning a majuscule *B*.[29]

Despite the significant absence of any textual or literary engagement with Chaucer, Loskey's marginalia must be understood alongside his relation to this book (*"liber iste"*) which he insisted he owned, and inside which he marked out spaces for practicing both secret and conventional methods of writing.[30] In this way, the printed page appears to be a neutral and personal place, shielded from the demands and rigor of public life, in which a young gentleman could safely hone the arts of writing. Yet Loskey's marginal notes also suggest that the annotator's intimacy with the page is threatened by a more public arena of other readers and claimants, like the Armisteads. His ciphers thus attempt to circumscribe and delimit the public space of the page while betraying an inevitable anxiety towards the book's future readers.

Such readers were evidently numerous. On a series of six rectos between "The Franklin's Tale" and "The Wife of Bath's Tale," an annotator contemporary with Loskey has inscribed the names of different women in the margins, using the same large letters and brown ink: "Elizabeth Metcalfe," "Margaret Pulleyne" and "Elianor Metcalfe," "Elizabeth Barrett," "Beatrice Mau," "Margery Trewman," and "Beatrice Mauleverer," with the names of Elizabeth Metcalfe and Beatrice Mauleverer also accompanied by their anagrams.[31] The hand's letter forms are regular, although significant blotting suggests haste or inexperience in writing. This succession of women's names—one echoing the Thomas and George Mauleverer whose names appear elsewhere in the copy[32]—may have collectively formed a type of *album amicorum* that gathered and preserved the names of those worthy of inclusion.[33] The anonymous annotator could have been a reader of Chaucer or may simply have been looking for a place to write, and like Loskey, found that place in the blank paper of this Caxton. Either way, the recording of these six names is an act invested with social and symbolic meaning, and the choice of this volume as a ready *album* in which to collect them demonstrates the versatility of the book as object.

There is evidence of connections between two families named Mauleverer and Metcalfe in the parish of Ingleby Arncliffe, North Yorkshire, in the mid-seventeenth century. James Mauleverer (1590/1–1664) had a wife called Beatrice (*née* Hutton, 1596–*c*.1640), as well as a daughter (b. 1624) and also a granddaughter (1651/2–1691) of that name. A son of James and Beatrice Mauleverer, Timothy (1627–1686/7), married a woman born Elizabeth Metcalfe (1625–1674), the daughter of George Metcalfe of nearby Northallerton.[34] Another Mauleverer, Thomas, of Allerton Mauleverer (d. 1687), had his will witnessed by one Christopher Metcalfe.[35] That these are the Yorkshire families among whom the book circulated during the seventeenth century is further suggested by a deed from December 25, 1627. James Mauleverer is the named lessor, and one Edmond Troutbecke of Bramham is the lessee, while a "Mr. Loskey, gent." is also mentioned in the deed as a landlord whose grounds Troutbecke also had "in his tenure."[36] From the late sixteenth century, the Mauleverer family seat was the manor called Arncliffe Hall, which the family owned until the early twentieth century.[37] The large number of early modern names in this volume indicates the book's centrality within the larger household but also suggests its mobility beyond the Mauleverer family.

The women's names and Loskey's signatures and ciphers collectively refine the narrative of how the book was conceived by its annotators in the seventeenth century. First, all of these notes underscore the conventionality of readers' marginal comments and marks, most recently classified by William H. Sherman and Heidi Brayman Hackel, who enumerate various categories that could be said to comprise early modern marginalia.[38] The conventional quality of these early modern notes, however, resides not only in their textual burden—names, anagrams, maxims, ownership notes, pen trials—but also in their relative location within the book's margins. When these individual readers chose to scribble, sign their names, or test a pen in the Bodmer Caxton, they authorized and reaffirmed the book's pages (and especially its rectos) as a place for exactly these types of uses.[39] By the late seventeenth century, Chaucer was being read in the classically styled folio volumes edited by Thomas Speght, which included not only *The Canterbury Tales*, but both genuine and spurious texts that purported to represent all of his "Workes," as well as features like a "Life" and a glossary of hard words, intended to aid the reader in understanding Chaucer's biography and his language.[40] Alongside such editions, which advertised their "newly Printed" status, older volumes like the Bodmer Caxton could conceivably be seen by some users as less valuable or useful for the reading of Chaucer than their more recent counterparts.

Caxton on the Market

The copy's value, both cultural and economic, was more prominently evaluated in the late nineteenth and early twentieth centuries. Sometime after its association with Loskey and the Mauleverers around the middle of the seventeenth century, the book entered the collections of the Royal Society, whose modern binding it still bears. It may have entered the library with the founding bequest made by Henry Howard, Duke of Norfolk in 1667; if it ever bore a stamp or inscription marking such a provenance, this has since been lost.[41] In the early 1920s, the Council of the Royal Society contemplated selling off the remaining non-scientific books from the collection.

The decision had been brewing for some decades, as an article published in *The Times* on December 1, 1880, relates:

> In regard to the library, a question has arisen as to how far purely literary works, which occupy much space, should be retained. Among them there are, doubtless, some which add neither to the utility nor to the importance of the library, but there are also some early printed books, bibliographical treasures, which are worthy of a place in any collection. It is proposed to have these carefully put in order, and to place them in a case by themselves. Among these, there may be mentioned: "Caxton's Chaucer," 1480, "Pynson's Chaucer," 1492, "Speght's Folio Chaucer," 1598.[42]

Having already sold or exchanged its non-scientific manuscripts for scientific books with the British Museum in 1829, the Society finally decided to dispose of the remainder of its non-scientific (or "miscellaneous") printed books, including those from Norfolk's founding bequest, around 1923.[43] The announcement triggered a debate in the *Times* letters pages surrounding the legal and moral rights of the Society to dispose of a collection entrusted to it over 250 years prior. The Royal Society's President, C.S. Sherrington (1857–1952), wrote in defense of the ruling on March 26, 1925: "These volumes, it has been decided, after careful deliberation, to sell because they have no scientific interest or are duplicate copies."[44] A riposte by R. T. Gunther (1869–1940), later founder of Oxford's Museum of the History of Science, cautioned that any "scientific interest and value" of future acquisitions could not be compared to the more laudable "value [of] general culture" esteemed by the founding members of the Royal Society when they established their Library.[45]

Our copy featured prominently in discussions of the sale. It is once again listed in *The Times*, in an article of March 26, 1925, announcing the Sotheby's auction, and the details of its sale also appear in the newspaper's account of the auction published on May 5: "two early editions of Chaucer's 'Canterbury Tales,' one of Caxton's second edition, 1484, with 283 leaves (there should be 312 [sic])—£660, and the other printed by R. Pynson, 1490, 321 leaves (wanting three leaves, one of which is a blank)—£560 (both bought by Quaritch) [sic]."[46] The Royal Society's Caxton and Pynson were listed in the Sotheby's catalogue as "Exceedingly Rare" and "Extremely Rare," with the further notes that thirteen and three copies of each edition survive, respectively. Beside the Pynson's greater degree of rarity, its better condition, and its "old calf" binding, the Caxton's higher selling price in this sale is noteworthy.

By 1941, the book was in the possession of the Philadelphia collector A. S. W. Rosenbach (1876–1952), who had advertised it at a price of $32,500.[47] Its buyer was Martin Bodmer (1899–1971), a Swiss philanthropist and bibliophile, who acquired it for his ambitious collection of world literature by engineering a deal with Rosenbach.[48] Also interested in the first edition of Shakespeare's *Sonnets* (1609) listed at $78,500 in the catalogue, Bodmer offered to pay the significantly lower sum of $60,000 for the pair. His proposal, made during a period of wartime austerity, was accepted by Rosenbach, and the books were kept in storage in New York until the end of the war permitted their safe passage to Switzerland.[49] The pair of books remains at the Fondation Martin Bodmer in Cologny, Geneva, where they number among a collection of 174 English books printed before 1700, representing one arm of Bodmer's vast library of world literature.[50] For Bodmer, the Caxton acquisition formed a key addition to his Chaucer collection, which includes a fifteenth-century manuscript of *The Canterbury Tales*[51] (formerly Phillipps MS 8136 and now Bodmer Cod. 48); Richard Pynson's trilogy of *The Canterbury Tales, The House of Fame,* and *Troilus* (all *c.* 1526); and editions of the *Workes* by William Thynne (1532, and two copies of the *c.* 1550 edition) and Thomas Speght (1598, 1602).[52] In total, there remain nine printed Chaucer volumes at the Bodmer, several of which were also purchased during the 1940s. Apart from these, the archives indicate that the library once owned a single leaf of Caxton's first edition of the *Tales*. The *c.* 1483 edition of the *Tales*, however, is the only English incunable still at the Fondation Bodmer.

A "very poor copy"?
The Bodmer Caxton lacks thirty-one leaves, and already had several leaves damaged and torn in its premodern history. An early owner made a series of extensive repairs to these leaves, patching many tears and holes, furnishing partially torn leaves with new paper, and recopying the sections of missing text back into the book on the fresh paper at five points (Figs. 3 [a] and [b]).[53] One of the newly added leaves retains its watermark, a large fleur-de-lis in a shield with the initials "WR" at the base, tentatively suggesting a sixteenth- or seventeenth-century date for the repairs.[54] Similarities between the supplied text and Richard Pynson's *c.* 1492 edition (*STC* 5084) indicate that Pynson was the repairer's source text.[55] The physical and textual mending of this copy by a premodern user illuminate certain bibliographic expectations about the early printed book. First, the likely use of a Pynson incunable over more recent editions available by the end of the seventeenth century might reflect the repairer's view of a Caxton not as a superseded edition of *The Canterbury Tales,* but as an old and valuable book worth preserving for its own sake. In addition, the new scribe supplied the missing text in

a stylized script that approximates the black letter in which Chaucer would be printed in all editions until the eighteenth century. Significantly, this scribe also reproduced extraneous physical details from the printed edition no longer necessary in a manuscript copy: the indented spaces left blank for decorated initials at the beginning of tales and prologues, page signatures, and a catchword (Fig. 3b).[56] Here is a copyist who not only sought to restore the textual integrity of this copy of Caxton, but who deliberately imitated the conventions of the early printed page while doing so.

This impulse to perfect and preserve incunabula is also evident in another copy of Caxton's second edition of the *Tales* formerly owned by Thomas Grenville (1755–1846), and now in the British Library. Slips in Grenville's hand recount their owner's admiration of his book: "the singular beauty of this Copy, induced me to incur a heavy expense in copying the defective leaves from that in St John's College Oxford." Another note adds the

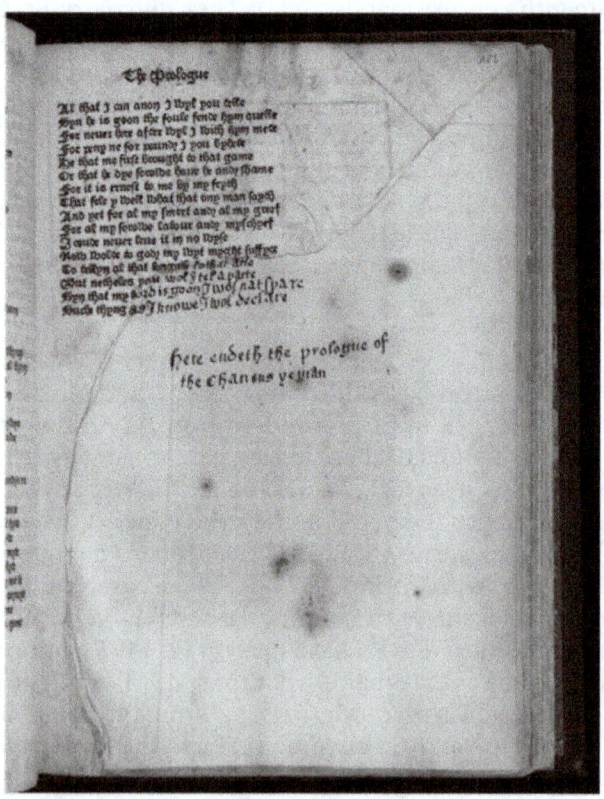

Figure 3a. Leaf from CYP/CYT showing premodern repairs.

facsimilist's name: "This beautiful Copy of mine wanting several leaves I had them supplied in facsimile by Harris from the Copy at St. John's [Oxford]— it is now quite perfect."[57] Agents like the prolific facsimilist John Harris (1791–1873), those who hired him to perfect their works, and the early repairer of the Bodmer Caxton all shared an antiquarian sensibility toward ancient works and a desire for their completeness and authenticity. The cachet that the first printed books could hold for later readers is most dramatically illustrated by another volume, Cambridge University Library, Syn.5.53.1. This is a fragment of William Thynne's 1532 edition (*STC* 5068), which was furnished with a spurious title page claiming a new provenance: "Westmestre, enprynted Wyllyam Caxton, MCCCCLXXXI [1481]."[58]

Where the Grenville copy has been professionally perfected and is lauded for its beauty, the Bodmer Caxton is imperfect, with missing leaves and roughly repatched areas. It was labelled a "very poor copy" by De Ricci

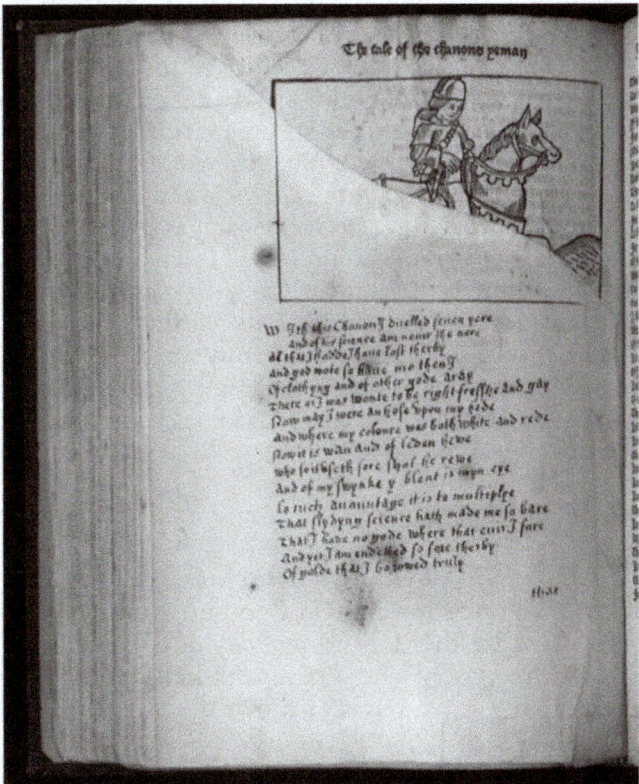

Figure 3b. Imitation blackletter script, offset initial, and catchword (sigs. 2d7r and 2d7v).

owing to these missing leaves, although the Sotheby's sale catalogue professed, "apart from the defects mentioned this copy is in very fair condition with good margins."[59] But the "good margins" that made this particular copy a desirable collector's item by the late nineteenth century were also an object of the bibliophile's disdain, encapsulated in William Blades's assessment of the then–Royal Society copy as bearing "manuscript disfigurements."[60] The physical feature that rendered the book a convenient place for early modern scribbling no doubt impacted nineteenth-century assessments of the copy's worth and collectibility.

The fortunes of the Bodmer copy thus track shifting attitudes to Caxtons between the book's publication and the present day. Events like the publication of Blades's two-volume biography of the printer (published from 1861 to 1863) and the South Kensington Quadricentennial exhibition (1877) saw the Caxton brand reach a new zenith during the mid- to late nineteenth century.[61] The concomitant appetite of collectors for England's earliest printed books was served by professional pen- and type-facsimilists like Harris whose business was the completion, restoration, and making good of old books. The repairs in the Bodmer Caxton, too, show that the anxiety over bibliographic completeness had its precedent in early modern repairs to damaged old books.[62] But where more immaculate copies had many of their marginal notes zealously cropped or washed by their collectors, the Bodmer Caxton's heavily annotated state suggests a relative neglect that results, ironically, in its significant interest to today's historians of reading. From its attentive, commonplacing readers to its use as a writing surface for ciphers and signatures, and ultimately to its pairing with a coveted Shakespeare edition in the sale to Bodmer, this copy's provenance demonstrates some of the hallmarks of Chaucerian reading alongside the lesser-studied histories of writing, rejection, and desire that also characterize the reception of England's earliest printed books.

University of Geneva

Acknowledgments
All images feature Fondation Martin Bodmer, Cologny, Inc. B. 70 and are courtesy of The Bodmer Lab, University of Geneva. I am grateful to Jacqueline Cowan and Jason Scott-Warren for their comments on an earlier draft of this essay. Any errors remain my own.

NOTES

1. *STC* 5083.
2. On book use, see William H. Sherman, *Used Books: Marking Readers in Renaissance England* (Philadelphia: University of Pennsylvania Press, 2007).
3. Sigs. B.5^r; B.7^v. My thanks are due to Katherine Hindley for help in transcribing the annotations of this reader.
4. See Alison Wiggins, "What Did Renaissance Readers Write in their Printed Copies of Chaucer?" *The Library* 9 (1) (2008): 16–17.
5. *The Riverside Chaucer*, ed. Larry D. Benson, 3rd edn. (Boston: Houghton Mifflin, 1987), 216 (VII. 940).
6. Sig. I.5^r.
7. Sig. a.2^r. These leaves are wanting in the Bodmer copy and were consulted in the Grenville copy of the second edition (British Library, C.21.d), discussed below and viewable online at "Treasures in Full: Caxton's Chaucer," British Library, accessed 20 March 2017, https://www.bl.uk/treasures/caxton/search.asp.
8. On the commonplacing of Chaucer, see Wiggins, "Printed Copies of Chaucer," 17. The two editions were printed in 1598 (*STC* 5077, 5078, and 5079) and in 1602 (*STC* 5080 and 5081).
9. Compare Wiggins, "Printed Copies of Chaucer," 29, who records a total of seventy-six names in her census of fifty-four copies.
10. One of his signatures is dated: "John Loskey Booke 1641." Sig. r.5^r.
11. Sigs. k.2^r, r.2^r, 2a.3^r.
12. Sig. r.2^r.
13. Loskey wrote his name in standard characters at seven different places in the book.
14. Sig. l.5^r.
15. On the uses of ciphering, see James Daybell, *The Material Letter in Early Modern England: Manuscript Letters and the Culture and Practices of Letter-Writing, 1512–1635* (New York: Palgrave Macmillan, 2012), 148; William H. Sherman, "Decoding the Renaissance: 500 Years of Codes and Ciphers," *Folgerpedia*, http://folgerpedia.folger.edu/Decoding_the_Renaissance:_500_Years_of_Codes_and_Ciphers [accessed January 9, 2017].
16. "This is my book I can swear / If it should be stolen John is named / He who wrote these words shall have his right hand blessed / He who wrote this poem, Loskey is his name." Sig. p.5^r. I thank Benjamin Cartlidge for advice on Loskey's Latin.

17. Daniel Wakelin, "'Thys ys my boke': Imagining the Owner in the Book," in *Spaces for Reading in Later Medieval England*, ed. Mary C. Flannery and Carrie Griffin (New York: Palgrave Macmillan, 2016), 32.
18. Nadine Akkerman, "Enigmatic Cultures of Cryptology," in James Daybell and Andrew Gordon, eds., *Cultures of Correspondence in Early Modern Britain* (Philadelphia: University of Pennsylvania Press, 2016), 69–84.
19. Wakelin, "'Thys ys my boke,'" 16.
20. Ibid., 17.
21. A similar use of code to establish ownership—of ideas, rather than books—was employed by scientists including Galileo Galilei (1564–1642), Christiaan Huygens (1629–1695), and Robert Hooke (1635–1703), who published their findings in anagrams so as to hide their discoveries while still safeguarding their claims to priority. See David Wootton, *The Invention of Science: A New History of the Scientific Revolution* (London: Allen Lane, 2015), 94–95.
22. To do this, Jefferson prefixed a *T* to pages signed *I* (J) and added a *J* to pages with signature *T*. A similar practice was adopted by Oxford antiquary Philip Bliss (1787–1857). See David Pearson, *Provenance Research in Book History* (London: British Library, 1994), 12–25; Margaret Nickson, "Sloane's Codes: The Solution to a Mystery," *Factotum* 7 (1979): 13–18; Christopher De Hamel, "Was Henry Yates Thomson a Gentleman?" in *Property of a Gentleman: The Formation, Organisation and Dispersal of the Private Library 1620–1920*, ed. R. Myers and M. Harris (Winchester: St Paul's Bibliographies, 1991), 77–89; and E.M. Sowerby, *Catalogue of the Library of Thomas Jefferson* (Washington, D.C.: The Library of Congress, 1952), 1: xii.
23. Wakelin, "'Thys ys my boke',"19.
24. British Library, Ames III/1190. See Pearson, *Provenance Research*, 21.
25. "Anthonie Armistead is the true owner of this book." Sig. o.1^r.
26. Wakelin, "'Thys ys my boke',"23.
27. Adam Smyth, *Autobiography in Early Modern England* (Cambridge: Cambridge University Press, 2010), 136. See Jason Scott-Warren, "Reading Graffiti in the Early Modern Book," *HLQ* 73, 367, who notes that "John Finet" wrote his name not only on the title page and flyleaf of CUL Pet.F.3.12, his Latin prayer book, but also repeated his name or initials nearly fifty times throughout the volume.
28. Sig. i.4^v.
29. Sig. q.7r.
30. Another ciphered note on sig. 2a.3^r reads, "learne to redeme the precious time here sent thee / shune false allurements, and courts subtilitie. / resolve herein, of thine amisse repent thee; so maist thou vanquish

chance and debilitie. / ʒo John Loskey." A Latin proverb and its English translation, in Loskey's italic and mixed secretary hands, also appear in the margins of sig. d.7^r: 'Fide sed ante fide qui fidet nec bene fidet / Faliter ergo fide ne capiare fide / He that trusts before he trie / May repent before he die.'

31. Signatures p.4^r, p.8^r, r.3^r, r.4^r,s.3^r,s.4^r. The anagrams for Elizabeth Metcalfe and Beatrice Mauleverer are "Habet faciam Stelle" and "Let vertue imbrace 'er" respectively, on sigs. p.4^r, s.4^r.

32. The names of Thomas Mauleverer and George Mauleverer appear together twice, and in the same hand, on sigs. B.5^v, h.1^r.

33. See G.D. Hobson, "Et Amicorum," *The Library*, 5th ser., 4 (2) (1949): 87–99. See also Helen Smith, "'Rare poems ask rare friends': Popularity and Collecting in Elizabethan England," in *The Elizabethan Top Ten: Defining Print Popularity in Early Modern England*, ed. Andy Kesson and Emma Smith (Burlington, VT: Ashgate, 2013), 84.

34. The Yorkshire Archaeological Society, *The Yorkshire Archaeological Journal* 16 (1902), 203. See also William Brown, *Ingleby Arncliffe and its Owners* (Leeds: John Whitehead and Son, 1901), 83–85.

35. "Will of Sir Thomas Mauleverer of Allerton Mauleverer, Yorkshire," The National Archives, accessed 12 January 2017, http://discovery. nationalarchives.gov.uk/details/r/D745575.

36. William Brown, ed., *Yorkshire Deeds* (Cambridge: Cambridge University Press, 1914), 2: 115.

37. See Brown, *Ingleby Arncliffe*, 6, who records that it was "left untenanted" until this time despite Mauleverer ownership since the early fifteenth century.

38. Sherman, *Used Books*, 16–17; Heidi Brayman Hackel, *Reading Material in Early Modern England: Print, Gender, and Literacy* (Cambridge: Cambridge University Press, 2005), 138–139.

39. By my count, 75 percent of the book's incidental marginalia (all marks excluding finding notes and textual commentary, where the location of the note is predetermined) appear on rectos.

40. Derek Pearsall, "Thomas Speght (*c.* 1550–?)," in *Editing Chaucer: The Great Tradition*, ed. Paul Ruggiers (Norman, OK: Pilgrim Books, 1984), 71–92.

41. Marie Boas Hall, *The Library and Archives of the Royal Society 1660–1990* (London: The Royal Society, 1992), 3, notes that books from the founding bequest were stamped "ex dono Henrici Howard Norfolciensis".

42. "The Royal Society," *The Times*, December 1, 1880.

43. Boas Hall, *Library and Archives of the Royal Society*, 44–46.

44. C.S. Sherrington, letter to the editor, *The Times*, March 27, 1925.

45. R.T. Gunther, letter to the editor, *The Times*, March 28, 1925. Letters

condemning the decision were also published in *The Times* on April 1, April 30, and May 5 of that year.

46. In fact, the annotated catalogues at the Huntington and in the Quaritch archives both confirm the £660 sum for the Caxton, but disagree as to the buyer, naming "Quaritch" and "J.P" respectively. I am grateful to both institutions for providing me with copy-specific information from their annotated auction catalogues, *Catalogue of valuable printed books, sold by order of the President and Council of the Royal Society, which will be sold by auction ... on Monday, the 4ᵗʰ of May, 1925* (London: Sotheby, 1925), no. 40. The Royal Society Pynson was lot no. 41.

47. *English Poetry to 1700* (Philadelphia: The Rosenbach Company, 1941), no. 160.

48. Bodmer would go on to make a larger purchase from Rosenbach in 1951 to 1952 when he purchased his Shakespeare collection. See Edwin Wolf and John F. Fleming, *Rosenbach: A Biography* (Cleveland: The World Publishing Co., 1960), 579–586.

49. Wolf and Fleming, *Rosenbach*, 502. An article by A.S.G. Edwards, "'What's it Worth?': Selling Chaucer's *Canterbury Tales* in the Twentieth Century," *Chaucer Review* 48 (2014), 239–250, misstates the $60,000 figure as the price of the Caxton only.

50. See Lukas Erne and Devani Singh, *Shakespeare in Geneva: Early Modern English Books (1475–1700) at the Martin Bodmer Foundation* (forthcoming 2017).

51. This MS was bought from Rosenbach on another occasion for $46,500, down from a catalogue price of $85,000. See H.P. Kraus, *A Rare Book Saga: The Autobiography of H.P. Kraus* (New York: Putnam, 1978), 273.

52. *STC* 5086, 5088, 5096; 5068, 5073, 5074; 5078, 5080.

53. The leaves with substantial repairs and recopied text are sigs. c.5; p.2; 2d.7; 2f.1; E.2.

54. The watermark is most similar to those catalogued as Briquet 7210 and Heawood 1721, although the absence of any complete sheets of paper in the repairs prevents the identification of any countermarks. See C.M. Briquet, *Les Filigranes: Dictionnaire Historique des Marques du Papier dès leur apparition vers 1282 jusqu'en 1600*, 2ⁿᵈ ed., ed. A. H. Stevenson (Amsterdam: The Paper Publications Society, 1968), 3; and Edward Heawood, *Watermarks, mainly of the 17th and 18th Centuries* (Hilversum: The Paper Publications Society, 1950).

55. The details in the supplied manuscript text peculiar to Pynson 1492 are evident, for example, in the *CYT* where "white and rede" appears where all the other black letter editions have "fresshe and rede"; and the inversion of the lines "There as I was wont to be right fresshe and gay / Of clothynge and of other good aray" (sig. 2d.7ᵛ).

56. Ink transfer onto the original pages suggests that the pages were physically repaired and then rewritten, rather than vice versa, eliminating the practical need for catchwords or page signatures.
57. British Library C.21.d, "Treasures in Full: Caxton's Chaucer," British Library, accessed 20 March 2017, https://www.bl.uk/treasures/caxton/search.asp.
58. Hope Johnston, "Readers' Memorials in Early Editions of Chaucer," *Studies in Bibliography* 59 (2015), 61.
59. *Catalogue of Valuable Printed Books*, 8. De Ricci measures the book at 273 x 197 cm in its modern binding, larger than nearly every other copy of this edition listed in his *Census*. Only the Pepys copy at Magdalene College, Cambridge is larger. Seymour De Ricci, *A Census of Caxtons* (Oxford: Bibliographical Society, 1909), no. 23: 9.
60. William Blades, *The Life and Typography of William Caxton* (London: Trübner & Co, 1863), 2, no. 57: 6.
61. On Caxton's reputation at the time of the exhibition, see David McKitterick, *Old Books, New Technologies: The Representation, Conservation and Transformation of Books since 1700* (Cambridge: Cambridge University Press, 2013): 159–182.
62. Ibid., 37–56.

The Fragments of a Middle English *Melusyne* Edition: Some Further Clues

LYDIA ZELDENRUST

A recent volume of this journal featured a fascinating contribution by Tania M. Colwell, in which she describes a group of printed fragments of a Middle English prose *Melusyne* found in the Bodleian Library in Oxford.[1] Six fragments of an edition printed in folio format survive, the various folios having been brought together after they were scattered among the Bodleian's collections.[2] These fragments have long remained relatively unknown to scholars, although they are listed in a number of catalogues, including the *Short Title Catalogue* (STC 14648) and the *Universal Short Title Catalogue* (USTC 501139).[3] The printed fragments are also rarely mentioned alongside the two better-known surviving manuscript versions of the English *Melusine* and *Romans de Partenay*, translations that each go back to a different French exemplar.[4] Colwell is the first to consider all six surviving printed fragments together, and she not only gives a thorough description of their stylistic, linguistic, and iconographical features, but she also makes crucial observations on the likelihood that this prose edition was printed by Wynkyn de Worde around 1510.

Colwell's note on these fragments also raises several interesting follow-up questions. One further avenue of inquiry in particular immediately resonated with me: that of the relationship between the English prose edition and the various *Mélusine* incunabula and early fifteenth-century editions that appeared on the Continent. During my recent research on the various Western European translations of this romance, I have uncovered some additional information about the English fragments that highlights their connection with European book production and trade networks. Such findings not only illustrate how many early *Mélusine* printers—including de Worde—benefited from cross-cultural connections and exchanges in the production of their books, but they may also have important implications in terms of the dating and potential source of the prose edition. This note, then, offers a complement to Colwell's, providing further clues in the mystery of the *Melusyne* fragments.

Since Colwell's description of the fragments is so detailed, it will suffice to give only a brief introduction here, before turning to these additional clues. The six surviving *Melusyne* fragments are now found in a guard-book under the Bodleian's shelfmark Vet. A1 d.18. Each of these paper fragments has been cropped, although the degree of resizing varies per folio.[5] The text of the romance is arranged in two columns, and the different episodes are introduced by separate headings. Those headings that are still complete have been numbered: they run from chapter lvi to lxxiii, but there are significant textual lacunae. The text of the fragments describes events found toward the end of the romance, around the key moment when Mélusine's great secret—that she becomes a half-serpent once a week—has been revealed, and she is forced to depart her family and her home. Fragment 1 begins at the point in the narrative where Melusine's son Geffray Great Tooth battles the giant Guedon, and fragment 6 ends with Geffray's visit to his father, Raymondin, who has become a hermit at Montserrat. The fragments also feature a total of four woodcuts, which illustrate scenes from the accompanying text. Most of the woodcuts have been cropped along with the rest of the folio; only the image on fragment 1r remains intact.

There is no surviving title page, and none of the fragments bears a colophon or any other printing marks, which means we cannot be entirely certain of the exact date of this edition nor of the identity of the printer. However, as Colwell shows, it is highly likely that the edition was published by de Worde, as the printing of the *Melusyne* romance would have been consistent with his output after 1500, both in terms of genre and of the edition's production and stylistic features.[6] I agree with Colwell that de Worde is the most likely candidate. However, I have been unable to find any concrete evidence as to why this edition is thought to have been printed specifically in 1510. After puzzling together various comments made by Robert Nolan, who is one of the first to discuss these fragments in his unpublished doctoral thesis, it appears that the Bodleian Library's catalogue first dated the fragments to 1510.[7] This date then led Nolan to postulate that de Worde must have been the printer, an idea that was then copied by other scholars. I have been in contact with librarians at the Bodleian's Rare Books collection in an attempt to track down the specific justifications for this date. However, the original catalogue slips give no details as to whether the dating of this edition is based on, for instance, type or deterioration of woodcuts. In fact, the edition was given a more cautious date of "*c.* 1510" in the original paper catalogue, but somehow this became 1510 exactly when the records were transferred to the digital catalogue and the STC.[8]

It is tempting to suppose that this dating was based on the partial watermark found on fragment 1. The mark is rather unclear and is also found in the middle of a woodcut. Colwell notes that the mark resembles "horns or the vertical spokes of a crown," but I would say that it bears a closer resemblance to those listed as "monts," or mountains, by Charles-Moïse Briquet, in which case it is upside down.[9] However, it must be said that one could also imagine that this is a mark depicting a flower, a leaf, or even a star—there is simply not enough left of the watermark to be able to make any definite claims about what it might represent, let alone about the dating of the paper. Colwell's discussion of the type used for the body of the text and for the headings also does not give us a very specific range of dates.[10] With such a lack of concrete evidence, it would be sensible to remain skeptical of this 1510 date, especially when trying to determine the possible source of this translation.

There is almost certainly an affiliation between the text of the fragments and that of the only known manuscript of an English prose *Melusine*— London, British Library, Royal, 18. B. II. This translation is based on the text of a printed edition of Jean d'Arras's Middle French *Mélusine ou la noble histoire de Lusignan*, most likely that of the *editio princeps* published by Adam Steinschaber in Geneva in 1478.[11] According to Nolan, although the text of the fragments is reduced by a quarter of its original size and is divided into a larger number of chapters, the fragments are so similar to the prose manuscript that they must represent an abridged version.[12] Carol Meale also comments on the many similarities between the manuscript and the fragments, but she argues that it is possible too that they represent separate translations that go back to a common exemplar.[13] Nonetheless, both scholars agree that the manuscript—usually dated to around 1500—was not copied from the printed text.[14] Naturally, the uncertainty surrounding the exact date of this edition is not a very helpful factor in trying to determine whether there is only one or if there are two English prose *Melusine* translations.

It is not my intention here to examine the exact relationship between the edition and the prose manuscript, although it is worth noting that a close examination of their philological relationship is severely complicated by the fragmented state of the prose edition. Instead, I am interested in the connections with editions printed on the Continent, and how such connections might help us track down the French source text. Crucially, although the prose translation is almost certainly based on the text of Steinschaber's *editio princeps*, this does not necessarily mean that the translator worked directly from an exemplar of this edition. This is because Steinschaber's text was copied—with very few minor orthographical adjustments—in several later *Mélusine* incunabula and early fifteenth-century editions.[15] Colwell already touches on this when she rightly points out that most of the commonalities between the manuscript and the edition—as noted by Nolan and Meale—reflect features found in all French *Mélusine* editions printed before 1517.[16] In fact, later printers made such extensive reuse of Steinschaber's text, layout, and chapter divisions that it is entirely possible that this text was mediated through a later edition. This means that we are looking at a much larger number of possible source texts than previously thought.

At this point, I want to draw attention to a hitherto neglected link with the French *Mélusine* edition printed by Martin Husz in Lyon sometime after 1479. In describing the only surviving copy of Husz's *Mélusine* edition, Arthur Rau notes that it was found in England soon after this edition was printed.[17] Rau adds that this particular copy of Husz's edition can also be linked to a London workshop printing for William Caxton, and he even suggests that it may have been among the books Caxton imported to England in 1488.[18] Rau bases his comments on the copy's binding, noting that the plates are similar to those attributed to the man now known as the Caxton binder. More recent research has shown that this binder worked for both Caxton and his successor de Worde, and that the known examples of manuscripts and books he covered date from around 1477 to 1511.[19] I have been unable to view the original binding myself, but if this copy indeed belongs to one of the groups of bindings that came from Caxton's bindery, then this raises a number of interesting questions.

For a start, although Rau does not comment on any connections with the English version, his observations open up the possibility that Martin Husz's edition is the source of the English prose translation. Husz's edition is the second earliest known edition of this romance in French, and it copies Steinschaber's text with only some minor differences in orthography. So, could this be the common exemplar postulated by Meale? Alternatively, if we follow Nolan's argument that the edition is an abridgement, is this the source of the translation found in the prose manuscript? If the latter is true, could it be that Husz's edition was brought to the printing workshop not as a model for the translator, but to serve as a guide in setting the prose translation to print?

Such questions of course depend on when exactly this copy was found in a London workshop, and on who might have ordered it and why. It is tempting, though, to wonder whether, if the copy was there in the late 1480s or early 1490s, its presence might indicate that there was an earlier English *Melusyne* edition, perhaps even printed by Caxton. If this surviving edition is one of de Worde's many reprints of works first printed by his former master, then this might explain why the prose *Melusyne* is in folio—a format favored by Caxton—while most of the romances newly printed by de Worde were in quarto format.[20] However, it is equally possible that the copy of Husz's edition was brought to London at a later stage, and that it was de Worde who made use of his connections with French printers and booksellers in order to obtain it. After all, we know that de Worde imported quite a large number of books—he is on record for having imported at least twenty-nine shipments between 1503 and 1531—many of which came from presses in cities like Paris and Lyon.[21] Of course, it could also be that this copy was imported and sent to the bindery by someone else entirely. It is difficult to provide a definitive answer when still so little is known about the printed fragments, or about the exact history of this particular copy of Husz's edition, but the possible link with a London workshop certainly is intriguing.

This connection becomes even more interesting when we consider that there is undoubtedly an iconographical link here, as there are some striking similarities between the woodcuts that illustrate the *Melusyne* fragments and the images of Husz's edition. Colwell already observes that some of the English cuts share features in common with images found in French *Mélusine* incunabula, and with the group of incunabula printed in Lyon in particular.[22] This group includes the edition printed by Husz. Colwell highlights that the woodcut on fragment 4v in particular, which depicts Melusine's son Geffray entering a cave in pursuit of a giant, bears a much closer resemblance to that depicting the same scene in the editions printed in Lyon than the woodcut found in Steinschaber's edition.

To this I want to add another example: as I have noted elsewhere, it is possible that the heavily damaged woodcut on fragment 3v also shows a similar scene to that found in the Lyon editions.[23] Although it is difficult to make any definitive claims about the small strip that remains, from what is left of the surrounding text it can be gleaned that this image accompanies the scene where Melusine is about to depart the human world and transform into a serpent. The placement of this cut makes it likely that it depicts Melusine's metamorphosis, as the transformation image is typically found before the description of Mélusine's parting words in the French editions too. Furthermore, the woodcut is found underneath a heading with the remaining words "(...)e of a serpent."[24] The components discernible in what is left of this image—part of a building, rocks, a tree, and what might be a bent arm—match features also found in the transformation woodcuts of the Lyon editions. Such iconographical links strengthen the possibility that Husz's edition was used as a model for the English edition, if not for the text of the translation then at least for some of its illustrations.

However, there are a few crucial factors that complicate such attempts at tracing the cross-cultural influences among the images of early *Mélusine* editions. For a start, Martin Husz's edition is itself already a product of a cross-cultural exchange: its images are derived from a set of woodblocks originally designed to illustrate the *editio princeps* of the German *Melusine* translation, printed by Bernhard Richel in Basel between 1473 and 1474.[25] Colwell notes that the images of the incunabula printed in Lyon were closely modeled on the woodcuts of Richel's edition, but they are in fact derived from the exact same woodblocks.[26] Some further modifications must be made: there are not three Lyon incunabula but four, and the edition printed in 1493 was published not by Martin but by Matthias (or Mathieu) Husz.[27] The Lyon editions printed by Martin Husz after 1479, by Gaspard Ortuin and Pierre Boutellier (or Schenck) around 1485, by Guillaume Le Roy around 1487, and by Matthias Husz are often referred to as a group because they are virtually identical in text, layout, and illustration.[28] It is likely that Martin Husz was the person who first obtained Richel's woodblocks, as we know that he worked as an apprentice in Basel and that he acquired some of Richel's printing materials in 1476.[29] He then came to Lyon and worked there as a printer from 1477 to circa 1481. Richel's woodblocks were reused again for subsequent *Mélusine* incunabula printed in Lyon, although in Matthias Husz's 1493 edition Richel's images are mixed with smaller copies and woodcuts derived from other editions, possibly because the original blocks had become damaged from constant reuse.[30]

The story then becomes even more complicated, as the influence of Richel's iconography is not limited to the Lyon editions alone. Richel's woodblocks were also used to illustrate the earliest known edition of the Castilian translation, the *Historia de la linda Melosina*, printed by Juan Parix and Estevan Cleblat in 1489.[31] Parix and Cleblat borrowed almost the entire set of woodblocks from printers in Lyon, and the blocks were sent back afterwards to be reused again for Mathias Husz's edition.[32] Aside from these instances of actual reuse of the same woodblocks, there are also a great number of early *Mélusine* editions whose iconography is modeled on that of Richel's edition. In fact, it would be too much to describe here the full extent to which Richel's images had an impact on the iconographies of editions printed in various languages.[33] Suffice to say that, because of printers' frequent image copying and reuse, the illustrations in most *Mélusine* incunabula—and some editions printed shortly after 1500—can in some way be traced back to Richel's images, making it difficult to pinpoint any direct iconographical links between the various early printed versions. To give an example, although it is true that some of the English *Melusyne* woodcuts match the composition of the woodcuts of the Lyon editions, they are also very similar to the woodcuts of the edition printed by Pierre le Caron in Paris after February 1498, and those of the second Parisian edition printed by Thomas du Guernier around 1503. This is because the images of these editions can also be traced back to Richel's: le Caron's woodcuts are copied after those of Matthias Husz's edition—which were derived directly or indirectly from Richel's woodblocks—and le Caron's images were then in turn copied in du Guernier's edition.[34]

This makes it rather confusing to try to narrow down the possible source or model for the English *Melusyne* images, especially when there are only four woodcuts left, most of which are incomplete. The problem also lies in defining when a close resemblance between images gives us enough proof to claim a direct line of influence. However, despite such reservations, I have found one very clear link between a *Melusyne* woodcut and an illustration that appears in at least one French *Mélusine* edition. It concerns the image on fragment 4r, which has been cropped at about a quarter from the top. We can still see that it depicts two armored figures raising their arms, as if they are about to strike each other. The figure on the right is larger than the one on the left, and although it is just possible to tell that the figure on the left is wearing a helmet, we can no longer see the heads of these figures or any weapons they might be holding. Behind the person on the left is a castle wall. This woodcut is found alongside a passage describing Geffray's battle with the giant Grymauld, for which it makes a fitting illustration, considering the height difference between these figures.

There is a particularly close resemblance between this image and a woodcut illustrating the same episode in a *Mélusine* edition printed by Jean II Trepperel in Paris sometime between 1527 and 1532.[35] The woodcut in Trepperel's edition is still intact, and it clearly shows that the man on the right is much larger than the one on the left, which would identify him as the giant. Geoffroy is holding a sword and the giant raises a scimitar, while in the top left corner of the image we see two figures looking at this scene from behind the castle wall. At first glance, it appears that the English woodcut is a simplified version of the image found in Trepperel's edition, as it depicts fewer rocks in the foreground and the lines on the giant's greaves are less intricate. Still, the rest of the image matches Trepperel's so closely—from the detailed patterns on the armor to the stones of the castle and the exact stance of the figures—and both images are so different from images that illustrate the same scene in other *Mélusine* editions that there must be a relationship between these woodcuts.

Colwell does not discuss this particular woodcut in detail, although she does note that it is listed by Edward Hodnett as appearing in at least three of de Worde's editions of the *Chronicle of England*, printed between 1515 and 1528.[36] She adds that "it may have an alternative line of descent."[37] I have examined various French *Mélusine* editions printed before Trepperel's, but none of the surviving copies features this same woodcut. However, the same image does appear in the 1511 edition of *Godeffroy de Boulion*, printed in Paris by Michel le Noir for Jean Petit, and in the 1522 edition of Antoine de la Sale's *La Salade*, again printed in Paris by Michel le Noir.[38] Since Trepperel is known to have copied various images from le Noir's *Mélusine* edition of 1517—and from the edition published by Michel's son Philippe le Noir around 1525—it is possible that the same image was used there, too.[39] The Trepperel and le Noir printing families were connected—most obviously through the marriage of Michel and Jeanne, the sister of Jean I Trepperel—and in some cases even worked together.[40] In all likelihood, it would not have been difficult for Jean II to obtain either the original woodblocks used by Michel le Noir or for him to have copies made. Still, these various editions postdate the date usually given to the English fragments, so we may wonder if there is an even earlier source.

It is also not clear whether this image was originally designed to illustrate a scene from the *Mélusine* romance or if it simply found its way into these various editions because it could be used as a generic illustration of a one-to-one combat scene. Certainly, one feature particular to this romance has been obscured here: because the visor on Geffray's helmet is down, we cannot see his characteristic great tooth sticking out from his bottom lip. This tooth is a monstrous token that Geffray inherited from his mother, and whenever we see him depicted in the French incunabula, the tooth typically functions as an identifying marker.[41] In this woodcut, however, the figure that supposedly represents Geffray is rather nondescript, so one could imagine that this knight in full armor could stand in for a host of different characters from different texts. It appears that le Noir saw this potential too: in his *Godeffroy* edition, the image represents the battle between the swan knight Helias and the count of Frankfurt, while in *La Salade* it accompanies an exemplum on military strategy taken from Simon de Hesdin's translation of Valerius Maximus. Since it is quite common to find Geoffroy depicted with his large tooth in the images of the early French *Mélusine* editions, it is entirely possible—even likely—that this image was designed for a different text.[42]

It is clear, then, that the English *Melusyne* woodcuts are derived from a mix of different sources, which would be in line with de Worde's usual *modus operandi*. It is also evident that the images rely heavily on French models, which, again, is quite common for de Worde. It has often been noted that he seems to have been particularly keen to copy illustrations from editions published by the notable printer and bookseller Antoine Vérard, but many of de Worde's books also feature images copied after woodcuts in French editions published by other printers—including Martin and Matthias Husz, le Noir, and Trepperel. Moreover, de Worde was not the only printer to make use of French image models: for instance, his main competitor, Richard Pynson, also regularly relied on woodcuts from French editions for the illustrations in his publications. As such, the *Melusyne* woodcuts provide yet more evidence that the history of woodcuts in English editions is intertwined with the history of wood engraving in a French context.[43]

However, some of the images discussed here also illustrate that, just as early English printing relied heavily on French models, early French printing in turn often relied on German models. In the case of the *Mélusine* romance, it was undoubtedly the great success of the first editions of the German translation that led to the printing of a French version, and the early printers working in Paris and Lyon—many of whom came from German-speaking regions themselves—then looked to earlier German image models when illustrating their books. The French editions contributed even more to the popularity of this romance, so much so that it was then further translated into Castilian, Dutch, and English.[44] The illustrators of these different versions also looked to earlier models—in this case both French and German exemplars. So, when we talk about de Worde copying existing woodcuts to illustrate his *Melusyne* edition, it is important to realize that this is all part of a larger process of copying and recycling, which happened on an international scale.

The downside of this constant image reuse and recycling is that it makes for a rather complicated web of connections, and so it can be difficult to trace these iconographical links. This is especially true for those editions, such as the prose *Melusyne*, where the woodcuts are derived from different sources. Of course, this makes it all the more important to determine whether the only surviving copy of Martin Husz's edition was indeed bound by the Caxton binder, and if and when it might have been found in a London (or Westminster?) workshop. Only by putting together the different scraps of evidence—not just typographical and iconographical links, but also the known connections between printers, binders, and booksellers—can we come closer to solving the mystery of the English printed *Melusyne* fragments and to pinpointing their exact source. My intention here has been to bring forward various additional clues that may in the future allow us to do just that. Most of all, though, I hope that this discussion has shown that it pays to look at the wider, European legacy of a printed text, especially considering that printing at this stage was not necessarily bound by conventional geographic or linguistic boundaries, and there was a constant movement of texts, materials, and people. Such a broader view reveals further evidence of the relationship between English and continental book production and trade, uncovering crucial cross-cultural links which are so easily overlooked when we focus only on the local context.

University of York

NOTES

1. Tania M. Colwell, "The Middle English *Melusine*: Evidence for an Early Edition of the Prose Romance in the Bodleian Library," *Journal of the Early Book Society* 17 (2014): 259–287.
2. Colwell, "The Middle English *Melusine*," 276, note 6, for an overview of the collections in which these fragments were found.
3. A. W. Pollard and G. R. Redgrave, *A Short-Title Catalogue of Books Printed in England, Scotland, & Ireland, and of English Books Printed Abroad, 1475–1640*, 2nd ed., rev. W. A. Jackson and F. S. Ferguson, compl. Katharine F. Pantzer, 3 vols. (London: Bibliographical Society, 1976–1991); *Universal Short Title Catalogue*, http://www.ustc.ac.uk (accessed 20 March 2017). Two of the fragments are also reproduced on EEBO: *Early English Books Online*, https://eebo.chadwyck.com/home (accessed 20 March 2017).
4. Although both manuscripts are based on a Middle French exemplar, the English translations represent two distinct translations of two separate French redactions. As noted below, the prose translation is based on a printed edition of the prose *Mélusine* by Jean d'Arras. The verse translation—found in manuscript Cambridge, Trinity College Library, R. 3. 17—is based on a manuscript of Coudrette's verse *Roman de Parthenay*.
5. For the measurements of each folio, see Colwell, "The Middle English *Melusine*," 260.
6. Ibid., 260–261.
7. Robert Joseph Nolan, "An Introduction to the English Version of *Mélusine*. A Medieval Prose Romance" (PhD diss., New York University, 1970), 22.
8. Email correspondance with Jo Maddocks, Assistant Curator of Rare Books at the Bodleian Libraries, 18 January, 2017.
9. Charles-Moïse Briquet, *Les filigranes: dictionnaire historique des marques du papier dès leur apparition vers 1282 jusqu'en 1600. A facsimile of the 1907 edition with supplementary material contributed by a number of scholars*, ed. A. Stevenson, 4 vols (Amsterdam: Paper Publications Society, 1968).
10. Colwell, "The Middle English *Melusine*," 260–261.
11. USTC: 71174. Incunabula Short Title Catalogue (hereafter ISTC), http://istc.bl.uk (accessed 20 March 2017), no. ij00218380. Gesamtkatalog der Wiegendrucke (hereafter GW), http://www.gesamtkatalogderwiegendrucke.de (accessed 20 March 2017), no. 12649.
12. Nolan, "An Introduction," 20–22.
13. Carol M. Meale, "Caxton, de Worde and the Publication of Romance in Late Medieval England," *The Library* 6th ser., 14 (1992): 287, note

15. Meale leaves open whether this common source could be English or French.

14. On the dating of the manuscript, see Nolan, "An Introduction," 18–19. The dates Nolan mentions for the watermark of the paper vary from 1515 to 1546, which might mean that we are actually looking at a more general date of "early sixteenth-century."

15. On the reuse of the text of Steinschaber's edition, see Hélène Bouquin, "Éditions et adaptations de 'l'Histoire de Mélusine' de Jean d'Arras (XVe–XIXe siècle): Les aventures d'un roman médiéval" (PhD diss., École nationale des chartes, 2000), 62–64.

16. Colwell, "The Middle English *Melusine*," 266–267.

17. Arthur Rau, "La première édition Lyonnaise de Mélusine," *Bibliothèque d'Humanisme et Renaissance* 18, no. 3 (1956): 431. This copy was for some time presumed lost but is now found in the Bibliothèque nationale de France, shelf mark Res Fol-NFR-129.

18. Rau cites: Nelly J. M. Kerling, "Caxton and the Trade in Printed Books," *The Book Collector* 4 (1955): 190–199. Kerling mentions that Caxton received at least 1,100 books from various shipments in early 1488.

19. The books covered by the Caxton binder originate from both England and the continent. See Alexandra Gillespie, "Bookbinding and Early Printing in England," in *A Companion to the Early Printed Book in Britain, 1476–1558*, ed. Vincent Gillespie and Susan Powell (Cambridge: D. S. Brewer, 2014), 82–83; Mirjam M. Foot, "English Decorated Bookbindings," in *Book Production and Publishing in Britain 1375–1475*, ed. Jeremy Griffiths and Derek Pearsall (Cambridge: Cambridge University Press, 1989), 73–74. Howard Nixon divides up these bindings into five groups, coming from one or perhaps two shops: Nixon, "William Caxton and Bookbinding," *Journal of the Printing Historical Society* xi (1976–77): 92–113.

20. Both Colwell and Meale have speculated about the reason for this folio format, suggesting that de Worde adapted his method to suit the length of the romance, as the quarto format would have made for a hefty volume. Compare Colwell, "The Middle English *Melusine*," 265; Meale, "Caxton, de Worde," 292.

21. C. Paul Christianson, "The Rise of London's Book-Trade," in *The Cambridge History of the Book in Britain. Volume III: 1400–1557*, ed. Lotte Hellinga and J. B. Trapp (Cambridge: Cambridge University Press, 1999), 140.

22. Colwell, "The Middle English *Melusine*," 262–263.

23. Lydia Zeldenrust, "Serpent or Half-Serpent? Bernhard Richel's *Melusine* and the Making of a Western European Icon," *Neophilologus* 100.1 (2016): 38–39.

24. Compare the heading found at the start of this episode in the English prose manuscript: "how Melusyne in fourme of a Serpent flough out at a wyndowe" (folio 187v).
25. ISTC: im00476000; USTC: 747181; GW: 12656. Ursula Rautenberg, "Die 'Melusine' des Thüring von Ringoltingen und der Basler Erstdruck des Bernhard Richel," in *Melusine (1456) Nach dem Erstdruck Basel, Richel um 1473/74, Volume 2*, ed. André Schnyder and Rautenberg, 2 vols (Wiesbaden: Reichert, 2006), 62; Laurence Harf-Lancner, "L'illustration du *Roman de Mélusine* de Jean d'Arras dans les éditions du XVe et du XVIe siècle," in *Le livre et l'image en France au XVIe siècle* (Paris: Presses de l'Ecole normale supérieure, 1989), 33–35.
26. Colwell, "The Middle English *Melusine*," 263.
27. There is often some confusion in secondary sources between Martin and Matthias Husz, both of whom were active as printers in Lyon in the late fifteenth century. The confusion is made greater by the fact that the two were probably related and both learned their craft in Basel. However, Martin was no longer active in Lyon after the 1480s, while Matthias started printing a few years later than Martin and continued until at least 1500. Matthias also inherited much of Martin's printing materials after his death.
28. Lyon, Martin Husz, after 1479 (ISTC: ij00218385, USTC: 71175, GW: 12560); Lyon, Gaspard Ortuin and Pierre Bouttellier (Schenck), c. 1485 (ISTC: ij00218390, USTC: 71176, GW: 12651); Lyon, Guillaume Le Roy, c. 1487 (ISTC: ij00218400, USTC: 71177, GW: 12562); Lyon, Matthias Husz, after 26 March 1493 and before 12 March 1494 (ISTC: ij00218405, USTC: 71178, GW: 12654).
29. See entry 74 in Guillaume Fau, et al., "Dictionnaire des imprimeurs et libraires lyonnais du XVe siècle," in *Le berceau du livre: autour des incunables. Etudes et essais offerts au professeur Pierre Aquilon par ses élèves, ses collègues et ses amis*, ed. Frédéric Barbier (Geneva: Librairie Droz, 2003), 230.
30. My observations about Matthias Husz's edition are based on personal consultation of the copy now in the Bibliothèque du Château de Chantilly (formerly Musée Condé), VI.I 30.
31. ISTC: ij00218430, USTC: 344879, GW: 12666. There is also a later Castilian edition, printed by Jacobo and Juan Cromberger in Seville in 1526 (USTC: 337807).
32. Ana Pairet, "Intervernacular Translation in the Early Decades of Print: Chivalric Romance and the Marvelous in the Spanish *Melusine* (1489–1526)," in *Translating the Middle Ages*, ed. Karen L. Fresco and Charles D. Wright (London: Ashgate, 2002), 142; Francis William Bourdillon,

"Some Notes on Two Early Romances: *Huon de Bordeaux* and *Melusine*," *The Library* 4, no. 1 (1920), 36–37.

33. For a more detailed discussion of the impact of Richel's iconography and how these images became what Martha Driver has called an "influential prototype," see Zeldenrust, "Serpent or Half-Serpent," 19–41.

34. Bouquin, "Éditions et adaptations," 270–278.

35. USTC: 72937. This edition may have been printed for Alain Lotrian. Around the same time, Trepperel also printed an edition of *Geoffroy a la grand dent*, which takes out some of the episodes found towards the end of the *Mélusine* romance to create a separate chivalric romance starring Mélusine most famous son. An earlier edition of this spin-off was likely published by Michel le Noir in 1517.

36. The image corresponds to Hodnett no. 902, which is also found on folio 17vb in the *Chronicle* editions printed in 1515 (USTC: 501314, STC 10000.5); 1520 (STC 10001); and 1528 (USTC: 502093, STC: 10002). Edward Hodnett, *English Woodcuts, 1480–1535*, rev. ed. (Oxford: Oxford University Press, 1973), 261. The woodcut appears much less worn in the *Melusyne* fragments, suggesting that this is an earlier imprint.

37. Colwell, "The Middle English *Melusine*," 263.

38. Compare folio 23v of *La genealogie avecques les gestes et nobles faitz d'armes du tres preux et renomme prince Godeffroy de Boulion* (USTC: 26217), and folio 13v of *La Salade* (USTC: 8378).

39. Bouquin, "Éditions et adaptations," 217–219.

40. Philippe Renouard, *Imprimeurs parisiens, libraires, fondeurs de caractères et correcteurs d'imprimerie, depuis l'introduction de l'imprimerie à Paris (1470) jusqu'à la fin du XVIe siècle* (Paris, 1898; reis., Paris: M. J. Minard, 1965), 354–355.

41. On Geoffroy and his monstrous tooth, see Harf-Lancner, "L'image et le monstrueux: Geoffroy la Grand Dent, le sanglier de Lusignan," in *Melusine. Actes du Colloque du Centre d'Études Médiévales de l'Université de Picardie, 13-14 janvier 1996*, ed. Danielle Buschinger and Wolfgang Spiewok (Greifswald: Reineke, 1996), 77–92.

42. It is worth noting that de Worde printed an edition of Robert Copland's *Helyas, the Knight of the Swanne* in 1512 (USTC: 501227, STC: 7571), and possibly again in 1520 (USTC: 501690, STC: 7571.5). This work is a translation based on the early chapters of *Godeffroy*. Hodnett does not list the woodcut depicting two figures in combat among the woodcuts attributed to de Worde's 1512 edition, but since it is found in le Noir's edition—and possibly also in that printed by Jean Petit in 1504—we may wonder whether this is how this particular image found its way into de Worde's stock. Hodnett notes that several woodcuts of the 1512 *Knight of the Swanne* edition have a French origin: *English Woodcuts*, 23.

43. Many scholars have commented on early English printers' use of French iconographical models, and on de Worde and Pynson's engagement with French exemplars in particular. See, for instance, Martha W. Driver, "Woodcuts and Decorative Techniques," in *A Companion to the Early Printed Book in Britain*, 99; Jordi Sánchez-Martí, "Illustrating the Printed Middle English Verse Romances, c. 1500–c. 1535," *Word and Image* 27 (2011): 90–102; Gillespie, *Print Culture and the Medieval Author: Chaucer, Lydgate, and Their Books 1473–1557* (Oxford: Oxford University Press, 2006), especially chapter 3; Driver, *The Image in Print: Book Illustration in Late Medieval England and Its Sources* (London: British Library, 2004), chapter 2; A.S.G. Edwards, "Continental Influences on London Printing and Reading in the Fifteenth and Early Sixteenth Centuries," in *London and Europe in the Late Middle Ages*, ed. Julia Boffey and Pamela King (London: Queen Mary and Westfield College, 1995), 229–256.

44. The edition printed by Gheraert Leeu in Antwerp in 1491 is the earliest known witness to the Dutch translation (ISTC: ij00218420, USTC: 436129, GW: 12665). It was reprinted in 1510 by Henrick Eckert van Homberch and in 1602 by Hieronymus I Verdussen. On the Dutch translation and its images, see Zeldenrust, "The Lady with the Serpent's Tail: Hybridity and the Dutch *Meluzine*," in *Melusine's Footprint: Tracing the Legacy of a Medieval Myth*, ed. Misty Urban, Deva Kemmis, and Melissa Ridley Elmes.

The Copyist of *Les Cronicles* in Leiden, Universiteitsbibliotheek, MS VGG F 6

JONATHAN BRENT

The initial and primary section of Leiden, Universiteitsbibliotheek, Vossius MS Gallici F.6 comprises a full copy of Nicholas Trevet's Anglo-Norman universal history, known by its medieval title as *Les Cronicles*.[1] This portion of VGG F 6, which runs from folio 1r to folio 93v, ends on its final page six or so lines before the bottom of the would-be text block, the extent of which bleeds through from the folio's recto. Just below this space, left of center, the initials "W.W." place a bow on the preceding work (Fig. 1). Readerly

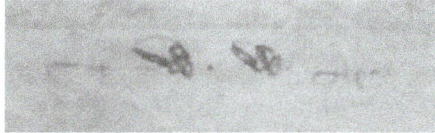

Figure 1: f. 93v.

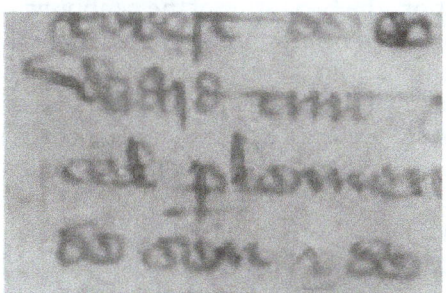

Figure 2: f. 93v.

annotation is a frequent sight in the Leiden manuscript, which is also signed in more than one place by an early modern owner.[2] These letters, however, seem to have been written by a scribe: not only do the flourishes accompanying the initials appear as line-filler throughout the text (e.g., fols. 22r, 39r, 65r, 85r), but the *W*s themselves seem to be a more careful execution of the preceding script (Fig. 2). An obvious explanation for these initials is that they are those of the scribe, who has signed his work after he finished copying it. This notion is complicated, however, by the multifariousness of the text as a whole, a feature that has led previous commentors, who have not noted the signature, to the modest suggestion of multiple hands. These are not necessarily conflicting determinations,[3] but it is worth pointing out that the justification for multiple hands, where it exists, is apparently flawed. In what follows, I look at the argument for multiple hands, as well as several difficulties presented by VGG F 6 respecting the distinction of scribes. I suggest, as an alternative, that *Les Cronicles* could instead be the product of a single copyist, working with a variety of materials over an extended period of time.

Previous work on the handwriting of VGG F 6 has been very brief, and makes no mention of the signature at the end of *Les Cronicles*. As far as I have been able to determine, there is only one extended paleographical description of the Leiden manuscript, written in 1962 by the eminent Anglo-Normanist Ruth J. Dean, and its entirety runs as follows:

> L [i.e., VGG F6] was transcribed by two or more copyists in the second half of the fourteenth century, probably in the fourth quarter. It seems later than A [London, BL, ms. Arundel 56] and not unlike S [Stockholm, Kungliga Bibl., ms. D.1311a], although it does not have the spiky character of S except for a suggestion of this in descenders. The ordinary and the tilted-back *e* are used, but the o-shaped one with heavy downstroke in the center is frequent. The first hand has the *q* with backward-curving tail carried up to make an abbreviation-stroke; but another hand has a distinctive *q* with a strong diagonal stroke down to the left carried back up under the bow. When this *q* has a superscript abbreviation-stroke it is usually quite separate, not carried up directly from the backward stroke as in some of the manuscripts; it is, however, sometimes made without lifting the pen after the lower loop has been completed.[4]

Unless I am mistaken in my identification, the two forms of the *qe* abbreviation Dean suggests as distinguishing one hand from another are actually both present throughout *Les Cronicles*, sometimes even occurring right next to each other (Fig. 3). The *q* with a "strong diagonal stroke" appears to be preferred whenever there is an abbreviation within a word (e.g., "evesqe"), because there would not otherwise be space for a full loop. Indeed, this is the normal form for *q*, and when it is considered apart from its use within abbreviations, it is ubiquitous.[5] Sometimes, though, a certain form is preferred, or even used technically. So, for example, in the text's preface, on folio 1r, the first form of *q*, with the abbreviation stroke making a circle round the letter, is used in conjunctive phrases (for example, *pur ceo qe, si qe*), while the second form is used as a relative pronoun (e.g., *ceux qe sount*). Without an obvious change in hands, however, we find the encircled *q* used as a relative later on folio 1r, after a gap denoting the beginning of the text proper. Both forms are used after the break as conjunctions.

Given such apparent haphazardness, it is difficult to attribute with certainty stints in which one form is preferred or even exclusive to a number of scribes rather than, say, a single scribe varying his habits. The same can be said for other variants that occur throughout the text but are sometimes found within the same stint, for example, the more and less ornate abbreviations of *er/re* (Fig. 4); varying methods of abbreviating *cristien-* (e.g., fol. 74r) and *Israel* (e.g., fol. 16r); several versions of the Tironian *et*; rounded and straight abbreviation marks in general; and the various forms of "capital" *A*, *B*, and *D*. On folio 8r, for example, a clear change in aspect marks a new stint at the beginning of *Les Cronicles'* Book of Joshua. The ink in this new section is apparently darker and in some places thicker, and the lines, which are fairly well spaced at the top of the page, become much more vertically compressed. Does this stint change also signal a change in scribe? At the top of the page, the copyist writes "Israel" (*isrl*) with a short or "sigma" *s*. This scribe uses a straight *i longa* at the head of proper names, and deploys a rather innocuous abbreviation for *ur* (Fig. 5). Below the break, we find nearly exclusive use of a looped *i longa*, resembling a modern letter *J*, as well as a much more

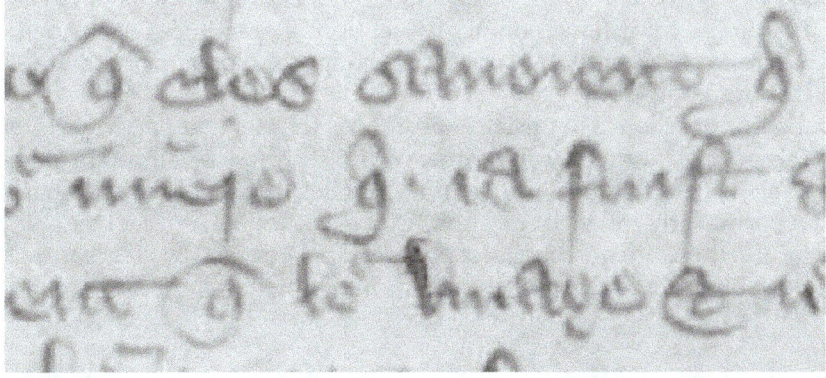

Figure 3: f. 4v.

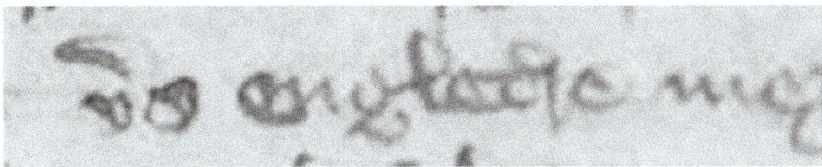

Figure 4: f. 55v.

audacious version of the same abbreviation (Fig. 6). *Isrl*, meanwhile, is written with a long *s*. And yet, we also find the same inoffensive abbreviations for *ur* throughout the latter stint. The straight *i longa* is there, too, and again becomes widespread by the end of the page. Finally, with no clear aspectual change marking a reversion of scribes, we see *isrl* written with a sigma *s* eight lines from the bottom.

Changes in aspect are themselves fairly frequent, and also a matter of some confusion. Take, for example, the first few folios of VGG F 6, especially folios 1v–2r. These are well spaced, fairly neat, and do not suffer much vertical compression. By the bottom of folio 2r, the script has started to undergo some compression, though this trend is not carried to the top of folio 2v. Then, halfway through folio 2v, the script regains its compression while taking on a saturated and pronounced chiaroscuro effect. The lines here run unevenly and more closely together, almost touching at points, before the ink begins to even out at the bottom of the page. The next folio has a different aspect, reinforced by the layout of the text into a single block. The chiaroscuro effect is less pronounced, if it is there at all, and the lines are (slightly) better spaced. Elsewhere in the manuscript, differences in aspect are far subtler and linked to variation in elements such as stroke thickness, line spacing, ink density/saturation, letter size and precision, and overall neatness. It is unclear in some stretches exactly what is going on. Variation seems too irregular always to signal a change in hand, though the role of image quality cannot be discounted for its effect on my perception.[6] Sometimes I am convinced that there exist real and obvious scribal changes at play, and at other points, I doubt this completely.

Lending credence to the latter position is the fact that *Les Cronicles* does have a sense of aesthetic unity. Most obviously, the script used throughout is a straightforward fourteenth-century Anglicana, which, as Dean suggests, is not particularly spiky: for example, except within the frequently deployed *st* ligature, there are no rising ascenders on the letter *t*. Another feature that seems stable is the choice of sigma *s* in the initial, prevocalic position of shorter

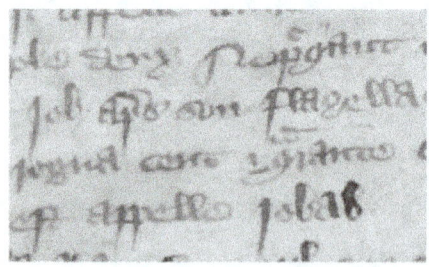

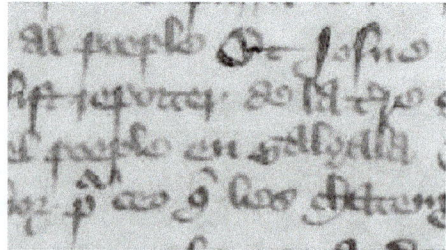

Figure 5: f. 8r. Note "nepurqant" in line 1, "Job" in line 2, and "Jobab" in line 4.

Figure 6: f. 8r. Note "Josue" in line 1, "pur" in line 4.

words such as *sa* and *son*, in contrast to the long *s* preferred by the scribe who copied the last item in the manuscript. There are two forms of *w*, each double-bowed. The letters *h* and *m* are frequently underscored by a familiar "strong diagonal stroke" extending left from their final legs, and there is a preference for round *r* after *o*. Sometimes this round *r* has an extra flourish extending down and to the left from its baseline joint, and it is even used on occasion following the letter *a*. A strikingly tall shape resembling the number 9 is used to signify *us*. The frequency and form of abbreviations are also fairly consistent, and again, the letter *q* is not drawn with a pointy descender.

Definitive judgments remain difficult, particularly without the benefits afforded by working with the manuscript *in situ*.[7] Rather than multiple hands, however, it is plausible that a single scribe—a certain "W.W."—is responsible for the entire work. Variation, in this case, could be explained by the scribe's using a variety of materials, and lapsing in and out of certain habits over an extended period of composition, itself due to sporadic availability of the exemplar, or if this manuscript was written as a side project, perhaps even by sporadic interest. What can be said for certain is that Dean's division based on separate *q*s is insufficient. The distinction of multiple scribes in *Les Cronicles*, if it is possible at all, would require a more complex set of criteria.

University of Toronto

NOTES

1. VGG F 6 contains a B-family version of *Les Cronicles* and two short polemical works, which were added later to fill out the final quire. The first (fols. 94r–95r) takes the form of a "deceitful" letter against English claims to the French crown, written in Latin and supposedly presented to Sigismund, Holy Roman Emperor, by "certain cleric of France." This was copied in a neat, small-bodied Secretary which gradually admits a number of Anglicana features and was partially edited in the nineteenth century. See Kervyn de Lettenhoe, ed., *Oeuvres de Froissart: Chroniques, IV* (Brussels: Comptoir universel d'Imprimerie et de Librairie Victor Devaux & Cie, 1872), pp. 443–444. The final item (fols. 95v–956r) is a defense of English claims written in French in a messier Anglicana/Secretary hybrid. Each of these texts is supported by a genealogical diagram, similar to those found in the body of *Les Cronicles* itself. For more on these charts, as well as the provenance of VGG F6, see Heather Pagan, "Trevet's *Les Cronicles*: Manuscripts, Owners and Readers," in *The Prose Brut and Other Late Medieval Chronicles: Books Have Their Histories*, ed. Jaclyn Rajsic, Erik Kooper, and Dominique Hoche (York: York

Medieval Press, 2015), 160–163, and cfr. John Spence, *Reimagining History in Anglo-Norman Prose Chronicles* (York: York Medieval Press, 2013), 19. For the division of *Les Cronicles* manuscripts into families, see Ruth J. Dean, "The Manuscripts of Nicholas Trevet's Anglo-Norman Cronicles." *Medievalia et Humanistica* 14 (1962), 100 n. 11, and, *inter alia*, Robert M. Correale, "Gower's Source Manuscript of Nicholas Trevet's *Les Cronicles*," in *John Gower: Recent Readings*, ed. R. F. Yeager (Kalamazoo: Medieval Institute, 1989), 133–135.

2. The name "William Aylesbury" appears at the tops of 1r and 96v, the first and last pages of the manuscript. Pagan suggests that this Aylesbury might have been a government official by the same name who lived in Amsterdam during the middle of the seventeenth century. See Heather Pagan, *op. cit.*, 161.

3. The initials could be those of a master, or perhaps simply a sign that the final scribe was self-aggrandizing.

4. Ruth J. Dean, *op. cit.*, 102. Dean, who discovered Trevet`s presence in VGG F 6, notes that fuller paleographical details are available in her doctoral dissertation (1938) for all the manuscripts of *Les Cronicles* except VGG F6, which she did not see until 1948, "and then only briefly." Gumbert's catalogue entry simply leaves it at "several hands." See "Medieval Manuscripts in French in the Leiden University Library," in *Medieval Codicology, Iconography, Literature, and Translation: Studies for Keith Val Sinclair*, ed. Peter Rolfe Monks and D.D.R. Owen (Leiden: Brill, 1994), 37.

5. It should be noted, in this connection, that there is at least one more abbreviation for "qe" used throughout *Les Cronicles*, formed by affixing what looks like a round *r* to the right side of Dean's "strong diagonal" *q*.

6. Lacking other means, I have consulted the manuscript via Leiden's online viewer (available, as of 31 Dec. 2016, at https://socrates.leidenuniv.nl/R/-?func=dbin-jump-full&object_id=2884199). As an example of the difficulty involved—in addition to general uncertainties respecting the manner in which the photographic medium has affected the appearance of the ink—the parchment in several places (e.g., fol. 67v and fol. 2v, the section just described) has not been completely flattened. The resultant ridges, which are easily missed when zoomed in enough to view the script critically, have the potential to explain at least some of the apparent compression.

7. Chief among these is the ability to compare pages rapidly. See Stephen Partridge, "The Legacy of John Shirley," in *New Directions in Medieval Manuscript Studies and Reading Practices*, ed. Kathryn Kerby-Fulton, John J. Thompson, and Sarah Beachle (South Bend: University of Notre Dame Press, 2014), 442–443.

An Unstudied Fragment of Wynkyn de Worde's Edition of *The History of Troy*[1]

HEDWIG GWOSDEK

The library of New College, Oxford, possesses a hitherto unstudied fragment of Wynkyn de Worde's edition of *The History of Troy*, adding a new witness to de Worde's edition, which he printed in London in either 1502 or 1503. The date in the colophon varies in the extant copies.[2] Wynkyn de Worde's edition is a reprint of William Caxton's English translation of Raoul Lefèvre's *Le Recueil des histoires de Troyes*, which Caxton published about 1473 or 1474. Lefèvre's work reflects the fashions and literary tastes of the court of the dukes of Burgundy, who traced their mythological ancestry to the Greek heroic age, and Caxton's edition is itself closely linked to the Burgundian court through the Duchess of Burgundy's patronage to which it refers.[3] Caxton himself did not reprint this chivalric work.[4] It was his assistant and successor, Wynkyn de Worde, who reprinted it almost thirty years later under the title *The recuyles or gaderīge to gyder of þe hystoryes of Troye how it was destroyed ȝ brent twyes by þe puyssaunt Hercules ȝ þe thyrde ȝ generall by þe grekes.* The reprint suggests that Caxton's work was still popular but that copies were no longer available. There must have been renewed interest from clients, presumably all belonging to the upper classes, who wanted to read about Greek mythology, heroes and chivalric ideals at the end of the fifteenth and the beginning of the sixteenth centuries, even though in Caxton's own words, chivalric ideals no longer existed in England of his time.[5] This apparent demand must have been enough to convince Wynkyn de Worde that it would be commercially advantageous to issue a new edition of Caxton's large volume a short time after he had moved his printing shop from Westminster to the sign of the Sun in Fleet Street in the City of London at the end of 1500.

The fragment in New College library, Oxford, consists of two conjugate leaves, Hh2 and Hh5 (shelfmark MS391: Folder 4, folio 12). In its complete form, Wynkyn de Worde's reprint is in folio and collates 2°: aa^4 A–Z^6 Aa–Kk^6. The text is set in de Worde's type 4: 95 G.^{6} It is a volume of 202 leaves, printed in double columns, each of 42 lines on a normal page of type with no headlines, no catchwords, and no numbers to the foliation. The text is divided into three books. They are preceded by the "Tabula," i.e., short passages summarizing the individual chapters of the three books (aa1^v to aa4^v), and Caxton's and Raoul Lefèvre's prologues (A1^{r-v}). Book one begins on A2^r and ends on column 2 of P1^r. The second book follows immediately, ending on column 2 of Aa4^v. The third book occupies leaves Aa5^r, column one, to Kk6^v.

The rediscovered leaves from gathering Hh belong to book three. Each of the leaves, however, is defective. Several lines at the top of both leaves have been cut off unevenly, and in addition, Hh2 has been sliced vertically with the result that the text of half of one column on each page is missing.^{7} More specifically, six lines are missing at the top of Hh2^r with only the descenders of line six of the left-hand column being partly visible. Moreover, half of the text of the right-hand column on the recto is wanting, including the signature "Hh ij," as seen in other copies. At the same time, half of the left-hand column on the verso is also missing, as well as the first six lines of text from the top of the left column, with only the descenders of line six being visible. The right column of this page lacks only five lines at the top. The second extant leaf, Hh5, in contrast, preserves both columns on both recto and verso, except that at the top of the recto page it lacks five lines of the left column, leaving only the descenders of line five. Of the right column, it lacks four lines completely and also the ascenders of line five. On the verso, it lacks five lines at the top of the left-hand column, leaving only the descenders of line five. The right column of this page similarly lacks the top five lines almost completely. The text on the two leaves contains four two-line printed initials: initial A is used on Hh2^r, Hh5^r and Hh5^v. Initial O is used on Hh5^v.^{8} The text area on Hh2^r is about 170 x 108 millimeters; that on Hh5^r measures about 172 to 174 x 139 millimeters, the difference in the vertical measurements reflecting the fact that the leaf was cut unevenly. The lines on leaf Hh2 recto and verso are not in register, unlike those on Hh5.^{9} The two leaves were used as pastedowns in the cover of another book. They were cut to fit the new purpose and trimmed accordingly. Hh2 measures about 216 x 133 millimeters, and Hh5 measures approximately 216 x 205 millimeters. Their lower margin is torn to an uneven edge. There is no visible watermark. The paper of the inner and lower margins of the conjugate leaves is damaged and shows signs of being extracted from the binding of another book. The leaves also exhibit a few small holes which were probably caused when the leaves were taken out from the previous binding, some of them affecting the text.

It has not been possible to trace the provenance of these leaves. They and other printed fragments in New College Library were sent to the Bodleian Library for conservation in 1987 to 1988 and are now stored in a guardbook provided by the Bodleian. There is no information about how they were stored earlier. When the fragments were removed from the boards of a binding of another book, information about the "parent" book was not recorded.[10]

Other surviving copies of this book from Wynkyn de Worde with the colophon show two different dates, 1502 and 1503.[11] Of the extant copies held by libraries in the United Kingdom, each lacks a few leaves. The only copy with the date 1502 in the colophon is located at Cambridge, Pepys Library, Magdalene College.[12] A copy with the date 1503 in the colophon is located in the library of King's College, Cambridge.[13] The copy held at the British Library, London, lacks the colophon.[14] Two perfect copies of de Worde's edition are located in American libraries with the date 1503 in each of their colophons. One copy is held in The Morgan Library & Museum in New York; the other copy is in the Library of Congress in Washington, DC.[15] One other fragment has been recorded. It is held at All Souls College, Oxford, and consists of no more than the fore-edge strip of leaf Ff5.[16] The fragment in New College library, Oxford, studied here, not only adds a further witness of Wynkyn de Worde's reprint of William Caxton's first book printed in English, but at the same time represents one of numerous examples of early printed books which were famous in their own time but have come down to us only in a few complete and incomplete copies.[17]

University of Munich

ACKNOWLEDGMENTS

The four fragments of *The History of Troy* reprinted by Wynkyn de Worde on the following pages are located in New College Library, Oxford, MS391, folder 4, fol. 12 and are reproduced with the permission of the Warden and Scholars of New College, Oxford.

APPENDIX

The History of Troy reprinted by Wynkyn de Worde, leaf Hh2ʳ.

The History of Troy reprinted by Wynkyn de Worde, leaf Hh2ᵛ.

The History of Troy reprinted by Wynkyn de Worde, leaf Hh5ʳ.

The History of Troy reprinted by Wynkyn de Worde. leaf Hh5ᵛ.

NOTES

1. The fragment was actually known and identified between 2007 (at least) and 2014. The record was then mistakenly removed from the *English Short Title Catalogue Online, 1473–1800*. The British Library and *ESTC/ North America*. It is abbreviated as ESTC and accessible at http://estc. bl.uk/.

2. See A. W. Pollard and G. R. Redgrave, *A Short-Title Catalogue of Books Printed in England, Scotland, and Ireland and of English Books Printed Abroad, 1475–1640*. 2nd edn., rev. and enl. Begun by W. A. Jackson and F. S. Ferguson. Completed by Katharine F. Pantzer. 3 vols. (London: Bibliographical Society, 1976–1991). (Abbreviated as STC). It accords these copies the status of two editions, nos. 15376 and 15377. It is not possible to ascribe the unstudied fragment to one or the other edition of de Worde's reprint.

3. See Norman F. Blake, ed. *Caxton's own Prose* (London: André Deutsch, 1973), no. 50, "History of Troy (c. 1473)," 99–100; *Catalogue of Books Printed in the XVth Century Now in the British Library*, part xi. *England*, ed. Lotte Hellinga (t'Goy-Houten: Hes & De Graaf Publishers BV, 2007), 7. (Referred to as BMC xi); also Yu-Chiao Wang, "Caxton's Romances and their early Tudor Readers," *Huntington Library Quarterly* 67.2 (2004): 173–188, at p. 174.

4. Cf. Blake's 1975 article, "Caxton's Reprints," *The Humanities Association Review* 26, 169–179, at pp. 170–171.

5. Blake, *Caxton's own Prose*, no. 80, "Order of Chivalry, *c.* 1484," pp. 126–127, and p. 170; also Lotte Hellinga, *William Caxton and Early Printing in England* (London: The British Library, 2011), 19–26. On the ownership of Caxton's books, see Margaret Lane Ford, "Private ownership of printed books," in *The Cambridge History of the Book in Britain*, Lotte Hellinga and J. B. Trapp, eds. (Cambridge: Cambridge University Press, 1999), 205–228, at pp. 213–218 and p. 227.

6. It can be identified as Duff type number 4. See E. Gordon Duff, *Fifteenth Century English Books. A Bibliography of Books and Documents Printed in England and of the Books for the English Market Printed Abroad*. Illustrated Monographs, 18 (Oxford, 1917; repr. Hain: Meisenheim, 1964). For an updated version of this catalogue, see Lotte Hellinga, ed., *Printing in England in the Fifteenth Century. E. Gordon Duff's Bibliography with Supplementary Descriptions, Chronologies and a Census of Copies* (London: The Bibliographical Society, and The British Library, 2009), plate XIV. For further information on this type, see Joseph J. Gwara, "Dating Wynkyn de Worde's Devotional, Homiletic, and Other Texts, 1501–1511," in *Preaching the Word in Manuscript and Print in Late*

Medieval England. Essays in Honour of Susan Powell, ed. Martha W. Driver and Veronica O'Mara (Turnhout: Brepols, 2013), 193–234, especially pp. 194–203. Figure 4 reproduces sig. D3ʳ of de Worde's edition of *The History of Troy* (STC 15377, 1503).

7. See the reproductions of the two leaves in the appendix.

8. Since 2ʳ and 5ᵛ are on the same forme, there are at least two different versions of the A that are part of de Worde's standard lombardic set 11. Cf. BMC xi, 378–379.

9. A comparison of the same leaves with the copy of the British Library, London (shelfmark G. 10509), showed that the register on Hh2 is also not perfect. This can most clearly be seen when looking at its verso that the printed columns are not in exact correspondence. I owe this information to Christian Algar, Curator, Printed Heritage Collections, of the British Library.

10. I am grateful for this information to Naomi van Loo, New College Library, Oxford.

11. The two ESTC records indicate that the only difference between STC 15376 and 15377 is their colophon date. A textual comparison of the relevant pages of the copies of Magdalene College, Cambridge (STC 15376), and of the Library of Congress, Washington DC (STC 15377), shows that there is no difference between the 1502 and 1503 variants and therefore it is impossible to determine the fragment's date from the text either.

12. The copy of Pepys Library, Magdalene College, Cambridge (shelfmark PL 1996), wants four leaves. Only this copy has the 1502 date and is the only known copy of STC 15376. On its date see Gwara, "Dating Wynkyn de Worde's Texts, 1501–1511," 203. For bibliographical references see *Catalogue of the Pepys Library at Magdalene College Cambridge.* Volume 1: *Printed Books.* Compiled by N. A. Smith (Cambridge: D. S. Brewer, 1978), no. 1996; also E. Gordon Duff and F. Sidgwick, *Bibliotheca Pepysiana. A Descriptive Catalogue of the Library of Samuel Pepys.* Part II: *General Introduction and Early Printed Books to 1558* (London: Sidgwick & Jackson, Ltd., 1914; repr. Cambridge: Cambridge University Press, 2009), no. 1996, p. 36. This copy is reproduced in *Early English Books Online, 1475–1700* (referred to as EEBO) and accessible at http:// eebo.chadwyck.com/.

13. This copy (shelfmark M.24.22) is described in their online catalogue at http://library.kings.cam.ac.uk/. It wants five leaves. According to STC 15376 this copy is a variant of the 1502 edition where it is said that the date is altered in manuscript to 1503. However, after it was personally inspected, I was informed that "the date printed in the colophon is unambiguously 1503. There is one manuscript annotation on the front

flyleaf, also saying '1503,' which may be the source of the confusion. In any case, there is no sign that this book claims to be from 1502." Therefore this copy does not conform to the STC description, but must in fact be a copy of STC 15377, not STC 15376 as listed. I am grateful to Gareth Burgess, librarian of King's College, Cambridge, for this information.

14. The British Library copy (shelfmark G. 10509; STC 15377), wants the first leaf and the last four leaves; leaves 2, 3, and 4 are slightly mutilated. Since the colophon of the BL copy is missing, this could be a copy of STC 15376 or STC 15377. See also *Catalogue of Books in the Library of the British Museum Printed in England, Scotland, and Ireland, and of Books in English Printed Abroad to the Year 1640.* Vol. II (London: Printed by Order of the Trustees, 1884), 938. The text is reproduced on EEBO.

15. For the copy at The Morgan Library & Museum, New York (shelfmark PML 741; STC 15377), see *CORSAIR Online Collection Catalog* at http://corsair.themorgan.org/; and The Morgan Library & Museum, *Catalogue of Manuscripts and Early Printed Books from the Libraries of William Morris, Richard Bennett, Bertram, Fourth Earl of Ashburnham, and Other Sources, now forming Portion of the Library of J. Pierpont Morgan,* 4 vols. (London: Chiswick Press, 1906–1907), vol. 3: *Early Printed Books,* no. 741. For the second copy with the same date, see Library of Congress, *A Catalog of the Gifts of Lessing J. Rosenwald to the Library of Congress, 1943 to 1975* (Washington, DC: Library of Congress, 1977), no. 1211. This copy has been digitized and is available on the Library of Congress website.

16. The fragment of All Souls College, Codrington Library, Oxford (shelfmark LR.6.a.13a(1)), is described at http://solo.bodleian.ox.ac.uk/.

17. I would like to thank Naomi van Loo, New College Library, Oxford, for allowing me to examine the fragment under her charge and for sending me further information about it. I also owe thanks to the librarians of the following libraries for additional information about their copies: King's College Library, Cambridge; Pepys Library, Cambridge; The British Library, London; All Souls College Library, Oxford; The Morgan Library & Museum, New York; and Library of Congress, Washington, DC. I have benefited from the advice and expertise of Professor Joseph Gwara and Dr. Oliver Pickering, to whom I owe thanks.

An Unnoticed Borrowing from the Treatise *Of Three Workings In Man's Soul* in the Gospel Meditation *Meditaciones domini nostri*

LAURA SAETVEIT MILES

This note identifies the only known borrowing from an unusual devotional tract from late medieval England, *Of Three Workings in Man's Soul*, by the equally understudied Middle English gospel meditation *Meditaciones domini nostri*. Quite possibly written by Richard Rolle, the section borrowed from *Of Three Workings*—a detailed description of Mary reading, meditating, and rapt in spiritual ecstasy just prior to Gabriel's arrival at the Annunciation—draws attention to the importance of the Annunciation scene as a model of contemplative practice crucial for readers of the lives of Christ genre.

Meditaciones domini nostri (hereafter *MDN*) is a neglected example of the many surviving vernacular gospel meditations produced in medieval England. The Latin title is taken from the incipit to the short Latin prologue before the Middle English text, as contained in one of its two manuscript witnesses, Bodleian Library MS Bodley 578. MS Bodley 578 contains only this text, and dates from the first half of the fifteenth century, with an unknown medieval provenance.[1] The other witness is a larger religious miscellany, Cambridge, Trinity College MS B.15.42 (fols. 5–42v), which also dates from the early to mid-fifteenth century.[2] Its medieval provenance is unknown beyond the ownership inscription of the brother ("frater") William Caston dated 1468 on the back flyleaf; its combination of vernacular and Latin texts supports a clerical origin, as well as a sophisticated interest in contemplative and visionary activity not unlike that demonstrated by the Carthusians or Bridgettines, for example. Here the *MDN* lacks some four folios in the middle and four folios at the end, but is otherwise the more careful copy.

The *MDN* has only been edited as a 1992 doctoral dissertation by Elisabeth Blom-Smith;[3] before and after Blom-Smith's efforts, the text has received scant attention.[4] This life of Christ sorely needs a new published critical edition so that scholars can analyze it properly. As is often typical for the genre, the text begins with Mary's genealogy; follows Christ's birth, life, death, and resurrection; and continues on to cover the Pentecost and more on Mary's life. Thus, in its Latin explicit before the Middle English text, the Bodley witness claims only partially accurately that *MDN* is "a meditation on the life and passion and resurrection and ascension into heaven of Jesus Christ according to Bonaventure out of his third, and shortest—though best—edition."[5] This somewhat academic comment identifies an authorizing source in the pseudo-Bonaventuran *Meditationes vitae christi*, one of the most widely read lives of Christ in medieval Europe, and well known in England by this time due to Nicholas Love's English translation, *The Mirror of the Blessed Life of Jesus Christ*, from around 1410. However, less than half of the *MDN* text is actually from the *Meditationes vitae christi*.

Rather, many other sources are woven into *MDN* by the compiler. Typical for vernacular lives of Christ, *MDN* incorporates Bible verses translated directly from the Vulgate and accompanied by careful explication, some apocryphal gospels, various patristic sources such as Jerome, excerpts from Bernard of Clairvaux's sermons, and small parts of Nicholas of Lyra's *Postilla*. In addition, the compiler drew extensive material from Bridget of Sweden's *Revelaciones* and her *Sermo Angelicus*, as well as Elizabeth of Hungary's *Revelations*, the *Legenda Aurea*, *The Pricking of Love*, and Mandeville's *Travels*.[6] The compilation proudly announces its reliance on Bridget's *Revelaciones* through red underlining in the Bodley manuscript and the marginal apparatus in the Trinity manuscript. In Trinity, nine large rubricated notes contain some variation on "Birgitta" besides the main text, in the scribal hand (out of the twelve total marginal source attributions).

One of these other marginal attributions in *MDN* identifies the *auctor* "Ricardes de Sancta Victore." The Trinity manuscript uses its usual rubricated marginal script (fol. 8r), while Bodley identifies the source within the text body using its usual textura hand with red underline (fol. 5v). In Trinity the main body text marked by this note reads, "And as a gret clerk seith is called Richard of Seynt Victores in a boke that he made off contemplation. Thus glorous virgyn about the tyme of the comynge of the Angell" (fol. 8r–v). Previously unidentified, these words signal a long borrowing from an anonymous Middle English tract known as *Of Three Workings of Man's Soul*, a late fourteenth-century devotional text featuring a translation of Richard of St. Victor's *Benjamin major*, and surviving in four manuscripts.[7] It was first edited in 1896 by Carl Horstman, then more fully in 1995 by Stephen B. Hayes, and again in 2007 by Ralph Hanna, who supports Horstman's suggestion that the author may be Richard Rolle.[8] Like the *MDN*, *Of Three Workings* has received barely any other scholarly attention, much less extended analysis.[9] Of the four manuscript witnesses to *Of Three Workings*, the *MDN* borrowing most closely matches in text and orthography Cambridge, Magdalene College, MS Pepys 2125 (fols. 80v–82v), though several variants suggest it was not the exact copy text. While MS Pepys 2125 apparently comprises two manuscripts later bound together, the part containing *Of Three Workings* possibly connects to the Brigittines of Syon Abbey, or neighboring Carthusians: it includes a short treatise on the contemplative and active life translated from Bridget of Sweden's *Revelaciones*, and some texts seem to have been revised for a male readership.[10]

In total, nearly 40 percent of *Of Three Workings* has been included in *MDN*. Together, these lines constitute one of the largest sections of borrowed material outside the *Meditationes vitae Christi* itself. *Of Three Workings* dominates the Annunciation scene, which in turn comprises 15 percent of the entire *MDN* text—a very high proportion of the narrative compared to other lives of Christ (especially considering this scene does not even feature Christ himself, per se).

Though it is conspicuously marked as Richard of St. Victor's in the margins of *MDN*, nothing by "this worthi clerke" actually remains in this borrowing, which is only of the second half of the source text. Containing the sole moment where Richard is mentioned, the first few lines of *Of Three Workings* are closely retained as the opening of the borrowing in *MDN*; but *Of Three Workings* continues on to translate a large part of Richard of St. Victor's *Benjamin major* on the tripartite hierarchy of thought, meditation, and contemplation. Compare the opening of *Of Three Workings* to the beginning of the borrowing in *MDN* quoted above, with omitted text underlined: "A grett clerke þat men calles Richard of Saynt Victoures settes in a boke þat he made of contemplacyon thre wyrkynges of Crystyn man saoule, qwylke are þise: Thoght, Thynking and Contemplacyon."[11] The *MDN* does not borrow any of the translation of Richard's *Benjamin major* from *Of Three Workings* (about one-quarter of the treatise), and it also omits the second section, on the role of grace in contemplation (likewise about one-quarter of the treatise).[12] These omissions fit in with the compiler's general tendencies to focus on visual details and to avoid more meta-commentary on devotional process or experience.

MDN picks up again in its borrowing to include almost all of the second half of *Of Three Workings*, an extended meditation on the moments leading up to the Annunciation, when the Virgin Mary is reading and meditating on the prophecies foretelling the Incarnation (Isaiah 7:14) just before the angel Gabriel's arrival. The *MDN* compiler includes most of the text at this point, except for a somewhat long passage on the nature of the "bodely ymagyn-acyon" and its relation to the soul.[13] Otherwise, the compiler switches the order of a few phrases, and omits brief moments where the narrative voice speaks directly to the reader—"And I schall tell thee," etc. Nonetheless, the compiler retains a few direct commands to the reader to "busily behold," a tone that is completely different from the rest of this compilation (he has carefully scrubbed most of that kind of language from the *Meditationes vitae Christi* passages). A comparison of the opening passage demonstrates the relationship between the source and the host. The text of *Of Three Workings* is taken from Cambridge, Magdalene College, MS Pepys 2125, the surviving version most closely related to the borrowing in *MDN*:

Of Three Workings	***Meditaciones domini nostri***
(MS Pepys 2125, fol. 81v; Hanna, l. 96–116; underlining indicates lines omitted in *MDN*)	(Blom-Smith, p. 13, l. 13–p. 14, l. 6; bold indicates additions, extra spaces added to help comparison)

Fyrst þu schall ymagyn in þi sowle a fayr chamber, and in þat chamber þu schall þen se sittyng at a wyndowe redyng on a book owre lady Saynte Mare. And þu schall sette þiself in som corner of þat chamber bisily beholding hire þer she sytteþ, and namly þe contenance and þe manere of hire havyng of hir body. Beholde howe deuotely she sytteþ and hir book bifore hire liggyng on a dext and she a partye stowpyng toward þe boke and redyng pryualy withowte shewyng of voys. And what þu shalt þenke þat she radde y shal telle þe. Þu shalt þenke þat she radde wordes of þe prophecie [howe it was sayde] of Ysaye [þe prophete][14] þat	And as a gret clerke seith is called Richard of Seynt Victorus yn a boke that he made off contemplacion, **thus glorious virgyn about the tyme of the comynge of the angell** sche was in hure chambur sittynge at a wyndowe

and hure boke liggynge in a dexe and sche in a part stowpynge toward the boke and redynge preuely without schewyng of voys

of the profecie, how it was seide of Ysaie the profyt that a |

a mayden sholde bere a childe, þe whvtche sholde saue al mankynde. And how sche ymagyned desiryng þat hit myȝt be in hire dayes, þat she myȝte ones see oure blessid lord þat she hadde servyd in þe temple in þe schappe of owre kynde. And bihald bisily vnto hire, and þu shalt se hire in þis ymagynacyon in hir sowle sittyng vpryȝt [in hyr body] lenyng þe lokyng of þe boke & lokyng vppe in to heuen. Bihold þen bisily þat blessid louely swete vysage of oure lady, howe deoute hit is, þe swete mouth cloos and þe eyȝen closed and þerwiþ no breþ passyng owt neyþer of hire mowþ ne nose. And [behalde þerwyth] se how paal she ys and no blood ne rode in hir vysage.

mayde schulde bere a child the whyche schulde saue mankynde. And scheo ymagined, desirynge that hit myȝt be yn hure dayes, that scheo myȝt see oones our blessid Lorde that scheo serued yn the tempull yn the schappe off our kynde. Byholde besyly vnto this blessid lady how that scheo settith hure vpryght yn body lenynge, lokynge yn the boke and lokynge vp to heuen. Byholde that blessid lowly visage of this lady how deuoute it is, the swete mowthe close and the hyen closid and therwith noone **euell** brethe passynge out of hure mouthe ne nose, and byholde therwith how pale scheo is, and no blood ne rode yn hure vysage.

The *MDN* compiler was likely drawn to the unusual way in which *Of Three Workings* focuses on Mary's precise meditation on the scriptural verse, her transition to reflective contemplation, and her physiological transformation into a trance-like state of rapture. Unlike *Of Three Workings'* first section translating Richard of St. Victor, the entire second half focusing on Mary at the Annunciation seems to be an original composition in Middle English and perhaps most suggestive of Rolle's devotional innovations. It is, as Hanna observes, "marked by considerable rhetorical cleverness,"[15] and its extended description makes it stand out from other lives of Christ representations of Mary reading at the Annunciation, such as found in Aelred of Rievaulx's *De institutione inclusarum*, Love's *Mirror of the Blessed Life of Jesus Christ*, and *Speculum Devotorum*.

This compiler seems less concerned with educating his readers about the technical aspects of *how* imagination and meditation work, but rather focused on exercising that imagination through this visualization—through plot-driven narrative. However, he retains the unusually detailed physiological description of Mary's ravishment partially quoted above, and how that may demonstrate bodily the experience of desire for the love of God. This static moment of deep concentration on the body in stillness, with the text's long description enforcing the reader's slow contemplation of the ravished body, is a striking contrast to the continuous action of the rest of the life of Christ—an unstoppably unfolding linear narrative. This last part of the text offers a visualization exercise in the tradition of guided meditations but also promotes an active emulation of the Virgin as a model contemplative. Readers witness her engaged reading of the Bible as an example that should be imitated in their own reading of either scripture or devotional texts such as *MDN* itself. Strategically placed towards the beginning of the story of Christ's life, the scene of Mary's reading becomes a necessary opportunity for learning and self-reflection to prepare the reader for imaginatively engaging with the rest of the narrative, culminating in Christ's passion and resurrection.

Mary's model of conceiving Christ, the *logos*, while reading the Word should be understood in the light of the compilation's frequent excerpting from Birgitta's *Revelaciones*: holy women channel God in powerful ways, this text emphasizes, and can facilitate the reader's own spiritual conception of Christ by means of text-based meditation. Identifying *Of Three Workings* as the source of this section of *Meditaciones domini nostri* helps to connect the gospel meditation to a new matrix of devotional texts, manuscripts, and known authors such as Richard Rolle. The strong presence of visionary holy women in both these works strengthens the possible Carthusian and Bridgettine inclinations of Trinity College MS B.15.42 and MS Pepys 2125, as these enclosed communities display a consistent interest in Mary, Bridget, and other Continental and insular visionaries. Hopefully further analysis of both texts will illuminate their importance to our understanding of late-medieval devotional culture and its holy women.

University of Bergen

NOTES

1. See the catalogue entry in Richard Hunt and Falconer Madan, *A summary catalogue of western manuscripts in the Bodleian Library at Oxford which have not hitherto been catalogued in the Quarto series* (Oxford: Oxford University Press, 1895–1953), 5:326–327.
2. On CUL MS B.xv.42, see M. R. James, *The Western Manuscripts in the Library of Trinity College, Cambridge: a Descriptive Catalogue* (Cambridge: University of Cambridge Press, 1904), 510–513. The full dissertation can be viewed online at http://trin-sites-pub.trin.cam.ac.uk/james/viewpage.php?index=244 (accessed 1 Dec 2016). CUL MS B.xv.42 manuscript also has an entry in Linne R. Mooney, *The Index of Middle English Prose Handlist 11: Manuscripts in the Library of Trinity College, Cambridge* (Cambridge: Cambridge University Press, 1995), 19–20.
3. Elisabeth Blom-Smith, "The Lyf of Oure Lord and the Virgyn Mary

edited from MS Trinity College Cambridge B.15.42 and MS Bodley 578," (PhD diss., King's College, London, 1992); a full PDF can be found online at https://kclpure.kcl.ac.uk/portal/files/2926635/418745.pdf (accessed 1 Dec 2016). She uses Trinity as the base text, supplementing with Bodley when gaps occur. Blom-Smith's adopted title, *The Lyf of Oure Lord and the Virgyn Mary*, does not actually occur anywhere in the text; she apparently derived it from an expansion of the first line of the Latin prologue in the Bodley manuscript. I will use the Latin title from the prologue itself.

4. Elizabeth Salter includes this life of Christ in her work on Love's *Mirror* and other translations of the *Meditationes vitae Christi*, where she grouped it with the *Speculum Devotorum*, a similar text; see chapter IV in *Nicholas Love's "Myrrour of the Blessed Lyf of Jesu Christ," Analecta Cartusiana* 10 (Salzburg: Institut fur Anglistik und Amerikanistik, 1974), esp. 106, n. 188. Roger Ellis and Barry Windeatt both mention it in passing as part of their discussions of Birgitta's revelations in medieval England; see Ellis, "Flores ad Fabricandum... Coronam: An Investigation into the uses of the revelations of St. Bridget of Sweden in fifteenth-century England," *Medium Aevum* 51 (1982), 163–186, esp. 180; and Windeatt, "1412–1534: Texts" in *The Cambridge Companion to Medieval English Mysticism*, ed. Samuel Fanous and Vincent Gillespie (Cambridge: Cambridge University Press, 2011), 199. (In both Ellis and Windeatt, the mistaken shelfmark Trinity College MS B.v.42 should read B.xv.42).

5. MS Bodley 578, f. 47v: "meditaciones de vita et passione et resurreccione et in celum ascencione Ihesu Christi secundum Bonaventuram ex tertia sua et brevissima licet fortisissima edicione."

6. For more on sources see Blom-Smith, vii–xiv.

7. In Blom-Smith's edition, the borrowing extends from p. 13, l. 12 to p. 16, l. 10; in Bodley, ff. 5r–v; Trinity, ff. 8r–9r. The final words are "Thus sythe Rechard de Sancto Victore."

8. Ralph Hanna edits the text from Cambridge, Trinity College, MS O.8.26: *Richard Rolle: Uncollected Prose and Verse with Related Northern Texts*, EETS o.s. 329 (Oxford: Oxford University Press, 2007), 84–88, and lxviii–lxix where he discusses its affinities with Rolle's œuvre. Stephen B. Hayes also uses Trinity O.8.26 as a base text with same-page variants from Cambridge, Magdalene College, Pepys Library 2125 and Cambridge University Library MS Dd.5.64, and helpfully prints in parallel the shorter version found in BL, Sloane MS 1009; "Of Three Workings in Man's Soul: A Middle English Prose Meditation on the Annunciation," in *Vox Mystica: Essays for Valerie M. Lagorio*, ed. Anne Clark Bartlett, Janet Goebel, and William F. Pollard (Cambridge: Cambridge University Press, 1995), 177–199 (Hanna did not appear to be aware of Hayes'

edition; though Hanna's edition follows more careful editorial procedures, Hayes' parallel layout and commentary remains useful). The text
was first edited from the shortest surviving version, CUL Dd.v.64, by
Carl Horstmann, *Yorkshire Writers: Richard Rolle of Hampole, an English
Father of the Church, and His Followers* (London: Sonnenschein, 1896),
1:82. The text is item M.5, O.15 in P.S. Joliffe, *A Check-list of Middle
English Prose Writings of Spiritual Guidance* (Toronto: Pontifical Institute of Mediaeval Studies, 1974); and no. 5 in R.E. Lewis, N.F. Blake,
and A.S.G. Edwards, *Index of Printed Middle English Prose* (New York:
Garland Publishers, 1985).

9. For instance, Jennifer Bryan, *Looking Inward: Devotional Reading and
the Private Self in Late Medieval England* (Philadelphia: University of
Pennsylvania Press, 2008), 55, fn. 72.

10. For a full description of the manuscript, see Rosamund McKitterick
and Richard Beadle, *Catalog of the Pepys Library at Magdalene College
Cambridge. Volume 5. Manuscripts: Part 1: Medieval* (Cambridge: D.S.
Brewer, 1992), pp. 54–61, as well as Hanna, *Richard Rolle*, pp. xliv–xviii.
Hayes also suggests a possible Bridgettine provenance for MS Pepys
2125 ("Of Three Workings in Man's Soul," p. 186).

11. Hanna, p. 84, l. 1–4.

12. In Hanna's edition of *Of Three Workings*, these omissions correspond
to l. 2–95 (out of a total of 180 lines), so almost exactly the first half.

13. Hanna, *Of Three Workings*, l. 128–143.

14. Bracketed variants are found in Trinity College, MS O.8.26 and CUL
Dd.v.64, and omitted in MS Pepys 2125 (and MS Sloane 1009, a greatly
abbreviated version). This suggests that the *Of Three Workings* copy text
for the *MDN* compiler was a version related most closely to MS Pepys
2125, but also related to Trinity College, MS O.8.26 or CUL Dd.v.64.

15. Hanna, *Richard Rolle*, lxix.

Descriptive Reviews

CHRISTOPHER DE HAMEL
Meetings with Remarkable Manuscripts.
London: Allen Lane, 2016.
632 pp. Numerous color illus.

Christopher de Hamel, longtime director at Sotheby's and now emeritus librarian of Corpus Christi College, Cambridge, has produced a wonderful volume. Intended for the general trade (and initially on the shelves in time for last year's Christmas coffee-table-book rush), this is nonetheless a rich and genially presented volume. It energetically presents our trade to a broad audience and offers rich gleanings on any variety of fronts.

At the center of the book are encounters with a dozen famous manuscripts, mainly ones from the glitz end (de Hamel begins his account by comparing his project with Sunday supplement celebrity interviews) of the production scale. Whatever their beauty (as opposed to the browned and dusty messes we very frequently deal with), these manuscripts have been carefully chosen to suggest the breadth of the field. Each book represents a century, from the sixth to the sixteenth, and de Hamel has carefully chosen his exhibits from a variety of genres.

In addition, all de Hamel's "interviews" occur in situ: the book has a certain travelogue quality, one that introduces general readers to the experience of libraries, some of them, of course, quite elegant spaces. This situational diversity complements that of the books themselves. And de Hamel carefully attends to a fact we all know and deal with on a daily basis; like every word, each with its unique history, he attends carefully—portraits of a number of rogues and villains, for example—to the biography of each celebrity, its descent and provenance. The volume traverses Europe in its visits both to the manuscripts' homes but also to the places where they were produced and their uneven descents to their current institutions. Readers of this journal will probably be most interested in the insular examples, here richly illustrated and interrogated. These represent mainly older materials: de Hamel's longtime companion, "The Gospels of St. Augustine" (Corpus Christi's MS 286), the "Codex Amiatinus" in Florence, and (how could one not?) Trinity College Dublin's "Book of Kells." The one later insular book discussed (another "how could one not?") is the National Library of Wales's Hengwrt *Canterbury Tales*, with copious attention to recent discussions of the scribe stimulated by Linne Mooney's identification of that scribe as Adam Pynkhurst.

Although, as indicated, the volume is largely intended for a nonprofessional audience, one persistent detail in de Hamel's presentation deserves highlighting. He insists throughout, in his discussions of his witnesses' production, upon the discontinuous quality of medieval books. Consequently, every chapter aligns its production narrative with a full collation of the volume in question (first at page 38 n), and de Hamel insists early on (6–7) that his lay readers internalize what a collation diagram is and how to use it. This seems to me a salutary lesson and one that all scholars, particularly anyone offering a description, should heed.

We should be very grateful to de Hamel for hinting to a broad public something of our craft and its fascination. In this hefty and richly illustrated volume, someone we already know well as a brilliant conversationalist and raconteur offers general readers an account genially mild yet authoritative and thoroughly enjoyable—though a bit shy on the dust and bookworms.

Ralph Hanna, Keble College, Oxford

WOLFGANG MAGER, ED.
The Middle English Text of Caxton's Ovid, *Books II–III.*
Middle English Texts 53.
Heidelberg, Germany: Universitätsverlag Winter, 2016.
xxxiii + 220 pp.

VALERIE EDDEN, ED.
Þe Instytucyonys and Specyal Dedys of Relygyows Carmelitys.
Middle English Texts 54.
Heidelberg, Germany: Universitätsverlag Winter, 2016.
xxvi + 252 pp.

In current times postgraduates and postdoctoral students are (mistak-enly) discouraged from undertaking cataloguing or editing on the grounds that such tasks take too long, do not attract funding, and are no substitute for the monograph, which is where we are all supposed to make our mark. While some of this is true (any worthwhile cataloguing or editing project cannot be rushed, and funding bodies do tend to favor the quantifiable spectacular enterprise), it is a very rare monograph that has the longevity or impact of an edition or catalogue. It is refreshing, therefore, that Wolfgang Mager saw fit to do an edition of part of William Caxton's *Ovid* manuscript for his dissertation at the Ludwig-Maximilians Universität in Munich under the supervision of Hans Sauer (one of the Middle English Texts series general editors); the dissertation was approved in 2009 and has now appeared in published format seven years later. Such a time frame is not unexpected for editing work, where a degree of maturation is required both as a step up from the thesis itself and to allow for further consideration of various editorial and textual points; would that some similar pause for thought could routinely be allowed before some monographs are rushed into print for good or ill. In this review, Mager's edition is coupled with one from an experienced scholar, Valerie Edden, who has devoted herself over the years to a study of the Carmelites, the one religious order that figures rarely in Middle English studies.

Mager begins his introduction (a multiplicity of short sections according to the usual Germanic format) with an overview of Caxton, who interestingly tells us that he finished his translation on April 22, 1480—a Saturday. The source, about which Caxton is silent, was a French moralized version of the text, the *Ovid Moralisé en Prose II*, which is edited here alongside the English. If some of us are less familiar with *Caxton's Ovid* than we should be, there is a reason for this, as Mager makes clear in his discussion: "there was no edition of books I–IX and the two partial editions of books X–XV from the early nineteenth and the early twentieth century are rare and difficult to obtain," while "Caxton's French source . . . has not been edited at all" (ix–x). Having given a few details about Caxton's life and works, the editor then asks the important question: was Caxton's manuscript translation ever printed? By analogy with his other translations and given what Caxton says in his 1483 *Golden Legend* prologue, the strong implication is that it *was* printed. Yet there is no solid evidence for this, and Mager, before returning an open verdict, makes the important point that if it had been printed, it is very odd that no editions whatsoever should survive of such a substantial work, as Ovid's *Metamorphoses* comprises no fewer than fifteen books and some 250 legends.

There is only one surviving copy of Caxton's translation, one manuscript historically intended as two volumes, apparently copied from Caxton's draft by a professional scribe and with a set of incomplete illustrations. Because these two volumes, Cambridge, Magdalene College, Old Library, MS F.4.34 and Cambridge, Magdalene College, Pepys Library, MS 2124, have been described many times, Mager is economical in his own description. Given this, the lack of pagination or foliation, and the general difficulties of gaining a sustained period of time in the Pepys Library, one can understand his decision to an extent, even if one would have liked a little more detail. Although the purpose of the English copy is not clear and ownership unknown until about the later sixteenth century, the three surviving manuscripts of the French source, which are all related in terms of chronology and Burgundian provenance, were associated with regal or noble owners (see xvi). Having provided an informative explanation of the development of moralized interpretations of Ovid from the early fourteenth century in France, Mager then discusses the relationship of the French manuscripts and Caxton's translation. Weighing matters up, he concludes that "The cumulative evidence thus makes it likely that Caxton used a manuscript now lost which was similar

to, but not identical with S" (xx). However, Mager does not use S (a manuscript in St. Petersburg) as his base text for the French but instead one in
Paris. The explanation for this is in note 22: the St. Petersburg manuscript
came to his attention too late to be considered. This is most unfortunate,
but regrettably such things can sometimes happen.

As it stands, Mager does a good job, over an extended part of the introduction, of discussing Caxton's translational technique, together with his
syntactical and lexical choices. He then follows with a facing-page edition
of the French and the English; he is to be commended for this because the
setting out of the text will have been time-consuming as well as necessitating
the incorporation of two sets of critical apparatus. There is a strong narrative drive in the work, made more pronounced by the chapter summaries
at the beginning of sections, for example, "How Iupyter sent Mercurye for
to kepe hys oxen on the montayne. Capitulo 24°" (91, ll. 7–8). And the text
itself is engaging; here, for example, in the story of Bacchus and Pentheus,
is Acoetes, explaining himself before the angry Pentheus, "'Myn name',
sayde he, 'is Acotes . . . I have nothyng but that I hade of my fader. . . . So it
happed on a day, by aventur, that I wente to Delon ledynge my ship'" (179,
l. 32 to 181, l. 9).

The edition concludes with a commentary and a glossary, though the
commentary could be much fuller; I fear that Mager credits his readers with
more classical knowledge than they may have, although he does provide a
very helpful descriptive index of classical names (204–210). Overall this is
a useful edition to have, forming as it does a follow-up volume to MET 43
(2011) by Diana Rumrich, who has edited Book I of *Caxton's Ovid*. Mager
notes (x) that both volumes are part of an editing project; we look forward
to the remaining twelve books.

The second edition reviewed here, Þe *Instytucyonys and Specyal Dedys
of Relygyows Carmelitys*, edited by Valerie Edden, is also a translated text.
The Latin source, *De institucione et peculiaribus gestis religiosorum carmelita-
rum decem libri in lege veteri exortorum et in nova perseverancium* (commonly
called *The Book of the First Monks*), which was of fundamental importance
for the history and identity of the Carmelites, seeking as it did to argue for
the antiquity of the order, was no doubt produced after 1379 by the Catalo-
nian provincial, Felip Ribot (d. 1391). It is extant in ten manuscripts divided
into an earlier and later recension. Ribot's text is in turn, he says, based on
four other named authorities, all of which are regarded as false attributions.
Edden helpfully provides a short summary of each of Ribot's ten books (xii–
xiii). The fifteenth-century translation, by the Norwich Carmelite Thomas
Scrope (also known as Bradley), who was born around 1400, is found in
only one manuscript, London, Lambeth Palace Library, MS 192. This

contains the Latin text in its first volume, and in its second volume, alongside the translation, the Middle English *Rule of St. Linus* for lay hermits, which may likewise have been by Scrope.

As the editor notes in her biographical discussion (xv–xx), Scrope "was a prolific writer, who had a long and colourful life" (xv). This included, according to the later John Bale, leaving his Norwich friary and wandering the streets "wearing sackcloth and a girdle of iron fetters and proclaiming the imminent end of the world and the appearance of the Bride of the Lamb" (xv). Later he settled in an anchorite cell in Norwich, traveled to Rome in 1449 to be consecrated Bishop of Dromore, became rector of Sparham near Norwich in 1454, and was a papal legate in Rhodes probably at some point between June 1466 and December 1468. Alongside all this, he was suffragan bishop of Norwich from 1450 to 1477 and held a number of benefices in East Anglia until his death in Lowestoft on January 15, 1491. While Scrope's other writings, all in Latin (listed on xviii), were aimed at fellow Carmelites, Edden reasonably argues that this translation may have been intended for a more general clerical audience or indeed even for the Guild of St. George in Norwich, of which he himself was probably a member. Not to be underestimated in this respect is what the translation has to say about spiritual development.

Edden concludes the introduction by looking at Scrope's translational method before moving to a manuscript description and a very short comment on date and provenance where much information is telescoped into a single paragraph. The evidence strongly implies that Scrope produced his translation in the Norwich Carmelite house in the 1440s. The Lambeth copy (which apparently dates from the second half of the century) would likewise appear to have been produced there, though Edden says that it is not in Scrope's hand nor corrected by him. She notes that there are several surviving examples of his hand but does not list them; one has to recall examples mentioned earlier (xviii–xx). Likewise, the detail about the dialect is very limited, with references simply to *A Linguistic Atlas of Late Mediaeval English* for the two main hands localized in Suffolk and Norfolk; it would have been good to have had a more expanded account. Be that as it may, Edden has produced a careful edition of a text that is itself scrupulously laid out in a schematic fashion, with a general summary at the beginning of the whole, prefaces at the start of each book, and (like *Caxton's Ovid* above) little summaries encapsulated in every chapter title, for instance, "The secund chapter [of Book VI] makyth mende that to the old professowrys of this relygion a tyme was sygned to hem in the which blyssed Mary schul be born" (90, ll. 17–19). The whole is concluded with a painstaking commentary and glossary, and a bibliography.

Overall, despite the few misgivings expressed here, it is good to have these editions. Both editors have expended time and energy editing texts that have not been edited before—and substantial material at that, as each text comprises almost two hundred pages. We should be grateful to them for doing this work.

Veronica O'Mara, University of Hull

PETER KIDD

500 Years: Treasures from the Library of Corpus Christi College, Oxford.
London: Scala, 2017.
63 pp. 48 color plates.

This delightful small Scala volume contains a selection of the manuscripts and printed books exhibited in 2017 (the quincentenary of Corpus Christi College, Oxford) at the Folger Shakespeare Library, Washington, DC, and the Center for Jewish History in New York.[1] Both the exhibition and the Scala volume are the work of Peter Kidd, and the book itself is lavishly illustrated, with foldouts of the front and back cover that illustrate the library, which is still largely in its sixteenth-century state.

The foreword by the president of the college, Richard Carwardine, briefly summarizes Corpus's claim to being "the first Renaissance institution in Oxford," founded by Richard Fox (d. 1528), bishop of Winchester and one of the most powerful men in England in the early sixteenth century. As a humanist foundation, the college promoted Greek and Hebrew alongside Latin as languages of scholarship, particularly scriptural scholarship. As a late foundation, the library also houses a large collection of printed books, with 280 incunables in a collection of more than twenty thousand pre-1830 printed books.

The seven sections of the book illustrate the library's founding by Fox. "Fox's Foundation" begins with a woodcut from Wynkyn de Worde's *Contemplacyon of Synners* (1499), which shows Fox receiving de Worde's book, and continues with a metalcut frontispiece from a 1497 Basel edition of St. Jerome's letters, which illustrates Greek, Hebrew, and Latin New Testaments in Jerome's study, and pages from the 1589 catalogue of the library, 310 of whose 371 titles are still in there today (nos. 1–3). Prominent in the early history of the library were Fox himself, who left ninety extant volumes, and the first president of Corpus Christi, John Claymond (d. 1536), who left seventy volumes, including seven Hebrew manuscripts.

The next three sections of the book illustrate the library's well-founded claim to being "The Trilingual Library." "The Latin Library" has a Venice edition of Cicero (1470) and an Italian parchment manuscript, both in humanist script, and a Gothic commentary on the Book of Job (nos. 4–6). "The Greek Library" has a Florentine Aristotle written on parchment by the scribe Iohannes Scutariota, one of several Greek manuscripts bought by Claymond in 1521 from William Grocyn's estate; a stunning Venetian edition of 1500 of the commentary on another Aristotle, printed in gold; and an *Iliad* decorated by the Cretan scribe Ioanne Rhosos in the third quarter of the fifteenth century (nos. 7–9). "The Hebrew Library" has rather more examples, several donated by Claymond: a late-twelfth-century parchment manuscript written in Arabic using the Hebrew alphabet; three parchment manuscripts with Hebrew and Latin side by side; a Basel edition (1535) of the Psalms in Hebrew and Latin, bought new by Claymond just before his death; and a copy of the seminal text for Hebrew biblical study, Rashi's Commentaries, stolen from the Hebrew scholar Robert Wakefield by Richard Collier, vicar of Sittingbourne (nos. 10–15).

"British Manuscripts" are illustrated by the Corpus Irish Gospels, the Lapworth Missal, the Corpus *Canterbury Tales* (MS 198), the Corpus *Piers Plowman* (MS 201) with a unique initial depicting Will dreaming his dream, and a royal genealogy in late Middle English (nos. 16–20). "Biblical Translations" begins with a page from the notes taken during the discussions of the King James Bible committee, spearheaded by the Corpus President John Rainolds (d. 1607), continues with a Netherlandish parchment manuscript of Erasmus's revision of his Latin New Testament, and concludes with a beautifully illustrated parchment manuscript of Desmoulins's *Bible historiale* (nos. 21–23). Finally, "Astronomy" has designs for sundials by Henry VIII's clockmaker, Galileo's *Sidereus Nuncius* (Venice, 1610), and a letter from Newton discussing the great comets of November and December 1680 (nos. 24–26).

Altogether this little book is a charming and beautifully illustrated introduction to a remarkable library and an exhibition that perhaps few of us may have been able to visit.[2]

Susan Powell, University of Salford (emerita)

NOTES

1. The full list of exhibits is given at 62–63.
2. However, a small exhibition of early printed books was on display at Corpus itself 7 September 2017, in conjunction with the conference "Renaissance College."

PETER KIDD
A Descriptive Catalogue of the Medieval Manuscripts
of the Queen's College, Oxford.
Oxford Bibliographical Society Special Series: Manuscript Catalogues 1.
Oxford: Oxford Bibliographical Society, 2016.
303 pp. 68 B&W figs., 48 color plates.

There is any number of reasons to welcome Peter Kidd's catalogue of
Queen's College manuscripts. Not only does this opulent volume represent
Kidd's return to cataloguing (following his meticulous 2001 bout with the
Bodleian's Buchanan manuscripts) and an important stage in replacing
Henry O. Coxe's 1852 catalogue with one attentive to modern bibliographi-
cal requirements, it also brings a new player, the Oxford Bibliographical
Society, into the production of full-collection catalogues (the dust jacket
promises two further volumes in progress, for Christ Church and Trinity).
Moreover, the production values on offer are impressive; the typesetter,
Paul Nash, has done an outstanding job in converting Kidd's careful descriptions and abundant visual materials into a book that is as elegant as it
is richly informative.

Queen's is not one of the larger collegiate collections in Oxford. As one
might surmise from the college's visual impact when viewed from Oxford
High Street, the Queen's library, like much else, was subject to a rage for
modernization and in the sixteenth century jettisoned its medieval holdings.
The roughly sixty books described here are thus all modern donations and
form a slightly artificial rather than organic grouping. The collection is particularly heavy on biblical materials, about a quarter of the whole (including
one volume in Greek and two Wycliffite Bibles); another half dozen volumes
could be described as fully "commentative." A further half dozen books are
liturgical, mainly Books of Hours (including one full Middle English primer).

Yet donors were scarcely as monotonal as this. MS 320 is the first half of a tenth-century two-volume set of Isidore's *Etymologies*. There are interesting twelfth-century books as well, a perhaps Continental copy of the Latin Josephus (MS 106) and a glossed Horace (MS 202). And among other nonpatristic offerings are a copy of Higden's *Polychronicon* (MS 307) and an Italian volume with two late antique epics (MS 314).

The descriptions, enhanced by book designer Paul Nash's magnificently open layout, are crisp, informative, and authoritative. I would particularly draw attention to one of Kidd's careful innovations. Books produced fascicularly are noted as such, for example, in MS 161 (an interesting Scots chivalric compilation, described at 76–80), the description signals the bibliographical independence of text items 1 to 9, 10, 11 to 21, and 22 to 26. One hopes that this presentation will become universal in catalogues. (Kidd here accords with a recent volume intended for general readers, Christopher de Hamel's *Meetings with Remarkable Manuscripts* [London: Allen Lane, 2016], see review in this issue, and de Hamel persistently demonstrates the importance, even to his "lay" readers, of recognizing such divisions.)

Navigating Kidd's volume is facilitated by unusually careful support material. There is a full list of incipits, often absent from recent catalogues. There are multiple topical indexes (e.g., authors and texts, iconography, second folios), not the single amalgamated lists of many recent examples. In these indexes, Kidd's references are keyed to precise portions of the descriptions, as opposed to simple references to packed pages.

I have only two qualifications to universal approbation. I understand Kidd's reluctance to take on a full account of the now-extinct medieval library. At the same time, having a full library history in a single volume would be useful. To construct that, interested readers will need also to consult Rodney M. Thomson and James G. Clark's *The University and College Libraries of Oxford* (reviewed here at pp. 317–319), 2:1232 to 1241, 1264 to 1295 passim, 1376 to 1377, and 1382 to 1383.

I have already noted the visual appeal of the volume, both as produced book and as one elaborately illustrated. Every manuscript is somehow depicted, whether in a full-page black-and-white "snapshot," or a detailed color plate, or both. The first group of images, a full page adjacent to each of the individual descriptions, I find problematic. The images should be valuable for offering samples of scribal hands and revealing more clearly than a verbal account aspects of mise-en-page. But the universal full-page reproduction (marked as "reduced," but never by how much) renders many of the scribal hands illegible in this form. And many images reproduce pages of solid textblock; this does give the viewer a sense of gross mise-en-page but offers no hint as to the *ordinatio* imposed on the text. I wonder whether some indication of the selective procedures underlying these images might be helpful (perhaps descriptive captions indicating salient features). And perhaps one might consider some more flexible illustrative program (images chosen to display scribal hands offering, as necessary, only part of the leaf at actual size, for example).

But, on the whole, Kidd, Nash, and the Oxford Bibliographical Society have combined in a contribution for which we should be grateful for many reasons.

Ralph Hanna, Keble College, Oxford

JULIA MARVIN
The Construction of Vernacular History in the Anglo-Norman Prose Brut
Chronicle: The Manuscript Culture of Late Medieval England.
Writing History in the Middle Ages, vol. 5.
York, UK: York Medieval Press in association with
The Boydell Press, 2017.
314 pp. 2 color + 26 B&W illus.

The importance of the Anglo-Norman prose *Brut* cannot be gainsaid. Originating in northern England around the end of the thirteenth century, some fifty or sixty French versions are extant. It was soon translated into English, and such was its popularity that three or four times as many versions remain in English. There were translations, too, into Latin, a few, perhaps, into Welsh, and with continuation and expansion it was to become "the medium in which secular Middle English historiography developed" (2)—as many as thirteen different editions were in print before 1528. In 2006, Dr. Marvin published the first scholarly edition of *The Oldest Anglo-Norman Prose* Brut *Chronicle*, its seventy-one-page Introduction tightly focused and dealing with such matters as the five manuscripts of the Oldest Version (OV), their relationships, and materials appropriate to the establishment of the edited text (Marvin distinguishes the *Oldest* from the Oldest Version [OV], that is her edited text). Her 2006 edition is now complemented by a splendid analysis not just of the OV but of its place within the wider *Brut* tradition. The book is simply structured: the "Introduction" (1–18) is followed by two parts, "Construction" (19–128) and "Reconstruction and Response" (129–229), with a "Conclusion" (231–259). Prefatory materials include two pages of well-chosen "Abbreviations" and a most helpful "Note on Proper Names, Transcriptions, and Translations." A "Bibliography," a "General Index," and a lengthy "Index of Manuscripts Cited" complete the book.

Nowadays we tend to view prose *Brut*s with suspicion, dismissing them as "derivative and middlebrow" (15), but Marvin reminds us that they were consulted as a source for history into the seventeenth century, and she argues that the prose *Brut* "set the context, form, and matter for vernacular historical writing in England" (2). In particular, the OV marks "a key moment in the larger *Brut* tradition," providing the core text for "a new British history" and serving as a catalyst for historical writing in the vernaculars of medieval England (16).

Five aspects of the "Construction" of the new British history are treated. The first of these chapters shows how the OV's author creates his New Troy in a vocabulary that is "fairly narrow" and "repetitive" (24). It is a history of rulers who are good or bad, for audiences "with relatively little immediate access to, knowledge or memory of, or investment in previous versions of the matter of Troy" (35). Even the founding of Rome is omitted, and Rome is first named in the story of Belin and Brenne. What matters in the OV is what happens in Britain and to its rulers: "Imperial Rome becomes an entirely negative exemplar" (54). From the first leader, emphasis is placed on "the centrality of the people's support—and counsel—to Brut's success" (27).

The second chapter shows how the OV promotes "the ideal of a cohesive community" (57) in which the right of rebellion is "presumed and enacted" (60). There are few descriptions of warfare, rather of negotiations and outcomes than of deeds. Just as the OV takes little interest in depicting war, so, too, chapter 3 shows, it "displays no sympathy for 'romantic,' sexual love" (78). Yet some women's stories are elaborated, and in interesting ways. For example, the narrative of Edward the Martyr's wicked stepmother is played out across three reigns (84). Marvin suggests that the OV displays "a demystifying attitude towards rape" (91) and that its presentation of women straightforwardly "as human beings, plain and simple" is "extraordinary in and of itself" (92).

A whole chapter is given to "Social Arthur," a model king and implicitly the forerunner of Edward I (107). The final chapter in Part I explores how the OV created a "common heritage" in which insular readers could "consider themselves descendants of Brut" (127). Ethnicities are blurred in a country of multiple identities. This is the true history ("le dreit estorie"), even to the land's renaming as "Engistlonde" and then "Engleterre" (117–118) by a writer "eager to demonstrate the genealogical credentials of the house of Plantagenet" (123).

Whereas Part I is a literary analysis of the OV set within the context of its sources and analogues, "Part II: Reconstruction and Response" examines four aspects of the history of material books in the French prose *Brut* tradition. Its twenty-eight images, two in color, are contextually apposite, contributing to points under discussion. In the first of these chapters, Marvin begins by dispelling the sense of solidity given by the OV text. Despite its strong common core, of the five manuscripts from which it is constructed, each one lacks text present in others. What, she asks, is the evidence for a lay market in England for Anglo-Norman texts? Even copies of the Short Version that look so alike as to be regarded as twins are shown to be markedly dissimilar. Anglo-Norman *Bruts* come in a variety of scripts and layouts, and must have had "many different points of origin" (153). Doubt is cast upon the presence or absence of verse prologue as the criterion for dividing the Short Version into two groups; and indeed, if the prologue is in its own separate quire, could it constitute evidence for an earlier stage of the Short Version?

Chapter 7 looks to the texts that travel with Anglo-Norman *Bruts*, a task complicated by the frequent loss of beginnings and/or endings and the general lack of original bindings—about 40 percent are today single codices. Nevertheless, the wealth of detail accumulated bears out Marvin's conclusion that the Anglo-Norman prose *Brut* and what we think of as romance are "understood and consumed in different ways" (174). These *Bruts* were taken seriously, keeping company with French and Latin rather than English, alongside historiography and such edifying works as the *Image du monde*. Despite the acknowledged hazards of an "incompletely known manuscript tradition" (45), in the opening paragraph of chapter 8 Marvin states firmly: "Each of the major versions of the Anglo-Norman prose *Brut* has a characteristic *ordinatio*" (177). Here she reflects on how texts are organized, on side notes, annotations, marginalia, and other forms of markup.

In Part II's last chapter, "History Illustrated," Marvin begins by reminding us how rare illustration is throughout the prose *Brut* tradition. Three late deluxe manuscripts were produced on the Continent, but only a few insular manuscripts of the Anglo-Norman *Brut* have any illustrations. Marvin's survey of these manuscripts bears out her suggestion that there was not "much in the way of a iconographic tradition" (205).

But what is Merlin's role in a serious historical work that prompts its audience to think about what they read? In her "Conclusion," Marvin contends that in its depiction of Merlin, the OV is "a precociously humanistic text" (258). Its Merlin is not so much a prophet as a sage, a reader of signs. Emphasis is placed on wisdom rather than magic, and his access to occult powers is downplayed. By contrast, the Long Version "makes a retrograde move," shifting "power from the reader back to the exceptional, superhuman figure of the prophet" (255).

A short descriptive review can do no more than attempt an overview of this deeply learned book. On page after page are nuggets prompting recognition and speculation. So just what history of England was chained in Winchester cathedral? (124) How large was "the sheer number of people involved in the making of prose *Bruts*"? (133) In what ways do "the manuscripts bear witness to different choices about how to accommodate the material," even what to include? (150) Overall, this is an important book to be treasured for its insights into historical writing and Arthurian chronicle, to be combed assiduously for its wealth of codicological detail. Yet it is so well written as to be thoroughly readable.

Jane Roberts, University of London

MYRA D. ORTH
Renaissance Manuscripts: The Sixteenth Century.
A Survey of Manuscripts Illuminated in France. 2 vols.
London and Turnhout, Belgium:
Harvey Miller Publishers for Brepols, 2015.
721 pp. 321 B&W, 55 color illus.

Myra Orth, who died in 2002, was without a doubt a leading expert on Renaissance French manuscript illumination, and these two beautifully produced volumes attest to her erudition and her long scholarship in that area of study. I remember Myra's showing me her proofs for the book during our last lunch in Boston some fifteen years ago. In its foreword, the publisher notes that publication of these much-awaited volumes was held up by the need to acquire and select the color illustrations, but that its decision was "to publish Myra's work with as little change as possible," updating only the bibliography (7). Many people, including Mary Rouse, had a hand in finishing these volumes, for which we must all be grateful.

In "French Renaissance Manuscripts and *L'Histoire du Livre*" (*Viator*, 32 [2001]:245–278), Myra wrote that the Renaissance manuscript is worthy of study because it remained an important force in book production well into the sixteenth century; further, she advocated contextualization. Miniatures need to be understood not in isolation but through study of the whole codicology of the book, the conditions of its production, and "the how and who of its readership," along with its text (247). These goals are more than met in her Survey catalogue.

Like many of the books in the Survey of Manuscripts series, Orth's book is in two volumes. Volume 1 contains text and illustrations, including appendices with biographies of the artists and scribes. Here we meet court portrait artists such as Jean Clouet (*ca.* 1485–1540) and his son, François (*ca.* 1520–1572), who produced both drawings and paintings of the French royal family and collaborated with manuscript illuminators; Guillaume II Le Roy (d. 1528), who was both an illuminator and a woodcut designer; the well-documented Noël Bellemare (fl. 1515–1546); and the much-studied Master of Claude de France (fl. *ca.* 1510–1525). There is also a section providing brief biographies of authors and translators, for example, Catherine d'Amboise (d. 1550), Guillaume Budé (1468–1540), Anne de Graville (d. *ca.* 1540), Marguerite d'Angoulême (1492–1549), Clément Marot (1496–1544) and his father, Jean (*ca.* 1464–1524 or 1526), to name a few. Another section gives short biographies of patrons, dedicatees, and first owners, among them Catherine de' Médici, queen of France (1519–1589), Claude de France, queen of France (1499–1524), Edward VI, king of England (1537–1553), Louise de Savoie (1476–1531), and others.

There are also helpful family trees of royal and noble houses (Orleans-Valois, House of Lorraine, House of Bourbon Vendôme, for example), as these lineages are sometimes hard to follow for those outside the immediate period. The volume closes with a list of illustrations (which rather oddly recurs at the end of volume 2 as well, though this may prove convenient for users of these books). All of this apparatus is helpful when studying the images that volume 1 contains.

And what images! These are crisply and cleanly reproduced on every page. Among the highlights of the color pictures are reproductions of a 1531 embroidered binding now in the Russian National Library (Col., Plate 1); an illumination made about 1530 of a printer's shop that was copied from the Parisian printer's mark of Josse Bade, showing the press, tools, and men at work, including a proofreader, along with two customers, from a compilation of Rouen Puy poetry (Col., Plate 17, see also Plate 96); a color reproduction from *La Coche* painted about 1541 from the work by Marguerite de Navarre, who provided detailed descriptions of each illumination for the artist (Col., Plate 37); and a painting of the Shroud of Turin displayed by three priests before an altar, from the Hours of Marguerite de France, made in 1559 (Col., Plate 54), a manuscript also located in Turin. Some of the color plates feature works in grisaille (Col., Plates 2–4), a fashionable form of illustration that continues into the sixteenth century.

Among the black-and-white reproductions, there are many miniatures of royalty or the nobility receiving manuscripts from their makers. These include Louise de Savoie (Plates 55, 100), Marguerite de Navarre (Plate 56), François I (Plates 59, 178, 202), Queen Claude de France (Plate 68), the nobleman Girard de Vienne (Plate 168), and Anne de Pisseleu, duchess of Etampes (Plate 173). François I (1494–1547), king of France and great patron of the arts, is everywhere: he is hunting (Plate 1), crossing the Alps (Plate 3), in battle (Plate 150), and listening to a reading by a translator with his court (Plate 153, "Antoine Macault reading his translation to François I and his Court"), among other activities. There are scenes showing the court of François I and other kings (Plates 89, 90, 91, 92, 93, 236, 237), and stationary portraits of various important rulers: François I again (Plate 250), King Louis IX (Plate 249), Louise de Savoie (Plate 265), Marguerite de Navarre as Bathsheba (Plate 266), and Catherine de' Medici (Plate 269). Martin Luther (Plate 94) preaches to two lewd allegorical women in the *Panegyricus*, a virulent anti-Protestant text, while Dante and Beatrice are shown several times (Plates 64, 65, 66) in a copy of the *Paradiso* made about 1520.

As Orth points out, one third of the books catalogued here are Books of Hours produced in France, and many of the reproductions show iconographies that have not changed a great deal since earlier periods. There are many scenes of the Annunciation, Nativity, and Crucifixion, and of Bathsheba in various stages of undress. Despite this, there are some unusual illuminations, including a scene of a bare-breasted Judith with the head of Holofernes (Plate 242), a head reliquary of Mary Magdalene that shows her skull (Plate 48), and a schoolhouse scene of the birching of a student from cuttings from a calendar in a Book of Hours (Plate 167a). Other religious works of instruction are illustrated by a donkey reading a book (Plate 210) and a curious scene of Christ exhorting Henri, Marguerite, and their court to take up their crosses (Plate 88). There are also allegorical scenes of various kinds, but the best of all is an illumination of God in his library holding a large Bible with clasps and brasses in his lap, his many books on shelves surrounding him, and various men exhorting him for copies of the book (Plate 97). In the volume's final picture section, "Comparative Illustrations," there are reproductions of drawings, woodcuts by Albrecht Dürer and Hans Holbein the Younger, and examples of woodcut that illustrate early printed Hours, for example those published by Geofroy Tory. Volume 1 is visually sumptuous and stimulating to study.

Volume 2 is the manuscripts catalogue. This provides clear bibliographic information about each manuscript as well as naming artists when known, citing the approximate date and place of making, and describing the binding, collation, initials, frames and borders, text contents, and provenance, with a selected bibliography at the end of each of the one hundred entries. This is clearly written, and each manuscript is fully described. The history for each book is very clearly laid out. The volume of Puys verse, for example, that contains both the scenes of the printing press and of God in his library (item 36, 135–140), had many makers. This is a record of the fifty winning poems at the annual Rouen competitions, copied about 1530, that includes poetry that dates between 1519 and 1528, and its fifty full-page miniatures have been illuminated by three artists.

Orth's list of each of these images further includes the refrain of each poem along with the author and date if known. She discusses the more interesting texts at some length, including the poem accompanying the il-lumination of the printing press (139) and the poem about God's library (138). For the *Panegyricus* (item 35, 132–135), she explains the history of this anti-Protestant text as a reaction to the desecration of a Marian statue in Paris in 1528. The mutilated statue (which is also illustrated in this manu-script) was replaced by a silver statue of Virgin and Child given by the king. Each entry is full of useful and interesting information about the period.

At the back of this second volume is "Additional Literature and Exhibits" (335–342), compiled after Myra's death, along with a glossary of terms, an index of iconographic subjects, an index of types of books by subject (Bibles, allegory and moral instruction, education, poetry), an index of provenance, and an index of manuscripts by location.

Myra Orth was a long-time member of the Early Book Society. She spoke in our sessions at the annual meeting at Western Michigan University and published three important essays in this *Journal*: "Dedicating Women: MS Culture in the French Renaissance, The Cases of Catherine d'Amboise and Anne de Granville," 1 (1997):17–47; "Family Values: Manuscripts as Gifts and Legacies among French Renaissance Women," 4 (2001):88–111; and "Manuscript Production and Illumination in Renaissance Paris (1500–1565)," 6 (2003):125–135. These two long-awaited Survey volumes teach us still so much and add to our knowledge of sixteenth-century book production.

Martha W. Driver, Pace University

JANE ROBERTS
Guide to Scripts Used in English Writings up to 1500.
Liverpool, UK: Liverpool University Press, 2015.
xvi + 294 pp. 8 color and 105 B&W plates.

Jane Roberts's *Guide to Scripts Used in English Writings* was first published by the British Library in 2005 and was positively received: in the *Journal of the Early Book Society*, volume 10 (2007: 275–276), Susan Powell judged it excellent. The book has since become a standard work of reference and a standard aid in the teaching of paleography with any focus on English. However, its price, even when bought second hand, had risen uncomfortably high, making the book a difficult purchase for new graduate students.

This new edition makes the *Guide* affordable again but is otherwise almost identical to its predecessor. Apart from a number of silent corrections and a brief additional note (xv), it is an exact reprint. The pages and the plates themselves have remained almost exactly the same size. Since the pagination is identical to the first edition, any teaching materials that refer to the book need not be updated. The printed blacks and grays of the handwriting in the plates do "pop" less in the images, because the book is printed using a different combination of ink and paper. The black-and-white plates therefore look slightly more faded than those in the British Library edition. However, this minor change is the only regrettable alteration, and in every other respect the Liverpool University Press edition is simply a slightly improved version of an already valuable tool. Readers are referred to Powell's review for a fuller description of its contents.

Given the largely unchanged nature of the *Guide*, it seems appropriate to consider the book in its teaching context, which certainly is changing. Is a directed guide dominated by black-and-white plates still useful in a time when an increasingly large number of manuscripts are accessible through digital facsimiles in full color? If anything, the welcome proliferation of manuscript images online has made books such as this one even more vital. Digital facsimiles tend to come without either transcriptions or commentaries on script; we can now quickly access a mass of evidence, but comprehensive training and contextualization are not (yet, at least) so widely available through the Internet. The *Guide* fills that gap and is an excellent paleographical companion for the exploration of medieval English writing both online and in physical manuscripts. Furthermore, the black-and-white plates in the *Guide* provide a useful experience for new students. Studying Old and Middle English in manuscript can still entail the reading of black-and-white facsimiles on paper or microfilm, especially when research wanders beyond a relatively narrow circle of canonical books. Digitization programs have, understandably, focused on famous and beautiful manuscripts in large repositories. Even when digital facsimiles are available for less popular texts, those facsimiles are sometimes themselves digitized microfilms. So some work with black-and-white images is not only acceptable but also an asset in itself.

Two features of remit should perhaps be picked out, not for criticism but as matters that we might bear in mind when using the *Guide*. First, Roberts makes occasional references to codicological evidence such as pricking (138) but does not set out to offer a codicological manual, and the growing mass of digital facsimiles found online also do little to teach readers about the physical analysis of codices. The necessary skills must still be acquired separately, ideally through the handling of many manuscripts in person. This limitation on codicological training might remain in place forever; it is hard to see how printed or online handbooks can replace the experience of trying to understand a manuscript in the flesh or on paper.

Second, while Roberts is careful to describe how scripts were adapted from their use in writing Latin, and while many bits and pieces of Latin can be found in the plates, the book necessarily makes English central. This is what the title promises, and it is also what those of us who study and teach medieval literature written in English need, but students, amateur bibliophiles, and scholars might all need to remember the fact that the plates are not a neutral sample from all the manuscripts of medieval England. Every tool has its limits, and these qualifications do not make the achievement of the *Guide* any less impressive. It remains an excellent tool for reference or training, and the best single, unified aid for work with the scripts that transmit Old and Middle English. We owe Jane Roberts and her editors a considerable debt of gratitude for their efforts to make this book available once again.

Daniel Sawyer, University of Oxford

R. M. THOMSON
A Descriptive Catalogue of the Medieval Manuscripts in the Library of
Peterhouse, Cambridge.
Cambridge, UK: D. S. Brewer for Peterhouse, Cambridge, 2016.
xli + 230 pp. 112 color (plus frontispiece) and 1 B&W plates.

Rodney Thomson's march through the ancient college libraries of England continues apace. With Peterhouse, he is dealing with the oldest college in Cambridge, having already covered Merton and Corpus Christi in Oxford (in 2009 and 2011 respectively). Although the history of the Peterhouse library is "fairly opaque" (xvii) before the start of the fifteenth century, the earliest donors can, it seems, be traced to before the foundation of Peterhouse as such, to the group of scholars at the hospital of St. John, who moved from there in 1284 to form Peterhouse. In the fourteenth century, individual donations of books for the curriculum were augmented by acquisitions from higher-status men such as Thomas Arundel, archbishop of Canterbury. With the fifteenth century comes more information about the library and its management. Indeed, 1403 to 1404 marks the first mention of a library room; an inventory of books was made on Christmas Eve 1418 and was added to until the 1450s, and by 1472 to 1473, there was a room for a librarian.

Thomson writes interestingly about the nature, function, and architecture of this library in the fifteenth century. Its expansion appears to have been the result of more substantial donations from the early fifteenth century onwards, the earliest from John Newton, Master from 1382 to 1397, who died in 1414 as treasurer of York Minster.[1] A later, long-serving Master, John Warkworth (1475–1500), was Peterhouse's most generous medieval donor of books; during his lifetime, he gave a dozen service-books for the chapel and 54 other books, of which as many as 47 survive.

Warkworth is of interest to the present reviewer in relation to her editing of the accounts of Lady Margaret Beaufort, whose secretary and dean of chapel (and later chancellor) was Henry Hornby, Master of Peterhouse soon after Warkworth (from 1501 to 1518). Among many bequests, Hornby gave £40 to the Master and Fellows of Peterhouse to be placed in the common chest where, his will states, Warkworth's money was kept, and altar cloths specifically for Warkworth's chantry chapel.[2] Most of Hornby's books went to St. John's College, Cambridge, which, as an active executor, he had helped to establish after Lady Margaret's death, but he left Peterhouse library four volumes of the Bible with Nicholas of Lyra's commentary and another four volumes of Peterhouse's choosing (he left a similar eight volumes to Clare College).

There is no mention of Hornby's bequest in Thomson's introduction, which ends the list of donors with Warkworth's successor (briefly), Thomas Denman (or Deynman), most likely another Lady Margaret nominee. Presumably no trace of Hornby's books survives, nor does his more substantial bequest to St. John's. Warkworth's books, it seems, were standard for the time, and Thomson cites Roger Mynors's characterization of them as "secondhand, predigested knowledge" (xxx). The eight volumes (seven titles) with Denman's ex libris are suited to his role as one of Lady Margaret's physicians—five titles can be characterized as "Medica," one as "Astronomica," and another is a volume of the *Epistolae* of St. Augustine (MSS 88, 95, 139, 145–146, 168, 182, 250).

Thomson's brief does not, of course, include printed books, which only really began to be acquired with Master Andrew Perne's "huge bequest of printed books" (no number is given) in 1589 (xxxi). Like manuscripts, before this date printed books were slow in coming (and late, compared with Lady Margaret's comparatively recent foundations of Christ's College and St. John's College, where printed books were the norm from their foundation at the start of the sixteenth century). However, Denman's MS 250 is a Sammelband, donated in 1501. The period between, roughly, the Hornby and Perne bequests saw a drop in the numbers of manuscripts in the library, partly perhaps because they were replaced by printed books, partly as a result of unreturned borrowings by Fellows and others, as when John Dee took what is now Cambridge, Magdalene College, Pepys 2329 (xxxvii–xxxvii). Thomson prints an analysis of the manuscripts and printed books in a shelflist of the library (MS 400), which was made just before Perne's donation (xxxii–xxxvii). There is no mention of the effect on the holdings of Edwardian and Marian visitations (on which see the review of *The University and College Libraries of Cambridge*, ed. Peter D. Clarke, *JEBS* 12 [2009]: 269), but the surviving books are mutilated by the removal, certainly by the mid-seventeenth century, of "nearly all" the decorated initials, some carefully but many roughly (xxxviii).

By the late eighteenth century, the books were clearly in a lamentable state (at least 73 were given a standard college binding at this time, of which process some interesting details are known, and more recent binding has been equally damaging to the evidence of their medieval origins). Thomson ends engagingly, but not, I suspect, mischievously: "Today they are as safe and secure as they have ever been: deposited in the University Library and subject to an ongoing programme of repair and conservation" (xxxix).

As for the descriptions of the manuscripts, they are workmanlike and useful, but not illuminating of the texts themselves, although the provenances are well described. To cite a few of Warkworth's donations: the two volumes of *Decretals* that form MS 10 came from Ramsey Abbey and have interesting notes from approximately the date of the second volume, the early fourteenth century (the first is late thirteenth-century). MS 132 is a *Legenda aurea* of the same period, either late thirteenth or early fourteenth century, also from Ramsey, with a likely pledge-note, and Thomson provides interesting information on the binding of the late-fifteenth-century *Distinctiones*, also by Jacobus de Voragine, which survives in MS 165. M. R. James recorded a binding now lost, presumably through the work of the Cambridge firm of John Gray in the early twentieth century (although one should perhaps blame the college for the specifications rather than the binders), but the back label (as in Syon books) survives, although now protected not by horn but by plastic.

The text of Thomson's catalogue ends with an appendix of "Manuscript Fragments in Peterhouse Printed Books," of particular interest to readers of this journal, and a second appendix of "Medieval Peterhouse Manuscripts No Longer in the Main Collection." The plates are excellent and provide valuable evidence of early bindings and of pastedowns and inscriptions, as well as decoration; included are some photographs that show surviving features of the fifteenth-century library, such as the outline of the desk lectern and bench on the wall of the Perne Library. The frontispiece shows the first leaf of the 1418 library catalogue, and the plates that illustrate manuscripts are headed "Bindings and Other Physical Features," "Owners, Donors and Users," "Scribes and Annotators" (some on binding strips and pastedowns), and "Decoration." Of the manuscripts mentioned in this brief review, MS 10 has one plate that shows the mark of the hooped iron chain-staple on the rear pastedown and other plates with the Ramsey and Warkworth ex libris (Plates 3, 10, 45). There is a full plate of the binding (with unidentified stamps) of MS 250 (Plate 6). Denman's ownership inscription in MS 182 is shown in Plate 69 (fol. 173v, but the catalogue entry has 273v).

The catalogue owes some debts to the living and the dead, and Thomson acknowledges the bibliographical help of others (ix and xl), particularly the college archivist, Roger Lovatt, and the former Kennedy Professor of Latin (1944–1953), Roger Mynors, whose annotated James catalogue Thomson is lucky enough to possess.

Susan Powell, University of Salford (emerita)

NOTES

1. York Minster prefers to use a variant (but rather antiquarian) spelling, "Neuton."
2. TNA PROB 11/19/69.

RODNEY M. THOMSON, ED., WITH JAMES G. CLARK
The University and College Libraries of Oxford.
Corpus of British Medieval Library Catalogues 16.
2 vols. London: British Library for the British Academy, 2015.
xlvi + 1728 pp. 8 B&W illus.

One welcomes the appearance of the most recent volume of the Corpus, a series under the able editorship of Richard Sharpe. Here, Rodney Thomson offers a definitive account of the surviving (and sometimes not surviving, e.g., the important but now long-lost indenture between William Rede and Merton College, UO49, 855–874) evidence for most institutional book collections in Oxford. The volume is obviously important in its documentation of one great intellectual center of late-medieval England. This, like other volumes in the Corpus, will be an utterly central first-recourse research tool—and, given its extent and the care that has gone into it, a much used one.

The volume shows the customary usefulness of the Corpus. This series gathers into one place studies previously dispersed, often difficult to access, and most frequently presented with insufficient annotation to be readily useful without further research. For example, Thomson here authoritatively replaces earlier accounts of Duke Humfrey of Gloucester's three famous gifts to the University Library (UO1–3, 8–54); one need no longer scrounge through either the summary account in *Bodleian Quarterly Record* 1 (1914–1916), 131–135, or A. Sammut's study of 1980, not available outside serious research libraries. To this convenience and wealth of information, Thomson's Corpus adds new materials, as well as copious indexes (on pages 1393–1728!), these the work of the largely unacknowledged James Willoughby (but see vii).

Further, although Thomson's contribution appears late in the Corpus series, one might see his work here as bringing to fruition the initiatory and inspiring origins of this hugely collaborative project, closely associated with the indispensable *Medieval Libraries of Great Britain* (N.R. Ker's work, now integrated with materials from published Corpus volumes, including this one, is now available online at http://mlgb3.bodleian.ox.ac.uk.) Thomson offers concise organization and annotation of such classics as F. M. Powicke's *Medieval Books of Merton College* (Oxford, 1931), now replaced by twenty-four Merton College documents; N. R. Ker's *Records of All Souls College Library*, Oxford Bibliographical Society ns 16 (Oxford, 1971), now seventeen lists; and a list of all entries in A. B. Emden's *Biographical Register* mentioning book materials, prepared by Andrew G. Watson (unacknowledged; now expanded to seventy-three separate annotated lists of individual donors).

Indeed, bringing the volume to completion has involved further hands (cf. Henry Mayr-Harting's preface, vii). The Oxford Corpus was begun in the early 1990s by Christian Jensen. Upon his decision to engage in cataloguing the Bodleian Library's incunables, James Clark, then a Brasenose Junior Research Fellow, took up the project for a decade; Thomson has constructively extended his fragmentary materials. Thomson is particularly suited for this culminating work; he draws on vast experience in college libraries, most particularly the central Corpus Christi and Merton, for both of which he has recently produced whole-collection catalogues. Both these earlier presentations, in addition to a guide to the current collections, demonstrate an impressive grasp of collegiate archival collections, from which most of the evidence here assembled derives.

Finally, as already noted, utterly integral to the volume are Willoughby's indexes. Corpus volumes are not quite constructed for continuous bedtime reading, and the usefulness of materials Thomson has gathered is substantially enhanced by Willoughby's contribution, one that, given Willoughby's familiarity with other collections, will also have added immensely to the richness of the volume's annotation. The indexes are also useful because Thomson does not provide a global survey of Oxford institutional libraries but of the "secular colleges" only. The index integrates information from these institutions and references to booklists from two important monastic colleges, not yet available in the Corpus. In the index, "BC" refers to Canterbury College booklists, and "BD" to Durham College booklists.

The volume necessarily relies on various materials, 158 documents in all. These range from catalogues, *stricto sensu*, to *electio* lists (whereby college fellows borrowed books from their institutions' circulating collections), to legal records, principally bequests by individual donors (often of only a few books). More than half the catalogue is given over to the extensive records of three colleges: the already-mentioned Merton and All Souls Colleges, and New College (eleven documents). One is particularly grateful for Thomson's headnotes to each of these entries; in addition to considering the diplomatic context of each document, he provides succinct library histories, typically beginning with the founders' statutes. In these accounts, Thomson shows a special interest in evidence for the physical state of book storage and eventually (sadly) of medieval library dispersal: deliberate and ubiquitous sixteenth-century culling of collections to make room for voluminous new acquisitions.

Corpus volumes customarily take their terminus ad quem from the various reports of John Leland and John Bale. Importantly, this volume goes well beyond them to the mid-sixteenth century. This decision allows inclusion of the quite unusual survivals, library lists prepared for the Marian visitors of 1556 (UO20 from All Souls College, UO23 from Brasenose, and UO68 from Merton; UO78 from New College may represent a partial draft). One late outlier is the first catalogue of Corpus Christi College (1589, UO33). This extension of interest is important. It allows volume users to track, in a major intellectual center, two seminal transitions. First, and more important intellectually, is the effect of the Cromwellian visitation of 1535, with its insistence on Greek and Hebrew and on "New Learning" generally. Perhaps equally important from a book-history perspective are the gradual shift to printed materials from the 1480s on and the encroachment on existing college collections of Reformation theology and polemic.

The only downside to this impressively useful volume is a decline in the British Library's production values. The boards are not very heavy (and do not quite match the hue on earlier volumes); the paper shows similar decline in quality, and the eight booklists illustrated appear on normal paper, not the glossy sheets to which one is accustomed. But well done, Rod and team (stretching back to Powicke)! While few may own a copy, this is a volume that will be a constant and welcome mine of information for researchers.

Ralph Hanna, Keble College, Oxford

Notes on Libraries and Collections

The Pilot Project for the Mohamed Tahar Library in Timbuktu

MURIEL ROILAND

On the fringe of the Saharan desert, nestled in the elbow of the Niger River, Timbuktu is one of Africa's most fabled cities. Myth envelopes the city. In his historical work *Tārīkh al-Sūdān,* a local scholar of the seventeenth century, Abd al-Sa'dī, speaks of an "exquisite city, pure, delicious, and illustrious." In the Middle Ages, the city of Timbuktu fascinated Arabs and Europeans. The Arabs knew of the richness of the Songhai Empire (1464–1492) and the Askia Dynasty (1493–1595); Europeans spoke of the treasures transported in caravans toward the city in the midst of the sands. The name "Timbutch" and that of the emperor Mansa Musa were inscribed on a Catalan atlas made in the fourteenth century for King Charles V of France. Muslim Africans have a completely different image of Timbuktu. They speak primarily of a center for the transmission of knowledge. In the sixteenth century, the city contained a "virtual industry for the copying of works coming from the North."[1] It was also a center of diffusion for Muslim mysticism. Timbuktu was known as the city of 333 saints, 333 being a symbolic and magical number.

At the beginning of Islam, from the eighth to the eleventh centuries, sub-Saharan Africa was considered a territory with many riches: gold, ivory, precious species of wood, and slaves. Ibadite Berbers from the Maghreb developed commerce along the caravan routes, but few traces remain of the Islamization of that time.[2] In the thirteenth century, Timbuktu became a way station at the heart of Saharan commerce.

In 1352, when Ibn Baṭṭūta undertook his voyage into the Bilād al-Sūdān, he described the city of Timbuktu.[3] He knew the story of Mansa Musa, the emperor of Mali, whose caravan passed through Cairo in 1324 on the pilgrimage route to Mecca.[4] Musa was the emperor who built the main mosque and University of Djingareyber, and made Timbuktu a center of cultural influence, both Islamic and economic. The historian Ibn Khallikān tells us that the emperor brought back many manuscripts on the return trip. Thus, as of the fourteenth century, tradesmen and scholars who visited Fez, Cairo, and the Hejaz in Arabia took with them manuscripts that were used for teaching in Timbuktu and that were also recopied there. According to Leo Africanus (d. 1552), "it was here that various manuscripts and written books were brought from the Barbary Coast, and were sold at a higher price than any other merchandise."[5]

By the time the city fell into the hands of the pasha Jouder of Morocco in 1591, Timbuktu had become a major center of Islamic learning. Ahmad Baba al-Timbukti (d. 1627), the most highly regarded scholar in the city,[6] tells us that there were more than twenty thousand students in Timbuktu. They attended universities attached to three mosques: Sankoré, Sidi Yahya, and Djingareyber.[7] During this period, Moulay Ibrahim, the ancestor of Abdul Wahid Haidara, collected the first manuscripts that would later form the basis of the Mohamed Tahar Library.

History of the Mohamed Tahar Library

Today, thirty-six private libraries still exist in the city. The Ahmad Baba Public Library is the most important of the city's libraries, but its collection is presently in the southern Mali city of Bamako because the manuscripts were moved there in 2012, during the occupation of Timbuktu by Islamic fundamentalists.[8] The library building is situated in the Sankoré quarter, which was formerly one of the three teaching centers in Timbuktu. At present it is being rehabilitated by UNESCO. The Mohamed Tahar Library reflects the history of the region of Timbuktu since the end of the fifteenth century. Abdul Wahid Haidara, former employee of the Ahmed Baba Institute, has been the owner of the Mohamed Tahar Library since 2003.

According to the family tree found in one of the manuscripts,[9] the ancestor of Haidara's family, Moulay Ibrahim, came from Yanbū' in the Arabian Peninsula and settled in Arawan in the sixteenth century. Situated six days by camel to the north of Timbuktu, Arawan was founded in 1385. By the fourteenth century it was a crossroads for caravans transporting salt and was also the birthplace of many famous scholars, among whom was Ahmad Baba.

Moulay Ibrahim acquired the first manuscripts now found in the library. At that time, in addition to the Koran, scholars would own manuscripts on grammar, theology, Islamic law (*fiqh*), and sometimes medicine and astrology. In the Mohamed Tahar Library, as in other private libraries in Timbuktu, the oldest books date from the fifteenth century. The oldest manuscript in the city is a Koran dating from the late twelfth century, copied in al-Andalus and kept in the Fondo Ka'ti Library.

Another eminent member of the Haidara family, known by the name of Baba Chirfi, lived in the seventeenth century; the family library was founded by one of his sons. Since that time, the library has been entrusted to the member of the family who knows Arabic best and who is committed to preserving the family patrimony. Today the library bears the name of Mohamed Tahar, a scholar of the family who left Arawan in the nineteenth century and settled in Timbuktu. He was a well-known jurist, one of the best calligraphers in the region, and taught grammar and religious science in Timbuktu.

The Collection and Particularities of the Manuscripts

The Mohamed Tahar library contains about two thousand manuscripts kept in iron trunks. Like the famed libraries of Chinguetti in Mauritania, the private libraries in Timbuktu hold a large number of manuscripts: between three hundred in the smallest and up to eight thousand in the Fondo Ka'ti Library. The great majority of the texts are in Arabic, but in Timbuktu there are many ethnic groups, including the Fula or Fulani, also known as Peul, the Tuareg, the Songhai, and the Hausa, and their languages are reflected in the manuscripts. Some manuscripts are written in Hassaniya Arabic, a dialect found in the Sahara, as well as in Songhai and more rarely in the Hausa language.[10] Some of these languages are written in Arabic letters.

Certain manuscripts are voluminous—more than three hundred folios—but many others contain only a few leaves. This is the case for contracts, short treatises on Islamic law, Sufi prayers, poems, and magic recipes, for example.

The oldest books in the Mohamed Tahar Library are fragments of the Koran and religious texts. There are three mystic Muslim texts (*taṣawwuf*) by the same Maghrebin author, 'Alī Ibn Maymūn al-Fāsī (d. 1511), which are assembled in a single manuscript. Several works by that author remain unpublished, and surviving witnesses are rare. The author was a scholar from Fez who lived in Cairo and then in Damascus, where he wrote ten treatises on Muslim mysticism. Only two texts have been published in recent years. Abdul Wahid Haidara agreed to photograph one of these texts, the *al-Risāla l-Maymūniyya fī tawḥīd al-Ājurrūmiyya*, an esoteric commentary on one of the most famous treatises on Arabic grammar, *al-Ājurrūmiyya*.[11] An edition and French translation are being prepared by Clara Murner at the University of Strasbourg as part of her doctoral thesis.

It is difficult to date the arrival of the first Arabic manuscripts in the region historically known as the Western Sudan. Ibn Baṭṭūṭa in the fourteenth century spoke of children learning Arabic in Koranic schools in

Timbuktu. He reported that the children used wooden tablets (*lawḥa*) and that they made their own pens and ink, just as they do today.

The manuscripts that arrived by caravan from the Orient or the Maghreb could be very expensive. Such is the case for the Korans, for example. A copy of the famous *Shifā'* by Qāḍī 'Iyāḍ (d. 1149) was sold for 45 mithqals of gold in 1486.[12] But when teaching began at Sankoré University in the sixteenth century, Timbuktu became the most important center in Africa for copying manuscripts. The number of local scribes increased, and prices of manuscripts varied according to the reputation of the scribe, the quality of the paper, and the type of transcription. Most of the manuscripts in the Mohamed Tahar Library were copied in Timbuktu or the surrounding region during the seventeenth and eighteenth centuries, but in some cases they are the only witnesses to medieval texts, as is the case with the treatises by Ibn Maymūn.

Additions often found in the manuscripts are a source of precise information on textual transmission. The first or last leaf occasionally contains the contract made between the scribe and his client, with a mention of the price of the copy and the signature of two witnesses, as required by Muslim law.[13] An example of this appears in a copy of a volume concerning the life of the Prophet Mohammed, *al-Sīrat al-Kalā'iyya*, written by Sulaymān b. Mūsā al-Kalā'ī (d. 1237), a thirteenth-century Andalusian scholar who lived at the time of Averroës. This is the only work by that author found in manuscript; others are lost. At the end of the last leaf, an addition in a hand other than that of the scribe tells us that the transcription was bought for three ryal on behalf of Ahmad Baba of the Sufi brotherhood of Aḥmad al-Bakkāy ibn Yaḥyā and that the sale was made according to the rules. The copy was thus made at the latest at the beginning of the seventeenth century.

Many copies contain numerous additions in the blank spaces, grouped around beautiful central decorations that are typical of manuscripts from Timbuktu. In other cases, completely unrelated texts were copied onto blank folios.

Codicological Elements

Most of the manuscripts in the Mohamed Tahar Library are copied on paper with a watermark, usually composed of three crescents (this replaced earlier watermarks with representations of the cross or angels; three crescents were thought more appropriate for Arabic texts). The watermarked paper was made in Venice and Genoa in Italy and dates from the sixteenth century. So-called Arabic paper has no watermark. Until the fifteenth century, Fez had the largest number of paper-makers in the western Maghreb. Thereafter, non-watermarked paper was made in Cairo and arrived in Timbuktu with the caravans, but this was not as popular as the watermarked Italian paper.[14]

The manuscripts of Timbuktu are made not of quires but of loose leaves, often unnumbered and without catchwords, which complicates the reassembling of a text if the leaves are in disorder. This is, unfortunately, frequently the case. Conservation conditions in the Mohamed Tahar Library are precarious. Timbuktu manuscripts are affected by the dry climate but also by the periodic rainstorms; homes are not watertight, and flooding is frequent. The paper is often fragile and brittle, and manuscripts are subject to damage by voracious insects. The manuscripts are kept in iron trunks that are often moved about and sometimes buried in the sand during conflicts. They were hidden for a year during the last occupation of the city in 2012. Many books have no bindings; such bindings as do exist are generally made of goat or sheepskin. Bindings may or may not have a flap, and sometimes there are leather ties to keep the book closed. As with the paper, the leather also arrived by caravan, but there was also important production in the city of Gao, some 200 miles east of Timbuktu.

The different types of writing in the Saharan manuscripts have been little studied. The calligraphy was originally adopted from that used in Muslim Andalusia and the medieval Maghreb, with the same idiosyncrasies in the writing of certain letters. According to Malians, a type of writing called *sūdānī* was created in Timbuktu in the sixteenth century before spreading to the Sahara. This writing was adapted by different ethnic groups into *hausawī* (from the name of the Hausa people), *al-takrūnī* (from the Toucouleurs), and *al-sūqī* (from the name attributed to the Tamasheq Kel as-Suq or Tuareg ethnic group in the region of Adrar), and finally the *sahrawi* writing (in the Sahara). One book that is frequently read in Abdul Wahid Haidara's family contains a poem by Ibn Wāhib, an author from the region of Timbuktu, written in *khaṭṭ al-sūqī*. The people of Timbuktu recite the poem for several days before the feast of the birth of the Prophet.

Representative Manuscripts

All the disciplines taught during the golden age of Timbuktu are present in the Mohamed Tahar Library: religion, grammar, history, literature, and science. Certain texts are found in most libraries of the Muslim world, but others are unusual. The authors of the oldest manuscripts are mainly from the western Maghreb and the Timbuktu region from the seventeenth century onward. They also attest to the notoriety of certain texts in the Saharan world.

Religion (*dīn*) is understandably the most frequently represented, with five full Korans and a large number of fragments. One manuscript, *Naẓm ṣughrā al-Sanūsī*, was written by a local author, Muḥammad b. Aḥmad al-Wankarī, who died in 1655. Al-Wankarī comments in verse on the theological work of al-Sanūsī, who lived in the fifteenth century at Tlemcen, in what is now northwest Algeria, and rejuvenated the Ash'arite school of Sunni Islam. His works were taught in Timbuktu in sixteenth-century universities.[15]

The occult sciences include treatises on magic, which are numerous in the library, and this is the case throughout the Muslim world. Few comparative studies exist of the texts on magic in Africa and elsewhere.[16] We find many spells for reconciliation of spouses, religious formulas, invocations to angels, and magic squares. One manuscript contains an astrological treatise by Muḥammad Baghayogho (d. 1593), a well-known scholar in Timbuktu in the sixteenth century. Baghayogho, imam at the Sidi Yahya Mosque, was one of the rare scholars who was not deported to Morocco after the city of Timbuktu was captured and the Songhai Empire fell in 1592. The manuscript is the only known copy of this text in Timbuktu.

Islamic law (*fiqh*) in the library is represented by many tracts by Malikite authors and commentaries on Malikite treatises. Malikism is the school of Sunni Islamic law adopted in the Maghreb and Sahara and is the subject most represented in the Mohamed Tahar Library. Certain of these texts are little known, for example, a beautiful manuscript containing a commentary by a local author, 'Alī al-Ḥarīshī, on the founding text of Malikism, *Irshādāt al-sālik fī sharḥ Muwaṭṭa' Mālik*. Law was fundamental in university teaching, and all scholars were required to study it. The large number of manuscripts on law is also explained by the fact that the ancestors of Abdul Wahid Haidara were jurists (*fuqahā'*). Consequently, along with the law treatises we find many contracts.

Sufi mysticism (*taṣawwuf*) is represented by texts by Shadhili authors, including works by 'Alī Ibn Maymūn. The Maghrebin jurists of the fourteenth, fifteenth, and sixteenth centuries, authors of works that are found in the library, were for the most part Sufis. The Sufi order of Sunni Islam known as Shadhili was very influential in the Maghreb and the Sahara in the sixteenth century. There are also texts by authors of the Sufi order known as Qadiri, which established itself in Timbuktu in the seventeenth century, and texts of the Tijaniyya, which developed in the Sahara in the eighteenth century. Today, the family of Abdul Wahid Haidara is in the Tijani order. According to him, the library attests to the harmony that exists between the Sufi confraternities in the city. The library contains a copy of the *Dalā'il al-khayrāt* by Muḥammad b. Sulaymān al-Jazūlī (d. 1465), a major work of Sufism found throughout the Muslim world. In Timbuktu it is read on feast days and at ceremonies to ward off war or drought. There is also a copy of *al-Ra'iyya*, a famous poem in 103 verses by Sīdī Abū Madyan al-Andalusī (d. Tlemcen, 1197) that is well known to the Maghrebin Sufis and exists only in manuscript form.

Many documents in the Mohamed Tahar Library complement documentation by the Timbuktu-based Institut des hautes études et de recherche Islamique–Ahmad Baba (IHERI-AB) on the local history of the eighteenth and nineteenth centuries, in particular, several letters written by Aḥmad al-Bakkāy al-Kuntī. Sheikh of the Qadiriya brotherhood and a political leader, Aḥmad al-Bakkāy was the author of a vast correspondence housed at IHERI-AB, currently in Bamako, and also in Timbuktu and in the Bibliothèque nationale de France in Paris. It would be very useful to collect, catalogue, and digitize these letters and documents in order to broaden our knowledge of nineteenth-century Mali.[17] Many of them, kept in private libraries such as the Mohamed Tahar Library, are still unknown, and many texts by local authors are still unpublished. An inventory and digitalization of the Mohamed Tahar Library is now in process in cooperation with the Institut de recherche et d'histoire des textes (IRHT), and UNESCO has just finished work on restoring the building.

IRHT-CNRS, Paris

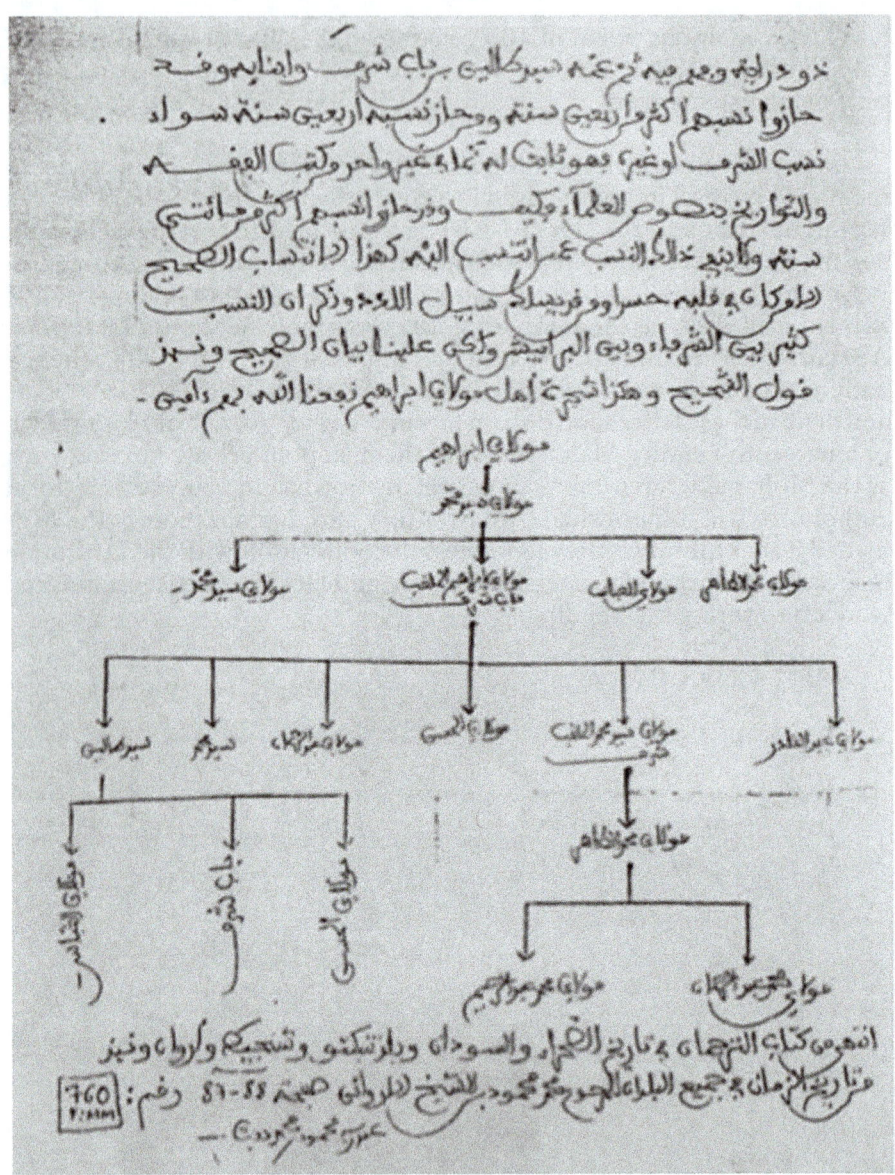

Family tree of Mohamed Tahar in the *Kitāb al-turjumān fī tārīkh al-saḥrā' wa-l-sūdān wa-balad Timbuktu wa-shinjīṭ wa-arawān*, Muḥammad Maḥmūd b. al-shaykh al-Arawānī (IHERI-AB, ms. 762). Reproduced with the permission of the IHERI-AB, Bamako.

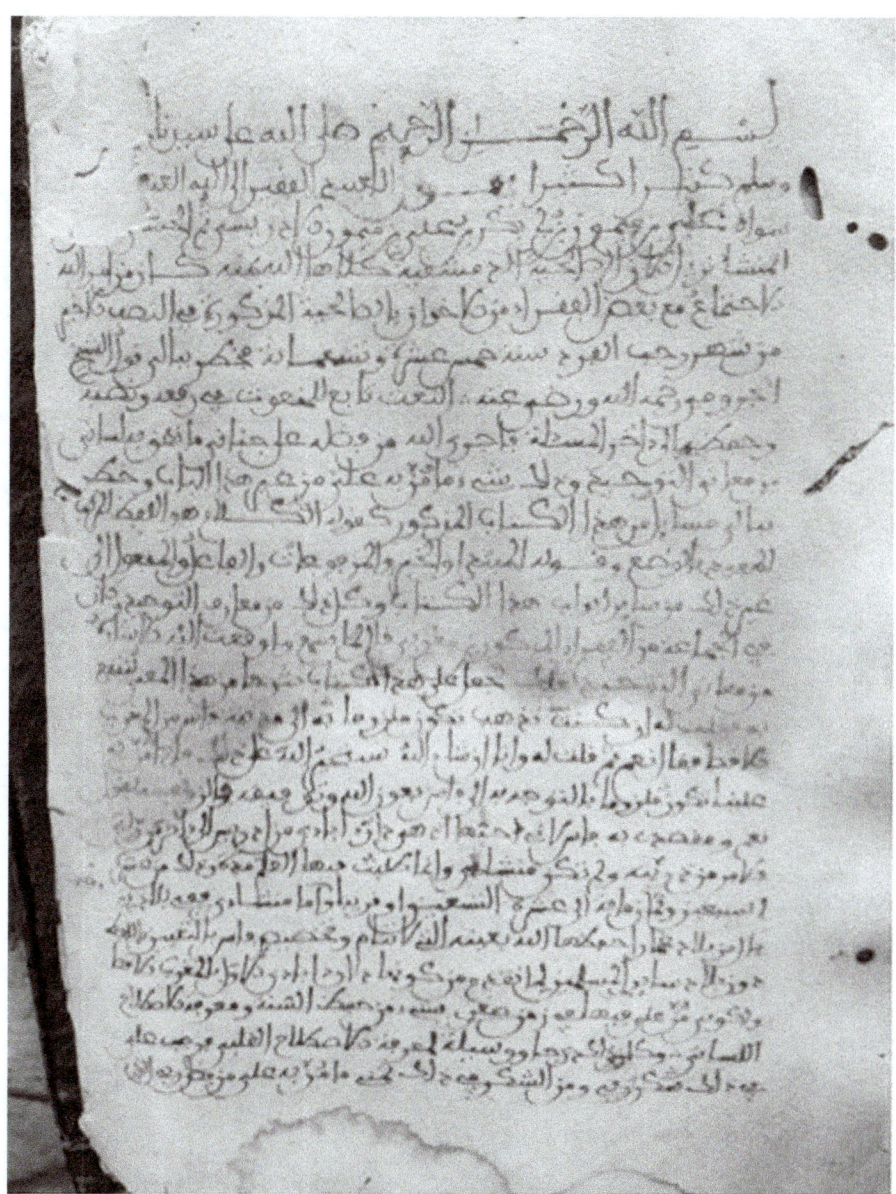

Ibn Maymūn (d. 1511), *al-Risāla al-Maymūniyya fī tawḥīd al-Ājurrūmiyya,* folio 1.
By permission of Abdul Wahid Haidara, Timbuktu, Mohamed Tahar Library.

Colophon of the *al-Sīrat al-Kalā'iyya,* Sulaymān b. Mūsā al-Kalā'ī (d. 1237).
By permission of Abdul Wahid Haidara, Timbuktu, Mohamed Tahar Library.

An astrological treatise by Baghayogho (d. 1593), folio 23.
By permission of Abdul Wahid Haidara, Timbuktu, Mohamed Tahar Library.

Irshādāt al-sālik fī sharḥ Muwaṭṭa' Mālik, 'Alī b. Aḥmad al-Ḥarīshī, folio 1.
By permission of Abdul Wahid Haidara, Timbuktu, Mohamed Tahar Library.

NOTES

1. J.-L. Triaud, "La fabrication du savoir," in J.-M. Dijan, *Les manuscrits de Tombouctou: Secrets, mythes et réalités* (Paris: Éditions Jean-Claude Lattès, 2002), 117.

2. Three hundred epigraphic inscriptions in Arabic and Tifinagh deciphered in the work of Paulo Fernando de Moraes Farias attest to the ancient Arabization and Islamization, but none of the inscriptions come from the area of Timbuktu; Paulo Fernando de Moraes Farias, *Arabic Medieval Inscriptions from the Republic of Mali: Epigraphy, Chronicles and Songhay-Tuareg History* (London: British Academy, 2004). See also J.-L. Triaud, "L'éveil à l'écriture: un nouveau Moyen Âge sahélien," *Afrique et Histoire* 4 (2005):185–241.

3. Ibn Baṭṭūṭa recounts that in the house of an emir near Timbuktu he read a copy of the work of Ibn al-Jawzī (the famous Hanbalite from Bagdad who died in 1200) on the lexical difficulties in the Koran (*Gharīb al-Qur'ān*).

4. Many chronicles, such as that of al-'Umarī (d. 1384), *Masālik al-abṣār fī mamālik al-amṣār*, tell of Ibn Baṭṭūṭa's encounter with the Mameluke sultan of Egypt, al-Nāṣir Muḥammad Ibn Qalā'ūn. One also finds the story of his voyage in the works of Abū Sa'īd 'Uthmān al-Dukkālī, Ibn Khaldūn, and Ibn Baṭṭūṭa himself; see also Abd al-Sa'dī, *Tarikh es-Soudan*, trans. Octave Houdas (Paris: Adrien Maisonneuve, 1964).

5. Léon l'Africain, *Description de l'Afrique*, trans. A. Epaulard (Paris: Adrien Maisonneuve, 1956), 468–469.

6. He is the author of fifty works. Copies of some of his texts are found in the Mohamed Tahar Library, and his name is often cited in the margins of manuscripts.

7. Maḥmūd Katī, *Tarikh el-fettach*, ed. M. Delafosse, trans. Octave Houdas (Paris: Adrien Maisonneuve, 1964), 316, recounts that there were also between 150 and 180 Koranic schools for young boys.

8. The 38,000 manuscripts and most of the material in the library were exfiltrated by members of the Institut des hautes études et de recherche islamique–Ahmad Baba (IHERI-AB).

9. An entry concerning the family of Abdul Wahid Haidara is found in a local chronicle entitled *Kitāb al-turjumān fī tārīkh al-saḥrā' wa-l-sūdān wa-balad timbuktu wa-shinjīṭ wa-arawān* (ms. 762 in the library of the IHERI-AB). The author is Muḥammad Maḥmūd b. al-shaykh al-Arawānī. See the family tree reproduced in the first illustration.

10. This language is spoken mainly in Niger and Nigeria, as well as other West African countries.

11. Other copies of this text are in Cairo, Rabat, and Berlin. The esoteric commentary on grammar is an important literary genre in Arabic that

was initiated by Qushayrī in the tenth century with his treatise *Naḥw al-qulūb* [The Grammar of the Hearts]. See F. Chiabotti, "Naḥw al-qulūb al-ṣaġīr: La 'grammaire des cœurs' de 'Abd al-Karīm al-Qušayrī," *Bulletin d'études orientales* 58 (2009):385–402.

12. A mithqal equals about 3.5 grams. This is reported by the Arab geographer al-Bakrī (1094) in his *Kitāb al-Masālik wa-al-mamālik*. The *Shifā'* of Qāḍī 'Iyāḍ, on the merits of the Prophet, continued to be read and taught in the Sankoré Mosque in the sixteenth century, according to al-Sa'dī, *Tarikh es-Soudan*.

13. The price can also be stated in bartered merchandise or animals.

14. J. M. Blood, "Paper in Sudanic Africa," in The Meaning of Timbuktu, ed. Shamil Jeppie and Suleyman Bachir Diagne (Cape Town: HSRC Press in association with CODESRIA, 2008), 45–55. In the seventeenth century, goods were transported via Tripoli.

15. According to Khassim Diakate, "Al-Sanûsî, un africain ash'rite au 15ème siècle", Ethopiques, 66–67 (2001). http://ethiopiques.refer.sn/spip.php?article1279#nb36

16. In the Middle Ages, the opinions of jurists and scholars on this subject were often divided between condemnation and acceptance: magic was accepted by a famous Malikite jurist named Ibn Abī Zayd al-Qayrawānī (d. 996) and condemned by a Malikite scholar, al-Maghīlī (d. *ca.* 1500), advisor to sovereigns in western Africa such as Askia Muḥammad Toure. See C. Hamès, "Problématiques de la magie-sorcellerie en islam et perspectives africaines," *Cahiers d'études africaines* 189–190 (2008):81–99.

17. This correspondence was partially studied in two doctoral theses: Abdelkader Zebadia, "The Career and Correspondence of Ahmad Al-Bakkay of Timbuctu: An Historical Study of His Political and Religious Role from 1847 to 1866" (London, SOAS, 1974); and Ismail Traore, "Les Relations épistolaires entre la famille Kunta de Tombouctou et la Dina du Macina (1818–1864)" (Université de Lyon, ENS, 2012).

About the Authors

Bart Besamusca is Professor of Middle Dutch Textual Culture from an International Perspective at the Utrecht Centre for Medieval Studies, Utrecht University. He has published widely on medieval narrative literature, manuscripts, and early printed editions. He manages the research tool Arthurian Fiction in Medieval Europe (www.arthurianfiction.org) and is currently co-supervising the research project "The Changing Face of Medieval Dutch Narrative Literature in the Early Period of Print (1477–c. 1550)" (www.changingface.eu). His most recent book publication is *The Dynamics of the Medieval Manuscript: Text Collections from a European Perspective* (2017), which he edited jointly with Karen Pratt, Mathias Meyer, and Ad Putter.

Jonathan Brent is a graduate student at the University of Toronto's Centre for Medieval Studies. His research focuses on multilingual historical literature in late medieval England. His current project is a bilingual student edition of Nicholas Trevet's *Les Cronicles*, a universal history written in Anglo-French.

Marleen Cré is an independent scholar affiliated with the Ruusbroec Institute at the University of Antwerp, Belgium. From October 2013 to March 2017, she was the postdoctoral researcher on the Swiss National Science Foundation project "Late Medieval Religiosity in England: The Evidence of Late Fourteenth and Fifteenth Century Devotional Compilations" carried out at the University of Lausanne, Switzerland. With Diana Denissen and Denis Renevey, she is currently editing a collection of essays entitled *'This tretice, by me compiled': Late Medieval Devotional Compilations in England.* She has published *Vernacular Mysticism in the Charterhouse: A Study of London, British Library, MS Additional 37790* (2006), and essays on the Julian of Norwich manuscripts, the Middle English translation of Marguerite Porète's *Mirror of Simple Souls*, and *The Chastising of God's Children*.

Sonja Drimmer is Assistant Professor in the Department of the History of Art and Architecture at the University of Massachusetts, Amherst. Most recently she has published "The Manuscript as an Ambigraphic Medium: Hoccleve's Scribes, Illuminators, and Their Problems" in *Exemplaria*.

Martha W. Driver is Distinguished Professor of English and Women's and Gender Studies at Pace University in New York City. A co-founder of the Early Book Society for the study of manuscripts and printing history, she writes about illustration from manuscript to print, manuscript and book production, and the early history of printing. In addition to publishing some 55 articles in these areas, she has edited twenty-two journals over twenty years, including *Film & History: Medieval Period in Film* and the *Journal of the Early Book Society*. Her books about pictures (from manuscript miniatures to woodcuts to film) include *The Image in Print: Book Illustration in Late Medieval England* (British Library Publications and University of Toronto), *An Index of Images in English MSS*, fascicle four, with Michael Orr (Brepols), and *The Medieval Hero on Screen* and *Shakespeare and the Middle Ages*, with Sid Ray (McFarland). She contributed to and edited *Preaching the Word in Manuscript and Print in Late Medieval England: Essays in Honour of Susan Powell* with Veronica O'Mara (Brepols, 2013). She also oversees the Texts & Transitions book series published by Brepols.

Hedwig Gwosdek has taught until recently as an Associate Professor of English Language and Medieval Studies in the English Department of the University of Paderborn, Germany. She is the editor of *Lily's Latin Grammar in English* (Oxford University Press, 2013) and has published on early printed Latin grammars in English and on the history of education.

Megan J. Hall is an administrator and instructor in the Medieval Institute of the University of Notre Dame. She specializes in Anglo-Saxon and Early Middle English literature, carrying out research on manuscript studies, women's literacy, digital humanities, and book history. Currently she is working on a book manuscript, *Learning and Literacy Outside the Convent: Early Middle English Women Readers and the Ancrene Wisse,* as well as a digital project exploring the intersections of physical space and spiritual life in the medieval anchorhold

Ralph Hanna is Professor of Palaeography emeritus and emeritus fellow of Keble College, Oxford. His most recent major publication is *The Penn Commentary on Piers Plowman*, Volume 2: *C Passus 5-9; B Passus 5-7; A Passus 5-8* (Philadelphia, 2017). Other publications include editions for the Early English Text Society, *Richard Rolle: Uncollected Verse and Prose, with Related Northern Texts* (o.s. 329, 2007), *Speculum Vitae: A Reading, Editions I and II* (o.s. 331-2, 2008), and *Editing Medieval Texts* (Liverpool, 2015).

Carissa M. Harris is an Assistant Professor of English at Temple University. She has published on medieval rape narratives, Middle English pastourelles, and obscenity in fifteenth-century manuscripts of Chaucer's *Canterbury Tales*. Her first book, *Obscene Pedagogies: Transgressive Talk and Sexual Education in Late Medieval Britain*, explores obscenity's usefulness as a tool for educating audiences about sexuality, violence, consent, and desire, and is currently under review.

Maidie Hilmo taught Chaucer at the University of Victoria, as well as Art History and English at Northern Lights College. Her most recent publication is "The Visual Semantics of Ellesmere: Gold, Artifice, and Audience," in *Chaucer: Visual Approaches* (2016). She is a co-author, together with Kathryn Kerby-Fulton and Linda Olson, of *Opening Up Middle English Manuscripts: Literary and Visual Approaches* (2012), and co-editor, with Kathryn Kerby-Fulton, of two collections of essays on the medieval reader. She is the author of *Medieval Images, Icons, and Illustrated English Literary Texts: From the Ruthwell Cross to the Ellesmere Chaucer* (2004) and of articles on illustrated medieval manuscripts, including the Pearl-Gawain manuscript.

Jessie Labadie is Visiting Assistant Professor of French at Randolph-Macon College. Her research treats Early Modern French and Spanish literature, women writers and book history. She teaches courses in French language, culture and literature.

Laura Saetveit Miles is Associate Professor (førsteamanuensis) of English literature at the Department of Foreign Languages at the University of Bergen, Norway. She researches religious culture and women's writing in late-medieval England, and has published on such topics as St. Bridget of Sweden, Julian of Norwich, Syon Abbey, and the Carthusians. Her current book project examines the history and meaning of Mary's book at the Annunciation.

Veronica O'Mara is Professor of Medieval English Literature in the School of Arts/English at the University of Hull. Her main research areas are Middle English religious literature, female literacy, preaching, and the relationship between manuscript and print. She edited (with Martha W. Driver) *Preaching the Word in Manuscript and Print in Late Medieval England: Essays in Honour of Susan Powell*, Sermo, 11 (Turnhout: Brepols, 2013), and (with Virginia Blanton and Patricia Stoop) *Nuns' Literacies in Medieval Europe: The Hull Dialogue*, Medieval Women: Texts and Contexts, 26 (Turnhout: Brepols, 2013), and *Nuns' Literacies in Medieval Europe: The Kansas City Dialogue*, Medieval Women: Texts and Contexts, 27 (Turnhout: Brepols, 2015).

Susan (Sue) Powell is Professor Emeritus of Medieval Texts and Culture (University of Salford) and a Visiting Research Fellow at the Institute of English Studies, University of London. She is an editor of manuscripts and early printed books, and her research focusses on religious and devotional texts and institutions. Her latest books are *Saints and Cults in Medieval England* (Donington: Shaun Tyas, 2017) and *The Birgittines of Syon Abbey: Preaching and Print* (Turnhout: Brepols, 2017).

Jane Roberts is a Senior Research Fellow at the Institute of English Studies and Emeritus Professor of English Language and Medieval Literature in the University of London. Her recent publications include: *A Guide to Scripts used in English Writings up to 1500* (London: BL Publications, 2005); with Flora Edmonds, Christian Kay, and Irené Wotherspoon, *TOE Online* (2005); with Alastair Minnis, *Text, Image, Interpretation: Studies in Anglo-Saxon Literature in honour of Éamonn Ó Carragáin* (Turnhout: Brepols, 2007); with David Ganz, *Lambeth Palace Library and its Anglo-Saxon Manuscripts* (London: Taderon Press, 2007).

Raphaela Rohrhofer is a doctoral candidate at the University of Oxford, where she is writing a thesis provisionally entitled "The Increase of the Wound of Love: The Dialectical Forces of Love and Dread in Late Medieval Contemplative Literature in England." Building on a background in medieval literature and art history, she is interested in the nuanced articulation of contemplation and the spectrum of responses to religious texts and images, as well as the relationship between the visual and the verbal in manuscripts from the high to the late Middle Ages. Her first book, *Familial Discourses in* The Book of Margery Kempe: *"Blyssed be the wombe that the bar and the tetys that yaf the sowkyn"* (2014), has won the Dr. Maria Schaumayer Prize, among others.

Muriel Roiland is a researcher in the Section for Arabic manuscripts at the Institut de Recherche et d'Histoire des Textes (IRHT, CNRS, Paris). She is responsible for the section's library of printed books and for its collection of reproductions of manuscripts in Arabic, and she manages the prosopographical database *Onomasticon Arabicum*. She has published on manuscripts of chronicles and biographical repertories from the Mameluke period. She recently published two articles in the periodical *Der Islam* on the textual transmission (13th to 15th century) of the work of an author in Damascus. She is also engaged in a project that is undertaking the renovation, preservation, and scholarly enhancement of a library in Timbuktu.

Daniel Sawyer is Postdoctoral Research Assistant in the English Faculty and a non-stipendiary Junior Research Fellow at Corpus Christi. He is currently at work on the "Towards a New Edition of the Wycliffite Bible" project at Oxford. Alongside his work on the Wycliffite Bible, he is writing a history of reading for later Middle English poetry. He has published on manuscript fragments, rediscovered Middle English poetry, and the use of physical navigational aids in medieval reading. He teaches paleography and medieval English literature.

Devani Singh is a Postdoctoral Research Associate at the University of Geneva. Recent or forthcoming publications include a *Chaucer Review* essay on the paratexts of Speght's Chaucer and a critical edition of the early modern printed commonplace book *Belvedere* (co-edited with Lukas Erne) to be published by Cambridge University Press. Her primary interest is the relationship between early printed texts and their readers, a topic investigated in current research on Chaucer's Renaissance reception and on the emergence of printed epistles to readers

Sian Witherden is a doctoral student in English at Balliol College, Oxford. Her thesis focuses on touch in late medieval English biblical drama. She has recently contributed to *Revolting Remedies from the Middle Ages*, edited by Daniel Wakelin and compiled by students of the University of Oxford (Oxford: Bodleian Library, 2017).

Lydia Zeldenrust is an Associate Lecturer in Medieval Literature at the University of York. She has published articles exploring the role of the early print market in the shaping and spread of inter-vernacular translations, and on literary motifs of women who transform into dragons. Lydia is currently working on a book examining the late medieval and early modern translations of the romance of Mélusine, which looks at both manuscripts and printed sources to trace the story's popularity and spread across Western Europe.

The twentieth volume of the *Journal of the Early Book Society*
was published in Fall 2017
by Pace University Press

Cover and Interior Layouts by Elliane Mellet
The journal was typeset in Arno Pro
and printed by Lightning Source in La Vergne, Tennessee

Pace University Press

Director: Sherman Raskin
Associate Director: Manuela Soares
Graduate Assistants: Elliane Mellet and Bryan Potts
Student Aide: Erica Magrin